The Fur Trade Gamble

Beaver Dens on the Banks of the Missouri, Karl Bodmer.
From Reuben Gold Thwaites, *Early Western Travels*, Vol. 25,
Cleveland: Arthur H. Clark Company, 1906.

The Fur Trade Gamble

North West Company on the Pacific Slope 1800–1820

Lloyd Keith and John C. Jackson

Washington State University Press
Pullman, Washington

Washington State University Press
PO Box 645910
Pullman, Washington 99164-5910
Phone: 800-354-7360
Fax: 509-335-8568
Email: wsupress@wsu.edu
Website: wsupress.wsu.edu

First printing 2016

Library of Congress Cataloging-in-Publication Data

Names: Keith, Lloyd. | Jackson, John C., 1931-
Title: The fur trade gamble : North West Company on the Pacific slope, 1800-1820 / by Lloyd Keith and John C. Jackson.
Other titles: North West Company on the Pacific slope, 1800-1820
Description: Washington State University Press : Pullman, Washington, [2016] | Includes bibliographical references and index.
Identifiers: LCCN 2015044936 | ISBN 9780874223361 (hardbound; alk. paper) | ISBN 9780874223408 (pbk.; alk. paper)
Subjects: LCSH: North West Company (1967-) | Fur trade--Northwest, Pacific. | Explorers--Northwest, Pacific. | Businessmen--Northwest, Pacific--History--19th century. | Indians of North America--Northwest, Pacific--History--19th century. | Northwest, Pacific--Discovery and exploration. | Northwest, Pacific--Commerce--History--19th century.

Classification: LCC F851 .K35 2016 | DDC 338.4/56852409795--dc23
LC record available at http://lccn.loc.gov/2015044936

On the cover: Trapping Beaver, Alfred Jacob Miller, commissioned by William T. Walters, 1858-1860. *Courtesy of the Walters Art Museum.*

Table of Contents

Illustrations and Maps

Dramatis Personae

Frequently mentioned individuals:
Montreal, London, and New York management

John Jacob Astor, New York entrepreneur competing for the fur trade of the Pacific Northwest.

John Fraser, agent for purchasing trade goods and selling the returns of the NWC in London.

Henry Hallowell, Montreal and New York agent for McTavish, Frobisher and Company.

Alexander Henry (the elder), pioneer of the Northwest fur trade of London marketing.

Alexander Henry (the younger), experienced NWC partner, drowned at mouth of the Columbia.

Duncan McGillivray, nephew of McTavish, partner in McTavish, Frobisher & Company and visionary of western expansion until his death in Montreal in 1808.

Simon McGillivray, nephew of McTavish who worked in McTavish, Fraser and Company, London office.

William McGillivray, eldest nephew of McTavish and director of NWC operations from 1784 to 1821.

Simon McTavish, of Garthbeg, Scotland, founding member of North West Company and McTavish, Frobisher and Company who experimented in the China trade in 1791.

William Seton, principal in Seton, Maitland and Company, merchants of New York.

NWC Wintering Partners and Clerks

Simon Fraser, NWC wintering partner led Peace and Fraser River explorations.

James Keith, sent west as a NWC clerk; he was promoted to a partnership and supervision of Fort George.

Finnan McDonald, Thompson's assistant in establishing the upper Columbia.

John McDonald (of Garth), facilitator of expansion and activities at sea or on the Columbia River.

Duncan McDougall, former PFC partner instrumental in the sale of Astoria and made a NWC partner.

Donald McKenzie, former PFC partner who led NWC Snake Brigades.

Donald McTavish, organized Isaac Todd voyage to Astoria/Fort George.

John George McTavish, on personal initiative arranged purchase of Pacific Fur Company.

John Stuart, brought New Caladonia connection from Fraser River to the Columbia.

David Thompson, recent NWC partner, led first expansion across northern Rocky Mountains; traded and explored until 1810.

Introduction

Bon Voyageur

The Columbia River once dominated the Pacific Northwest. Today it passively blocks travel or adds a sparkling view along the interstate highway. The Pacific Northwest, through which it flows, occasionally merits mention in weather reports, but its history is little remembered. Popular understanding of the region's early nineteenth-century legacy usually begins with a New York entrepreneur's frustrated ambition for Astoria and ends in the well-documented records of the Hudson's Bay Company. All but forgotten are two decades of dedication by the North West Company of Montreal to the earliest economic development of a new country.

In the late eighteenth century a passage across the northern Rocky Mountains by some western river was the dream of fur traders who reached the head of the Saskatchewan River. Such a passage would lead eventually to *La Chine* (China) and potential riches.

An initial trickle of intrusive Montreal "pedlars," as the rival Hudson's Bay Company of London disparaged their trading competitors, into the northern Canadian plains in the last half of the eighteenth century soon became a flood. The Montreal entrepreneurs who brought the trade store to the hinterlands faced economic challenges because they had to make capital-intensive, long-distance arrangements to import British merchandise, arrange credit, assemble goods, and transport those investments to increasingly distant trading posts. Those "outfits" had to be shipped westward in large freight canoes about a thousand miles to a depot at Grand Portage on the north shore of Lake Superior. From there, the goods were transferred to more maneuverable twenty-five-foot-long "north" canoes driven by five to six paddlers, loaded with about a ton and a half of cargo, and transported another two thousand miles. Because beaver was the only fur that repaid the costs of acquisition and transportation, finding new sources of those pelts became crucial.[1]

Unprofitable competition between rival traders forecast the necessity of a consolidated organization, and in April 1784 eight Montreal fur trading interests formed a sixteen-share partnership named the North West Company that would extend their business beyond Grand Portage, perhaps as far as a route to the western sea.[2] One of the partners was a Milford, Connecticut, fur trader named Peter Pond, whose previous experience on the middle Saskatchewan River introduced him to Indian descriptions of great mountains and a river that they called the *Naberkistagon* running down to the western sea.[3] After 1787 Pond shared responsibility for the North West Company operations in the Athabaska department with an ambitious clerk named Alexander Mackenzie. After absorbing Pond's ideas regarding northern geography, Mackenzie's first exploration to find a commercially feasible line of communication to the Pacific Ocean led to a dead end at the Arctic Ocean. In spring 1793, Mackenzie, his clerk Alexander McKay, and eight voyageurs set out in a north canoe in search of a freshwater "Northwest Passage through the northern Rocky Mountains."

Mackenzie came upon a large river flowing southward, the present Fraser River, but soon found it too dangerous to descend. Returning upstream Mackenzie and his men took a cross-country route to the coastal home of the Bella Coola Indians and finally reached salt water. He marked his accomplishment with a sign painted in vermillion and grease on a rock that proclaimed, "Alexander Mackenzie from Canada, by land, the twenty-second of July, One thousand seven hundred and ninety-three." But a full year before that seemingly impossible crossing by land, a new drainage had been discovered on the Pacific Coast. On May 12, 1792, the Boston coastal trading ship *Columbia Rediviva* had

1 For a comprehensive history of the development of the North American fur trade *see* Hanson, *When Skins Were Money*. Full citation to works found in the notes are provided in the bibliography to this work.

2 Davidson, *The North West Company*, 9; Campbell, *The North West Company*, 19. The founding members were Simon McTavish, Benjamin and Joseph Frobisher, George McBeath, Robert Grant, Patrick Small, Nicholas Montour, Peter Pond, and William Holmes. Wallace, *North West Company*, 8.

3 Wallace, *Pedlars from Quebec*, 14-15. An informative biography of Peter Pond is Innis, *Peter Pond*.

entered an unexplored river. According to European traditions of discovery, the experienced Boston sea-otter trader Captain Robert Gray claimed all the drainage of the river for the United States, naming the massive watercourse "Columbia" after his vessel.[4] If British traders were to challenge that discovery, they had to find another way to cross the northern mountains. What follows is the description—part narrative, part documentary proof—of how that missing link was connected.

The authors have undertaken to narrate the neglected role of the North West Company of Montreal in the development of the Pacific Northwest, and its lasting heritage. Over many years of extensive research H. Lloyd Keith tracked down a body of business documents and private correspondence revealing how that partnership opened a vast new region and developed its potential. These largely unexamined and unpublished letters between Montreal management and western wintering partners revealed deeper insights into the vision, organization, and implementation of a business conducted on the edge of the continent with the promising potential of a Chinese market.

Keith visited repositories that include the Archives nationales du Quebec, the University of Montreal, the Library and Archives of Canada, Ottawa, and the Archives of Ontario, Toronto. In Scotland he rediscovered revealing data at the University of Aberdeen and in the British National Archives in London. An indefatigable scholar, he probed the Baker Library of the Harvard School of Business Administration and the Yale University Library, New Haven. On many visits to Winnipeg, Manitoba, he drained the extensive records of the Hudson's Bay Company.

Unfortunately my good friend died before he could complete the documentary history with which he intended to extend the record he published in his ground-breaking *North of Askabaska*. As an associate with similar background, and at the request of his widow, Karen Keith, this study combines our mutual understanding into a narrative history of the opening of the Pacific Northwest to the fur trade and the world. My studies include a comprehensive background in the development of the continental fur trade from the earliest beginnings in New France, New York, and the expanding North American frontier. Published books

4 The Papal Theory of the Priority of Discovery served old world explorers well, but became inconvenient to the British Empire when an upstart North American nation used it. *See* Miller, *Native America, Discovered and Conquered.*

range from histories of early exploration to the expansion of the fur trade in the Canadian Northwest and the Rocky Mountain beaver hunt.

From our combined research Keith and I gained insights contradicting some traditional understandings of western fur trade history. It was apparent that the North West Company's expansion plans were doomed by a flawed business plan, but the individuals, great and minor, who tried to implement that plan created a more lasting human heritage. In the final accounting, the NWC's lasting contribution came from those almost-forgotten boatmen, packers, and trappers who for more than a quarter-century of intense labor and personal dedication had made the business function. As one historical era of development ended, it was replaced with the initial settlement of a new country by the former workmen and beaver-trapping freemen and their "country marriages" to native women and their mixed-families. This French-speaking, Catholic-believing community became the original multicultural population base and human heritage of the North West Company Columbia Adventure.

John C. Jackson[5]
April 2015

5 John C. Jackson passed away August 15, 2015.

Simon McTavish, of the North West Company's "McTavish, Frobisher and Company" agency, ca. 1800. *Library and Archives Canada, C-000164/MIKAN 2895450.*

William McGillivray of the North West Company's "McTavish, McGillivray & Company" agency. *Library and Archives Canada, C-000167.*

Chapter One

"Oh Caledonia, Stern and Wild"

Duncan McGillivray, Simon Fraser, 1793–1808

THE REALIZATION OF A transcontinental trade route from western North America to an oriental market was the long-sought goal of fur trade merchants in North America.[1] Because beaver was a fur that repaid the costs of acquisition and transportation, finding new sources of those pelts became crucial to those engaged in the fur trade. As distances stretched ever farther into the remote north, logistical problems became acute. Northern streams and lakes were only free of ice for five months, barely enough time to deliver packs of furs to the Grand Portage on Lake Superior, take on new cargoes of trade goods, and make it back to a distant western post in a short traveling season. Expansion into each new river's drainage system increased the deadly risks of being stopped by ice. As the costs of three- to four-thousand-mile round trips approached the value of the furs to be sold, further northern expansion would eventually become a money-losing proposition.

Alexander Mackenzie's overland route of 1793 to the Pacific had proved to be a barren accomplishment, but using the familiar Saskatchewan River approach might be a better answer and he professed interest in "the broad continental strategy of the trade."[2] Having marched upstream in lockstep with other Montreal competitors and the rival Hudson's Bay Company, the partners of the North West Company considered finding a way to break over the imposing barrier of the Rocky Mountains to open a potential bonanza of beaver swimming in the waters of the Columbia River. However, due to founding member Simon McTavish's

1 "Caledonia" in the chapter title refers not to the French Pacific Island, but the upper Fraser River country of present British Columbia.

2 Lamb, ed., *Journals and Letters of Mackenzie*, 23.

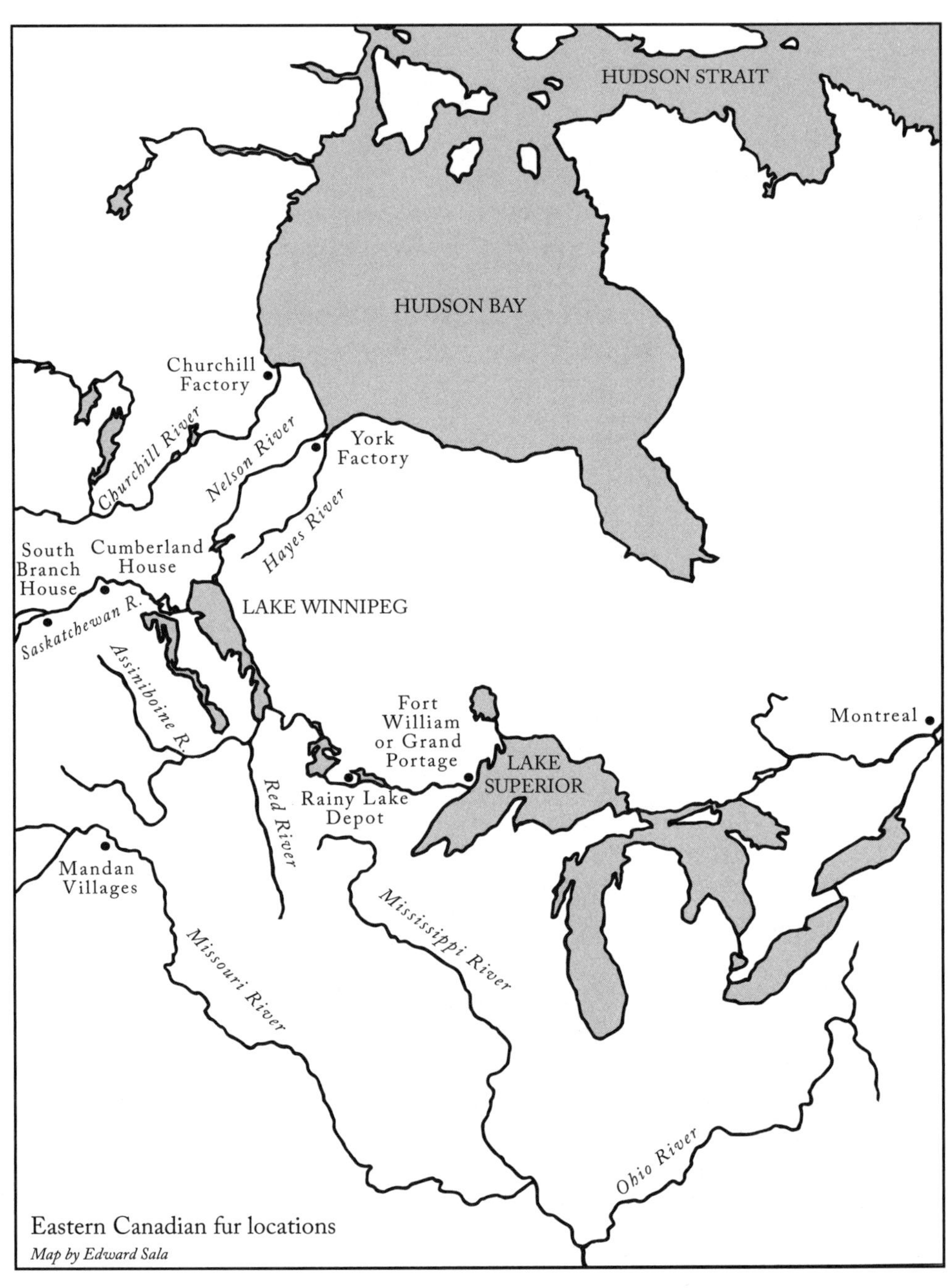

Eastern Canadian fur locations
Map by Edward Sala

experiments in maritime trade and reluctance to undertake expensive new ventures, western expansion did not get underway until the first year of the nineteenth century.

But McTavish's caution was more than an ambitious NWC partner like Alexander Mackenzie could endure. His explorations had confirmed the Fraser River was too dangerous to descend and gained him notoriety and British honors. Throwing in with rival Montreal interests, Mackenzie made himself the inspiration for a "New North West Company," which eventually took the more illustrious (and just a tick imperious) designation, "Sir Alexander Mackenzie & Company." Despite his easily consulted book, *Voyages From Montreal On The River St. Lawrence... To The Frozen And Pacific Oceans* (1801), Mackenzie actually hindered British trade expansion by distracting western impetus.[3] As far as the North West Company was concerned, Mackenzie's competition drew off the resources necessary to support worthwhile expansion.

During the month preceding his 1802 knighthood, Mackenzie wrote a letter to Lord Hobart, the Secretary of State for War and Colonies that included an enclosure he titled "Preliminaries to the establishment of a permanent British Fishery and Trade in Furs &c on the Continent and West Coast of North America." Among proposals in this communication was his recommendation that a British settlement be established "in the River Columbia."[4] He was too late again. The mercantile development of the Pacific Northwest had already begun—with a whisper that was almost lost to history.

While Alexander Mackenzie's ghost-assisted book was being tidied up for publication in London, a more conservative approach to western expansion in the fur trade was being explored on the upper reaches of the Saskatchewan River. The visionaries driving that plan were well-placed nephews of Mackenzie's aging nemesis Simon McTavish. Despite criticism by other partners, their inclusion into the fur trade wasn't nepotistic; it was just clannish.

3 Mackenzie, *Voyages from Montreal.* Eight years after his explorations, Mackenzie's field journals were edited for publication by a London hack named William Combe who did not hesitate to incorporate visionary material from other published sources.

4 Lamb, *Journals and Letters of Mackenzie*, 504.

William,[5] Duncan,[6] and Simon[7] McGillivray were sons of McTavish's sister, Anne, who had married a poor Inverness-shire tenant farmer. The three boys faced an unpromising future in Scotland until their successful uncle brought them to Montreal to learn the northwest fur trade. While William and Duncan were being groomed for a larger role in the operations of the McTavish, Frobisher & Company agency of the North West Company, their lame brother Simon was sent to the London agency.

William entered business in 1784 at age twenty, and six years later had saved enough to buy the share of the retiring Peter Pond and become a wintering partner in the NWC.[8] "Wintering partners" were part owners in the concern and lived year round in the interior, returning east only for the summer "rendezvous" at Grand Portage (later Fort William) on the Great Lakes. They were responsible for supervising the trade in the districts assigned to them. As field managers, they sought Indian groups, developed new transport routes, and even altered the prices offered for furs. Wintering partners chose their post sites, selected and requisitioned trade goods, enticed Indians to trade, and drove the men under their command to render a profitable return on their time.

William McGillivray's experience as a trader in the Red River, English River, and Athabaska districts gave him a broad understanding of fur trade geography and a taste of competitive tactics. He had learned provisioning in the Red River pemmican trade and the problems of transport in the Athabaska department two years before fellow partner Alexander Mackenzie's 1793 journey to the Pacific Ocean. Forgoing barren discovery, McGillivray returned to Montreal where he was made a partner in the agency of McTavish, Frobisher & Company that handled the downstream business for the inland-locked North West Company.[9]

McGillivray's younger brother Duncan began his career in the NWC along the North Saskatchewan River as a clerk for Angus Shaw, a some-

5 Ouellet, "William McGillivray," *Dictionary of Canadian Biography* (hereafter *DCB* 6), www.biographi.ca/en/bio/mcgillivray_william_6E.html, accessed June 10, 2014.

6 Kirk and Brown, "Duncan McGillivray," *DCB* 5, www.biographi.ca/en/bio/mcgillivray_duncan_5E.html, accessed June 10, 2014.

7 Simon McGillivray was lame and better suited to work in the McTavish, Frobisher and Company London office. He became a partner of the NWC in 1805. Ouellet, "Simon McGillivray," *DCB* 7, www.biographi.ca/en/bio/mcgillivray_simon_7E.html, accessed June 10, 2014.

8 Innis, *Peter Pond*, 112.

9 Ouellet, "William McGillivray."

times ruthless trader. During the winter of 1794–95 Duncan learned the hard rules of "the skin game" from a master. Fort George was sandwiched between the hunting ranges of the beaver-producing Strong Woods Cree Indians and the provision producing northern plains tribes. According to the personal journal Duncan kept (perhaps for his older brother's edification) "7 different nations" of Indians traded there.[10]

McGillivray was dismissive of the northern plains tribes because they preferred to trade provisions and did not actively trap beaver. When NWC operations moved up the Saskatchewan River in 1796–97 to build NWC Fort Augustus within musket shot of the HBC's Edmonton House, he became quarrelsome and aggressive with his neighbor William Tomison, the rough-hewn HBC inland master. Duncan declared in a letter written between November 8 and 14, 1797, "I am a young Man in the beginning of my Career, I have all to gain & nothing to lose but my reputation & Life...and I will always hold it ready to be sacrificed in support of the former and of the Interest of my employers."[11]

Having proved himself as an Indian trader, in 1798 Duncan McGillivray returned to Montreal where he was also made a partner in McTavish, Frobisher & Company. William and Duncan McGillivray realized that the way across the mountains had to be launched from the upper Saskatchewan, and in September 1799 his associate, John McDonald, ascended the upper Saskatchewan to build closer to the "Stoney Mountain."[12] The Nor'wester was trailed by the ever-watchful HBC inland master, James Bird, to the fork of the Saskatchewan and Clearwater River where Bird built Acton House to oppose McDonald's Rocky Mountain House.[13] The primary objective of both parties was to have a more convenient place to receive the trade of the Piikani (Peigan) and Kainai (Blood) Blackfeet, as well as that of the "Southern" (western Cree) Indians. Both houses also hoped to attract Kutenai from across the mountains.

Preceded by former HBC clerk David Thompson, who had a reputation as a surveyor, Duncan McGillivray hurried to the recently established

10 Morton, ed., *Journal of Duncan McGillivray*, viii-ix.

11 Morton, ed., *Journal of Duncan McGillivray*, 31, 43, 45, 56, 57, 62; Johnson, ed., *Saskatchewan Journals*, xxxi, xl-xlvi.

12 Livermore and Anick, "John McDonald."

13 Edmonton House Journal by James Bird, 1799-1800, Hudson's Bay Company Archives (hereafter HBCA), B60/a/5, extracted from Johnson, ed., *Saskatchewan Journals*, xxxi, xl-xlvi.

Rocky Mountain House in fall 1800 with the responsibility of extending the search for new beaver resources. Recognizing that something more than trading was up at Rocky Mountain House, Bird accompanied McGillivray upstream where they arrived on October 23, 1800.[14]

By the time they arrived Thompson had just sent off some visiting Kutenai, who agreed to guide two men engaged by the NWC west across the Rocky Mountains where they would winter and induce Indians to hunt and properly prepare beaver pelts. Although Thompson did not acknowledge Bird's presence, the bayman observed the departure of McGillivray and Thompson to visit to the scattered Piikani winter camps southwest of present Calgary, Alberta.

Bird remained at Acton House through most of the winter, watching the Nor'wester activities and some trade from Kutenai who were eager to obtain guns and ammunition. Before he returned downstream in mid-February 1801, Bird was on amiable terms with the Piikani, whose chief promised to steer Kutenai to Acton House when they next appeared.[15] But the bayman suspected that Duncan McGillivray had come to Rocky Mountain House with a larger purpose than running a store for the Blackfeet or Kutenai.

Duncan McGillivray and David Thompson returned from visiting the Piikani at the beginning of December, believing (or perhaps claiming) that a Piikani civil chief had made no objection to the introduction of contracted trappers on the South Branch of the Saskatchewan.[16] By now, unfettered competition on the upper Saskatchewan from multiplying competitors threatened the extinction of beaver. Traders could no longer depend on tribal hunters to meet their needs. To increase production two Montreal operations had already taken to importing contracted Nipissing, Ojibwa, and Iroquois First Nation people, whose steel traps swept beaver from the streams or lakes. It was no surprise that imported Iroquois trappers were unwelcome by resident tribes who also depended on that hunt.

Duncan McGillivray envisioned the extension of the hunt across the mountains, where there were believed to be untouched sources of beaver

14 1800-1801 Edmonton Events, reconstructed from Johnson, Edmonton Journals, in Coues, ed. *New Light*, 2:567, 640, 703-04.

15 Johnson, ed., *Saskatchewan Journals*, lxxviii, 194, 208-10, 212, 214.

16 Belyea, ed., *Columbia Journals*, 12-20.

skins. His visit to the Piikani winter camps near present-day Calgary was intended to get their agreement to tolerate the presence of the NWC's contracted Iroquois trappers. Piikani, who were the best beaver hunters among the northern plainsmen, were unlikely to welcome competitive strangers or the introduction of arms and ready supplies of ammunition to peoples they customarily intimidated. But in the longer view, McGillivray needed their cooperation if operations were extended to the Pacific Slope.[17]

Believing the opinion of a civil chief represented the temper of the tribe, the Nor'westers now had to find a suitable road across the mountains, because the trail Kutenai recently used from the headwaters of the Red Deer River was open to Piikani harassment. Raiders used several other trails to mine Kutenai pony herds, but McGillivray was looking for a practicable way to transport outfits to his traders and return peltry.

A second exploration caused bayman James Bird to comment on NWC plans to go in the summer of 1801 to "examine the country west of the mountain as far as the borders of the South Sea & ascertain if possible whether as is supposed an advantageous trade can be carried on with those parts or not either from hence to China." This time Bird made sure that a trustworthy HBC clerk went along.

> ...in Decr. last Messrs. Mc Gilvery & [the HBC clerk John Peter] Pruden sett off with men to ascertain if possible the truth of this report: after traveling many days thro" the mountain in which they never saw the mark of a Beaver their guide by accident was unable to accompany them farther; the former Gentlemen however proceeded on alone til the snow had increased to the depth of five feet and the precipices became so high & Steep that he could find no method (being unacquainted with the proper passes) of descending one which he made a shift to Climb from this side much more to descend others which presented themselves beyond; he was Consequently under the necessity of returning.[18]

Blocked by deep snow that aggravated his rheumatism, Duncan McGillivray failed to find a practicable passage through the awesome

17 Johnson, ed., *Saskatchewan Journals*, 208-10, 212, 214.

18 Bird to Tomison, Nelson House, 19 February 1801, B.49/c/1, fos.1-4, in Johnson, ed., *Saskatchewan Journals*, lxxviii to lxxxi. This interest preceded the publication of Mackenzie's book.

mountains.[19] In spring when the ice finally broke on the upper Saskatchewan, he hobbled to the canoe, a mountain-broken man who only stopped at Fort Augustus long enough to convince the NWC clerk James Hughes to make another attempt at finding a road across the mountains suitable for a pack train.[20] That became the exploratory failure on the Ram River recorded by Thompson in his "discovery" book and blamed on the Indian guide.[21]

Discovery devolved on the two almost anonymous NWC engagés Thompson had sent off from Rocky Mountain House with the Kutenai. In October 1800 the dutiful Charles La Gassé and the lower Saskatchewan River mixed-blood Pierre Le Blanc trailed a band of twenty-eight Kutenai men and seven women across the northern Rocky Mountains. The pair was equipped to spend the winter with those western Indians, learning what they could of their curious lisping language.[22] Despite the levy that Piikani made on their horses and packs of furs, La Gassé and Le Blanc encouraged Kutenai to risk bringing their trade to Rocky Mountain House.[23]

The two traders *en derouine* should have guessed that they were being asked to do more than accompany Indians.[24] Around Rocky Mountain House the two men had only seen the mountains at long-distance, a string of jagged teeth biting the sky, and La Gassé and Le Blanc were not

19 Thompson wrote that McGillivray suffered frostbite and rheumatism due to his failure to look after himself, but failed to say anything about what Pruden also endured.

20 Proof is lacking, but McGillivray may have had a hand in convincing a party of Iroquois contract hunters accompanied by four Canadians who left the mouth of the South Branch of the Saskatchewan on January 23, 1802, to try hunting near the mouth of the Red Deer River or in the Cypress Hills near present Medicine Hat, Alberta. Johnson, ed., *Saskatchewan Journals*, 311.

21 "Account of an attempt to cross the Rocky Mountains by Mr. James Hughes, nine Men & Myself, on the part of the N.W[t] Company; in order to penetrate to the Pacific Ocean. 1801," Vancouver Public Library manuscript.

22 Kootenay is considered a language isolate, different from Interior Salish. Frederick E. Hoxie, ed., *Encyclopedia of North American Indians* (Boston and New York: Houghton Mifflin Company, 1996), 56; *See Peter Fidler's Journal...1792-93*, Bruce Haig, ed., (Lethbridge, Alberta: Historical Research Centre, 1991), 16, 47-49, 50-52.

23 Charles La Gassé was listed in the Fort des Prairies complement as a *voyageur contremaitre* (a foreman) in 1804 and 1805. Pierre Le Blanc may have been the country son of Francois Le Blanc (Franceways or Sasswe as he was known in the early trade) and a Cree mother.

24 *En derouine* was a technical term meaning to go about drumming up trade. The practice initially developed in the greater northwest to reduce the subsistence demands on a trading post by sending extra hands to live with Indian bands during the winter.

mountaineers. Abstractions did not interest them as much as the footing of the horses they rode across steep shale slopes. But they were breaking into a new world.

Unfamiliar with the language of their hosts, questions about distances, geography, or tribal associations probably depended upon gestures, pantomime, or maps drawn in the sand. That they returned in late May by way of the headwaters of the Red Deer River suggests that they followed the Kootenay River as far south as the Tobacco Plains and their Kutenai guide took them back by a trail up the Elk River.[25] There was a close call when the guide was killed by Stoney Assiniboine, but La Gassé and Le Blanc returned to Rocky Mountain House with that news before Thompson and Hughes left on their unsuccessful exploration on June 6 with a Cree guide in a party of eleven with thirteen horses. Perhaps discouraged by the failure of his exploration, David Thompson recorded very little about what the two men did west of the mountains.[26] His reticence makes it difficult to determine the value of their accomplishment, but that didn't matter because whatever they reported would not be put in motion for another six years.

Thompson stayed at Rocky Mountain House during the yearly Outfit 1801-02, cautiously trading with Piikani, Bloods, and Cree, and perhaps learning from visiting Indians that what the Piikani were willing to accept concerning imported Iroquois trappers failed to take into account the attitude of their surly Atsiina (Gros Ventre or Falls Indians) neighbors. Already in retreat up the South Branch of the Saskatchewan for a previous attack on trade houses, at the end of February 1802 Atsiina slaughtered fourteen Iroquois trappers and two Canadians. If that gruesome news reached Thompson before he left Rocky Mountain House in 1802, it may have chilled his illusion that northern plainsmen would welcome imported trappers.[27]

At the end of the 1802 trading season, both upper Saskatchewan trading houses were abandoned. The North West Company put the idea of

25 The need for supposition arises when faced with an obvious event lacking documentary proof. Absence of a paper trail does not mean that nothing happened. A matrix of peripheral evidence may suggest it, but that also requires a degree of deductive supposition.

26 Nisbet, *Sources of the River*, 68, 72; and Nisbet, *The Mapmaker's Eye*, 31-32. Thompson passed over their return lightly in the various versions of his travels.

27 Peter Fidler Chesterfield House Journal 1801-02, HBCA, B.34/a/3 in Johnson, ed., *Saskatchewan Journals*, 311-14.

extending operations across the mountains on hold so they could address the problems created by the visionary Alexander Mackenzie, who had joined their competitors.[28] When Alexander Mackenzie published *Voyages from Montreal* in 1801, he believed the large river he had come upon west of the Rocky Mountains, locally called the Tacoutche Tesse (now the Fraser River), to be the upper portion of the Columbia River.[29] Although he had not followed the Tacoutche Tesse to its mouth, Mackenzie was convinced, and convinced others, that it was a feasible route to the western sea.[30] Mackenzie proposed that the British government assist the merchants from Canada in extending fur trade routes to the shores of the Pacific Ocean and establishing depots at the mouth of the Columbia River or at Cook's Inlet for the transshipment of peltry to the markets of China. It would be to the advantage of British hegemony in North America, he asserted, if Canadian merchants were to unite with the Hudson's Bay Company but, short of that, some way had to be found to allow Canadians the right of passage from the west shore of Hudson Bay to the Columbia River and its tributary waters.

Initially led by the Montreal firms of Forsyth, Richardson & Company and Leith, Jamieson & Company, the upstarts were joined in 1802 by the newly knighted Sir Alexander Mackenzie, who brought influence, capital, and a new identity. The New North West Company would be known by the brand "XYC" stamped on their bales of goods, and later as Sir Alexander Mackenzie and Company.[31] From his previous experience in McTavish, Frobisher & Company, Mackenzie knew that it would be necessary to convince the East India Company to accommodate Canadian merchants by relaxing their strictures on British trade in Canton. Those "ideas" constituted "Mackenzie's Plan on Extending the Trade."[32]

28 The "General Return of the Departments and Posts of the North West Company for 1802" listed nine posts on the Saskatchewan River operated by two partners, sixteen clerks and 80 men. "Exclusive of the above...there are 80 to 100 Canadians and Iroquois Hunters with whom the North West Company had Contracts, but who are not considered Servants of the Company, ranging free over the Country wherever they find it convenient to hunt."

29 Lamb, *Journals and Letters of Mackenzie*, 412, and map following 238.

30 Mackenzie, *Voyages from Montreal*, 410.

31 A reliable and thorough source on the XY Company is the 1957 thesis by Pendergast, "The XY Company." *See also* Fleming, "The Origin of 'Sir Alexander Mackenzie and Company'."

32 For a summary of Mackenzie's plan, *see* Lamb, *Letters and Journals of Mackenzie*, 415-18 and 516-19. Arthur S. Morton's reference to the "Columbian Enterprise" can be found in

It should not be assumed that Mackenzie's plan and the North West Company's "Columbian Enterprise" were synonymous. The NWC agents in McTavish, Frobisher and Company were in agreement about establishing an Asian market for North American furs—which Simon McTavish had been trying to do since 1792. During the previous decade he made expensive attempts to profitably market beaver pelts in Canton. During his brief association with McTavish, Frobisher & Company, Mackenzie gained enough understanding of the difficulties to propose bypassing New York and London (and thereby Montreal) as transshipment points in favor of Hudson Bay and depots on the Pacific coast.

Not surprisingly, Simon McTavish and William McGillivray considered it undesirable to remove the center for doing business from Montreal.[33] McTavish felt expansion and solidification of the business could best be orchestrated from Montreal, where he enjoyed good connections with the London market. Expansion beyond the upper Saskatchewan and across the Rocky Mountains should be a slow, deliberate process, he believed, with care taken to establish a profitable business before attempting further exploration.[34]

Soon after old McTavish's death, the bitter competition between the rival North West Companies ended in a November 1804 merger. This significant agreement meant that capital and energy previously expended on competition could now be devoted to expanding the trade west of the Rockies. Those plans rested with William McGillivray, because Alexander Mackenzie had been excluded from the new organization. It was up to the McGillivray brothers' team to renew efforts to open the exploitation of the Peace River country.[35]

Each summer as many as possible of the wintering partners assembled at the new Kaministikwia depot on the north shore of Lake Superior, where the decision was made to push west from Athabaska. Although Archibald Norman McLeod represented the upper Peace River

---

A History of the Canadian West to 1870–71, 463ff. A critical exception to Morton's analysis can be found in Belyea, "The 'Columbian Enterprise,' 3-27; and Morton's response, "A Historical Exemplum."

33 For an understanding of Simon McTavish's character, *see* Ouellet, "Simon McGillivray"; for the organization of the NWC in 1795 *see* Elaina Allen Mitchell, "The North West Company Agreement of 1795," *Canadian Historical Review*, 36:2 (1958).

34 Chapter Six below has a fuller examination of the maritime experiments.

35 After closing Rocky Mountain House in 1802, David Thompson spent two years in the Peace River country.

department at the 1805 summer meeting, he chose not to lead an exploration. Because the other partner on the upper Peace, John Finlay, had retired, the task fell to Simon Fraser who had been advanced to partnership status in 1801. Fraser was given the responsibility of extending trade up the Peace River through the tangle of northern waters and of exploring the Tacoutche Tesse to its mouth.[36] Like Mackenzie, Fraser was under the impression that this river was the Columbia.

In the summer or fall of 1804, even before the proprietors of the North West Company decided to extend trade beyond the Rocky Mountains, senior clerk John Stuart established a new post on the Peace River. Also known as Rocky Mountain House, it would be a staging place for pushing into New Caledonia.[37] The southern or Parsnip fork of the Peace, and a small tributary flowing from Trout Lake were explored. The results led Fraser to decide on Trout Lake as the site for his first trading post beyond the portage.[38] Nor did he stop at Trout Lake, and during those busy months of 1805, Fraser explored across the height of land and into the Pacific Ocean watershed.[39]

Assisted by three clerks—John Stuart, James MacDougall, and Archibald McGillivray—and about twenty men, Fraser's first object was to open the trade in the new territory and then go on to explore the Tacoutche Tesse downstream, with the aim of linking it to the Columbia and an outlet to the Pacific Ocean.[40]

Between the fall of 1805 and the summer of 1807, Fraser directed the building of trading posts at Trout Lake (later called Fort McLeod), Stuart Lake (later Fort St. James), Fraser Lake (Fort Fraser), and a freight-forwarding station, Fort George, at the confluence of the Nechako and Tacoutche Tesse Rivers. The time and effort devoted to establishing these

36 Or so J. N. Wallace suggests. *See* Wallace, *The Wintering Partners*, 69.

37 Wallace, *Wintering Partners*, 70. Lamb states that "in the autumn of 1805 Fraser led a party of about twenty men up the Peace River and established a post at Rocky Mountain Portage," but John Stuart's journal states clearly that he sent James MacDougall up the Peace in 1804 to accomplish that task. *See* Lamb, *Simon Fraser*, 15-16; Burley, *Prophecy of the Swan*, 32-33, 65. The new post was located near the modern community of Hudson's Hope, British Columbia.

38 Lamb, *Simon Fraser*, 16; Burley, *Prophecy of the Swan*, 75.

39 Library and Archives of Canada (hereafter LAC), Selkirk Papers, MG 19, E1, 9326. Rocky Mountain Portage House was not the same as Rocky Mountain House on the upper Saskatchewan.

40 Lamb, *Simon Fraser*, 16, and LAC, Selkirk Papers, MG 19, E1, 9309-11, 9316.

posts underscore the priority given to business over exploration. The first three establishments were intended as bread-and-butter fur trading posts, while Fraser desired that Fort George serve as a provisioning post because of its strategic location as a jumping-off point for the journey down river.

That was not going to be easy because Indians encountered by the Nor'westers were salmon-dependent people whose concept of fur trading may have been colored by what they heard from coastal neighbors about ships that called into those fiords in search of sea otter pelts. They knew no more about European guns, animal traps, or trading than what they had heard second or third hand. If Indians were going to be useful participants in the fur trade, they needed to be converted to the hunting and exchange system. The Nor'westers, then, had to create their business from the ground up, communicating all the essential knowledge to the Indians with only a basic grasp of their unfamiliar languages.

Initially Fraser hoped to explore farther down the Tacoutche Tesse than Mackenzie had descended in 1793, if not to its mouth. Lack of provisions and sufficient boatmen thwarted his plans, and he had to delay the projected voyage down what they thought was the Columbia River. It was May 28, 1808, when Fraser, accompanied by John Stuart, Jules Quesnel, two Natives, and nineteen men in four canoes embarked from Fort George to descend the mighty river. This seasoned troupe of forward-looking explorers and traders knew little of the course of the river they were about to follow or the dangers it might pose, and were uncertain how the inhabitants along the way would receive them.

The river in the spring freshet proved extremely dangerous. Nevertheless, they managed to race in the canoes until June 10, 1808, when further water travel was deemed impracticable. The party continued on, mostly by foot, each man weighed down by an eighty-pound pack, until they passed the dangerous Fraser River canyon and on June 30 emerged in calmer waters where they acquired canoes from friendly Indians.[41] Although they managed to surmount the physical dangers presented and reached the river's mouth in some thirty-six days, they were discouraged by the hostile reception they received from the local Cowichan Indians.

The explorers did not dally along the salt water Strait of Georgia. Their return voyage was accomplished on August 6, a day less than the

41 Burley, *Prophecy of the Swan*, 76-101.

downstream leg of their journey had taken.[42] But this was no victorious homecoming. Fraser had failed to find a practicable or useful route for bringing trade goods into the interior or transporting returns to the sea. Nor had he found a connection to the Columbia River.

---

42 Burley, *Prophecy of the Swan*, 104-28.

Chapter Two

Into a Heart of Darkness
David Thompson

The move into New Caledonia had thus far been a long canoe-bound, portage-inflicted, end run around the Rocky Mountains, following rivers penetrating that barrier by torturous, winding courses adding miles to transport problems. A more direct approach was necessary and while Simon Fraser busied himself on the upper Peace and Fraser Rivers, another North West Company partner began a second probe westward from the head of the North Saskatchewan River.

David Thompson returned to Rocky Mountain House six years after he first thought the northern Rockies resembled "the Waves of the Ocean in the wintery storm...suddenly congealed and made Solid by Power Omnipotent."[1] His education in a London charity school had been enough to get him placed as a fourteen-year-old apprentice in the Hudson's Bay Company. By the time he was seventeen, he had been taken up the Saskatchewan River and sent *en derouine* to winter in a Piikani Blackfoot camp and learn their language.[2]

Well before 1784 HBC traders had been among the Piikani, but Thompson's experience during the 1787–88 winter made a lasting impression on the young bayman. He was appalled by the barbarity of returning war parties and eighteen years later he still distrusted those northern plainsmen who seemed capable of anything. Where horses could go, there would be dangerous Piikani, Siksiki, Kainaa, and murderous

1 Belyea, ed., *Columbia Journals*, 19. These are excerpts from Thompson's field journals and later revisions.

2 Thompson's opus on his early fur trade experience was published in Tyrrell, ed., *David Thompson*; and in the first of three projected volumes, Moreau, ed., *Writings of David Thompson*. Vol. 1 contains a full list of Thompson-related publications on page xiv, n.15.

Atsiina. How would they react when the North West Company opened trade with the Kutenai across the Rocky Mountains?

Another HBC traveler with the Piikani during the winter of 1792–93 had a less daunting winter. Peter Fidler met Kutenai who crossed through the Crowsnest Pass to the Old Man River in present southwest Alberta, bringing horses to trade to those buffalo hunters. During Duncan McGillivray's 1795–96 winter at Fort George, he noted that some Kutenai were determined to bribe or fight their way to the traders.[3] Both the Nor'wester John McDonald and the HBC's James Bird became interested in attracting the trade of the Kutenai Indians because their country was said to teem in beaver.[4]

But Kutenai and their Salish (Flathead) allies had a risky habit of crossing the mountains to hunt buffalo and carry dried meat home for winter provisions. As they moved into the hunting ranges of northern plainsmen, hostile clashes were inevitable.[5] To satisfy the social and political ambitions of rising leaders, northern plains warriors pulled off horse raids and provoked clashes. Seeing NWC-owned arms passed to western tribes would complicate the risks of tormenting western horse herders.[6]

During the previous winters of 1800–01 and 1801–02 at Rocky Mountain House, Thompson's opinion of Piikani had not improved. The post had been built to receive peltry from Piikani, Blood, Sarci, and Swampy Ground Assiniboine and the few abused Kutenai who survived Piikani harassment getting there. It was a lesson for him in October 1800, when twenty-six Kutenai men and seven women ran the hostile gauntlet to trade beaver and bear skins. When they headed home, Thompson had sent two of his men to winter with them.

---

3 Peter Fidler, "Journal of a Journey over Land from Buckingham House to the Rocky Mountains in 1792 & 3," Bruce Haig, ed., (Lethbridge, Historical Research Centre, 1991); Morton, ed., *Journal of Duncan McGillivray*; Johnson, ed., *Saskatchewan Journals*.

4 Edmonton House Journals, HBCA, B60/a/6, fo. 6; B60/a/7, fos. 4d, 6-8d; in Johnson, *Saskatchewan Journals*, lxxii, 211-12.

5 Anthropological evidence suggests Kutenai, who know themselves as *Ktunaxa*, were a northerly people who migrated south following the trails of large game animals and settled along the banks of the Kootenay River. Brunton, "Kootenai," 224-25.

6 This speculation into Thompson's mind as he prepared to cross the mountains is based on his previous experiences as a young man and his later concerns about Blackfoot hostility.

What Duncan McGillivray had hoped to accomplish then was establishing new business across the mountains. But that risked violating the symbiotic relationship already established with the tribes that traded at Rocky Mountain House, causing McGillivray to go out of his way to insure Piikani cooperation. It had been Atsiina who killed trappers coming up the South Branch of the Saskatchewan in 1802 when Thompson closed Rocky Mountain House and was sent to Athabaska.[7] Now, when he returned, the North West Company still intended to go behind the backs of the Piikani to provide arms and ammunition to their western victims. Crossing the mountains was not going to strengthen that relationship.

Dating when the actual decision was made to cross the Rocky Mountains is difficult, although the NWC historian Gordon Charles Davidson wrote, "Thompson probably received his orders at the general meeting preceding the amalgamation which would indicate that it was really part of the activity resulting from the reorganization of 1802."[8] However, when Thompson was sent west in 1806, not all the wintering partners were enthusiastic about what they foresaw as a difficult and expensive adventure. Protective of their share in profits, those hard Scots doubted that a surveyor could generate enough trade to pay expenses.[9]

After spending the previous winter lower on the Saskatchewan at Fort George, Thompson finally arrived at Rocky Mountain House in October 1806 to find the expansion was already underway.[10] During the summer Thompson's brother-in-law, the upper Fort des Prairies proprietor John McDonald, sent two mixed-blood clerks and a small crew to improve the trail the Kutenai used.[11] Before Thompson arrived, Jacques

7 Thompson's claim that McGillivray obtained the permission of the civil chief "Sac o tow wow" to bring Iroquois contract hunters into the mountains had been disproved in February 1802, when Atsiina warriors on the South Branch killed fourteen intruding Iroquois steel trappers and two Canadians for good measure.

8 Davidson, *The North West Company*, 98.

9 Details of these activities can be found in Thompson's writings and in Kyba, "Thompson's 1801 Attempt to Cross the Rocky Mountains," as well as in Belyea, ed., *Columbia Journals*.

10 Nisbet, *Sources of the River*, 50.

11 Journal 18 of Rocky Mountain House Occurences, October 11, 1806–July 26, 1807, by David Thompson, Archives of Ontario (hereafter AO19), Series F 443-1, microfilm MS 4426; W. A. Sloan, "The Role of Native People in Extension of the Fur Trade on the Upper Saskatchewan and through the Rocky Mountains 1784-1807," unpublished paper, n.d., 14-15, 27.

Raphael ("Jaco") Finlay and Nicholas Montour, accompanied by several engagés, had already worked to clear a packhorse trail from the upper Saskatchewan over a mountain pass to the western watershed.[12]

Hacking branches and fallen trees as they descended the western slope to a north flowing river, the workmen did their best to make a passage. Leaving Jaco Finlay building canoes, Nicholas Montour apparently visited the Upper Kutenai winter camps and advised them that a trader was coming. But as Thompson prepared to cross the mountains in spring 1807, he faced a labor problem.

Former engagés, who lost their jobs after the 1804 merger of competing operations, had to live by trapping. Previously, those "free men" had received what appeared to be high wages paid in the inland currency of *livres*. One hunter complained to the HBC's James Bird, "the NWCo will not pay them in money unless they take their outfits from them" at high inland markup. Refusing to pay hunters in cash meant that a freeman was essentially marooned on the upper Saskatchewan, unable to build up a nest egg to retire and in danger of falling into debt bondage.[13] North West Company regulations also prohibited freemen from carrying private packs of furs in company boats to search downstream for a better market. Some hunters threatened to take packs as far as York Factory in search of better prices. Expansion rested on the cooperation of an uncertain manpower base.

It was a full year before Thompson's party began moving the trading outfit toward the Continental Divide. On the height in June 1807, they came upon a watercourse he called the Portage River (present Blaeberry River). It flowed down to a larger stream flowing northwestward which he initially called the Kootanae River.[14] The name Columbia was not mentioned in Thompson's field journal, but it would soon be used in a letter with serious consequences for the NWC Columbia Adventure.

12 At least eight individuals were active west of the mountains before Thompson arrived at Rocky Mountain House in October 1806: clerks Finlay, Montour, and Jules Maurice Quesnel, engagés Michel Boulard, Bercier, Joseph Daniel, Drummond, Forcier, and Finlay's young Saulteur brother-in-law.

13 Edmonton House Journal, B60/a/7, fo. 4d. Bird comments that freemen are more productive trappers than Indians.

14 G. P. V. and Helen B. Akrigg, *1001 British Columbia Place Names*, 3rd ed. rev. (Vancouver: Discovery Press, 1973), 26. Thompson's Portage River did not become the Blaeberry (Blueberry) until Alexander Henry renamed it as he passed down it in fall 1813.

At the river's edge, Thompson was disappointed with the efforts of the trail cutters and canoe builders, raging in his field journal, "It may be seen how Jaco, McMter [Mr. Montour] & two men with them have earned their wages... Jaco ought certainly to be forfeited as he has done next to nothing."[15] In a later revision dated June 30, he wrote that he "visited the Canoes left by Jaco – found them unfit for carriage but handy for light voyaging."[16] Eventually Thompson realized that Jaco was unable to build a larger transport canoe because he lacked suitable birchbark. The best trees for bark didn't grow west of the mountains, a fact the critic soon learned firsthand, but he never rectified his judgment of Finlay. The criticism continued in letters he sent east in March 1808 to other partners at Fort Augustus.[17]

There is a suggestion that Jaco Finlay may have been the unidentified Canadian freeman who claimed to have taken six hundred beaver during the 1806–07 winter and later traded with the Hudson's Bay Company at Edmonton House. Finlay's name appears on a fairly accurate map of several tributaries of the Columbia River bearing that date which resurfaced in the papers of the HBC clerk Peter Fidler.[18] After returning to Rocky Mountain House and outfitting with the ammunition, traps, and food he needed to feed his family, Jaco Finlay turned south to trap in the Piikani country.[19]

On July 19 Thompson began building his first post, Kootenae House, on a lake near the head of the north-flowing Columbia River. He hoped to intercept hunters who previously carried their peltry to the British houses on the upper Saskatchewan. But it was soon apparent that neither the Upper Kutenai nor Lakes Indians were dedicated beaver hunters.

15 June 27, 1807, AO18.

16 Belyea, ed., *Columbia Journals*, 215 citing AO18, adds an expanded criticism, apparently taken from his field journal and copied later into the report sent to Duncan McGillivray which became the Royal Commonwealth Society Library version. However Belyea takes her version from AO20, dated June 30, which on page 49 suggests that Thompson's indignation may have softened when he wrote to James Hughes on July 5 and sent the letter back with Indians. *Columbia Journals*, 49, 50.

17 Contrary to accepted understanding, it was not Thompson but the engagé Jean Baptiste Buché who set to work on August 10 building the first split cedar plank canoe that became the prototype of the boats used during Thompson's years on Columbia waters. Belyea, ed., *Columbia Journals*, 222.

18 The Finlay map is reproduced in Nisbet, *Mapmaker's Eye*, 37.

19 Thompson to Dear Gentlemen, March 4, 1807, HBCA, A67/1, fos. 8-13d.

They would have to be taught how to take and properly prepare peltry before they could become productive trading partners.[20]

Thompson's immediate problem was feeding the seventeen men, women, and children who accompanied him. Scrambling for a sparse diet ranging from deer, dogs, swans, or porcupine to rotten horseflesh must have made Kootenae House a hungry place where the children whimpered in their beds. The traders were unsuccessful with the nets they set to catch the lake trout, mullet, or sturgeon they had known in more familiar waters. Two Kutenai were persuaded to hunt food for the strangers, but the game population was limited at a time when the area's Indians were waiting for salmon to return.

The salmon that came at the end of August were scarred and tattered survivors of proud silver fish that instinctively climbed a thousand miles up an unrelenting river, driven to return to the gravel beds where they found life, and where most would spawn and then die. The first fish spotted were fugitive, but the clerk, Finnan McDonald, speared one that weighed 26½ pounds on the steelyard meant to appraise beaver pelts. The arrival of late-summer salmon should have eased the food problems for the human population, but the exhausted fish were lean and their flesh was poor food for hard-working house builders.[21]

The main body of Kutenai was returning from crossing the mountains with their Salish neighbors to hunt buffalo and dry the meat. The heavy packs they brought back represented winter food stocks that they were reluctant to share with the traders. However, hunting for deer, elk, or mountain sheep improved enough early the next winter that Thompson's men were able to dig a cave in a bank and pack ice around quarters of elk or deer to make a "glacier" that would stay frozen indefinitely.[22]

Kootenae House was still under construction on August 13 when two Kutenai men came from the south with the alarming news of a fight between the three "Blackfoot nations" and the Salish and Sahaptins (Nez Perce).[23] During the summer Piikani delegates arranged a peace meeting

20 Ibid.

21 Nisbet, *Mapmaker's Eye*, 46. In his correspondence, McDonald spelled his first name Finnan, which is the spelling used throughout this book.

22 Nisbet, *Mapmaker's Eye*, 50, 69. Thompson took elk quarters from the glacier in February 1809 to make jerky.

23 The Kutenai's neighbors to the north, south, and west spoke three of the seven Interior Salish languages, most of which differed from one another sufficiently to be mutually

with the Salish. It seemed to begin on friendly terms. All went well for a week filled with promising councils and agreement was reached. But as the conference was breaking up a fight erupted in which fourteen Piikani and four Salish were slain.[24] Already uneasy that he was violating the trading symbiosis, Thompson was alarmed that potential hostiles were loose on the west side of the mountains and seeking revenge for the deaths that occurred.

That bad news was compounded by Kutenai reports that forty-two strangers, led by an officer, had been present during the peace council. Thompson credited that report to Kutenai, but his first contact was with an obliging young Nez Perce (*Nimi-ipuu*) who delivered a shocking letter dated "Fort Lewis, Yellow River, Columbia, 10th July, 1807." Presenting a list of ten regulations stating how foreign traders were to conduct themselves in Upper Louisiana territory, the letter identified the party as Americans. Along with several paragraphs of specifics Thompson read:

> The new ceded Territories to the American States northward and westward of the Illinois, comprehend the Mississourie Red River and all the Lands westward to the Coast of California and the Columbia River with all its branches; of which we have now taken Possession and on which we are now settled down to the Pacific Ocean; extending northward to about 50 Degrees north Latitude, according to the Boundaries settled at the Treaty of Peace between the united States and the Court of Great Britain, although it is by no means allowed here nor does any of our Expressions bear the Sense that Great Britain has any special right to any of the Lands on the Pacific Ocean or to the Commerce of any of the Rivers that flow into the said Ocean, all of which we shall comprehend as within our said Territories until some further Explanation takes place on this head between the united States of America and the Court of St. James.[25]

The party was under the command of a Captain Zackery Perch and a Lieutenant James Roseman. The astonished Thompson realized this was another American force larger than the previous Corps of Discovery led

---

unintelligible. They had the most intimate relationships with the Shuswap, Lakes, Kalispel, Pend d'Oreille, and Flathead. Other Salish people, including the Okanogan, Spokane, Coeur d'Alene, and Columbian, visited infrequently with the Kutenai. Brunton, "Kootenai," Table 1, "Language Classification," 51.

24 Entries for August 13, September 25, 1807, in Belyea, *Columbia Journals*, 60, 69.

25 Edmonton House Journal, November 10, 1807, HBCA, B60/a/7, fols. 6-8d.

by Lewis and Clark. As confirmation, the Nez Perce courier recognized former members of the Lewis and Clark Expedition and asserted that two returning corpsmen were with the new party. Those were enough details that the British trader could not immediately question the authenticity of the letter and was unprepared to deal with an unanticipated intrusion of strangers.

That challenge to the legality of the western expansion was grave and Thompson admitted in his field journal and in the recap written later for Duncan McGillivray that:

> [A]bout 3 weeks ago [i.e., about 22 July, 1807] the Americans to the number of 42 arrived to settle a military Post, at the confluence of the two most southern & considerable Branches of the Columbia & that they were preparing to make a small advance Post lower down on the River.[26]

Thompson did not mention the letter in later copies of his daily journal, but on September 23 he sent his clerk Finnan McDonald and five men back to Rocky Mountain House with the damned thing.[27] In addition to the compilation of developments from May 10 to September 23 that was meant for Duncan McGillivray, the express may have carried letters to Fort Augustus that have since been lost.[28] Thompson surely expected John McDonald and James Hughes would read his long account before sending it down the Saskatchewan to intercept the NWC winter express carrying mail to Fort William and Montreal. It was critical that the downstream partners know that Americans had returned west of the mountains.[29]

The couriers waiting at Rocky Mountain House received the packet and allowed the HBC clerk John Peter Pruden (the same who accompa-

---

26 "Thompson Journal 18," Archives of Ontario; T. C. Elliott, ed., "Narrative of the Expedition to the Kootanae @ [at or about?] Flat Bow Indian Countries, on the Sources of the Columbia River, Pacific Ocean, by D. Thompson on behalf of the N. w Company 1807," *The Quarterly of the Oregon Historical Society* 26:1 (March 1925): 28-49, at 43.

27 Belyea, ed., *Columbia Journals*, 28; Nisbet, *Sources of the River*, 100.

28 "Narrative of the Establishment on the Sources of the Columbia, addressed to Mr. Duncan McGillivray, Director to the N.W. Co^{y}, and the Gentlemen of the upper Fort des Prairies." Royal Commonwealth Society Library, Cambridge, England, and published as Elliott, ed., "Narrative of the Expedition to the Kootanae."

29 Thompson spent a good deal of time at his writing desk, evidenced by three overlapping versions of events up until McDonald departed with the packet as well as other letters.

nied McGillivray in 1801) to make a copy of what seemed to be a circular letter. This copy was passed on to the Edmonton House inland master James Bird who entered it into the house journal on November 10, 1807. Bird preserved a document his NWC competitors preferred to forget. As the express passed the Upper and Lower Forts des Prairies, other wintering partners became aware of a threat to the vast region of the Pacific Northwest that the North West Company intended to claim with its Columbia business adventure. The packet arrived at Alexander Henry's Pembina Post on March 31, 1808, and was forwarded to Fort William just west of Lake Superior on April 2, 1808.[30]

Included in the winter packet was a twenty-six page recap of Thompson's experiences crossing the mountains and establishing Kootenae House. Drawn from his original field journals numbered 18 and 19, it was addressed to his mentor Duncan McGillivray and filled in details about the unexpected appearance of Americans. A negative opinion from the partner responsible to making the expansion work was not good news.

Since 1803 the McGillivrays had tried to gain access from Hudson's Bay to shorten long canoe trips to distant posts, but HBC always refused. During the 1807–08 winter while waiting to learn how the western extension was going, Duncan composed a pamphlet titled "Some account of the trade carried on by the North West Company." This was intended to be circulated publically to pressure the British government into becoming involved in the expansion. McGillivray urged the government to support the North West Company's western enterprise in the Pacific because "a new field would be open for the consumption of British manufactured goods; and a vast country and population made dependent on the British Empire."[31]

After sending Finnan McDonald off with the packet, which he would deliver to waiting couriers from Fort Augustus, Thompson accompanied a Lakes Kutenai man to the headwaters of the Columbia River and across a short portage into a south flowing stream he named for the McGillivrays (present Kootenay River). But the short four-day trip ended as a mere gesture. It would be a week-long horse ride through an

30 Gough, ed., *Alexander Henry*, 1: 301.

31 Headed "Some Account of the Trade carried on by the North West Company" and finally titled "Sketch of the Fur Trade, 1809," PAC photostat. *See* Morton, ed., *Journal of Duncan M'Gillivray*, Appendix, p. 22.

intervening jumble of mountains and ridges to the Flat Bow country and Thompson turned back.[32]

Although he did not mention it again in recopies of his field journal, it is unbelievable that Thompson put the idea of an American presence out of his mind. He already revealed in the copy to McGillivray that he was considering shifting the NWC trade operations to the north. Then in early November the express party returned from Rocky Mountain House and delivered a purloined copy of one of Captain Meriwether Lewis's first reports of his Corps of Discovery undertaking. After reading this, Thompson copied it into his discovery journal.[33]

Not long after the Americans returned to St. Louis and wrote their first dispatches, someone, in the interest of the North West Company, made a copy of a letter that Lewis dated in September 1806. The recipient was not named, but the copy arrived at NWC headquarters in time to be forwarded up the Saskatchewan and across the mountains to Thompson.[34] The object of the Lewis and Clark Expedition, Nor'westers learned, had been the location of a portage between the Missouri and Columbia Rivers for the extension of United States commerce. Alarmingly for the NWC, Lewis suggested that it might be possible to bleed off the fur trade of the greater northwest by way of the Missouri River.[35]

Copies of that speculative vision must have blossomed like weeds in the garden of the Nor'westers. Duncan McGillivray represented the "Agents and Directors" at the meeting of wintering partners at the Fort William inland headquarters from July 10 to 31, 1807. The minutes, too, are in his hand. He would have read the purloined letter there and made sure it was forwarded to David Thompson. From the similarity of his phrasing, it appears that Sir Alexander Mackenzie had also read a copy of the Lewis letter during the winter of 1807–08. On March 10, 1808, he sent a memorandum to the British government commenting on the activities of the Americans, "who it is said have traversed the Country by Land and Water from the Missisipi to the Pacific Ocean...[and] that it is

32 Belyea, ed., *Columbia Journals*, 72-74. Thompson gives no indication that the possibility of encountering Americans influenced his decision.

33 Nisbet, *Sources of the River*, 106, dates this on December 11, 1807.

34 Journal of Occurences, AO20, page 291, Archives of Ontario.

35 The letter preserved in the Vancouver Public Library manuscript is similar to two others written at the same time and reproduced in Jackson, ed., *Letters of the Lewis and Clark Expedition*, 2: 336-43.

their intention to claim...exclusive Privileges to the intermediate Country, as well as to the Coast Northward from the Spanish Boundary to the Latitude of 50."[36] He urged, "The Fur Trade should be carried on from the Atlantic to the...mouth of the River Columbia...where a Commercial Colony might be planted."[37]

The Kutenai returned from Salish country with wracking coughs and a sickness that was fatal to children and old people. As the Old Chief's band moved toward Kootenae House they were stricken and had to camp to tend the sick. Pertussis (whooping cough) had traveled from the Osage on the lower Missouri River northward to the Mandan/Hidatsa villages in 1805. The next year it plagued the upper Saskatchewan posts and may have traveled up the Yellowstone. For an isolated people, innocent of Old World diseases, whooping cough could be deadly.[38]

Thompson and his men experienced difficulty getting Kutenai or Lake Kutenai (Flat Bows) to hunt beaver for them.[39] Never introduced to the symbiotic relationship of the fur trade, peoples west of the Rockies lacked enthusiasm for killing beaver to exchange for European commodities. There is no indication they were supplied with traps or instructed in their usage so they must have shot unwary animals or dug them out of their dens. To get the pelts he wanted, the best Thompson could manage was sending out men *en derouine* to live with the Kutenai and teach them how to hunt and properly prepare the furs.

As he settled into Kootenae House, Thompson faced another concern. He realized that Piikani were keeping this project under surveillance. Whether these natives were remnants of the broken-up peace delegation lingering in the Salish country to seek revenge, or just horse-shopping opportunists, was not clear to him. The first party of fourteen young Piikani dropped in on August 27, bringing a house-warming gift of provisions. Those twelve men and two women hung around until September

---

36 Mackenzie to Castlereagh, March 10, 1808, in Lamb, ed., *The Journals and Letters of Mackenzie*, 518.

37 Lamb, *Journals and Letters of Mackenzie*, 42.

38 Belyea, ed., *Columbia Journals*, 64-67, 69; Nisbet, *Mapmaker's Eye*, 46. No one, not even the traders, understood how easily epidemics traveled. Kutenai suffered previously when the great 1781 smallpox pandemic reduced them to a band of forty tents.

39 The band of the Old Chief were upper Kutenai favoring locations at Columbia or Windermere Lakes. The Flat Bow of Ugly Head were lower Kutenai living around present Creston, B.C., and on the lake into which "McGillivray's River" drained. Midway between lay the favored pastures of the Tobacco Plains.

1. Thompson should have been encouraged that they had women with them, which meant their intentions were not bad, when he wrote:

> I had expected them long ago, & it must be their Policy to be highly displeased with us being here, as we render all these Indians independent of them over whom from time almost immemorial they have held in dependence or as enemies & destroyed them. They have it in their power to be very troublesome to us & even cut us off.[40]

He could not believe the claim that they were "pleased that we are here" and that they had only come to steal Kutenai horses. Those insults included running off the old Kutenai chief's horses and exchanging shots with the posse. Thompson's concern heightened next day when three more Piikani arrived as heralds of a larger party following them. At midday on September 5, twenty-three Piikani men and a few women arrived, asking for rum—as was the usual expectation when Natives visited a trading house. Keeping them outside the palisades, Thompson traded the rum for a few scraps of meat. When they departed on the thirteenth, he gave small gifts of tobacco, ammunition, and vermillion, in return for the promise of their leaders to try to keep the young men from stealing horses. Some loiterers told Thompson:

> They denied any intention of the Chiefs of bringing on a Quarrel but owned that the young men would be glad of it, that they should have a pretence to plunder all Parties – I assured them that whatever they might think proper to begin they would meet with a warm reception, however numerous they might be. That the Peagans are highly jealous of the Kootenaes having a trading Post in their Country is certain & equally so that they may wish to find some means to drive us hence, but how they will act is yet to be learned.[41]

Thompson failed to grasp that the Piikani were doing business as usual in horse-raid gamesmanship. Despite his apprehension, the visitors made no hostile gestures toward the small party of traders, perhaps because they knew that might reflect negatively on their trading arrangement on the Saskatchewan. But Thompson's paranoia cast an undeserved cloud over what was actually a restrained Piikani reaction to the NWC's arming of their opponents.

---

40 Belyea, ed., *Columbia Journals*, 62.
41 Belyea, ed., *Columbia Journals*, 66.

In mid-December Thompson should have recognized that a political motive was still driving the Piikani fixation on a peace initiative. Despite heavy snow in the mountains, another delegation of five Piikani crossed the pass and announced that the Blackfeet and Cree were at war with each other, which precluded any intention of their making war west of the mountains. It was instructive that the Piikani stayed at the post until three Flatheads and two Nez Perce appeared a few days later. That had to have been more than a coincidence. When the old Kutenai Chief arrived with four lodges of his band on Christmas Eve, there were meetings and drumming to which Thompson was not invited. Apparently the tribes were trying to reschedule the previous summer's aborted peace initiative.

Thompson tried to forget about the American incident until December, when Salish and Nez Perce visitors delivered a second threat, this one directed specifically at him. Addressed to the "British mercht. Trafficking with the Cabanaws [Kutenais]," the document had been written by the same American officer, who dated it September 20, 1807, from Poltito Palton Lake [Lake Pend Oreille].[42] It threatened that "we have more powerful means of persuasion in our hands than we have hitherto used."[43]

Before the Christmas visitors left Kootenae House, Thompson made gifts to the visiting Salish to obligate them to collect beaver to repay what amounted to advances he had just given them. He promised to visit the Flat Bow Indians in the spring to collect the debt, and in March he sent two men to the Salish country to encourage the arrangement. Along the way, Michel Boulard and Augustin Boisvert were overtaken by a party of Piikani who followed them to the Old Chief's camp. A fight developed in which the old Kutenai chief was wounded, one Piikani was killed, and another wounded. The Kutenai herd was reduced by thirty-five horses that the retreating opportunists ran off. Instead of continuing south to connect with the Salish, Boulard and Boisvert headed into the Lake Indian country.

In early March Thompson wrote two long letters to his supporters admitting that he was having problems getting the expansion started but

42 The letter was written at Lake Pend Oreille on the Clark Fork of the Columbia River, but not delivered until Kalispel Salish and Nez Perce delegates came in December to meet Piikani at Kootenae House.

43 Actually, many of the 42 men with the captain were only nominal Americans. He was bluffing. Jackson, *By Honor and Right*, 228-29.

reassuring his supporters that "I know what I am about."[44] That included encouraging Iroquois or freemen trappers without families to bring their traps and take beaver. Hoping to trade for *castor gras d'hiver* (beaver clothing previously worn by the Kutenai) Thompson made his first exploration of McGillivray's River in spring 1808. But this visit to the Lake Indian country only yielded three packs, and one of those, bearskins and beaver, was lost in a flooding creek as Thompson struggled to return overland. High water to the south (or perhaps Thompson's concern for what the Americans might do) prevented the collection of the advances made the previous winter to the Salish.[45]

According to regulations that a wintering partner must accompany the fur returns, Thompson was obliged to go down the Saskatchewan to receive a new outfit at the inland refitting depot on Rainy Lake. That would also provide an opportunity to confer with other partners about how to react to the unforeseen appearance of the Americans. Passing Rocky Mountain House on June 24, 1808, Thompson picked up 182 beaver skins from independent trappers, including those from Jaco Finlay, who spent the winter trapping in the Piikani country in proximity to the same Indians Thompson feared.[46] The first returns from the Pacific Slope only amounted to fifteen packs, about as many, according to critics, as what the Kutenai had previously carried to posts on the east side of the mountains.

The March letters that Thompson sent to the Saskatchewan proprietors, John McDonald and James Hughes, and to his supporter Donald McTavish, were meant as reassurances. As he rode downstream in a light canoe, Thompson composed a pencil draft of a letter to his sponsor Duncan McGillivray describing his progress to date and registering a hint of uncertainty. "I labour under many disadvantages which only time and generous assistance can improve.…I leave to your judgment if we can with any propriety come to the [Country] of Lakes.[47]

---

44 HBCA, A67/11, 8-13d, preserves the March 3 and 4, 1808, letters from Thompson. Scholar Sean Peake found and noted copies in the HBCA file, A67/11, fos.8-13d. The copies were made by an HBC clerk when evidence was being collected for the Oregon Boundary decision.

45 Belyea, ed., *Columbia Journals*, 75-95.

46 Thompson to Hughes, McDonald, and Donald McTavish, March 4, 1808, HBCA, A6/11, fo. 9d.

47 Pencil draft in Thompson Journal Number 19, Ontario Archives microfilm, reel 2, series 1.

Along the way Thompson had opportunities to meet and confer with other NWC partners and by the time he reached the Rainy Lake depot, he already knew of Duncan McGillivray's death on April 9, 1808. There was no need to make a fair copy of his pencil draft. The account Duncan McGillivray was writing was also incomplete and the information about the appalling American territorial claim had not reached him in Montreal before he died. It was his grieving brother William who received Thompson's recap and the implications of proceeding in the face of a potential international incident.[48]

It was still uncertain who the American officer was and what he might be doing. When Thompson passed Fort Augustus on September 27, 1808, or later at Boggy Hall or Rocky Mountain House, he learned of the death of the American officer and realized that he could proceed to expand south. What was learned from Indians along the Saskatchewan River or west of the mountains in fall 1808 was that Captain Perch had crossed the mountains hoping to contact Piikani and convince them to reconvene the aborted peace council. But Bloods and Atsiina, like those he previously encountered on the Yellowstone River, and met again at the peace council, resented strangers meddling in their politics.

Somewhere on the rolling hills west of the Great Falls of the Missouri, they intercepted Captain Perch and his party of ten. James Bird at Edmonton House recorded:

> Several Blood Indians arrive'd with provisions &. These People it appears from a variety of Accounts, & from the spoils now in their Possession, discovered in their Summer War excursions, on a southern branch of the Missoury, two small settlements which they plundered of goods to a considerable amount, besides about 300 Beaver Skins. One of the men belonging to these settlements was killed & the rest (ten in number) after being stripped were permitted to escape - From some papers brought in by the Indians, the immediate Traders seem to have been Canadians; but from the situation of the Houses, & from the American Colors, which were taken from them, it is concluded that they must have been Subject to the United States.[49]

48 After making a few annotations, William McGillivray turned it over to other editors to publish.

49 Edmonton House Journal, Oct 2, 1808. HBCA, B60/a/8, fo. 4. The only parties operating on the upper Missouri at that time were the men with Captain Perch and four or more trappers with the Detroit trader Charles Courtin.

It would be at least thirty years before the entry in the Edmonton House journal was copied by HBC clerks to inform British diplomats arguing the question of a western boundary. David Thompson never knew the true identity of the presumptuous officer who briefly menaced him. Nor have most historians, who puzzled over the enigma of another United States officer west of the mountains only a year after the return of Lewis and Clark. Actually Perch, or as Thompson erroneously wrote Pinch, was an alias of former Captain of United States artillery, John McClallen, who resigned his commission in 1806 in order to undertake a secret mission to the Spanish Interior Province of New Mexico on behalf of the only general of the United States army, James Wilkinson.[50]

When a direct route was blocked by New Mexican-intimidated Pawnee Indians, McClallen turned north up the Missouri and Yellowstone Rivers expecting to outflank the blockade and enter Santa Fe by a backdoor. At the head of the Yellowstone, Crow Indians reported that British traders were expanding west of the Rocky Mountains. Recovering a sense of a more pressing duty, McClallen changed front to answer that challenge. Of course Thompson didn't know that, but what the Kutenai reported to him was true and supported by documentary evidence.[51]

After the American officer was killed, most of the free trappers who followed him across the mountains returned to the Yellowstone River and were probably absorbed into the operations of St. Louis traders from the mouth of the Big Horn River. An unknown number of others may have returned to the friendly Salish. When curious tribesmen came to check on Finnan McDonald's winter camp and store, they were accompanied by survivors of the American officer's party who were now living as free trappers.[52] In dealing with McDonald, they confirmed the death of the confrontational American officer. At the hangar and tents on the lower McGillivray's River, McDonald received the uncollected debts from the Kalispels and traded enough peltry from visiting Salish or freeman trappers to total thirty-two field packs. In the spring, Michel Boulard and Augustin Boisvert returned from the Lake Indian country with eighteen

50 Jackson, *By Honor and Right*.
51 Edmonton House Journal, October 2, 1808, B60/a/8, fo. 4.
52 Identities have been confirmed for only eight of the forty-two men with McClallen or Charles Courtin.

light packs of furs.[53] And at Kootenae House, Thompson received eight packs taken by five Iroquois trappers. When those returns were carried across the mountains to Fort Augustus, the total of sixty-two light field packs were pressed into forty-eight standard ninety-pound boat packs and sent on in two canoes under the supervision of the indispensable clerk James McMillan.[54]

After spending three leisurely weeks at Fort Augustus/Edmonton, David Thompson and Finnan McDonald left in mid-July to return to Kootenae House. Along the trail they met the Hudson's Bay Company clerk Joseph Howse, who was scouting the pass that would take his name. If the Edmonton House master James Bird intended to test the potential of the western trade, Thompson needed to expand his operations south and gain a hold on the Salish trade ahead of a competitor.

53 They were Boisvert and Boulard who had been sent in March 1808 to renew a contact with the Salish, and went on to the Lake Indian country. In addition to the packs he brought, Boisvert had acquired a country wife. Nisbet, *Sources of the River*, 134.

54 Those light field packs averaged 69½ pounds each. Later Thompson shipped packs from Salish House that weighed from 70 to 80 pounds each. Lighter packs were easier on the small, poorly fed packhorses. Entry for June 27 [28], 1809, Thompson's Journal 19, 23.

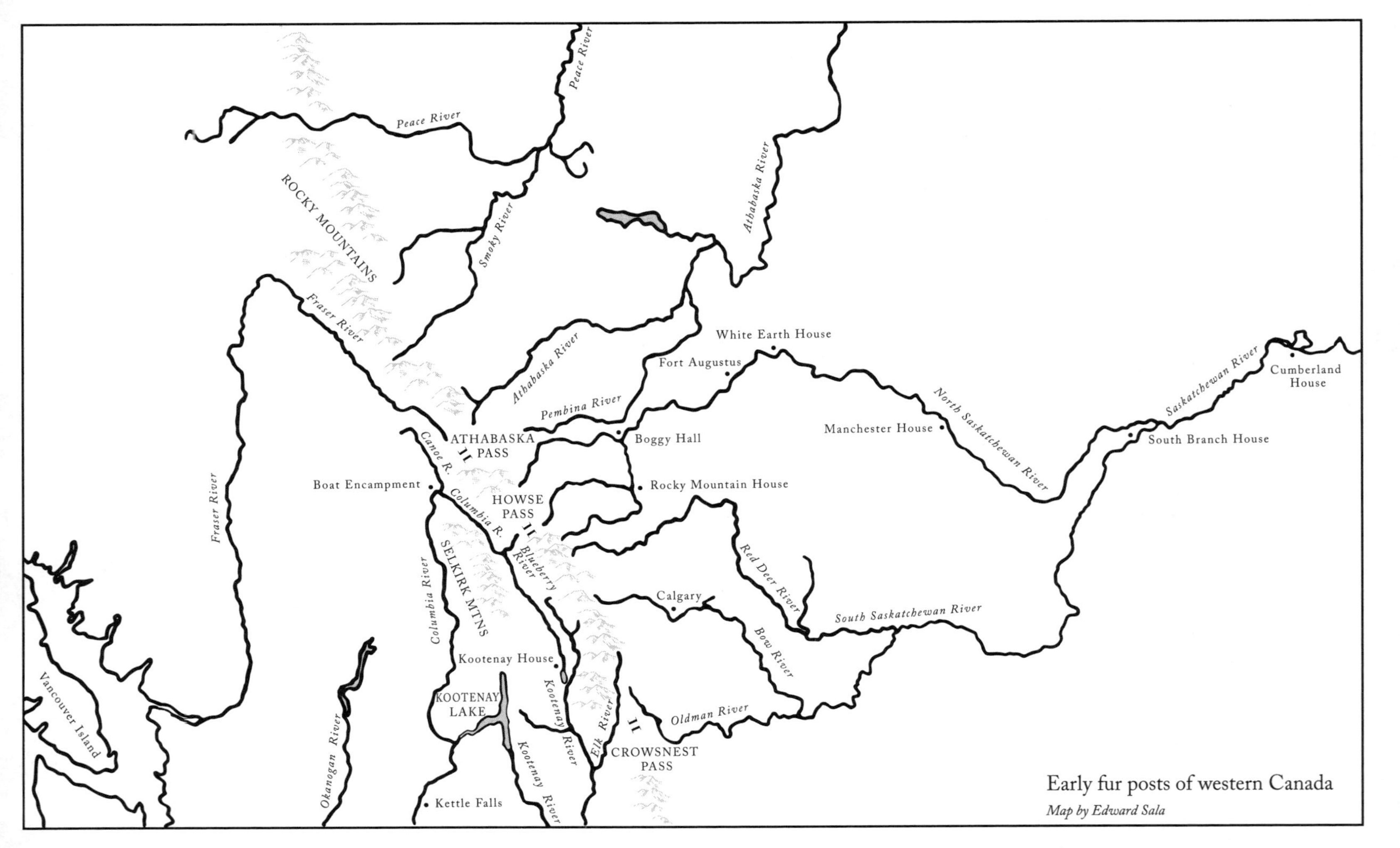

Early fur posts of western Canada
Map by Edward Sala

Chapter Three

Competing for the Columbia

North West Company on a Slippery Pacific Slope

UNAWARE OF THE PROBLEMS DEVELOPING with the Columbia Adventure, William McGillivray came to the 1808 North West Company annual meeting with the wintering partners of McTavish, McGillivray & Company. Despite unimpressive initial returns of skins from the West, the proprietors decided to extend operations on the Columbia and give it supply status equal to the highly productive Athabaska department. In the Lower Forts des Prairies department, the ailing John McDonald was replaced by the experienced Alexander Henry and given two canoes for the Fort Vermilion outfit. James Hughes remained at Fort Augustus on the upper Saskatchewan where he received ten canoes.[1]

William McGillivray left the meeting to return downstream before David Thompson arrived at Rainy Lake with the latest information about the American captain's threatening attitude. Learning of the death of Duncan McGillivray along the way seems to have discouraged Thompson from completing the letter he started in the back of his field journal asking Duncan if the western experiment should continue. The letter further suggested that despite an American intrusion, the greater part of the trade to the north was still left to the NWC.

Thompson' reputation as an explorer should be balanced against the reality of his obligations as a productive North West Company wintering partner. Establishing a viable business in a new region was his first responsibility; exploration of the Pacific Slope was a distant objective. As he returned to his western post, Thompson probably heard rumors of the death of the American officer. If true, Thompson could risk expanding

1 Wallace, ed., *Documents Relating to the North West Company*, 260, 262.

operations toward Poltito Palton Lake.[2] The Kalispels who visited Kootenae House in December 1807 had already provided Thompson with better understanding what he called the Salish River (present Clark Fork of the Columbia).

Stopping at Kootenae House, Thompson sent his clerk Finnan McDonald and a canoe party down McGillivray's (Kootenay) River, but they left too late in the season and were blocked by ice above the falls. Undaunted at being denied a comfortable winter among the Salish, McDonald built a *hangard* (storehouse) and set up tents to live in during the winter. After news of the new establishment spread among the tribes, Salish started coming from their Flathead Valley winter camps to do a bit of trading. Very likely they were accompanied by remnants of the American party, who confirmed the death of Captain Perch.[3]

It would take another year before that information reached Fort William or Montreal, but the downstream management had already dismissed the two threatening letters as meddling by some United States interest, perhaps Mr. Astor who was showing an interest in the western trade. Very likely, the mysterious St. Louis informant who intercepted and copied Meriwether Lewis's report on the exploration of the Corps of Discovery was still keeping his NWC connections informed.

Encouraged by what McDonald learned and reported during the winter, Thompson carried his returns only as far as Fort Augustus before returning and abandoning Kootenae House on August 29, 1809. He expected that the Salish would provide a more reliable source of provisions for the new post (or posts) he intended to build. Traveling down McGillivray's River past McDonald's winter camp and past the modern communities of Libby and Bonners Ferry, Idaho, brought Thompson's party to the northern terminus of what he later identified as the "Lake Indian Road."[4] Borrowing packhorses from the Lower Kutenai, they

---

2 Captain Perch, alias John McClallen, revealed his limited understanding when he referred to the Poltito Palton, Cabanaws, and Pilchenee, names he got from the two former corpsman then with him. Alvin Josephy Jr. unraveled the derivation of the term Pellate Paller (pello-ut pelu) that Lewis and Clark applied to certain Nez Perce living on the Clearwater River near present Kamiah, Idaho. Josephy Jr., *The Nez Perce Indians*, 649-51, n.30.

3 Alexander Henry at Fort Vermillion and James Bird at Edmonton heard Indian accounts of the death. The remainder of Captain Perch's large party or Courtin's smaller group would have informed McDonald.

4 Belyea, ed., *Columbia Journals*, 243.

trailed south, following the stream now known as the Pack River to Poltito Palton Lake (Lake Pend Oreille). Turning east along the north shore, Thompson located and built his second trading post, Kullyspell House.[5]

While the house was being built, Thompson made an abbreviated exploration of the river flowing out from the lake (Pend Oreille River), but turned back before finding where it ended. Leaving Finnan McDonald in charge of the new establishment, he then moved east up the Clark Fork and made an exploratory circuit overland to McGillivray's River to meet clerk James McMillan bringing the new outfit.[6] After consolidating stores at Kullyspell House, Thompson traveled some seventy-five miles up the Clark Fork to the place where it spilled over a chute likely to stop boats. On the east end of a meadow that promised grazing for horses, he built another house and named it Saleesh House, although it was still a discrete forty miles from the traditional Salish winter camps.[7] Thompson kept his distance from the Indian camps because another American party was there and he had no way of knowing if the previously stated United States trade regulations might be enforced.[8]

News of a convenient trading post attracted freemen living with the Indians and in need of supplies. Many of these men were a legacy of earlier American intrusion into the country. Some were trappers Captain Perch brought west in 1807; others had recently followed the trader/trapper Charles Courtin to the Three Forks of the Missouri and beyond. Courtin and his party had extended trading operations from Fort Remon at the mouth of the Yellowstone to the promising beaver workings of the upper Missouri, and the venture had at first proved rewarding. In February when the early Salish buffalo hunt started across the mountains, Courtin attempted to carry his packs gathered in the Columbia drainage to a large cache of beaver fur he had left near the Three Forks

5 Belyea, ed., *Columbia Journals*, 106; Elliott, ed., "The Fur Trade in the Columbia River Basin prior to 1811," 246. Elliott Coues placed the northern terminus of the Lake Indian Road nearer the Idaho/Montana border, relying, perhaps too uncritically, on Thompson's coordinates. See Coues, ed., *New Light*, 2:672.

6 White, ed., *Thompson Journals*, 43-58. Confirmed by the extensive field research and checking of Thompson's observations by Carl W. Haywood.

7 White, ed., *Thompson Journals*, 59-75. The exact location depends on the accurate reinterpretation of Thompson's compass bearings by Carl W. Haywood in his *Sometimes Only Horses to Eat.*

8 When clerk James McMillan returned from Rainy Lake with the 1809–10 Outfit, he may have carried encouragement for Thompson to proceed in the face of an as yet untested U.S. territorial claim and previously stated trading regulations.

of the Missouri River. In a narrow canyon leading east from the lower end of the Bitterroot Valley (near present Missoula, Montana), he was killed in a Blackfeet ambush. Thompson initially called that fatal channel "Courtin's Defile," but in later years it became known as the Hell Gate.

The breakup of the small American party produced significant returns for the NWC. Seen as the only apparent authority in the country, Thompson was called to the Salish camp by surviving trappers to adjudicate the dispersal of the recovered packs. After redistributing 454 poorly-dressed beaver to Courtin's men, Thompson then purchased those pelts, along with "the rest of the Furrs at the price mentioned in the accounts."[9]

Augmented by skins from Indians, the Nor'wester gained 496 pelts weighing about 907 pounds. When 431 pelts weighing 785 pounds previously received at Saleesh House were added, that totaled about 1,650 pounds of peltry.[10] Thompson and McDonald made up "22 pactons" (light packs) of seventy to eighty pounds each and sent these down to Kullyspell House on March 21, 1810.[11] Over half of that trade came from furs recovered from the slain American, Courtin. Much of the remaining peltry must have been produced by Salish who used it to buy about twenty NWC trade guns at a cost of from fifteen to twenty beaver skins a gun.[12] That confirmed the Piikani concern—that their enemies would be armed.

On May 17, 1810, Thompson's men began carrying forty-six light packs and six pieces of baggage north over the "Lake Indian Road" to McGillivray's River. Thompson's personal baggage went along because he had decided that his obligation as a partner had been met and he was owed an overdue furlough.[13] Drifting those packs from Saleesh House to the mouth of the Pack River was nothing compared to hauling them over that snow-bound trace with thin horses that were eating leaves to survive. Back on McGillivray's River they lacked bark to patch the battered canoes McMillan had used the previous October to bring the outfit

9 As far as known, account books for this interesting period have disappeared, along with a list of letters Thompson wrote to associates.

10 White, ed., *Thompson Journals*, 92-95.

11 An average weight of a beaver pelt at 1.86 pounds, taken from William Ashley's accounts at the 1825 American rendezvous, appears a bit too high.

12 Cox, *Columbia River*, 105.

13 White, ed., *Thompson Journals*, 117-18.

down. Boatmen paddled and poled against the current and the emaciated horses staggered along a shore trail. It took five trips to portage around the great falls below Finnan McDonald's abandoned hangard. Fourteen packs had to be shifted to horses to lighten the boats, but after three days that was given up to save the weakening animals.

Ominously, at the Canal Flats portage to the Columbia, tracks of "Peeagan spies" seemed to confirm Thompson's concern that the dread Piikani were hovering along the route.[14] After forty-two tortured days, the first significant fur returns from the west reached the mouth of the Blaeberry River. All that remained for tired porters and exhausted horses was an excruciating climb over the snow-bound Rocky Mountains.[15]

After slogging through four feet of snow over the pass and down the upper Saskatchewan, Thompson left McMillan at Fort Augustus with instructions to bring along the forty-six packs. Going ahead in a light canoe, Thompson reached Alexander Henry's new White Earth House on June 23. While his guest took a leisurely five-day rest, Henry realized that Thompson intended to take a furlough in Montreal and interceded with a more demanding obligation.[16]

Henry had traveled to Fort William in a light canoe the previous year to hurry more trade goods to the Saskatchewan and Columbia Adventures. At the rendezvous there were rumors of new American competition in the fur trade, but a more imminent threat loomed on the upper Saskatchewan—the Hudson's Bay Company intended to move across the mountains and open a rival trade. Henry sought to intercept Thompson and convince him he had to answer that challenge. Despite Henry's strongly held opinion, Thompson continued downstream with his family. But there must have been some kind of understanding as not long after McMillan arrived from Fort Augustus with the packs, he was sent back upriver carrying the goods Henry brought from downstream. Among the trade goods were two bundles of Thompson's property, including his

14 Belyea, ed., *Columbia Journals*, 111-16 (Sept. 27 to Oct. 6, 1809).

15 Extracted from White, ed., *Thompson Journals*, 113-26.

16 Wallace, *Documents Relating to the North West Company*, 210, 259-60. Thompson had been listed on the rotation list as eligible for leave in 1808 and was listed on the rotations for 1810. In a later letter to an old friend, he admitted that he had intended visiting Montreal in the summer of 1810 "but the critical situation of our affairs in the Columbia obligated me to return." Masson, *Les Bourgeois de la Compagnie du Nord-Ouest*, 41-42. Also quoted in Belyea, ed., *Columbia Journals*, 254.

precious books. The western partner expected to return to the Clark Fork with a new outfit.[17]

The NWC trade in the far west faced challenges from potential Piikani interference and possible HBC competition. Additionally, since 1806 the downstream agents McTavish, McGillivray & Company had been in negotiation with New York fur buyer John Jacob Astor. Well known in Montreal and sometimes an invited guest of the company's prestigious Beaver Club, Astor had frustrating dealings with the Nor'Westers over easing competition along the Great Lakes border.[18] About the time that they were reading the purloined copy of Meriwether Lewis's report to President Jefferson, or Captain Perch's American trade regulations Thompson had sent them in late 1807, Astor confided to United States Vice President De Witt Clinton "his plans on the Subject of a company for carrying on the furr trade in the United States even more extensive than it is done by the companys in Canada."[19]

In spring 1808 Astor confirmed his vision of a continental fur trade by first chartering the American Fur Company in New York State and soon offering to buy the Montreal-financed Michilimackinac Company, foundering on the shoals of American embargo.[20] Astor's plans for the western expansion of his business developed during a period when the United States felt beleaguered by an overbearing British Empire. Negative public feeling intensified after April 1809 when British ambassador David Erskine "misread his instructions from London and signed an agreement that led a gullible Madison administration to remove restrictions on trade with Great Britain. When London repudiated this generous conciliatory move, the American government was outraged

17 Gough, ed., *Journal of Alexander Henry the Younger*, 2:452, 454-55.

18 The account of Astor and his fur trade empire can be found in Haeger, *John Jacob Astor*. A recent but not consulted recap is Stark, *Astoria*.

19 Ronda, *Astoria and Empire*, 38-39.

20 The value of skins exported from Quebec to England in 1807 amounted to £240,000. Other furs worth £70,112 were also sent to the United States by way of Lake Champlain until the 1808 embargo lessened the demand from that quarter. "General View of the Imports and Exports of Canada from 1754 to 1808 (in sterling money)," John Lambert, *Travels through Canada, and the United States of North America, in the years 1806, 1807, & 1808 : to which are added biographical notices and anecdotes of some of the leading characters in the United States* (2d. ed., cor. and improved. London: Printed for C. Cradock and W. Joy, 1814), 206. A currency conversion table is included in Appendix B of this work.

and the exasperated President James Madison moved to reinstate non-intercourse restrictions and call up a "ten thousand man army" to demonstrate commitment.

Ever the entrepreneur, John Jacob Astor saw a way to use his American citizenship to get around such trade embargoes and supply the western Indian trade by launching a grand plan to dominate the fur trade on two fronts. His two-pronged strategy first combined his new firm, the American Fur Company, with the Montreal-controlled Michilimackinac Company into an umbrella concern to be dubbed the South West Company. Secondly, he envisioned making a similar arrangement with the North West Company in the far west, which might work because McTavish, McGillivray and Company, in addition to being agents for the North West Company, held interests in the Michilimackinac Company.

By 1809 the Michilimackinac Company, in the face of severe trade restrictions, was economically stressed. Astor could provide an alternative to business failure by offering to purchase the Michilimackinac Company, and at the same time suggest a joint venture with the North West Company into the Pacific. Suspicious of their wily rival, the Nor'Westers declined until Astor repeated his offer with more specifics. If the North West Company would purchase one-third interest in his Pacific venture, he would purchase one-half interest in the Michilimackinac Company. Interested but cautious, the Montreal agents informed Astor that they would have to consult other parties in Montreal and at Fort William.

When other Montreal interests bombarded the government with petitions to block Astor's plan, William McGillivray of McTavish, McGillivray & Company and John Richardson of Forsythe, Richardson & Company went to New York in February 1810 to see if Astor was willing to follow through on the Michilimackinac Company deal. When Astor held to his initial offer, they explained that it could only be decided at the summer meeting at Fort William. The Montreal representatives who left for the July 1810 inland rendezvous expected trouble from wintering partners. If there were objections, they did not appear in tersely written minutes only listing assignments for the next trading season. In 1811, after much stalling, the Nor'Westers and their Montreal agents finally came to terms with Astor regarding his South West Company. It would be the ensuing summer before a final agreement could be reached and meantime Astor went forward with his plans for the Pacific Fur

Company by recruiting partners and voyageurs in Montreal, activities that certainly were not to be missed in trade-sensitive Montreal.[21]

The meeting concluded before Thompson arrived at the Rainy Lake inland depot, but he learned about what was discussed as he met other partners. When he read his instructions Thompson found he was directed to rendezvous with the Pacific Fur Company and confirm that the North West Company had agreed to hold a one-third interest in an adventure that Americans would control. The dedicated astronomer now realized that he was tasked with completing the exploration of the Columbia River in order to confirm its feasibility as a transport route from the fur-rich interior to the coast. He already knew from the Meriwether Lewis report to Jefferson that the Columbia was navigable from the Snake River to the mouth.

David Thompson's journal from July 22 until October 28, 1810, has not been located. It would have accounted for his return trip to the Rocky Mountains, which has instead become the cause of much speculation and controversy among historians. Lacking knowledge of the documents clarifying the intention of the wintering partners, many writers have since argued erroneously that whoever first arrived on the Columbia would win control of its riches.

Consequently, some historians interpreted Thompson's turnabout at Rainy Lake as a "race to the sea," his presumed goal the establishment of commercial and national priority on the Columbia.[22] Hudson's Bay Company historian E. E. Rich, for example, wrote, "There [at Rainy Lake] he [Thompson] found urgent orders from the North West partners, stimulated into frantic activity by news that the American Fur Company had been formed by John Jacob Astor to take over the fur trade of the west. Thompson's orders allowed no further delay."[23] Arthur S. Morton argued that "he was sent back posthaste to reach the mouth of the Columbia and

---

21 These arrangements are discussed in Haeger, "Business Strategy and Practice," 192-94. The January 8, 1811, agreement between Astor and the Nor'Westers concerning the South West Company can be found in Wallace, ed., *Documents Relating to the North West Company*, 239-45.

22 Beyond discovery, national priority had already been established by three previous American parties: Lewis and Clark, John McClallen, and Charles Courtin. Now Astor was on the way to complete the commercial factor.

23 Rich, *Fur Trade*, 200.

to build a fort and raise the Union Jack on the breezes of the Oregon, before Jacob Astor's expedition should arrive."[24] But there *was* no "race to the sea" and the wintering partners, including Thompson, were simply acting on misinformation concerning a deal with Astor.[25]

Before leaving Saleesh House in spring 1810, Thompson was aware of the collapse of two American attempts to establish posts west of the mountains and a third on the Yellowstone River. The last, fielded by the reorganized St. Louis Missouri Fur Company, a syndicate of St. Louis entrepreneurs, seemed too distant to be a threat to his Clark Fork operations. But trading and trapping on the upper Missouri by Charles Courtin and others had proved rewarding.[26] From that location Americans were less than a week away from the NWC posts.[27]

When Thompson left Saleesh House in mid-May, nothing in his journal suggests that he knew that threat had been muted when the American trappers scattered on April 12 to begin a late spring hunt. About ten miles from the fort, Bloods and Atsiina fell on the parties killing several and sending the survivors fleeing to safety. After being penned in and frustrated by Native hostilities for over a week, the resident partner Pierre Menard wrote that he hoped to attract the Snakes or Flatheads. "My plan is to induce them to stay here if possible, and make war upon the Blackfeet so we may take some prisoners and send one

---

24 Morton, "North West Company's Columbian Enterprise," 284.

25 Thompson's *Narrative* is not much help in clarifying events at Rainy Lake in 1810 or during his return to the Columbia, and gives what editor Richard Glover considered a "remarkably false impression." *See* Glover, ed., *David Thompson's Narrative*, lvi-vii and 316n1.

26 Pierre Menard to Adrien Langlois, October 7, 1809, Kaskaskia Papers, Missouri Historical Society, in Oglesby, "Pierre Menard, Reluctant Mountain Man," *The Bulletin of the Missouri Historical Society*, vol. 24. "It is said that one cannot imagine the quantity of beaver that there is [at the forks of the Missouri], but there is the difficulty of the savage Black Feet who plunder often and who have kept our men during the last spring from making a fortune. They were obliged to retire from the beginning of the hunt after not only having [had] stolen some of their beaver, but also some of their horses, traps & arms, ammunition & excepting one party of 4 men, of which Case [Charles Courtin] brother of Bt. Fortin was one. He had in cache at the end of October of the past year 20 packs of Beaver and may have at the present at least 50 packs. His caches were in the 3 forks but there is no news of him since the past year."

27 This period is treated in *The Selected Papers of the 2010 Fur Trade Symposium at the Three Forks*, edited by Jim Hardee (Three Forks, MT: Three Forks Area Historical Society, 2011).

back with propositions of peace—which I think can be easily secured by leaving traders among them below the Falls of the Missouri."[28]

Nor would the British trader have known that another partner, Reuben Lewis, was less optimistic about prospects in a letter to his brother, Governor Meriwether Lewis. His "principal hopes are now on the Columbia," he wrote, because he felt that the Blackfeet "are urged on by the British traders in their country." Reuben Lewis believed that he and General William Clark should sell their shares in the St. Louis Missouri Fur Company and reinvest in the new Pacific Fur Company. One fearless young trapper even volunteered to make a circuit to the south, outflanking the hostile Indians, in order to reach Shoshones or Salish and induce them to become allies.[29]

In a second attempt to trap, the Missouri fur men went out on April 22, resulting in the gruesome deaths of George Drouillard and two of his Shawnee kinsmen, who were also killed by Bloods and Atsiina. At that time Thompson was drifting his returns down the Clark Fork and planning to send Finnan McDonald and seven men back to Saleesh House to gather provisions and remain as the summer complement guarding the house and the remaining goods.

One of the freemen left at Saleesh House with Finnan McDonald was a survivor of the party of the slain Charles Courtin. Michel Bourdeaux (hereafter Bourdon) had not forgotten the cache of beaver still buried at the Three Forks. He shared that interesting fact with McDonald and perhaps Thompson. The possibility of retrieving another bonanza of Yankee beaver skins left rotting in a hole in the ground was irresistible.[30]

Thompson instructed McDonald to send provisions over the "Great Road of the Salish" to intercept the packers and boatmen working returns up McGillivray's River and encourage the Salish buffalo hunters to make provisions for the traders and their families. McDonald took this as an excuse to cross the mountains with the buffalo hunters. There is no proof that the idea developed before Thompson left Saleesh House,

28 Menard to Chouteau, 21 April 1810, in Chittenden, *American Fur Trade*, 2:898. *See also* Aarstad, "This Unfortunate Affair," 62-67.

29 R. Lewis to M. Lewis, 21 April 1810, Meriwether Lewis Collection, Missouri Historical Society; John C. Jackson, "Reuben Lewis: Fur Trader, Subagent and Meriwether's Younger Brother," *We Proceeded On*, 38:4 (November 2012), 8-17.

30 This speculation dangles on several accounts of what resulted, HBCA B60/a/9, fos. 2-2d; Coues, *New Light*, 2:720-21.

and Thompson would have good reason to distance himself from what developed.

Unaware of the murderous Blood and Atsiina attacks on the Missouri Fur Company, Finnan McDonald, Michel Bourdon, and Jean Baptiste Buché accompanied the summer buffalo hunt. Following *Cokalarishkit*, the Salish road to the buffalo, brought them to the buffalo ranges along the Missouri River above the Great Falls, the area where Captain Perch had been killed two years previously. It was a dangerous year to be in the ranges of the northern plainsmen. HBC Edmonton House master James Bird observed warriors were on the war trail at the end of February 1810, some going to war upon the Snakes or riding south to attack Mountain Crows in their country. The Crow were getting arms and ammunition from the American fort at the mouth of the Big Horn, and those traders promised to join the Crow in an invasion of the South Branch of the Saskatchewan. Appalled Atsiina fleeing north were so desperate for ammunition that they threatened to rob Rocky Mountain House to get it.[31]

McDonald and Bourdon later provided Thompson with a description of what took place, which he dramatized in his later *Narrative*:

> Accompanied by Mr. Finan McDonald, Michel Bourdeaux and Baptiste Buché with ammunition tobacco &c to encourage them: they crossed the Mountains by a wide defile of easy passage, eastward of the Saleesh Lake, here they are watched by the Peeagans to prevent them hunting the Bison, and driven back, and could only hunt as it were by stealth; the case was now different, and they were determined to hunt boldly and try a battle with them: they were entering on the grounds, when the scouts, as usual early each morning sent to view the country came riding at full speed, calling out, the "Enemy is on us;" instantly down went the Tents and tent poles, which, with the Baggage formed a rude rampart; this was barely done, when a steady charge of cavalry came on them, but the Horses did not break through the rampart, part of pointed poles each party discharged their arrows, which only wounded a few, none fell; a second and a third charge, was made; but in a weak manner; the battle was now of infantry. The Saleesh, about one hundred and fifty Men, took possession of a slightly rising ground about half a mile in front of their Tents, the Peagans, about one hundred and Seventy men drew up and formed a rude line about four hundred yards from them; the Saleesh and the white Men lay quiet on the defensive; the Peeagans, from time to

31 Coues, *New Light*, 2:720-21.

> time throughout the day, sent parties of about forty men forward, to dare them to battle Buche, who was a good shot, said they were harder to hit than a goose on the wing the three men had several shots discharged at them, but their violent gestures prevented a steady aim in return; the three men were all good shots, and as I have noticed the Indians allow no neutrals, they had to fight in their own defense. Mr. Finan McDonald fired forty five shots, killed two men and wounded one, the other two men each fired forty three balls, and each wounded one man; such were their wild activity, they were an uncertain mark to fire at; the evening ended the battle; on the part of the Peeagans, seven killed and thirteen wounded; on the part of the Saleesh, five killed and nine wounded; each party took care of their dead and wounded; no scalps were taken, which the Peeagans accounted a disgrace to them; the Saleesh set no pride in taking scalps; This was the first time the Peeagans were in a manner defeated, and they determined to wreck their vengeance on the white men who crossed the mountains to the west side; and furnished arms and ammunition to their enemies.[32]

Those western hunters were now armed with twenty new guns sold to them at Saleesh or Kullyspell House, which Thompson rationalized as arming the Salish and Sahaptins against the depredations of enemies.[33] By siding with the Salish in what amounted to a Piikani turkey shoot, the Nor'westers unintentionally overplayed their hand.

At Hudson's Bay Company's Edmonton House, James Bird was sensitive to inter-tribal war games because he was sending the clerk Joseph Howse across the mountains to test the Salish trade. Howse left for the Columbia with nine men, including two Nipissings already familiar with the western country.[34] His Blackfoot interpreter was John Park, who had learned the Blackfoot language by living with the Piikani. Joseph Lewis became the third African American to enter the western country.[35] The party eventually grew to seventeen including four Cree hunters. On August 20, 1810, Joseph Howse wrote Bird from the "Cootenais R.," reporting that

---

32 Glover, ed., *David Thompson's Narrative*, 306.

33 There were eight additional guns in the 1810-11 outfit that the Piikani blocked later. The consequence of the arms business was an escalation of violence that continued for most of the century.

34 Three years later Toussaint Paquin presented a note for two thousand six hundred and thirty eight livres for the furs his brother Joseph Paquin gave to Mr. Howse on the Columbia.

35 The first was William Clark's servant in 1805 and the second John McClallen's waiter in 1807.

> Kootenae Indians warned that there had been a battle between Flat Heads and Muddy River Indians in which fourteen of the later had been killed...and that the Muddy River Indians in consequence are laying in ambush to intercept him, or any white man who might attempt to convey goods to the Flatt Heads.[36]

After being stalled for a time near abandoned Kootenae House, the HBC party was allowed to pack the HBC outfit on prairie ponies along the Kootenay River until their guides struck off above present Libby, Montana, to follow the Fisher River trail overland, bypassing Flathead Lake, to the usual Salish winter camps along the lower Flathead River.[37]

Concerned that the Hudson's Bay Company would carry competition for the Salish trade, Alexander Henry dispatched James McMillan and Nicholas Montour to "watch the motions of the H. B." and soon moved up from the White Earth location to Rocky Mountain House. His two observers were also intimidated at Kootenae House and only allowed to proceed because they were traveling light and carried no trade goods and no guns. Upon reaching the Clark Fork, McMillan and Montour found that McDonald had already abandoned Saleesh House and after tenting on the river twenty miles below retreated to the new house Jaco Finlay was building for the Spokane and Coeur d'Alene Indian trade.

Without actually touching base with McDonald, McMillan and Montour confirmed that the new HBC settlement was located above Saleesh House and about six miles below the confluence of the Flathead and Clark Fork Rivers, a place the Salish favored because those rolling hills offered grazing for their large horse herds.[38] Convinced that the HBC would take the Salish and freeman trade because of the lack of trade goods, the two Nor'westers left Kullyspell House on December 12.

During the winter, Howse had opportunities to associate with the mountain freemen gaining potentially useful geographic understanding. Despite the danger of bumping into outraged Piikani, he even accompanied the Salish winter buffalo hunt to the heights overlooking the

36 Howse to Bird, received October 31, 1810, Edmonton House Journal 1810-11, HBCA, B60/a/9, fo. 2.

37 Although speculation has placed the location in other places, being close to the trading Indians made proximity to their winter camps near the Horse Plains the logical place for Howse to trade and to cut off McDonald at Saleesh House.

38 Alexander Ross noted the location in his field journal on February 14, 1814.

country near the Great Falls and returned to the Salish winter camps in February 1811.[39]

Unaware of those developments, David Thompson and the new outfit in four canoes were returning to the mountains. Traveling ahead in a light canoe, Thompson reached the consolidated White Earth House on September 6, a day ahead of the three loaded canoes. Five days later, after refitting the canoes and engaging in an all-night party, the brigade of twenty-four men and three women carrying fifty-one packages of trade goods and provisions, continued up the North Saskatchewan River.[40]

In passing the upper Saskatchewan posts, Thompson told James Bird that he anticipated arriving at the mouth of the Columbia the following August and that the arrangement with John Jacob Astor remained effective. Thompson was in no hurry to arrive there before Astor's ship, the *Tonquin*, which they knew to be en route. He only had to meet the Pacific Fur Company and confirm the arrangement to share the western trade.[41] Sometime after Thompson went on, the gregarious Nor'wester James Hughes found time to visit his neighbor at Edmonton House. On October 31, James Bird wrote in his journal:

> The NWCoy. appear now to pursue their trade to that quarter with an avidity which can be created by prospects of great benefit only. They amuse us with Stories of their intention to send a Ship round to the Mouth of the Columbia in Pursuit of this trade, they tell us likewise that they are to hold a third part of the Stock of a large American Company which is formed in New York to undertake a trade up the Missowery & that River to the Pacific Ocean.[42]

Two weeks after Thompson left White Earth House, Alexander Henry rode to Rocky Mountain House with a small party. As they approached his wintering post on October 5, Henry was surprised to find it already occupied—by the "Columbia brigade." According to the explanation of those boatmen, in proceeding up the Saskatchewan they encountered four Piikani men of consequence blocking the trail across the mountains. Piikani later informed Henry that they had camped on the Kootenae

39 H. Christoph Wolfart, "Joseph House," DCB 8. Howse may have had a description of the fight from the freeman Michel Bourdon who instigated and participated in it.

40 Coues, New Light, 628; Gough, *Alexander Henry*, 2: 470-71.

41 Glover, ed., *David Thompson's Narrative*, 322.

42 Edmonton House Journal, HBCA, B60/a/9, fo. 2.

Plain in September, determined to prevent the trail being used to supply the Kutenais and Salish with more arms. Four chiefs were sufficient to stop and turn back the new outfit.[43] But where was Thompson?

Thompson also traveled on horseback with a few companions until they perceived signs of trouble. Without checking to determine what had become of the boat party, they retreated downstream to the mouth of the Brazeau River and made a carefully concealed camp. Later, when he was confronted by Henry, Thompson lamely explained that he failed to realize his brigade was already ahead of them. He had waited from September 15 to October 15 and was still waiting for them to come up the river.[44] A precious month had been lost until Henry broke into the Columbia packs to get liquor that would distract the Piikani hanging around Rocky Mountain House. The subterfuge allowed the canoes to slip down the river and rejoin Thompson. In a year when the "Adventure to the Columbia" needed to compete with the HBC, the misunderstanding meant that the Clark Fork trading houses would not receive trade goods.[45]

The Piikani blockade finally gave proof to the fear Thompson had felt for the past three years. Convinced that the trail was interdicted by hostiles, at the end of October he set out to find a way around the blockade. Thompson's detour—by way of the Brazeau River—required twenty-four horses, each carrying from 180– to 240–pound loads plus traveling provisions. The familiar Indian trail had been recently used by a party of freemen and Thompson hired one of them as his guide.[46]

The route led them north along the flank of the Rocky Mountains to the Athabaska River. Constant clearing of fallen timber ate up over a month of the advancing season until it was getting too late to attempt crossing the mountains. Realizing that his horses could not travel much beyond the valley of the Athabaska, Thompson brought materials to construct dogsleds and snowshoes for the men.[47]

---

43 Coues, *New Light*, 644.

44 Gough, ed., *Alexander Henry*, 2:470-87. The Coues and Gough editions of Henry's journals contain differences in transcription, sometimes changing the meaning in possibly significant ways.

45 Coues, *New Light*, 644-650; Gough, Alexander Henry, 2:481-485.

46 Gough, Alexander Henry, 2:486; Glover, ed., *David Thompson's Narrative*, 324 n1.

47 Thompson's description of that trying experience from October 29, 1810, to January 26, 1811, is in Belyea, ed., *Columbia Journals*, 117-41.

They were still struggling up the frozen and snow-covered Athabaska River on December 21 when Thompson wrote by firelight to his friend Alexander Fraser, reporting news of the deaths of a number of American trappers in two attacks near the Three Forks of the Missouri River. The hostility of Blood and Atsiina Indians had turned back an American challenge.[48]

The winter weather soon became an adversary as the struggling party bogged down in the snow. On December 29, 1810, Thompson abandoned his staggering horses, left a portion of the outfit to the care of a clerk, and prepared to continue with a dog train. Now the previously moderate weather turned bitterly cold, with temperatures plummeting to thirty-six degrees below zero.[49] As the men and dogs flagged, their loads had to be cut in half, and caches of goods began to mark the trail.[50] They crossed the pass where snow was seven-and-a-half feet deep. But across the height of land, temperatures rose and deep, melting snow became a new challenge. To add to their misery, just west of the Continental Divide, a January rain began falling. Finally, on January 26, 1811, some in the party had had enough. From a last camp beside the gloomy, drizzly snow-sodden banks of the Columbia River, three of the small party retreated back over the pass.

Until the snows melted, Thompson and the two loyal Canadians had to endure the rest of the winter at a junction of the Wood, Canoe and Columbia Rivers, a place to be known as Boat Encampment.[51] The search for a route around the Piikani blockade and over the Continental Divide in the middle of winter seems a desperately ill-advised move. How would Thompson have felt, had he known that Piikani departed from Rocky Mountain House by November 9, reopening what would be known in the future as Howse Pass?[52] All Thompson could do now was wait out the winter, try to reassemble the outfit scattered along the Athabaska

48 "Appendage to John McDonald of Garth Autobiographical Notes," Masson, ed., *Les Bourgeois*, 2:41-42. It was mid-January before this and other letters were sent by messengers back to Fort Augustus in time to catch the winter express going to headquarters.

49 Belyea, ed., *Columbia Journals*, 136, 141.

50 A five-pound bag of musket balls lost from one of these caches just north of the summit of Athabaska Pass was found in 1921 by a member of the Provincial Boundary Commission. Belyea, ed., *Columbia Journals*, 261-62.

51 Belyea, ed., *Columbia Journals*, 132-41.

52 Glover, ed., *David Thompson's Narrative*, lviii; Coues, *New Light*, 662; Gough, ed., *Alexander Henry*, 2:495-96.

River and Pass, and proceed to meet the Astorians at the mouth of the Columbia River.

Marooned on the upper Columbia, David Thompson was unaware of developments at the recent Fort William meeting. Wintering partners were not going to accept Piikani dictation of how their trade was conducted and flatly rejected Thompson's idea of shifting access to the Columbia father north to avoid the Piikani blockade. Western superintendence shifted to Thompson's pugnacious little brother-in-law, John McDonald, who vowed to put the pesky Piikani in their place. Mr. Thompson was left free to "prosecute his plans for discovery on the west side of the mountains towards the Pacific," including descending the Columbia to confirm the cooperation with Astor.

The Columbia outfit was increased to five canoe loads supervised by John McDonald, assisted by the clerk John George McTavish. Papers were read and laid on the table for discussion relative to the south trade and a proposal to buy stock in the Hudson's Bay Company. It might be presumed those subjects commanded attention for the rest of the day, and more, as protests were registered on July 15 against the stock purchase or a projected trade to China. Several parties involved with the Montreal agency for the Michilimackinac Company were not in agreement concerning the compact with Astor and those opposed chose to opt out of the combined agreement.[53] Their protest was registered just a month after Thompson arrived at the mouth of the Columbia River to confirm that deal.[54]

The new year of 1811 began with Thompson totally out of contact with everyone and still believing he was directed to descend the Columbia River and confirm a one-third interest in Astor's Pacific Fur Company. By mid–April 1811 the snows had melted enough for Thompson to continue his explorations westward. On May 3 his small party was working up the Columbia when they encountered two Nipissing trappers who had descended the Blaeberry River and were followed by others. Thompson hired the Grand Nipissing and Louis Iroquois to carry letters to William Henry and Nicholas Montour and assist them in bringing the

53 Wallace, *Documents of NWC*, 265-69. Details concerning these events can be found in Lamb, ed., *Journal of a Voyage*, 7-10.

54 Compare to David Lavender, *The Fist in the Wilderness* (1964, Reprinted Albuquerque: University of New Mexico Press, 1979), 138-140.

caches on to the Boat Encampment. Charles Iroquois was hired to be his bowman in the descent of the Columbia.

With most of the outfit stranded at various places along the Athabaska Pass, Thompson could only carry three pieces of trade goods and 180 pounds of dried meat, 10 of pemmican, 10 of grease, and a little flour in his leaky twenty-five-foot cedar plank canoe.[55] By the second week of May they passed the Blaeberry River, and not much later, deserted Kootenae House. While portaging from the upper Columbia to McGillivray's (Kootenay) River, his small party met several trappers who had wintered with Kutenai at the Tobacco Plains. Unmolested by Piikani, they intended to go trapping in the Salish country.[56]

Thompson's thin notation, "the HB are in the lake—just arrived from winter quarters," was his only recognition that the English had free rein in the Salish country.[57] Because the blockade had prevented new goods from reaching Finnan McDonald, Joseph Howse had all winter to exploit the trade that Thompson spent the last four years developing. He carried away thirty-six bundles of furs, more than the twenty-two packs that Thompson had shipped the year before.[58] The furs hauled back across the mountains and shipped downstream to York Factory on the bay were worth £1500/10/6.

James Bird met the men bringing those packs down the Saskatchewan River on July 30, 1811, and reported to an associate:

> [Y]ou will receive considerable satisfaction from hearing of the safe return of Mr. Howse & party from the Flat Head River with a trade sufficiently valuable to defray the Expenses of the Expedition and afford a considerable profit to the Company but you will partake of the mortification I feel at my being obliged to add that Mr. Howse has thought the danger too eminent to admit his attempt to return to that country this season.[59]

55 Nisbet, *Sources of the River,* 178.

56 The previous July, Alexander Henry saw Joseph Desjarlaix's son, F. Martin, and a young Saulteur taking their families to the Columbia. White, ed., *Thompson Journals*, 150-52, 163.

57 White, ed., *Thompson Journals*, 163.

58 "Joseph Howse," Appendix in Rich, ed., *Colin Robertson's Correspondence Book*, 222. The HBC paid its servants wages of £242 from a total expense of £576/5/5 ¼.

59 Bird to Auld, Grand Rapids, August 9, 1811, Churchill Correspondence, HBCA, B42/b/55, fos. 19-20.

As far as Bird was concerned, the Salish trade wasn't worth the risk to his HBC traders.[60] After wintering across the mountains, Joseph Howse visited England where he was interviewed by the HBC Governor and Committee. They gave him a present of £150 for his services in proceeding from York Factory to the Stoney Mountains in the years 1810 and 1811.[61]

Thompson reached the Clark Fork on May 26, 1811, and found Saleesh House deserted with no explanation from Finnan McDonald. But he may have learned more from Michel Bourdon who he now engaged, along with others, to descend the Columbia. Bourdon had helped create the Piikani blockade by siding with the Salish. After building another canoe and casting off below the chutes that would be known as Thompson Falls, the trader left a notice painted on a board "in case the Americans should pass."[62] As he already knew of the dispersion of the Missouri Fur Company party, his message must have been meant for the overland party of Astor's Pacific Fur Company.[63]

Despite Thompson's bias against Jaco Finlay, he had been re-engaged as a clerk to build another post among the Spokane Indians.[64] Leaving Lake Pend Oreille, Jaco traveled overland to an inviting yellow pine-lined meadow where the junction of the Little Spokane and Spokane Rivers would be a salmon-protein bonanza. There was a promising pasture, potential gardens, and room for a race track that would allow exciting pony races when Spokane, Kalispel, and Coeur d'Alene Indians congregated during the fishing season to take huge, forty-pound salmon by the hundreds. The return of the salmon even drew San Poil, Colvile, and Palouse away from their own fisheries to share in the festivities and trade fair.[65]

Realizing that the fight between the Salish and Piikani might invite retaliation, Finnan McDonald had abandoned Saleesh House in mid-

60 HBCA, A6/18, fo. 104; A1/50, fo. 149.

61 Archives of Manitoba: Hudson's Bay Company Archives, B60/d/2b;B239/d/147, 113-14.

62 White, ed., *Thompson Journals*, 172; Nisbet, *Sources of the River*, 180.

63 Thompson expected the overland Astorians to come up the Yellowstone and follow the Salish road to the buffalo in reverse.

64 March 27, 1810, "Jaco arrived. I engaged him in his old Capacity of Clerk & Interpreter." May 9, 1810; as Thompson was preparing to leave Kullyspel House he gave "Jaco his Summer orders." White, ed., *Thompson Journals*, 103, 114.

65 Ruby and Brown, *The Spokane Indians*, 40, 47.

summer and shifted the provisions he had collected to join Finlay at Spokane House. The big, red-bearded McDonald spent a miserable winter regretting the lack of goods to compete with the HBC and uncertain how to proceed.

At some point, an odd couple composed of two women came to visit. Finnan recognized one of them as Augustin Boisvert's former Lake country wife whom he had partnered with during the winter 1808–09 that he and Michel Boulard spent in the Flat Bow country. Unfortunately, her loose behavior around Kootenae House so offended Thompson he ordered the engagé to send her away. As the Lake Kutenai remembered, the large, young woman they knew as Q̲ánqon kámek klaúla, claimed the experience of having had a white husband had given her the spirit powers of a man. As spring 1811 returned to Spokane House, she reappeared with a wife of her own.[66] Soon she would play a unique role in the intrigue between the NWC and the Astorians.

Finnan McDonald wrote a letter, the contents of which can only be speculated at, dated April 5, 1811, and addressed to John Stuart at Fort Eskekakadine, New Caledonia.[67] Because Q̲ánqon and her partner knew the Flat Bow country, he gave it to them to deliver, expecting that they would take his letter overland to the Okanogan River where an Indian trail led north to the Fraser River trading posts.[68] If Piikani kept the road along the mountains closed and a new outfit failed to arrive, Finnan might have to depend on those posts for supplies.

Two months after sending that letter, Finnan received a note from Thompson, instructing him to bring horses and meet at the Kalispel camp below Lake Pend Oreille. Riding an unusually high spring freshet, Thompson's boatmen descended the Clark Fork River in record time, paddled across Lake Pend Oreille and about fifty miles down its outlet to a large camp at a lake and root grounds near present Usk, Washington. Receiving the horses that were sent to carry them and their gear

66 Nisbet, *Sources of the River*, 134-37.

67 At that time the NWC had posts at Stuart's Lake, McLeod's Lake, and Fraser's Lake near the great bend of the Fraser River, all blocked by Simon Fraser's conclusion that the Fraser could not be navigated to the sea.

68 Okanogan is also spelled Okanagan when in reference to people and places north of today's international border, and often interchangeably in reference to the native people of that name and some geographic sites. For consistency we have chosen to use "Okanogan" throughout.

cross country, Thompson and his party arrived at the newly built Spokane House on June 14.[69]

After reprimanding Finnan for the trouble he caused in siding with the Salish, and leaving that lucrative trade to Howse, Thompson ordered him to ascend the Columbia and bring down the outfit that had been left stranded at the Boat Encampment. The three packs containing trade goods brought with them from the delayed outfit would not be enough to satisfy the Salish if the Hudson's Bay Company returned, or if the overland Astorians came that way.

After completing arrangements at Spokane House, Thompson and his party rode northward to the Ilthkoyape (Kettle) Falls of the Columbia. They spent two weeks at that reeking Indian fishery building a split plank canoe and preparing for the journey to the river's mouth. Before the canoe was completed, Thompson received "gifts" from Q̲ánqon, sent to him from the Sanpoil River, about ninety miles downstream from the Kettle Falls. Her gift included "2 pieces of iron, 5 dressed Skins, 1 Beaver skin & 2 Horses to be paid for when I see her."[70] Somehow Q̲ánqon had learned at lot about Thompson's intentions, and of the presence of other whites on the lower Columbia River. The people of the great river regularly passed a stream of information or rumors up and down the current. The Columbia was the functioning inter-tribal connection between the interior and the coast; the latest news from downstream passed upstream with the summer salmon run and Finnan's mysterious letter, in the hands of the two couriers, began to develop its own "magic" properties, apparently spreading gossip and giving Q̲ánqon a tool to command respect among the tribes she met.

On July 5, 1811, David Thompson, seven boatmen, and two Sanpoil interpreters pushed their canoe into the current.[71] Still in no hurry to reach his ultimate destination, Thompson familiarized himself with the course of the river and the various fishing people living along its shores. He was traveling light with no intention of building a post anywhere along the river because the two companies would share the trade in the

69 A detailed analysis of Thompson's journeys through this part of the interior can be found in Allan H. Smith, "An Ethnohistorical Analysis of David Thompson's 1809-11 Journeys," 309-81. *See also* Elliott, "David Thompson's Journeys in the Spokane Country." More recently, Haywood, *Sometimes Only Horses to Eat*.

70 Nisbet, *Sources of the River*, 187.

71 Glover, *Narrative*, 339; Elliott, "Journal of David Thompson," 43.

lower Columbia. However, in his mind, that partnership should stop short of the trade he had developed over the previous years. To make sure, Thompson went ashore at the confluence of the Snake and Columbia Rivers and erected a pole with the following note attached:

> Know hereby that this Country is claimed by Great Britain as part of its Territories and that the NW Company of Merchants from Canada, finding the Factory for this People inconvenient for them, do hereby intend to erect a Factory in this place for the Commerce of the Country around. D. Thompson, Junction of the Shawpatin River with the Columbia, July 8th, 1811.

In a way, this may have been Thompson's delayed answer to the audacious claims of Captain Perch to the region, and to head off any Astorian ambitions. Thompson's sign was merely a gesture because the message he scrawled on a board at Saleesh House on the Clark Fork above Lake Pend Oreille showed that Thompson already knew overland Astorians were coming. Above Celilo Falls, Sahaptins fishing on the rocks pantomimed the arrival of a ship at the Columbia's mouth. At Tongue Point, just short of the American's new establishment on July 15, 1811, Thompson took the time to write a short letter informing the proprietors of Astoria of his arrival:

> Permit me to congratulate you on your safe arrival & building in the mouth of the Columbia River: Your situation is such as to enable you with the aid of good Providence to command an extensive commerce & humanize numerous Indians in which I wish you success.
>
> With pleasure I acquaint you that the Wintering Partners have acceded to the offer of Mr Astor, accepting one third share of the business you are engaged in, their share of Capital not to exceed £10,000 without further permission – I have only to hope that the respective parties at Montreal may finally settle the arrangements between the two Companies which in my opinion will be to our mutual Interest.
>
> Accept of my best wishes for your health & that of the Young Gentlemen with you.[72]

The next day, David and Robert Stuart, and Duncan McDougall, Astor's partners at Fort Astoria, responded:

---

72 Belyea, ed., *Columbia Journals*, 277.

> We have the pleasure to acknowledge the receipt of your Note of yesterday, communicating the pleasant intelligence of the Wintering Partners of the North West Company having accepted of Mr Astor's offer, of one third share of the Business we are engaged in, and with you sincerely wish that final arrangements may take place to the mutual satisfaction of both parties, which would inevitably secure to us every advantage that can possibly be drawn from the Business ...
>
> We beg leave to congratulate you on your safe arrival here and accomplishing so arduous an undertaking in the midst of dangers & privations that must have attended so unusual a route, we shall therefore esteem ourselves happy in affording you any assistance that may be in our power while you may remain here, or in returning to your establishments.[73]

The Astorians admitted that getting Astor's ship *Tonquin* across the Columbia bar cost eight lives. Duncan McDougal's and David Stuart's search for a building site found a place on the river's sloping south bank shore, backed by a towering wall of old growth fir trees, about twelve miles from Baker Bay on the north shore at the entrance to the river. Those former Nor'westers failed to see that the anchorage was poorly sheltered from the current of one of the great rivers of the continent.[74]

As far as David Thompson and the puzzled Pacific Fur Company proprietors at Fort Astoria knew, they were partners in this joint venture to the Columbia. However, the Astorians were suspicious. When their ship *Tonquin* sailed from New York harbor on September 8, 1810, they were under the impression that the partnership agreement had all but dissolved. It was a surprise when Thompson arrived with his "news," but it was possible something had been arranged later. Prudence suggested they play along without disclosing plans for an interior trade.[75]

In that they relied on a remarkable resource. Finnan McDonald's mysterious letter entrusted to Q̓ánqon and her partner and intended for the Fraser River had instead preceded Thompson down the Columbia.[76]

---

73 Bridgwater, "John Jacob Astor Relative to his Settlement on Columbia River," 52-53. The original document can be found among the John Jacob Astor Papers, Western Americana Collection, Beinecke Rare Book and Manuscript Library, Yale University, New Haven, Connecticut. *See also* Jones, ed., *Annals of Astoria*, 34-35.

74 Jones, ed., *Annals of Astoria*, 8-11.

75 See Thompson's journal entry for July 22, 1811, in Belyea, ed., *Columbia Journals*, 157, which explains why Thompson went ahead of the Astorians at the Upper Dalles on July 31. That is, he was bound north while he thought the Astorians would be headed southward. See Glover, ed., *David Thompson's Narrative*, 370.

76 June 15, 1811, Jones, ed., *Annals of Astoria*, 24.

The couriers should have taken the Indian trail north along the Okanogan River, but instead they had traveled to the Pacific. When Thompson arrived at Astoria, he found that the couple had arrived there a month earlier and had already provided the receptive Astorians with several maps of the interior.[77] A later observer noted

> Mr D. Thompson arrived at the moment Mr D. Stuart was preparing to be off for the upper Parts of the River & after a stay of a week they both started together - D^{d} Stuarts brigade consisting of 3 wooden canoes to man which he had only 3 Canad^{s} 2 Islanders & 3 Clerks—Ross, Pillet & McLennan[78]—This flotilla which D^{d} Thompson left between cascades & Dalles, proceeded to Oak [Okanogan] River where they formed an establishment[79]

When the boats arrived on July 22, Thompson did not doubt "but err now a coalition of the two companies had taken place."[80] As the flotilla crawled up the Columbia, the written record turned on the pen of one of several journalistic-minded clerks, Alexander Ross, a former school teacher who was about to fledge as a fur trader.[81] Navigating up the Columbia River must have seemed like a terrifying channel between over-looming cliffs. Ross's shipmates died just crossing the Columbia bar, and now he was helping drive a grotesquely carved cedar canoe past a burial rock covered with decayed coffins and ghastly bones. What had he gotten into!

When the joint North West Company and Pacific Fur Company canoes left Astoria, the Indian couple traveled with them. Suspicion may explain why, before setting out, Thompson contrived to exchange his man Michel Boulard, who had been with him since the first crossing the mountains, for a strong-armed Hawaiian named Cox. Thompson ingenuously described Boulard as "well versed in Indian affairs but weak for the hard labor of ascending the river."[82] However, Boulard had known

77 Nisbet, *Sources of the River*, 213-14.

78 The Astoria headquarters log names the boatmen as Ovid Montigny, Benjamin Roussele, and Jacques Lafantaise, but only one of the Hawaiians, Cox, can be identified because he was exchanged for Thompson's man, Boulard. Jones, ed., *Annals of Astoria*, 35.

79 Memorandum Book of James Keith, 1811-21, James Keith Papers, National Archives of Canada (hereinafter NAC), A-676, A-2, p.21.

80 Jones, ed., *Annals of Astoria*, 33-35.

81 Ross, *Adventures*, 155.

82 Nisbet, *Sources of the River*, 224, 226.

Qánqon since she attached herself to his trapping companion years earlier, and it is possible Thompson planted him in the Pacific Fur Company boat to keep an eye on her as well as the Astorians. Thompson neglected to mention any corporate espionage in his field journal, but two Astorian clerks described it later from the advantage of hindsight.[83]

The skin gamesmanship between the Cascades and The Dalles (Long Narrows) led Thompson to hope the Astorians planned to make a trading post on the lower river. But Pacific Fur Company strategists had already deprogrammed Qánqon about the disposition of North West Company posts in the interior, and David Stuart's party really intended to go beyond The Dalles. When Thompson got ahead and came to the Indian camps around the Walla Walla and Snake River mouths, he suggested those tribes divert the Americans up the Snake.[84]

Qánqon, in the meantime, used Finnan's letter to John Stuart as a source of power in order to exploit the river people they passed, accumulating from them in exchange for her magic and insider knowledge, a herd of twenty-six horses, robes, leather, and *higuas* (odd items) by the time they reached Okanogan. Ross does not mention if Qánqon and partner accompanied David Stuart to the Fraser River country, or if Finnan's letter ever reached Fraser, but she led the American competitors to a key place on the Columbia.

After returning to the Kettle Falls, Thompson worried that Qánqon might actually deliver Finnan's letter to John Stuart. He wrote a counter letter on August 28, 1811, describing his descent of the Columbia which he trusted to a native courier.[85] But it seemed obvious that competitive maneuvering was already muddying the pristine waters of the Columbia and no matter what the Astorians led Thompson to expect, they intended to open an inland post.

---

83 Ross, *Adventures*, 157. As the plot thickens, a wee touch of supposition seems permissible.

84 Nisbet, *Sources of the River*, 214, 225-28.

85 Lamb, ed., *Sixteen Years in the Indian Country*, 151. The letter was not delivered to Daniel Harmon in New Caledonia until April 6, 1812.

Horsemen descending to McGillivray River (present Kootenai), July 28, 1845, H. J. Warre.
Library and Archives of Canada, C-58144.

Chapter Four

"Doing Indian Business"
Spokane House and Okanogan

With the diplomatic mission to meet the Astorians completed, David Thompson and his crew paddled back up the Columbia River to the mouth of the Snake River where he sent a message to Jaco Finlay at Spokane House to bring horses and meet him on an Indian overland trail that ran along the Palouse River. Luckily, obliging tribesmen provided Thompson with horses because Jaco failed to meet the party as instructed. Thompson arrived at Spokane House on August 13, 1811, ahead of a chagrined Jaco, who dragged in that evening. Finlay confirmed that Finnan McDonald had gone to the upper Columbia to meet the marooned outfit being brought down from the Boat Encampment, and had not returned. Thompson spent four days "doing Indian business" and bringing up accounts. There were few furs to calculate, as he started to the Kettle Falls with only three packhorses. After a short week McDonald arrived on August 27, reporting that he had hiked past the Arrow Lakes but stopped short of the Little Dalles and Dalles de Mort without seeing anything of the incoming outfit.[1] Having failed to meet the expected new outfit, the resourceful clerk had built a canoe and paddled back to the Kettle Falls.

It was getting late in the season, and traders should have been allowing supplies to beaver hunters. The lack of goods could lose more business. Thompson anticipated the new outfit would be late as he had already started building a bateau to ascend the Columbia and retrieve last year's marooned outfit. Two days after hearing Finnan's negative report, Thompson took time to write a letter informing the Nor'westers

1 Belyea, ed., *Columbia Journals*, 168-69, 175.

operating in the Fraser River country of his descent of the river and return. Two freemen, Regis Bellaire and Michel Allaire, took the letter toward the Okanogan River with the intention of sending it on with Indians.[2]

Leaving the Kettle Falls on September 2, Thompson extended his survey of the upper river in a hard, 227-mile upstream pull, past several horrendous rapids. At the most difficult places, boatmen had to get out and pull the boat around rocks with a towline. The hungry crew completed the first navigation of the last section of the unexplored upper Columbia under morning mist, cold rains, and freezing snow, in weather too bad for hunting moose.

On September 21 they met two men in a small canoe who reported that the dutiful clerk William Henry brought the packs of last year's outfit down from the mountain. Two days later everyone arrived at the Boat Encampment where Thompson received dispatches from headquarters informing him that he was now free "to prosecute his plans of discovery on the west side of the Rocky Mountains toward the Pacific."[3] Thompson must have found that message ironic. He had just completed his obligation to examine the entire Columbia River, spent the previous winter in a miserable hut away from his family, traveled thousands of miles in continuing uncertainty, and endured hunger, biting insects, incompetent clerks, Indian mystics, and untrustworthy opponents. If Thompson sensed a dismissive tone in the minutes of the distant management, he made no comment in his journal.

The dispatches also confirmed that the agreement with the Pacific Fur Company had fallen through. Even before Thompson had started to descend the Columbia, the wintering partners and downstream agents meeting at Fort William knew that the one-third arrangement that might be made with Astor would be limited to Michilimackinac operations with the South West Company. After having completed a round trip from Kettle Falls to Fort Astoria and adding another 227 returning miles to the Canoe Encampment, Thompson now learned that there was no deal with the Pacific Fur Company. He had confirmed the naviga-

2 Belyea, ed., *Columbia Journals*, 171, 287. It is possible they were accompanied by Ignace Shoriowane, who had scouted the possibilities as he descended the river with Thompson.

3 Minutes of the deliberations and transactions of the North West Company assembled at Fort William at their regular meeting in the month of July, One Thousand Eight Hund[r] & Eleven, in Wallace, ed. *Documents Relating to the North West Company*, 265-66.

tion of the entire Columbia, and the potential of opening "a Trade from England and China to the North West Coast of America—" But the key to that opening was now in the hands of the Americans.[4]

Until a ship could be sent to the Columbia River to carry away skins traded from the Natives of the region, the North West Company would have to continue hauling their returns across the mountains. The Fort William meeting had already realized that the steep 3,500-foot climb from the Columbia River to the summit of Athabaska Pass would not serve as a freight route. No matter the threat from hostile Piikani, it was critical to regain control of the transport route along McGillivray's River (the Kootenay). What confused Thompson was that his pugnacious little brother-in-law, John McDonald, had been sent as the new western superintendent to do that.[5] There was much in that decision that David Thompson would not understand until much later, when simultaneous operations finally came together.

But at the moment, the Columbia Adventure was proceeding on parallel tracks separated by towering mountains and depths of misunderstanding. Unless a trustworthy Indian or casual freeman came along, the managerial line of communication ran back to the voyageur mainline, perhaps even to Fort William, distances measured in months instead of weeks or days. That added an additional burden to operations needing guidance about how to deal with the old rivalry with the HBC and the new threat of Mr. Astor's PFC. Nor could a western wintering partner ignore the St. Louis entrepreneurs from the Yellowstone or upper Missouri Rivers who loomed on the east side of the mountains and had already penetrated the Lewis (Snake) River. At a time when a coordinated effort was needed, two experienced proprietors might prefer to go home and leave the inevitable problems to clerks.

Much earlier in the season, on July 20, 1811, John McDonald and his clerk John George McTavish, guided by the experienced James McMillan, had left the Fort William meeting with a brigade of thirty men driving five canoes loaded with trade goods. Outfit 1811–12 represented a 25

4 Wallace, *Documents Relating to the North West Company*, 267-68. The length of the Columbia is usually given as 1243 river miles. Thompson had previously traveled about 106 miles between the present Blaeberry River and Columbia Lake.

5 Both McDonald and Thompson married Métisse daughters of Patrick Small. When Thompson returned west in 1810, he left his wife and children with McDonald's family living at the bottom of the River Winnipeg.

percent increase in inventory for the Columbian outfit, and doubled the manpower the North West Company would need west of the mountains.[6]

Already an old hand on the upper Saskatchewan, McDonald had initiated the move across the mountains and was a logical choice to continue the Columbia Adventure. The clerk he was bringing, John George McTavish, was a mature thirty-three years of age with previous experience challenging the HBC's monopoly of bay ports. The second son of an impoverished Chief of Clan McTavish, he had been brought into the fur trade by his distant kinsman, Simon McTavish. J. G. McTavish spent the 1808–09 winter at Fort Dunvegan in the Peace River country and saw the difficulties of operating long supply lines to the Fraser River posts. After spending the previous winter at Montreal in close association with the downstream agents, McTavish had a good idea of how the NWC intended to respond to encroachment of the Pacific Fur Company.[7]

When the reinforced supply brigade of five canoes and thirty boatmen passed the HBC's Edmonton House on August 14, 1811, McDonald could not resist telling his former acquaintance, James Bird, that a ship was also going to the Columbia in the NWC's interest.[8] If Piikani tried to object to using the mountain portage, the boat brigade included Joseph Paul, a "bold guide and old bully" who would be sent ahead from Rocky Mountain House "to take a Hunter, three more men, Bark & other materials for making of canoes & proceed across the mountains *by the route Mr Thompson* [previously] took & there on the sources of the River Columbia or Oregon & begin to make the ocean by the time I got there with the goods."[9]

McDonald soon had a taste of why Thompson wanted to avoid the Howse Pass route. Twenty-two young Piikani stopped Paul's party on the Kootenay Plains and "pillaged all they had and took their horses, arms and all."[10] As ominous as that might seem, the only hostile act by

6 Wallace, *Documents Relating to the North West Company*, 266, 269. When NWC management made that decision, they had no way of knowing if the HBC intended to return to the Salish country.

7 Van Kirk, "John George McTavish."

8 HBCA, B60/a/10, fol. 1.

9 Masson, ed., *Les Bourgeois*, 38; Gough, ed., *Alexander Henry*, 2:336.

10 Masson, ed., *Les Bourgeois*, 38-39. On November 7, Indians from Acton reported to Bird that the six Canadians that McDonald sent ahead on horseback were surprised by twenty-

the fearsome Piikani during their blockade was beating a few point men with their bows. That did not deter McDonald. With only a skiff of snow on the east side of Howse Pass in mid-September, McDonald's brigade reached the junction of Blaeberry Creek and the Columbia before the end of the month.[11] When he was much older, McDonald recollected,

> [W]e began canoe making to ascend & not descend. My object was not to descend the river which took an entire northerly direction round very high mountains which lay west of us. My business was to ascend & go south in the direction in which the Snake country lay where Mr. Thompson ensconced himself on Snake [Clark Fork] River."[12]

Although winter lay some weeks in the future, McDonald decided to winter at Kootenae House where he could interdict the Piikani blockade by occupying a strategic location guarding the Howse Pass. Unaware of McDonald's plans, Thompson was at that same time pushing his canoe up the Columbia under already challenging weather, confident that his recommendations to shift to the Athabaska Pass route had been accepted and the new outfit would come that way.[13] He expected to meet it at the confluence of the Canoe and Columbia Rivers, but to his disappointment Thompson found that William Henry brought down only part of the caches left along the trail the previous winter.

Before he could return downstream, Thompson had to ride up Athabaska Pass and get the rest. Along the way Thompson met two Iroquois bringing a letter from McDonald asking him to meet the brigade at the Kootenay Plains. Given his concern about the Piikani blockade, it was unlikely Thompson would have done that. The change of plans arrived too late for him to make the attempt in any event.[14]

Although the letter has not survived, Thompson would have logically assumed that, in the event the two parties failed to link up at Kootenay Plain, after crossing Howse Pass McDonald would descend the Columbia to the mouth of the Canoe River and meet him there. He had no idea that McDonald's party had already stopped at Kootenae House. After waiting

four Muddy River Indians at the Kootenay Plain on the east side of the mountains, who stopped, plundered and beat them with their bows. HBCA, B60/a/10, fo. 5.

11 Masson, *Les Bourgeois*, 38; Glover, ed., *David Thompson's Narrative*, 300n2; HBCA, B60/a/10, Edmonton House Journal by James Bird, entry for August 14, 1811.

12 Masson, ed., *Les Bourgeois*, 40.

13 Belyea, ed., *Columbia Journals*, 176-78.

14 White, ed. *Thompson Journals*, 175 n.1; Nisbet, *Mapmaker's Eye*, 123.

eight days as winter closed in, Thompson wrote a note on a board in case McDonald came that way, stowed the remainder of the previous year's outfit in his plank bateau, and started back down the Columbia. Passing dangerous, ice shrouded rapids in low water Thompson was back at Kettle Falls on October 30. After hiking seventy miles to Spokane House, he sent Jaco Finlay with horses to bring on the year-old trade goods.[15]

Thompson must have felt that his five years west of the mountains were less than a complete accomplishment. His descent of the great river should have been the crowning achievement of those trying years. Instead, he was caught in a muddle of unanticipated developments that called his management abilities into question. Two attempts to properly resupply western posts had failed—the first because of his reluctance to face down the Piikani blockade and the second due to the difficulties of a winter crossing of Athabaska Pass and the delay at the Boat Encampment. Misunderstandings between the Montreal management and a distant superintendent of field operations were beginning to split the cedar canoes he stitched together. Unless an efficient supply system could be put in motion, the Columbia Adventure might sink in McGillivray's River.[16]

The letter advising he should continue exploring was beginning to seem more dismissive. Thompson had turned back from a well-deserved furlough in the name of duty and tried to find a viable alternative to the Piikani blockade. But now those sacrifices were beginning to look like the end of his career as a Nor'wester.

Thompson had time to rethink his position as the boat returned to the Kettle Falls and the remains of Outfit 1810–11 were packed on horses to Spokane House. On November 11 he left Jaco Finlay, Paul the Iroquois, and Cox, the Hawaiian Islander, to winter at Spokane House.[17] A three day ride brought him to the Pend Oreille River where he met two of his men, returning from a disappointing trade with a band of Lake Kutenai.[18] In his journal, Thompson wrote:

> Learning from Bercier & Methode that the Lake Indians do not hunt, but only gamble & keep the men starving, I told them as the Season was fast advancing to lay up the Furrs they have, abt. 4 Packs, & make their

15 Glover, ed., *David Thompson's Narrative*, 383-84.

16 Putting thoughts in Thompson's mind may seem presumptive, but it is important to emphasize the problems of communication that seriously hampered western operations.

17 Elliott, ed., "David Thompson's Journeys in the Spokane Country," 171.

18 After leaving Pend Oreille Lake, the Clark Fork becomes the Pend Oreille River.

> best way back to Kinville [at Kullyspel House] & return to Skeetshoo (Spokane) River with the property &c as to keep up a Post there with so few goods is expense to no purpose.[19]

In Thompson's mind, raiders seemed everywhere. The two freemen told Thompson that Piikani had killed two Kutenai and then tried to make peace with others. Raiders also intercepted three Iroquois and their families, stripping them of their belongings.[20] Fearing that an accident had befallen McDonald's brigade, Thompson wrote a letter to the nearest partner on the east side and sent three men to follow the lower McGillivray's (Kootenay) River to the Columbia and go on over Athabaska Pass.[21] There was the possibility that at some point they might intercept McDonald.

Continuing up the Clark Fork by boat, Thompson was back at Saleesh House on November 19. Due to the lack of trade goods he had to send Finnan McDonald to "beg" provisions from the Salish camps. Six days later, the mystery of the missing brigade was answered: James McMillan arrived with John George McTavish and fifteen men leading ten horses loaded with fifteen packs. Outfit 1811–12 put the Columbia Adventure back in business.[22]

After McTavish explained the latest operational changes taking place at Fort William, he and Thompson spent two days breaking out goods to be left at Saleesh House. Most of the outfit would go on to Spokane House, the new center of operations. It would be up to McTavish to induce the Kalispel, Coeur d'Alene, and Spokanes to hunt beaver. Taking six horses, McTavish continued to Spokane House where Jaco Finlay would help him adjust to his duties.[23]

Still trying to coordinate, Thompson sent a letter to Kootenae House on December 3, 1811, and received a reply from McDonald on January

---

19 For lack of trade goods, Thompson had to abandon the Lake Indian country which he initially believed productive of beaver.

20 Elliott, ed., "Thompson's Journeys in the Spokane Country," 172. There is a small, intriguing mystery here. In August, two Salish reported a fight with the Meadow Indians (Piikani), which Mehode and Bercier confirmed. Although there are similarities, this does not appear to have been the same as the abuse of McDonald's advance party.

21 White, ed., *Thompson's Journals*, 178-79.

22 White, ed., *Thompson's Journals*, 182.

23 White, ed., *Thompson's Journals*, cxvii, 181-83. For attitudes toward Finlay *see* Meyers, "Jacques Raphael Finlay," 163-67; Wallace, *Documents Relating to the North West Company*, 220.

22, 1812. Whatever those exchanges contained required a response from Thompson after five days, and McDonald's reply by March 4. It might be presumed that there were some tart words about missed connections before general agreement that next spring furs would be carried east over the Athabaska Pass route. Thompson faced one last loop from Saleesh House, through Spokane House to Kettle Falls, where a boat brigade would carry the Clark Fork returns to Boat Encampment.[24]

Instead of ending five years of effort as the master of an inland trade empire, Thompson realized he had become a supernumerary. The tone in his journals suggests that he was just biding time at the high point of his business expansion until he could go out of the country with the next brigade. Not a grand example, Saleesh House consisted of three rooms: a storeroom, Thompson's bedroom, and another that had to accommodate the family of Finnan McDonald, his Kalispell wife Margaret and two children, and James McMillan's wife with three.[25] Whatever the living arrangements, those were close quarters and the post must have been an active, boisterous trading place. Fur trader's country wives were expected to earn their way and Mesdames McDonald and McMillan helped by preparing sinews for snowshoes.

Ensconced cozily for the winter, the Nor'Westers surely discussed how the Astorian David Stuart had ignored the understanding with Thompson and established the first inland post of the Pacific Fur Company at the mouth of the Okanogan River. From there he ventured north to the Shuswap country. Before Thompson left Saleesh House to descend the Columbia, he had known that another party of Astorians was making their way overland. But Thompson had no way of knowing their progress or the route they took.[26]

To escape the domesticity, Thompson made a trip to the south end of Blackhorse (Flathead) Lake, more for sightseeing than exploration

---

24 Belyea, ed., *Columbia Journals*, 171-78, 288-90; Elliott, "David Thompson's Journeys in Idaho," 172-73. Thompson, McTavish, and the boats departed on April 22, 1812.

25 Thompson's family resided east of the mountains at this time. For the families of McDonald and McMillan, *see* Wallace, ed., *Documents Relating to the North West Company*, 463; Jennifer S. H. Brown, *Strangers in Blood: Fur Trade Company Families in Indian Country* (Vancouver: University of British Columbia Press, 1980), 132; White, "Saleesh House," 255.

26 Donald McKenzie, two clerks, and eight hands arrived at Astoria January 18, 1812, in two canoes. The overland Astorians came by way of the Snake River with great difficulty. Jones, ed., *Annals of Astoria*, 68.

because he had already traveled the parallel Great Road of the Salish.[27] A second outing went south following Cokalarishkit, the Salish Road to the Buffalo, across a low divide into the north end of the Bitterroot Valley. Thompson already knew the general geography from Captain Lewis's description and specifics from what Charles Courtin's men described.[28] Looking into the maw of Courtin's Defile (the Hellgate) from a distance, Thompson wanted nothing to do with the dangerous place where Piikani killed Courtin and might still be lurking. Unlike his daring predecessor, Joseph Howse, Thompson declined the opportunity to see the western reaches of Louisiana Territory.[29]

Actually the "astronomer and surveyor," as he now liked to describe himself, had covered the major points of the Pacific Northwest, taking sun sights and recording calculations that he would later use to construct detailed maps. As a cartographer with an artistic bent, a mere outline wasn't entirely satisfying and Thompson filled in chains of mountains by shading and coloring. He also made long elevations (tinted drawings) of those high places, details that some later traveler might recognize and locate.[30]

As Indian leaders developed confidence in traders, they sometimes looked to whitemen for advice. Before descending the Columbia in 1811 Thompson had advised the Salish and Nez Perce to forego attacking their Okanogan neighbors and "hold themselves ready for [what he anticipated would be an inevitable] war with the Peagans by next September."[31] As Thompson was preparing to leave Saleesh House in April 1812, five considerable Piikani visited the Salish seeking to renew the 1807 peace initiative. When the Salish council asked Thompson's advice, he told them "not to make Peace with the Piegans – but if they came to serve them as they have often served the Saleesh & other tribes." Nez Perce were encouraged to work beaver so they could buy ammunition

27 Carl W. Haywood has located the exact spot where Thompson stood to get a distant view of the lake.

28 For an alternative to the accepted understanding of where he stopped, *see* Haywood, *Sometimes Only Horses to Eat*.

29 Howse to George Simpson, February 9, 1843 in Rich, *Colin Robertson's Correspondence Book*, 222.

30 Samples of maps are at the end pages of Moreau, ed., *The Writings of David Thompson*, vol. 1. *See also* Nisbet, *Mapmaker's Eye*.

31 Elliott, ed., "David Thompson's Journeys in the Spokane Country," 12.

for the war next summer.[32] It was reasonable advice as Piikani, who confessed to killing a free Canadian and two Iroquois on the borders of the Rocky Mountains, declared their intention "to kill every white man they may find west of the Rocky Mountains or on their way thither" who were supplying the Salish with firearms, which was the principal cause of their losses.[33] In spring 1813 Sarci trading at Edmonton House reported to the ever-vigilant James Bird that Bloods and Blackfeet lost fifty of their relatives killed by Flat Heads since the summer 1812. Thompson's advice to reject Piikani peace proposals insured those hostile exchanges would continue.

At some time, two freemen again accompanied the Salish going to buffalo. Michel Bourdon had been involved in the previous hostile encounter and Michael Kinville kept Kullyspell House until Thompson closed it. During a hostile confrontation, they fought alongside their Salish associates against the Piikani. In his narratives, written much later, Thompson claimed that Bourdon and Kinville were killed. "I deeply regretted them" as they were the last of 350 careless American free hunters. But Thompson's memory failed him and the recollection was a gross exaggeration.[34]

Lack of accounts or missing letters make it difficult to compile an accurate idea of the returns from the previous five years. In his *Narrative* Thompson claimed to have boated 122 packs up the new route via the Columbia, but those would have been the returns of two year's trade.[35] Roughly calculated, the returns of five years trading may have been only 243 light packs of mixed furs which, when repacked into ninety-pound boat packs, could have totaled 170. Shifting the route moved operations away from potential Piikani interference, but the upper Columbia River and the difficult long road across Athabaska Pass was an impossible and expensive way of getting furs to market.

---

32 White, ed., *David Thompson's Journals*, 208-10n107.

33 Edmonton House Journal, HBCA, B60/a/10, fol. 14; B60/a/11, fos. 8, 12. Bird's man with the Piikani in summer 1812 said that Atsiina and Bloods were more to be feared than the Muddy River Indians. More than the interdiction of the arms trade led Bloods to travel so far to the south that they killed Indians they had never seen before.

34 Glover, ed., *David Thompson's Narrative*, 392-03. Bourdon accompanied the spring 1813 brigade to the mouth of the Columbia and engaged as an interpreter for two years on July 27. He had another ten years of adventuring before Blackfeet ran him down and killed him. Jackson, *The Piikani Blackfeet*, 79.

35 Glover, ed., *David Thompson's Narrative*, 395-96; Nisbet, *Sources of the River*, 237.

The David Thompson era of the North West Company Columbia Adventure ended in 1812 when the pioneer Thompson and the present superintendent McTavish took the meager returns of two outfits across the Rocky Mountains. Thompson went on to Fort William and was allowed to retire from the partnership with the guarantee of income for three years and a rider that he work up his maps. Providing financial support to a cartographer was an unusual indulgence for hard-nosed wintering partners but the downstream agents may have seen an opportunity of using a public service to enhance their campaign to gain a royal charter for the west like the monopoly granted by the British crown to the Hudson's Bay Company on Rupert's Land. Myth holds that one copy hung in the great hall at Fort William where guides were permitted to see the overview of a geography they carried in their heads.[36]

David Thompson was not inclined to illuminate mistakes. He made no more than necessary of the shocking obstruction of Captain Perch, the death of Mr. Courtin, or the fights that Americans had with Bloods and Atsiina at the Three Forks. Thompson refused to connect Finnan McDonald's blunder in offending the Piikani with the blockade that delayed his descent of the Columbia. The gun trade and use of liquor is deliberately obscure.

That should be compared to what Thompson accomplished during the five years he spent west of the mountains. He opened the interior trade that would consistently supply the furs for the North West Company's projected maritime enterprise. He personally tested a good part of the Columbia River as the conduit to move packs to a shipping point and supplies to inland posts; he filled in gaps that might have disproved its value to a transportation system. Less successful as a fur trader in producing returns to support an expensive trade expansion, he left the country just as the rival Pacific Fur Company began spinning a competitive web over all the trading areas he opened, and some he hadn't.

After spending a winter at Kootenae House being entertained by Kutenai "hunting, dancing, singing and gambling, night and day," John McDonald "deadheaded" back to Rocky Mountain House leaving "Mr. Thompson, coast clear, to follow with Mr. McTavish."[37] Veteran clerks

36 A replica is still displayed in the reconstructed fort.

37 Masson, ed., *Les Bourgeois*, 2:40–41.

were left to answer the aggressive PFC expansion.[38] After misleading Thompson into believing that David Stuart and his men would "build a Factory somewhere below the Falls of the Columbia at the lower Tribe of the Shawpatin Nation," the Astorians went on to build their first inland post at the confluence of the Okanogan and Columbia Rivers.[39] Arriving at the mouth of the Okanogan River on August 31, 1811, they located on the left bank less than a mile from the Columbia River.

Already remarkably aware of the potential of the Shuswap country, Stuart took two men and rode north to confirm what he could only have known from the informant Qánqon. Crossing the height of land they descended to Thompson's River and spent the worst of the winter with receptive Indians. Let the skin games begin!

38 Nor'westers referred to the Pacific Fur Company as "the Americans," despite the fact that most of Astor's wintering partners and engages were actually British subjects.

39 Belyea, ed., *Columbia Journals*, 157.

Chapter Five

War and Robbery at Astoria

Compared to the problems the Nor'westers experienced getting established in the Salish country, the Pacific Fur Company campaign in the Northwest began as a model of corporate efficiency. Wilson Price Hunt was to accompany the ship *Beaver* on a voyage along the northwest coast to try to involve the Russians. Partner Robert Stuart and a small party would carry dispatches overland to New York informing Mr. Astor of progress. Entering the lower Snake River, Donald McKenzie and Alfred Seton intended to initiate a trading relationship with the Nez Perce. David Stuart's party dropped Alexander Ross and Donald McGillis off at Okanogan before proceeding to the promising Shuswap country.

After throwing up a sixteen- by twenty-foot house from handy driftwood near the Columbia and Okanogan confluence, by September Stuart felt confident enough to send two clerks back to Astoria with a progress report. Since Thompson passed downstream, interest in Okanogan had increased and the party returning to Astoria included two strangers who mysteriously appeared. One was Thompson's former downstream steersman Ignace Salioheni, who made a remarkably fast trip to Okanogan in company with the freeman Registe Bruguier, who was looking for an Indian courier to carry Thompson's letter to NWC traders on the Fraser River.[1] Other Astorians recognized Bruguier as a respectable Canadian country merchant who had been trading among the Indians on the Saskatchewan where he lost his outfit and drifted across the mountains as a

1 Thompson's letter passed from tribe to tribe until it was delivered to Daniel Williams Harmon at Stuart's Lake on April 6, 1812. Harmon's paraphrasing only indicates that Thompson informed fellow traders of his trip to the mouth of the Columbia. Lamb, ed., *Sixteen Years in the Indian Country*, 151-52.

trapper on the Clark Fork of the Columbia.[2] Stuart convinced Ignace and Bruguier to try their luck at Astoria.[3]

Surrounded by high barren hills that cut off the view, the clerk Alexander Ross found Okanogan a dreary and claustrophobic place where he was alone except for the dog he had picked up at Monterey and named Weasel. He later wrote:

> Only picture to yourself, gentle reader, how I must have felt, alone in this unhallowed wilderness, without friend or white man within hundreds of miles of me, and surrounded by savages who had never seen a white man before. Every day seemed a week, every night a month. I pined, I languished, my head turned gray, and in a brief space ten years were added to my age. Yet man is born to endure, and my only consolation was my Bible.

Ross, a former school teacher who signed on as an Astorian, was destined to become one of several chroniclers of Pacific Fur Company and North West Company operations on the Pacific Slope. It is presumed that he kept a journal that was eventually published as memoirs: *Adventures of the First Settlers on the Oregon or Columbia River* in 1849 and *The Fur Hunters of the Far West* in 1855.[4]

Ross expected David Stuart to return in a month, but it was 188 carefully counted days before he paraphrased Stuart's return on March 22, 1812, having

> bent our course up the Oakinacken, due north, for upwards of 250 miles, till we reached its source; then crossing a height of land fell upon Thompson's River, or rather the south branch of Frazer's River, after traveling for some time amongst a powerful nation called the She Whaps....The Indians were numerous and well-disposed, and the country throughout abounds in beavers and all other kinds of fur; and I have made arrangements to establish a trading post there the ensuing winter. On the twenty-sixth of February we began our homeward journey, and

2 Franchère, *Journals of a Voyage*, 91. When Bruguier arrived at Astoria, he performed services for the Astorians and was listed as a freeman and hunter in the 1813–14 list of persons on the Columbia.

3 Jones, ed., *Annals of Astoria*, 51.

4 Readily available to scholars and containing invaluable descriptions of events from 1811 to 1825, Ross's books continue to be quoted as fact although the author had a habit of inserting himself in events that he was not a party to or inventing facts to support his assertions.

spent just twenty-five days on our way back. The distance may be about 350 miles.[5]

During Stuart's absence, Ross claimed to have collected 1,550 beaver pelts "worth in the Canton market £2,250 sterling" for merchandize valued at only £25 sterling.[6] The following April the PFC partner Robert Stuart arrived from Astoria with a boat party bringing supplies. Making a quick turnaround they started back downriver with four canoes carrying a cargo of furs that had now grown to 2,500 beaver skins.

To the chagrin of the Nor'westers summer complement, Astorian John Clarke built a new trading post within a stone's throw of Spokane House and soon dispatched clerks and parties to trade with the Salish and Kutenai. James McMillan lacked the manpower to oppose them because Thompson and McTavish had taken thirty men to drive six boats laden with 122 packs up the Columbia to the Athabaska Pass route. The Nor'westers were clearly outmanned until John George McTavish returned from Fort William. The two other NWC clerks, Finnan McDonald at Saleesh House, and Nicholas Montour with the Kutenai, would have to use their influence to stretch arrangements with local tribes and freemen trappers that would keep them loyal in the face of a free-spending and aggressive opposition.[7]

James McMillan also had to deal with the belligerent John Clarke, who was reputed to be a relative of Astor's. Clarke had four clerks, twenty-one Canadians, six Sandwich Islanders, and an Indian guide working for him.[8] To answer this formidable competition, McMillan had only ten men at Spokane House when Clarke sent out three of his clerks

---

5 Ross, *Adventures*, 164.

6 Ross, *Adventures*, 163. His estimate must have been made later from the advantage of hindsight.

7 It is difficult to arrive at an accurate number of North West Company engages. Thompson named 19 men with him during the 1811–12 winter, plus 15 who came in with McTavish for a total of 34. But some of those may have been freemen or half-engaged men only employed when they were needed and free to trap or trade with Indians at other times.

8 Between his arrival and departure nineteen months later, John Clarke married, according to the custom of the country, Josephte Kanhopitsa who he later "turned off" to Jean Baptiste Boucher. Franchère, *Journal of a Voyage*, 155; H. Lloyd Keith, "The 'Dried Spider' and the Gadfly: The James Keith–John Clarke Confrontation at Mingan, 1831-32," in *New Faces of the Fur Trade Selected Papers of the Seventh North American Fur Trade Conference, Halifax, Nova Scotia, 1995*, edited by Jo-Anne Fiske, Susan Sleeper-Smith, and William Wicken (East Lansing: Michigan State University Press, 1998), 282-313. A picture of Josephte (Clark) Boucher can be found in Jackson, *Children of the Fur Trade*, 50.

with sufficient number of men to intimidate the Nor'Westers posted in Spokane's hinterland.[9]

To the south, the ambitious Americans sent Donald McKenzie with one boat and two canoes up the Lewis (Snake) River to establish a post among the Nez Perce. Astorians boasted that McKenzie had already found the Willamette Valley so full of beaver that another party consisting of two clerks and fifteen men would ascend that river in the fall to trade with those Indians.[10] Rubbing salt in the wound, they boasted that the two former Salish country freemen who went down to Astoria were provision hunting and trapping beaver with the Willamette party.

The Nor'Westers felt heavily outnumbered until the fortuitous appearance of Joseph Felix LaRocque at Spokane House brought McMillan additional trade goods that had been packed over Athabaska Pass.[11] LaRocque had transferred those packs to canoes at Boat Encampment and loaded them on horses at Kettle Falls. Arriving at Spokane House about mid-November, LaRocque remained there until McMillan sent him with a number of men to build a post on the Thompson River.[12] Along the way, they must have passed through Alexander Ross's "Oakinacken," although the Pacific Fur Company clerk made no mention of it until on a later visit to Kamloops when Ross observed "soon after Mr. Stuart reached his wintering place, the North West, jealous of that quarter, followed hard at his heels and built alongside of him."[13] Unlike the difficult relationship of Clarke and McMillan at Spokane House, the rivalry between Stuart and LaRocque remained friendly and profitable to both. After a winter of successful trading, LaRocque left the post early in the spring and returned to Spokane House.

Spread thin and not as lavishly equipped, four determined NWC clerks were holding their own in what had already become "the disputed

9 Jones, ed., *Astorian Adventure*, 100; Cox, *Columbia River*, 91, 109.

10 Jones, ed., *Annals of Astoria*, 89, 137.

11 Joseph LaRocque entered the fur trade as a fifteen year old in 1801 for the XY Company. His activities are known until 1806 when his biographer wrote "no details of his career are known until he appears in 1812 in the neighbourhood of Fort Kamloops among the Shuswap Indians." *See* E. E. Rich, "Joseph LaRocque," in *Dictionary of Canadian Biography*, 9:456-57.

12 The date the fall brigades reached Spokane House from Fort William varied, of course, but was almost always sometime in late October or November. *See* Jones, ed., *Astorian Adventure*, 107.

13 Ross, *Adventures*, 214, 222. Returning from Astoria, David Stuart left Okanogan for the Thompson River on August 25, 1812.

Oregon Country." Although the competing parties were private businesses, the contest was international, as it would be in the future when the boundary question stirred diplomatic waters in later decades.

The decisions to enter into a "trade from England and China to the North West Coast of America" made by the agents and partners at Fort William in 1811 sputtered due to misunderstandings between the summer headquarters on the north shore of Lake Superior and the downstream management of McTavish, McGillivray & Company.[14] Upon returning to the 1812 Fort William rendezvous, John McDonald, pleading sickness, insisted on going down to Montreal for treatment. But when Donald McTavish, a supporter of western expansion, was ordered to go to London, McDonald's health suddenly improved. McTavish was instructed "to set out immediately & proceed in the Columbia Business by sailing from England for the [North] West Coast, as soon as possible & conduct that Business in conformity to the Resolve of the Company last Year." Despite the expected competition with the Pacific Fur Company, the worried wintering partners were not going to let that already expensive adventure falter because of a damn fur buyer in New York.

That plan received a shock on July 15, 1812, when a Great Lakes' sailing vessel, the *Invincible*, arrived at Fort William.[15] The sometimes acrimonious deliberations among the NWC leaders were going on when former partner William McKay burst into the great hall shouting that war had been declared by the government of the United States against Great Britain.

The implications were far-reaching. For starters, if connections to Montreal were to be cut off, all the returns at Fort William, the operating capitol of the NWC, could be locked up. The meeting minutes state that "Mr Shaw with the Gentlemen going to Montreal, and as many more as could be spared, should set out in the *Invincible* with a supply of arms ammunition & Provisions for St. Maries—then to act as circumstances may require." Aside from this, however, most of the decisions

14 Wallace, ed., *Documents Relating to the North West Company*, 266, 268; Library and Archives, Canada (hereafter, LAC), Selkirk Papers, MG 19, E1, vol. 31, 9108-11.

15 The *Invincible* was probably the 120-ton vessel, capable of carrying six to eight guns, that the North West Company offered the British government to be put at their disposal during the war. *See* James Davie Butler, "Early Shipping on Lake Superior," in *Proceedings of the State Historical Society of Wisconsin* (Madison: Democrat Printing Company, 1895), 91-2. The date, July 15, is given in Glover, ed., *David Thompson's Narrative*, 398.

reached at the annual meeting would have been approved in spite of a state of war. Those plans were not wartime measures intended to oppose a national enemy, but strategies intended to outwit a crafty rival in John Jacob Astor.[16] Operations in the Pacific Northwest should not be put in jeopardy.

But the declaration of war threatened the company's plan to send a supply ship to the mouth of the Columbia River. When Donald McTavish reached London, he would have to seek a British naval escort and a bill of marque for the ship that was supposed to sail to the Pacific.[17] At the same time, Astor's representatives might try to get around the British naval threat by arranging to ship a cargo to the Pacific in a hired British vessel.[18] This sudden change in circumstances made it more difficult to supply the Columbia Adventure by sea. John Stuart was not present at the Fort William meeting when,

> he is appointed by Company to take charge of the Department of New Caledonia & combine his Plans & operations with the Gentlemen on the Columbia, & that Mr Stuart is to proceed next Spring as early as possible down to the Sea, there to form a junction with Mr J. G. McTavish and meet the Ship intended to come to the Columbia.[19]

Managers of distant places were only required to come as far as the bottom of the Winnipeg River (Bas de la Rivière Winnipeg) or the Rainy Lake inland depot to deliver returns and receive new outfits. Having inherited the supervision of the Columbia Department, John George McTavish missed hearing the war news at Fort William and was already hurrying the next outfit west to beat the winter to Athabaska Pass. Alexander Henry received the war news at Lake Winnipeg, and realizing

16 The North West Company agents in Montreal had conveniently forgotten their September 1809 memorial to the British ambassador in Washington, "…the Americans seem to aim at establishments in trade beyond the Rocky Mountains and on the River Columbia to which they have no pretensions of discovery either by water or land…No establishment of the States on that river or on the coast of the Pacific should therefore be sanctioned." "Memorial of the North West Company, Montreal, 10 September 1809," FO 115/20/3, PRO, cited in Ronda, *Astoria and Empire*, 56.

17 A letter of marque was a license granted by a sovereign to a subject to fit out an armed vessel and employ it in the capture of merchant ships belonging to the enemy's subjects.

18 Ronda, *Astoria & Empire*, 251-55.

19 Ronda, *Astoria & Empire*, 271-72. These instructions would have reached Stuart at Fort Chipewyan about the second week of September where he embarked with his brigade for New Caledonia, arriving there "with the news" on November 28, 1812.

the importance of informing the Columbia Department, turned back to catch up with the Columbia boats. On July 23 Henry encountered the HBC's ubiquitous James Bird at the north end of Lake Winnipeg and shared the war declaration with him. Then he raced on in a light canoe driven by ten men "to overtake the Canoes from the Columbia" before they passed his post.[20]

Meanwhile, Mr. Astor's adventure to the Columbia had gained momentum. Stepping back in time to Astoria, Donald McKenzie and the travel worn first overland Astorians arrived on January 18, 1812. Not quite a month later, Wilson Price Hunt and the main body appeared, followed later by a few stragglers.[21] After forces were consolidated, Astor's partners decided to send clerk John Reid east with dispatches reporting the company's progress to date. But when the party conducting him upriver failed to offer passage gifts to the Indians they encountered, Reid was wounded in a confrontation at the Long Narrows and his mission aborted.

With many mouths to feed, and to relieve the monotony of smoked salmon, the Astorians turned to the Willamette Valley as a source of elk and deer meat. After recovering from his overland ordeal, Donald McKenzie had taken two clerks and six men in two canoes to explore McKay's River (now the Willamette). Traveling about a hundred miles upstream, they trapped and traded for beaver with bands of Kalapooya Indians before returning to Astoria on May 11.[22] William Wallace and John Halsey were sent to the Willamette Valley to establish a provision post. If the local Indians were shocked to see strangers slaughtering deer and elk in inconceivable numbers to feed distant strangers, what could the inoffensive hunters and acorn gatherers do about it?

In May the supply ship *Beaver* had anchored off Astoria bringing trade goods and an additional twenty-seven men: six Canadians, fifteen mechanics, five clerks, and a new partner named John Clarke. In all, the Astorians then had eighty-three men plus four partners to flood the Columbia with Pacific Fur Company traders.[23] Because the depot was

---

20 Edmonton House Journal, July 23, 1812, HBCA, B60/a/11, fo. 1.

21 Jones, ed., *Annals of Astoria*, 68n149, 72n160.

22 Jones, ed., *Annals of Astoria*, 79, 85, 89.

23 The number has been compiled from a list of clerks and men of the former PFC, October 1813. *See* HBCA, F.4/61, fos. 3-7d, North West Company, Miscellaneous Accounts, 1808-1827.

unable to feed them, most of them had to be sent to inland posts, accelerating Pacific Fur Company inland expansion.

Astor's manager, Wilson Price Hunt, embarked on the *Beaver* "to perform a voyage on the Coast and return in the fall, Mr. McDougall is to take charge of the Factory, when it is intended he will go to winter in McKay's River or Wolamat."[24]

On June 29, 1812, the Astorians had started a brigade of sixty-two men up the Columbia.[25] An account of that departure described the send-off, when "A handsome salute was fired from the Battery of our Fortification or Factory, which was answered from the Boat with three hearty cheers, which altogether had a fine effect."[26]

John Clark's brigade arrived at the mouth of the Snake River and after muscling local tribes into providing packhorses, traveled up it to the mouth of the "Pavilion" (Palouse) River where a well-known Indian trail led overland to Spokane. They built a house post and sent off outposts.

According to Alexander Ross, it was late November or early December when J. G. McTavish passed Okanogan. When McTavish arrived at Spokane House, he was unpleasantly surprised to find that John Clarke, four clerks, twenty-one Canadians, and six Hawaiians had already built an impressive PFC house, almost at his doorstep, and already sent clerks to winter with the Salish and Kutenai. If McTavish was displeased to find he was nose to nose with an opponent, for the moment it was "hale fellow, well met," because it was customary to invite neighbors to share the regale celebrating the return of a brigade. Over a cup, McTavish had the satisfaction of displaying the war declaration to his crestfallen opponents. By then it was too late for Clarke to call in his outposts or make adjustments.[27]

The Nor'wester's brief visit must have been the reason Ross started on December 2, despite the weather, to go to Spokane House. After nearly freezing in a snow storm along the way and thawing out at Clark's fireplace, Ross described the new location.

> The spot selected for the forming of our establishment was a handsome point of land, formed by the junction of the Pointed Heart and Spo-

24 Jones, ed., *Annals of Astoria*, 15n39 for fuller description of PNC plans.
25 For confirmation of the makeup of this expedition *see* Jones, ed., *Astorian Adventure*, 100.
26 Jones, ed., *Annals of Astoria*, 100.
27 Jones, ed., *Astorian Adventure*, 107-08.

> kane Rivers, thinly covered with pine and other trees, and close to a trading post of the North West Company, under the command of a Mr. M'Millan, one of their clerks, who had ten men with him.[28]

Ross stayed from December 6 to 9, and then returned to dreary Okanogan to go north on December 20 to warn David Stuart at Kamloops.[29]

About this time at the confluence of the Snake and Clearwater Rivers (present Lewiston, Idaho), Donald McKenzie was increasingly peeved with the reception he received from the local tribes. The Nez Perce kept raising the price of the ponies he needed for provisions to feed his men. McKenzie found an excuse to make the four-day horseback ride to Spokane where McTavish had the satisfaction of watching him make a copy of the war declaration and hurry back to his post at the forks of the Snake.

Given the possibility of armed conflict extending into the Pacific Ocean, the Pacific Fur Company base of operations at Astoria could be vulnerable to British naval attack. Hastily closing shop on the Snake, McKenzie meant to transfer some of his stock of trade goods to Spokane. But realizing that snow blocked the horses, those packs were buried under the trade house and the house burned in hope the ashes would conceal the cache and keep Indians from breaking into it. McKenzie's clerk, Alfred Seton, detailed their cold retreat from the Snake River.[30]

When those twenty-two fugitives arrived at Astoria on the evening of January 16, 1813, all that the factory journalist discreetly noted was "that part of the country...did not answer the needs expected."[31] Despite an apparent setback, "a regal was given to all hands" which left them so overhung that they could not work the next day. It was not until January 25 that the log keeper recorded his reaction.

> The news Mr. McKenzie learned from the people of the N. W. Co. directly from Montreal, that War was declared between the U. S. and Great Britain, leaves every reason to suppose that another Ship will not be here next Spring. War was declared in June 1812 and the only hope to be cherished that a Ship shall be here in season is that Mr. Astor may have anticipated the event and arranged accordingly. We have now

28 White, ed., *Thompson Journals*, cxix.

29 Ross, ed., *Adventures*, 236. Ross did not mention the war and may have been wrong on his dates.

30 Jones, ed., *Astorian Adventure*, 106-08.

31 Jones, ed., *Astorian Adventure*, 145.

> stopped selling to the people [the Natives] every thing except what may be absolutely necessary for them.[32]

The strategic position was ominous and Duncan McDougall or Donald McKenzie were not the team John Jacob Astor would have preferred to be in charge at a critical time such as this. The depot could be attacked and taken by a British warship, perhaps even by the anticipated NWC supply ship. Suspending sales to the natives would only lead to trouble. Already short of provisions, Astoria was unable to call in the men at outlying posts. In response to the potential war threat, the two timid partners concocted a plan to move the stock of trade goods inland, beyond reach of the British navy. They tried to obtain enough packhorses to haul it back to St. Louis. Until spring, all they could do was wait and see what developed. Only thirty-one men remained to defend Astoria should enemies arrive in force.

By contrast, John George McTavish had the capacity to see through a couple of windowpanes like McKenzie or McDougall. But his position wasn't that good either and he was already breaking into the new outfit to supply too many outposts. How the Astorians would react must have been the topic of fireside debates with McMillan during the next couple of months when competitive advantage depended on which ship arrived first.

The dispatch pouch from Fort William contained the wintering partners' resolution to have a ship outfitted in London and dispatched as soon as possible to the Columbia.[33] By early spring 1813 McTavish had received reports from his scattered posts about a scarcity of trade goods. Getting a little desperate, he decided to go to the mouth of the Columbia to await the arrival of the ship.

When John George McTavish left Spokane House on April 2, he was accompanied by Joseph LaRocque, the apparently indispensible Michel Bourdon, and eighteen Canadians paddling two bark canoes.[34] Passing the mouth of the Snake River they saw that Indians had broken up Clarke's abandoned barge in revenge for his rough treatment of one of

32 Jones, ed., *Annals of Astoria*, 149.

33 Wallace, ed., *Documents Relating to the North West Company*, 271-72.

34 Jones, ed., *Annals of Astoria*, 171. This is the same Michael Bourdon whom David Thompson said had been killed by the Piikani in August of the previous year.

their own. Others were wearing blankets and trade items probably looted from McKenzie's caches on the Snake.

About ten miles above Celilo Falls, the Nor'westers met Donald McKenzie, the clerks John Reed and Seton, and seventeen men traveling in two lightly laden canoes. During the night they spent together it is not possible to say with accuracy what McKenzie told McTavish beyond his intention to trade for Nez Perce packhorses.[35]

McTavish expected to meet John Stuart and the New Caledonia brigade at the Okanogan River, but he felt that he couldn't wait until the Fraser River party arrived. McTavish and his canoes arrived at Fort Astoria on April 11, just nine days from Spokane House, and were disappointed that the NWC ship was not at anchor. But McTavish's timing was excellent as the next day was the anniversary of the PFC landing at Astoria. Voyageurs knew how to time the pace of their paddling and the thirsty Nor'westers arrived just in time for the regale.[36]

J. G. McTavish had matured under the guidance of old Simon and his McGillivray cousins, serving in some dubious attempts to gain access to the greater northwest from Hudson's Bay. Later in the Peace River country, he grasped the challenges of a long supply line. More than most wintering partners (which he hoped soon to become) J. G. McTavish understood what a long downstream outlet to the world could mean, and he was eager to greet the promised ship. Although he had no way of knowing the ship's name or if it had a Royal navy escort, he would stay until it arrived.

The Nor'westers had landed on a little bay a short distance downstream from the Astorian's fort and confidently began putting up a hangard (warehouse) for the goods they expected to receive. The obliging Astorian blacksmith even forged an iron hasp for the door and a large staple to lock it.

Their neighbor Duncan McDougall already understood the implications that a war between Great Britain and United States held for his little post on the far northwestern coast of nowhere when McTavish told him that their anticipated supply ship would be "equipped with everything necessary & adapted to Indian trade arranged by men possessed

35 Jones, ed., *Astorian Adventure*, 112-13; Jones, *Annals of Astoria*, 149n11; Lamb, ed., *Journal of a Voyage*, 117.

36 Jones, ed., *Annals of Astoria*, 172, 174.

of experience & a thorough knowledge of the business."[37] It might even carry a bill of marque allowing a private vessel to take enemy property during war.

For the next three months the crisis crawled in slow motion with both parties maintaining an amiable relationship. Short of food, McTavish offered to trade his entire assortment of goods (one bale) for provisions of equal value, which McDougall provided without hesitation. Fort Astoria continued to hum with activity as the large staff of smiths, sawyers, carpenters, coopers, and charcoal makers went about their chores. But there was no locking out the reality: those activities were not producing furs or resolving a dilemma.

After a frosty winter at Spokane House, the Pacific spring breezes were refreshing. Securing provisions was a problem because of the large concentration of hungry men. When the ooligan (smelt) run began in February, eight bushels of those delectable little fish were a treat. But the smelt run went on upstream to other rivers and since March the Astorians were on half rations. Sawyers with nothing to do only received one meal a day. Waiting impatiently for the promised ship, McTavish and LaRocque watched the Astorians' thin stew come to a boil.

The overstaffed Astorian enterprise was planning to retreat up the river and portage across the continent, but Mr. McDougall and his well-tooled carpenters were too casual. They didn't start bending boards or nailing plank barges together until June. Those looked too heavy to paddle and the men wallowing in the hospital from scurvy and venereal disease wouldn't be strong enough in another month to row against the Columbia freshet. McTavish hoped his voyageurs had the sense to stay away from the infected Clatsop women because the Astorian's medical chest had been exhausted.

Three months dragged by. Despite rumors of a sail on the horizon or guns fired offshore, hikes to high places to scan an empty ocean failed to answer McTavish's hope, or McDougall's fear that the PFC's *Beaver* would not return from the north in time to reship Mr. Astor's property. The arrival of inland traders from Spokane and Okanogan provided no answer to what had become of John Stuart, who was supposed to come from New Caledonia to also meet the ship. Although Nor'westers equated trading goods for provisions with eating beaver skins, McTavish

37 Jones, ed., *Annals of Astoria*, 172.

had been forced to do it. Dried or smoked salmon was purchased from the Chinook Indians; dried and strung ooligans were purchased by the fathom. One NWC hunter killed three elk a short distance from the fort; another time, a canoe McTavish sent to the Willamette returned loaded with venison.

By May 4 pressure to react in some way to an ominous possibility was building. McTavish and LaRocque accompanied McDougall to Chinook Point to scan the ocean, but no sail, Astorian or NWC or British naval, broke the horizon. On the May 22 someone thought he heard a ship's gun fired offshore and LaRocque made another trip to look in vain. The increasingly discouraged Astoria journalist described their shared dilemma in his entry for June 3.

> It is now too late to flatter ourselves longer in the hope of seeing a Ship. Our views & expectations are bent in different direction. The arrival of one for us would serve to facilitate business, but would not in the present crisis alter arrangements. The arrival of Mr. McKenzie in January with the news of a War in the U. States & the unpromising prospect in the interior of the country, gave a decisive blow & left no alternative but to decide upon such measures [as] are now soon to be put in execution, & for the forwarding of which every exertion has been made & suitable precaution used at this place to save property. Viz., That we decamp with everything valuable if possible by the 1st July & make the best of our way to St. Louis.[38]

This decision was announced to all the workmen at six o'clock that night and by the next day must have been communicated to the Nor'westers next door. Nine days later the interior brigade arrived, landing John Clarke, Donald McKenzie, and David Stuart, fifty-three men, and 116 packs of beaver and baggage. It was late June when the assembled partners of the Pacific Fur Company took actions consistent with McDougall and McKenzie's earlier decision to abandon the trade.

At that late point the Astorians realized the plan to return eastward would be delayed because they lacked horses to carry men and property across country. It would take another year to obtain them from the interior. After McKenzie had little success getting horses from the Nez Perce, he returned downstream and spent his time trading for dried salmon along the Columbia to feed the overstaffed post. Not until Octo-

38 Jones, ed., *Annals of Astoria*, 187.

ber 2 did he take twelve men and three clerks in two canoes upstream "for the purpose of bringing down the packs and Sandwich Islanders."[39] John Clarke went back to trade for horses and provisions from the Flatheads. John Reed would scour the Snake country.

During the three months that McTavish and LaRocque idled near Astoria, they observed how casually the Americans prepared for a retreat across the continent. They certainly weren't privileged to see what McDougall, or his writer, penned into the post log, but they saw cedar plank canoes and barges finally being built to carry property up to the forks of the Columbia. There Mr. Astor's property would be packed on overloaded wild horses and carried through the inhospitable Snake country, doubling transport costs of a stock of little further value.

A year's delay required the cooperation of the North West Company. J. G. McTavish was summoned to the fort and found himself facing Mr. Astor's downhearted wintering partners. Duncan McDougall, Donald McKenzie, David Stuart, and a reluctant John Clarke proposed a division of business for the ensuing year. The PFC proposed that they would give up their trade among the Kutenai and the Spokanes in return for a free hand among the Flatheads and on the Columbia River.[40]

McTavish found no long-term disadvantages in the Astorians' proposal and accepted their terms because his reserves had run out and the anticipated ship had still not appeared. What he would do was purchase about $850 worth of goods from the former adversaries, enough to tide him over during the trading season. That loan would be repaid "in any manner that shall best suit our purpose" at the forks of the Columbia next spring.[41]

After waiting three months without meeting their ship with supplies for a new outfit, McTavish and party hung around Astoria for the celebration of the Fourth of July and next day began a long pull upriver to Spokane and other inland posts to prepare for the winter trade.

---

39 Jones, *Astorian Adventure*, 125.

40 In order of publication, the documentation providing these details can be found in Irving, *Astoria*; Elliott, "Sale of Astoria, 1813," 44-46; Ronda, *Astoria and Empire*, 278, 281; and Jones, ed., *Annals of Astoria*, 197-99, 219. The most recent retelling is Stark, *Astoria*.

41 Jones, ed., *Annals of Astoria*, 199-200; Lamb, *Journal of a Voyage*, 119-20. The actual value of the goods was given as $850.80½. HBCA, F.4/61, fo. 9d. Jones describes the arrangement between Duncan McDougall and J. G. McTavish as "a market-sharing agreement" for the winter, with some posts abandoned to lessen competition among the parties.

Meanwhile in New Caledonia, bad weather prevented John Stuart from leaving Stuart Lake for the Columbia until May 13, 1813. The cost of sending supplies across the continent to the remote department and receiving returns the same way was too expensive. The Nor'Westers intended to supply those posts from the Columbia and bring out returns for marketing in China.[42] Stuart embarked with eight men in two canoes intent on finding a direct and feasible trade route between the Fraser River and the Columbia, the primary object of his exploration.

By using a combination of canoes where feasible, and packhorses where not, Stuart succeeded in pushing a route through. In August 1813, below the mouth of the Okanogan River, Stuart and McTavish finally joined forces. Finding no reason to continue on to the mouth of the river if there was no ship there, Stuart accompanied McTavish back to Spokane House. Business did not command McTavish's whole attention after he met Stuart's ward, the mixed-blood daughter of Roderick McKenzie, and took her as his second country wife.

McTavish and Stuart arrived at Spokane House early in September unaware that the peripatetic Wilson Price Hunt had returned to Astoria on the chartered *Albatross* on August 20. He was too late to head off the PFC's decision to abandon the country, unilaterally decided by McDougall, McKenzie, and others. After less than a week, Hunt sailed to Hawaii to arrange for a ship to carry the Astorians away.[43]

North West Company communications traveled at a frustrating pace. In May 1813 an express canoe left Montreal, traveling as fast as possible to the North West Company headquarters at Fort William. From there a second crew and a fresh canoe drove westward, with the best voyageurs and nothing more than a few provisions and a mail pouch. Sometime in September the express arrived at Spokane House delivering letters conveying important and urgent news.

---

42 Lamb, ed., *Sixteen Years in the Indian Country*, 154-55, 159. No records of the 1812 brigades between Fort William and New Caledonia have been found but, from Harmon in the source cited, it can be guessed that it took about two months between Fort William and Fort Chipewyan, another month to Dunvegan on the Peace River, and a fourth month between there and Stuart's Lake (Fort St. James) in New Caledonia. *See* Lamb, *Sixteen Years*, 110-18; 127-34.

43 Jones, ed., *Annals of Astoria*, 211-13. McDougall's notes for August 25 do not mention a tumultuous meeting on that day as described by Elliott, "Sale of Astoria," 46-47 or repeated by Ronda, *Astor and Empire*, 285-86.

Among the letters McTavish took out of the dispatch case was confirmation that the ship *Isaac Todd* had sailed from Portsmouth on March 18, 1813, bound for the Columbia River, and accompanied by the frigate *HMS Phoebe*. The naval escort carried orders "to take and destroy everything that is American on the Northwest coast."[44] McTavish and Stuart must have read that news with disgust, as they had been previously advised that the ship was to have sailed from England in October 1812.[45] Despite the delay, they were elated to learn that their supply ship was on its way, and under Royal Navy protection.[46]

No less gratifying, McTavish and Stuart also learned they had been made North West Company partners, which gave them greater latitude in making decisions.[47] Upon reading that, McTavish made the precipitous decision to return to Fort Astoria. Knowing the PFC was on the edge of collapse, an offer to buy them out would eliminate their need to haul property and furs overland. He was accompanied by a brigade of nine canoes and the manpower to receive and carry that cargo.

About one hundred miles above Astoria, somewhere in the area of The Dalles, McTavish and Stuart overtook the Astorians McKenzie and Clarke who were also returning to Astoria. The PFC clerk Alfred Seton recorded spending the night of October 2 with "The British party consist of 2 Bourgeois, viz Messrs McTavish & Stuart & 7 clerks, viz Messrs McMullen, Bethune, Henry, Jos. McGillvery, McDonald, Montour & Cox & about 40 common men."[48] McKenzie and Clarke tried to slip out during the night with the warning that a large party was coming that

44 Extract from a letter written by Montreal agent Angus Shaw to John George McTavish, dated Montreal, 9 May 1813, including information regarding the warship. *Message from the President of the United States communicating The Letter of Mr. Prevost, and other Documents, relating to the establishment made at the mouth of the Columbia River;* 17 Cong., 2d sess., H. Doc. 45 (Washington, D.C.: Gales and Seaton, 1823), 65.

45 Lamb, ed., *Sixteen Years*, 155.

46 This should be understood in the broader sense that *HMS Phoebe*, *HMS Cherub*, and *HMS Racoon* were sent to the Pacific in 1813 to search for and destroy *USS Essex*, which was attacking the British whaling fleet.

47 HBCA, F.3/2, fos. 115-16, letter dated Montreal, May 9, 1813, from William McGillivray to J. G. McTavish.

48 Jones, ed., *Astorian Adventure*, 126-27, 226-37. While Pacific Fur Company clerk Gabriel Franchère counted ten canoes containing seventy-two to seventy-four men, figures echoed by Alexander Ross, the estimates are probably exaggerations. The list of "People on the Columbia for the winter 1813/14," is a census of 176 individuals from both companies plus 10 freemen in the Salish or Snake country. Jones, ed., *Annals of Astoria*, 226-37.

might try to take over the PFC post. Leaving Stuart to follow with the boats and the rest of their men, McTavish raced after them.

But the NWC was not coming with conquest in mind, only bringing down enough hands to carry the anticipated new outfit to the inland posts. Meantime, that extra manpower could improve the depot McTavish had started at Astoria the previous spring. But when they arrived on October 7, 1813, his expectation of finding a ship at anchor, ready to be unloaded, was again disappointed.[49]

The newly minted proprietor John George McTavish wasted no time in taking the initiative. Less than twenty-four hours after arriving, he made an audacious offer—to purchase all the goods and furs belonging to the Pacific Fur Company. It probably did not occur to him that he had no authority to do so.[50]

The Astoria headquarters log reveals little of the undercurrents that surged until October 12, when Duncan McDougall came to an understanding with McTavish regarding the Pacific Fur Company's assets. When John Stuart arrived that evening with the NWC brigade, he expressed reservations regarding that understanding. According to the headquarters log,

> Mr. McTavish proposed purchasing the goods and Furs belonging to the company, here (as well as in the Interior) for cost and charges, excepting Articles damaged or in use. [On the 14th] Visited by Messrs. McTavish and Stuart and finally settled upon terms the property would be disposed for and the time for receiving payment.[51]

The next day, however, McDougall was surprised when McTavish wanted to change the terms. McDougall ended the discussions and to show his determination ordered "additional precautions [to be] taken about the fort that they should take no advantage of the hopes we before entertained, of coming to an amicable settlement with them."[52]

---

49 Wallace, ed., *Documents Relating to the North West Company*, 279.

50 Lamb, ed., *Journal of a Voyage*, 129. PFC clerk Gabriel Franchère rationalized that the offer was made out of necessity because the Nor'Westers were running out of food and "Tired of having to come to us for their subsistence, they finally suggested buying the post and its contents."

51 Jones, ed., *Annals of Astoria*, 220.

52 Jones, ed., *Annals of Astoria*, 221-23; and compare to Ross, *Adventures*, 246, which makes a dramatic narrative but raises a few questions regarding his veracity. In the headquarters log, McDougall noted the agreement was signed and made out in duplicate on October 16. Six days later he delivered the keys of the store to McTavish and Stuart.

In his account Franchère had little to say beyond how the negotiations dragged on.[53] Ross Cox, who had already become a Nor'wester, made no criticism of the proceedings and Alexander Ross, who was not present at the negotiation, invented his version of how the property negotiations were handled:

> One morning before daylight Messrs. McDougall and McKenzie summoned all hands together, seventy-two in number, and after a brief statement of the views of the North-West in reference to the negotiation, ordered the bastions to be manned, the guns to be loaded and pointed, and the matches lighted. In an instant every man was at his post, and the gates shut. At eight o'clock a message was sent to McTavish, giving him two hours and no more, either to sign the bills or break off the negotiation altogether and remove to some other quarters. By eleven o'clock the bills were finally and formally signed, and Astoria was delivered up to the North-West Company on the 12th of November, after nearly a month of suspense between the drawing and the signing of the bills.[54]

Alfred Seton, the only American among the scribblers with close ties to Astor, thought McDougall was a traitor to the cause. He made the flag, or rather the lack of a visible American flag, an issue when the arrogant Nor'Westers hoisted their Union Jack. In his mortification, Seton observed "20 men therefore under the guns of the Fort display the British colours while 60 men in a good fort surrounded with guns are fearful of offending these potent men."[55]

What the North West Company actually obtained from the Pacific Fur Company is evaluated in Article 4 of the sale agreement:

> And further it is hereby agreed & concluded upon by the said Parties that the following are the rates at what the Establishments, Furs & Stock on hand be valued at as follows
> Dry Goods, Stationary, Gun powder & leaf Tobacco 50 Pr Ct on prime cost of N York
> hip Chandlery 60 Pr Cent
> Shot, Ball, lead, Iron & Steel 100 Pr Cent

---

53 Lamb, ed., *Journal of a Voyage*, 142-43.

54 Ross, *Adventures*, 245.

55 Jones, ed., *Astorian Adventure*, 128-29. The events, the business, and the political consequences have been churned over by so many writers that the authors find no reason to repeat those speculations. For the two new NWC proprietors, it was just another accomplishment of skin gamesmanship.

Deduct^{n} in made up Iron works of 33 1/3 Pr Cent
Boats each £10 H^{x}C^{y} D^{o} in use 100/. H^{x}C^{y}
Shallop w^{t} Rigging complete £112.10
wo Blksth's Forges ea £25
Plug Tobacco 1/6 P$^{r\ lb}$ - d^{o} d^{o} Col. manuf. 1/3 P$^{r\ lb}$
Beads, assorted 5/. P$^{r\ lb}$
Arm's Cannon &c at Prime cost
Provisions at fixed Prices ... Provisions were not valued as all articles in use at Half Invent^{y} Prices - vizt at Hlf Prime cost
Horses ea 30/.
Buildings at £200
John Reids adventure to deduct 100 P^{r} C^{t} - say only 50 Pr Cent
Beaver 10/. P$^{r\ lb}$ Coating 8/4 ^{lb} Muskrats 7½^{d} Land Otters 2/6 & Sea 60/.
Signed 10th Octr 1813 & afterwards assumed & signed by W. P. Hunt on the Part of the P.F. C 10th March 1814.[56]

Finally, on October 16, 1813, Duncan McDougall for the Pacific Fur Company and John George McTavish and John Stuart for the North West Company, with seven clerks from both companies as witnesses, signed the bill of sale for a price of $58,291.02 plus other considerations.[57] A continent away, John Jacob Astor yelled out in his sleep, "Robbery!"

Interpretations of Donald McKenzie's behavior during that trying period have depended on what the admiring clerk Alexander Ross wrote about him. But the recent publication of the Fort Astoria headquarters log calls that appreciation into question. For the moment it was John George McTavish who was the mercantile hero.

William McGillivray's earlier letter of May 9, 1813, to McTavish was glowing in its praise.[58] It suggested that McTavish was considered indispensible and in line for something greater. His negotiated purchase was certainly influenced by McGillivray. As he settled into the Astorians' post, now rechristened Fort George, J. G. McTavish had no inkling that he would soon be knee deep in more senior partners.

---

56 National Archives of Canada, Keith Papers, A-676, Memorandum Book, p. 30.

57 Elliott, "Sale of Astoria, 1813," 49-50; HBCA, F.4/61, fo. 9; Jones, ed., *Annals of Astoria*, 221-22. Clerk Alexander Ross came from Okanogan with the PFC brigade and must have witnessed the sale, although he put the purchase price at $80,000. It is unlikely he would have been party to the negotiation, of which he nonetheless invented several pages of conversation.

58 William McGillivray to J. G. McTavish, Montreal May 9, 1813, HBCA, F.3/2, fos. 115-16.

When the Astorians and Nor'westers listed their combined forces for the winter 1813–14, there were 176 named individuals scattered in the Pacific Northwest as well as unassociated freemen living with the tribes. Before the Astoria ledger was closed, the profit and loss of Mr. Astor's company and the political significance and international consequences of the endeavor were matters of a well-conceived, but unlucky business venture. The human cost was another matter. Of the approximately 228 officers and workmen that the New York nabob sent to the Columbia, at least 66 lost their lives. Even by early nineteenth century standards of humanity, it was an appalling casualty count. Losses of 34 percent went far beyond those usually found acceptable by Montreal or London traders operating east of the mountains.[59]

The rest of October was spent arranging for a joint inventory of the stock of goods. McKenzie left as a passenger with Stuart and five canoes returning to inventory the inland goods. McDougall stopped keeping the log on October 28 and did not resume until his November 15 entry, which recorded the arrival by canoe of Alexander Henry, Alexander Stuart, James Keith, and sixteen men from Fort William.

59 Perhaps not by the armies, then meeting in bloody battles between young men who were born in North America.

Chapter Six

"a dull sailer"

The Tardy Voyage of the *Isaac Todd*, 1812

Given the difficulties the Astorians encountered just getting their ship *Tonquin* to the Pacific, Hawaii, and across the dangerous Columbia River bar at a considerable loss of lives, only to lose the ship and most of the crew in an encounter with hostile Indians somewhere along the west coast of Vancouver Island, John George McTavish was understanding of the disappointing failure of a North West Company ship to arrive. The delay was opportune, giving him time to present Mr. Astor's discouraged and fearful partners with an offer beyond refusal.

McTavish anticipated his appointment to a partnership would be confirmed. On November 14, just seventeen days after receiving the keys to the fort, two other partners and a clerk arrived by canoe. His status suddenly dropped to that of the least senior partner. As the month of November wore down, there was still no sail on the horizon. Only later would McTavish learn why. New plans had been made far from the Columbia.

The business of obtaining a suitable vessel to send out to the far northwest had begun eighteen months previously, in April 1812, when William McGillivray wrote a letter from London expressing his frustration that the East India Company was stonewalling his request for a license to trade in China, and that the British government would not give a straight answer to his petition for a charter for the North West Company. Launching such an ambitious enterprise required a considerable investment. Deadlines for outfitting and the best time to leave were fast approaching.

Still, McGillivray believed he was already ahead of the game because he had convinced Donald McTavish, a senior wintering partner, to delay his retirement for a year and take command of their "Adventure to the Columbia." When the wintering partners came to the Fort William annual meeting in July 1812 and read McGillivray's opinion, they also heard David Thompson's estimate of what might be expected from the Pacific Fur Company. That sounded like a challenge and they approved sending a ship to transport goods and additional staff to the Columbia River.[1]

John McDonald, the sometime superintendent of the lower Fort des Prairies department, had returned to Fort William in a "light" canoe, pleading illness. He quickly recovered, though, in time to join the party being assembled to go to England. Four clerks, a physician, six French Canadian voyageurs, and a Hawaiian Islander named Cox, who knew something about crossing the dangerous Columbia bar, would join the ship at Montreal.[2] The agents expected the ship would be fitted for a voyage of two to three years, to deliver European trade goods at the Columbia River, take on beaver skins, and, with an East India Company license in hand, trade those skins in China for either oriental goods to be sold on the return voyage, or specie (money in coin) which could be profitably exchanged in England.

Sometime before mid-October 1812, the *Isaac Todd*, commanded by Captain Frazer Smith, cleared customs at Quebec carrying the year's fur production.[3] Built at Trois Rivières, Quebec, about 1811, the *Isaac Todd* was owned by a nephew of William and Simon McTavish, and a cousin of Donald McTavish.[4] She weighed some 350 tons, mounted ten guns, and sailed with a crew of seventeen.[5]

1 Wallace, ed., *Documents Relating to the North West Company*, 268, 271; William McGillivray to the Gentlemen Wintering Partners of the North West Company, Fort William, April 9, 1812, LAC, Selkirk Papers, MG19, #1, vol. 31, 9121-26.

2 Davidson, *North West Company*; Masson, ed. *Les Bourgeois*, 43. For extensive notes on these passengers, *see* Coues, ed., *New Light*, 2:894-98.

3 An August 18, 1812, date is found in National Archives, Pubic Record Office, Colonial Office Papers (hereafter NA PRO) 42/149/95. If that date is accurate, the men made exceptionally good time from Fort William, especially considering the wartime conditions on the Great Lakes.

4 John McTavish would succeed to two shares in the Montreal agency of McTavish, McGillivray & Company in 1814 (Wallace, *NWC Documents*, 141, 301, 485). His role with the Montreal agency prior to 1814 is unclear, as is the reason for his ownership of the *Isaac Todd*.

5 NA PRO, Colonial Office Papers, London, England, series 42, vol. 82; cited in Davidson, *North West Company*, 136. In his autobiographical notes, eighty-five-year-old John McDonald of Garth misremembered that the ship carried a letter of marque, but that was not obtained until after the *Isaac Todd* arrived in London.

William McGillivray wrote to the wintering partners of the North West Company that "the East India Company still appear to be favorably disposed—the certainty of getting Dollars in Canton for our Beaver Skins removed a Barrier which last year I thought unsurmountable."[6] But McGillivray's enthusiasm was premature, as a careful reading of the twenty-two article license revealed:

> all the sales to be made of the Cargo of the said Ship...and all the money to be received at Canton or elsewhere in China or any Goods Wares or Merchandise whatsoever to be sold there by or on the account of the persons concerned in the Adventure hereby licenced shall be paid by their Agents into the Treasury of the said United Company [East India Company] at Canton for Bills of Exchange to be drawn by the said United Companys Super Cargoes on the Court of Directors of the said United Company payable in London three hundred and sixty five days after sight at the same rate of Exchange at which the said Super Cargos shall draw Bills on the said Court of Directors in the same Season.[7]

Thus, not only were the Nor'Westers barred from trading beaver skins for Chinese goods, they also were not allowed to transport specie to England and therefore could not benefit from a possible favorable exchange rate. Compelled to settle for bills of exchange, which did not appreciate in value as hard currency did, the fur traders could not expect payment for an entire year after the bills were presented.

Rather than return empty to England, the East India Company condescended to allow the *Isaac Todd* to transport a cargo of goods belonging to them to London for freight-money. The second half of the license detailed the conditions under which the goods were to be shipped, and circumstances under which payment could be withheld. It was not a good contract for the North West Company, but the company's London agent, Simon McGillivray, and wintering partner Donald McTavish, were blind to the ultimate consequences when they signed the document on January 13, 1813.

---

6 "Letter dated London April 9, 1812, from William McGillivray to the Gentlemen Wintering Partners of the North West Company." LAC, Selkirk Papers, MG19, E1, vol. 31, 9121-26.

7 LAC, Ellice Papers, A-19, 54, No. 19. Bills of the East India Company were issued at rates ranging from four shillings ten pence to six shillings per dollar, for bills payable 365 days after sight. *See* Morse, *Chronicles of the East India Company*, x.

After the Montreal cargo was unloaded at the London docks, Donald McTavish and John McDonald, assisted by the NWC's London agents, began outfitting the *Isaac Todd* for its next long voyage. Besides re-sheathing, re-caulking, and supplying new canvas, lines, and hawsers, the ship needed modification to accommodate twenty cannon. Because of the war, the fifty-four-gun American frigate *Constitution* was then preying on British vessels in the Atlantic and might be encountered somewhere off the coast of Africa near the Cape Verde Islands.[8] In the Pacific the Americans had the thirty-six-gun frigate *Essex* preying on British whalers.

Expecting danger from any quarter, the London agents petitioned for a letter of marque for the *Isaac Todd,* and a sloop of war to escort their ship and clear the North American coast of hostile vessels and settlements.[9] While guilty of some hyperbole in pressing their needs, the Nor'Westers insisted "the territorial possession of the Countries bordering on the Columbia River, and finally the whole Northwest coast of the Continent of America, will depend upon the measures to be adopted by His Majesty's government on the present occasion."[10]

Fitting out a ship carrying a letter of marque required time-consuming modifications to the deck to accommodate twenty guns. At Portsmouth Donald McTavish and John McDonald were delayed another month anxiously awaiting final government clearance. The six French Canadian voyageurs, brought along for service in the Columbia Department, were detained by a Royal Navy press gang.[11] Another distraction occupied the attention of the lusty little John McDonald who hired a local woman, Jane Barnes, to accompany him to the Columbia, ostensibly serving as the company's seamstress.

About a month before J. G. McTavish left Spokane House, anticipating the arrival of the *Isaac Todd* at the Columbia, the ship finally cleared Portsmouth on March 25, 1813.[12] The ship sailed in company with about forty other merchant ships and a naval squadron that included the *HMS*

---

8 LAC, Autobiographical Notes of John McDonald, A Partner in the North West Company, 1791- 1816, MG19-A17, 73.

9 The full text of these two petitions was published in Davidson, *North West Company*, 283-92. The request for military assistance can be found on pages 136-37.

10 NA PRO, Colonial Office Papers, PRO, London, England, series 42, vol. 149, 141

11 O'Neil. "Maritime Activities," 249; Masson, ed., *Les Bourgeois*, 44-45.

12 "Extract from Mr. McDonald's Journal," Payette, ed., *Oregon Country*, v.

Phoebe, assigned to accompany the *Isaac Todd* to the Columbia. Royal navy Captain James Hillyar carried secret orders to "render every assistance in your power to the British traders from Canada, and to destroy and, if possible, totally annihilate any settlements which the Americans may have formed."[13]

Problems soon hampered the *Isaac Todd.* An anchor and hawser were lost after departure from Portsmouth, and at Tenerife in the Canary Islands, the Canadian voyageurs had to be bailed after getting into trouble with Spanish authorities.[14] In an Atlantic storm, the merchant ship under sail with a full crew could not keep up with her escort sailing "under bare poles."[15] The weight of those twenty long guns on the *Isaac Todd*'s deck may have caused the ship to be a "dull sailer."

Enmity between Captain Frazer Smith and John McDonald appeared when McDonald invited the Captain and officers of the *Phoebe* aboard for dinner, wine, and porter, but neglected to invite Captain Smith and his officers. When the naval officers and their host sat down to partake of their meal, the fine dinner and drinks had been intercepted by Smith for his own mess and poorer fare substituted. Later, when confronting Smith, the pugnacious fur trader bragged "a serious row would have taken place, but McTavish & others came & took me away. No doubt that I would have punished some of them."[16]

After weathering the difficulties of an Atlantic crossing, the convoy arrived at Rio de Janeiro on June 11, seventy-eight days out of Portsmouth.[17] The *Isaac Todd* and *Phoebe* lay at anchor for nearly a month, making it necessary to hire twelve new men and two officers to replace those who, once ashore, deserted.[18] Perhaps that had to do with news that the American war ship, the *Essex*, Captain David Porter, and an armed tender were destroying or capturing British merchantmen in the Pacific Ocean. When Captain Hillyar protested that the *Phoebe* and the cumbersome *Isaac Todd* were inadequate to face such an imposing foe, Vice

13 Haeger, "Business Strategy and Practice," 195; Russell, "Chinese Voyages," 23. *See also* Haeger, *John Jacob Astor*, 160, 319.

14 Masson, ed., *Les Bourgeois*, 45-46.

15 Payette, ed., *Oregon Country*, v.

16 LAC, Autobiographical Notes of John McDonald, 75.

17 Green, "Analysis of the *Autobiographical Notes of McDonald*," 162.

18 Payette, *Oregon Country*, vii. Four of the new men were deserters from H. M. Cutter *Dart*, which was last seen sailing from Pernambuco on the Brazilian coast for England on October 27, 1813, and was never heard from again.

Admiral Manley Dixon, commander of the British navy's Brazil Station, decided to send the sloops of war *Cherub* and *Racoon* to the Pacific in support of the *Phoebe*. Now the *Isaac Todd* sailed under the protection of three of His Majesty's ships.[19]

Two days after clearing Rio on July 8, Captain Hillyar opened his sealed orders and immediately requested McDonald to come aboard the *Phoebe* to discuss what should be done in case the frigate should become separated from the *Isaac Todd* and arrive first on the Columbia. He felt a partner should be aboard to take charge of the company's affairs, as well as the Hawaiian Cox to find a passage over the bar at the river mouth. In compliance, the old fur trader had himself transferred to the *Phoebe* along with three Canadians and Cox. But not the seamstress; women were not allowed aboard a royal naval vessel and McDonald reluctantly left Jane Barnes in the tender care of Donald McTavish.[20]

After nearly losing sight of the *Isaac Todd* during a gale, Captain Hillyar spoke with the ship on July 23, 1813, about 550 miles east of La Plata (Argentina), and next week lost sight of the lumbering merchant ship entirely.[21] The convoy approached the boisterous seas surrounding Cape Horn at the worst possible time of year—winter. Lacking proper trim, the *Isaac Todd* struggled to keep up. The naval ships took nearly a month to double the cape and cast anchor at the Juan Fernandez Islands, west of Valparaiso, Chile, on September 11.[22] After waiting over a week for the merchant ship to appear, the three warships finally gave up and sailed on.

After consulting charts, Captain Hillyar realized that the mouth of the Columbia River was too shallow for the 700-ton *Phoebe* and decided he would send the smaller 423-ton *Racoon* across instead.[23] McDonald, the blacksmith, the Canadian engagés, and the Hawaiian Cox left the *Phoebe* and boarded the *Racoon* together with eighty-seven bales of

19 Masson, ed., *Les Bourgeois*, 46. *See also* Gough, "The 1813 Expedition to Astoria," 46-47; Hussey, ed., *Voyage of the Racoon*, xi. The original manuscript log is held by the Bancroft Library, University of California, Berkeley.

20 John McDonald's autobiography and logbook are the only records of the voyage that have survived.

21 Payette, ed., *Oregon Country*, viii; Hussey, ed., *Voyage of the Racoon*, xv, xxi, 19; Masson, ed., *Les Bourgeois*, 47; LAC, Autobiographical Notes of John McDonald, 79.

22 Masson, ed., *Les Bourgeois*, 47; LAC, Autobiographical Notes of John McDonald, 79; Payette, *Oregon Country*, ix.

23 *See* Hussey, ed., *Voyage of the Racoon*, xv, for a discussion of this ambiguity.

NWC trade goods and three casks of beef.[24] However, the warships sailed together from Juan Fernandez to somewhere off the coast of Panama, where Hillyar thought the *Racoon* could safely proceed to the Columbia alone. They could call at Cocos Island where the *Isaac Todd* was expected to take on wood and water.[25] But after waiting two days for the merchant ship to appear, the *Racoon*'s captain, William Black, ordered the ship's name chiseled on a rock and carved into the bark of a tree as signs for the *Isaac Todd* to follow, and put to sea for the Columbia.

Two weeks later, while test firing the *Racoon*'s guns, an accidental explosion injured twenty-one people, seven fatally, including the NWC company blacksmith.[26] McDonald suffered severe injuries, and the Hawaiian Cox received superficial burns. The scorched but otherwise undamaged HMS *Racoon* crossed the Columbia bar and anchored in Baker Bay on November 30, 1813, a week short of four months since sailing from Rio de Janeiro. To the disappointment of the British sailors, the unimpressive trading post established by the Astorians was already flying the Union Jack. There would be no battle, no prize of war—the fort was already British property.

By the standards of their association, the proprietors who came to the mouth of the Columbia were gentlemen and obliged to treat each other as such. But that mannerly veneer wore thin in those sagging cabins at the end of the world where John George McTavish quickly came under criticism. For two short weeks after negotiating his contract McTavish had basked in the accomplishment of his initiative—buying out the Pacific Fur Company and eliminating all competition.[27] When he made the contract in October 1813, with no sign of a ship, friend or foe, it did not occur to the aspiring proprietor that purchasing the assets of the PFC went beyond the bounds authorized to wintering partners.

24 Payette, ed., *Oregon Country*, ix, xi; Masson, ed., *Les Bourgeois*, 48; LAC, Autobiographical Notes of John McDonald, 81.

25 Payette, ed., *Oregon Country*, ix.

26 In his log written at the time and probably more accurate, McDonald specified twenty-one injuries from the explosion and identified the fatalities as J. Flett and a Canadian. *See* Masson, ed., *Les Bourgeois*, 49; LAC, Autobiographical Notes of John McDonald, 84; Payette, ed., *Oregon Country*, x.

27 That was affirmed when a special express brought Angus Shaw's letter making him and Alexander Stuart partners in the NWC.

But it had occurred to others, and leadership had been dispatched to aid in managing the department—leadership that would arrive at newly christened Fort George just days after McTavish had negotiated its purchase. At the 1813 Fort William rendezvous "It was therefore considered essential to the Interests of the Concern that a Partner with two able Clerks should still proceed to the Columbia in order to strengthen the Party already sent across the mountains."[28] The Hudson's Bay Company inland master James Bird gained an insight into feelings of NWC partners on August 5, 1813, when Alexander Henry, Alexander Stuart, and James Keith paused at Fort Augustus/Edmonton House on their way to the Columbia. Henry told his former neighbor that the Columbia Adventure had a hundred men and officers and expected to take possession of the American settlement. That would probably cost £50,000 and Henry did not believe it could be profitable despite the high opinion their agents had of it.[29] On the afternoon of November 14, Fort George at the mouth of the Columbia was surprised "By the Arrival of Messrs Alex. Henry, Alex. [Stuart] & Keith, with a Party of 16 Men, in two Bark Canoes, from Fort William, which place they left the 19th July last. They brought Papers from Canada as late as the 12th June."[30]

Alexander Henry was the more senior officer, with twelve years' experience as a partner in the North West Company.[31] His companion, Alexander Stuart, had been awarded a partner's share that summer and was no match for the domineering personality of J. G. McTavish. But confronting the seasoned Henry in a contest of wills was a challenge to McTavish. Friction between them led Henry to avoid using McTavish's name in the journal he returned to on November 15, 1813. Henry invented a pseudonym, "Mr. Thompson," although there was no one of that name at Fort George.[32]

Five days later the Nor'Westers moved into the fort. There is no hint in the headquarters' log revealing how they were accommodated or whom they displaced. It was just as well that John Stuart, Donald McKenzie,

28 Jones, ed., *Annals of Astoria*, 223; Wallace, *Documents of the North West Company*, 274.

29 Edmonton House Journal, August 5-7, 1813, HBCA, B60/a/12, fo. 1d.

30 Jones, ed., *Annals of Astoria*, 223n132.

31 Gough, ed., *Alexander Henry*, 418-419. Henry was about forty when he arrived at Astoria.

32 Gough, *Alexander Henry*, 2:616-17, 637; Franchère, *Journal of a Voyage*, 131-32; Jones, ed., *Astorian Adventure*, 142. On March 6 and 7, 1814, Henry again mentions Thompson visiting Hunt's brig *Pedler*.

and the men necessary to drive five canoes left for the interior with the winter's outfit and to complete the inventories at Spokane House and Okanogan, because Fort George was about to fill up with fur traders.

About noon on November 30 at half-tide "a large ship appeared in sight, standing over the Bar, with all sails spread, and a light breeze from the North East."[33] The *Racoon* had arrived. It successfully crossed the always dangerous bar and half an hour later anchored in Baker Bay. In this time of war, nerves were on edge, and, not knowing whether the vessel was friend or foe, McTavish ordered the peltry, arms and ammunition, and other valuables moved to Tongue Point, some distance away. McTavish and Henry remained at the fort, anxiously awaiting the results as the expendable Duncan McDougall and seven men were sent in a canoe to determine the ship's nationality. The ship flew a white flag at its foremost, a common signal for peace—but also used upon occasion as a ruse.[34]

Uncertain which party was in control of the fort, Captain Black had decided to anchor in Baker Bay on the north side of the river's mouth, away from any potential hostile fire. After securing the ship, he sent an armed cutter to reconnoiter the river channels and the fort. They soon came upon the canoe from the fort carrying Duncan McDougall, John Halsey, and crew, who the officer in the cutter invited aboard the *Racoon* to meet the captain. Drinks were shared all around to celebrate the occasion. While those remaining at the fort continued to fret about the intentions of the strange ship, the welcoming committee aboard the *Racoon* imbibed until it was decided that McDougall had best not attempt descending the boarding ladder. He remained aboard while a tipsy John Halsey herded the intoxicated canoe paddlers six miles upriver. About half past nine, the worried Nor'Westers in the fort heard singing coming from the direction of the river. Halsey and the drunken canoe crew joyfully reported that the ship was the HMS *Racoon,* Captain William Black commanding.[35]

Among the new arrivals was yet another NWCo partner. John McDonald, who remained on board, was just beginning to recover from severe injuries suffered in the explosion and would not be able to assume an active role in affairs for some time. That was just as well as many soon

33 Gough, ed., *Alexander Henry,* 2:615.

34 Off Cape of Good Hope on June 4, 1815, the *Isaac Todd* would come upon an American schooner "flying a white flag at the fore an indication of peace."

35 Gough, ed., *Alexander Henry,* 2:616.

had reasons to dislike the little man who did not hide his poor view of their actions, character, or courage.[36]

Captain Black considered Baker Bay a more convenient anchorage for a war ship, with access to wood and water and in an excellent position to guard the river's mouth from enemy ships.[37] That made for a tedious chore of unloading and delivering the ship's eighty-seven bales of trade goods and three casks of beef. The captain's reasons for his lack of accommodation is reflected in his clerk's record:

> This piece of business of buying the settlement of an Enemy's people (by which the North West Company by no means acted proper after petitioning to Government for a force to be sent to take the place, plant the British Flag, and establish it under their firm) in my opinion to all intents and purposes is diametrically opposite to the fundimental laws of great Britain under the head of assisting an Enemy, which purchasing the property and establishment of these people who were on the point of abandoning the whole on the approach of the Racoon planted the British Colours on the Fort (named it Fort George) in the Name of King George the Third [and] fired a salute in honor to the same, no doubt on an investigation in the Court of Admiralty it will be clearly proved the company of the Racoon are the captors of the aforesaid establishment and property belonging thereto [and] consequently will justly be entitled to the emoluments arising therefrom, which is estimated after everything settled to the amount of £50,000.[38]

The officers and crew of the *Racoon,* who expected prize money would be theirs, now had to be satisfied with the knowledge that they had done their duty "to the North West Company," as John McDonald put it.[39] Tensions increased when naval officers attempted to recruit some NWC engagés into the Royal service, and the sailors complained that the fur traders were stingy with their fresh provisions.[40]

36 LAC, Autobiographical Notes of John McDonald, MG 19, A-17, entry for December 1, 1813. McDonald did not leave the ship until December 7.

37 Hussey, ed., *The Voyage of the Racoon*, 11.

38 Hussey, ed., *The Voyage of the Racoon*, 5.

39 LAC, Autobiographical Notes of John McDonald, MG 19, A-17, entry dated just prior to "Astoria Dec[r] 1813." Further evidence the navy men expected a prize can be found in Jones, ed., *Astorian Adventure*, 142. Editor Jones asserts Seton was wrong to come to this conclusion for Captain Black stated he had no such expectation and cites as his source, Gough's article "The 1813 Expedition to Astoria," 50.

40 Hussey, ed., *Voyage of the Racoon*, xx, 6.

As far as Captain Black was concerned, his duty only required that he deliver up the North West Company's goods in his ship, claim British sovereignty over the surrounding country, and conduct a new survey of the mouth of the Columbia River. Black had no desire to remain longer, but stormy weather created conditions hazardous to moving the cargo. Swells created by current, ebbing tide, and high winds threatened more than once to swamp a ship's boat or the river schooner *Dolly,* loaded with bales of blankets or casks of beef.

With no prize money forthcoming, something had to be made out of this wild goose chase to the northwest coast. Decorum required a ceremony of "taking possession." At noon on Sunday, December 12, 1813, Captain Black went to the fort aboard the *Dolly* accompanied by John Clarke and Alexander Stuart, a midshipman, four marines, and three seamen. Earlier in the day the weather had been fair, but within the hour the wind whipped up a gale, creating a ferocious chain of breakers across the river. By three in the afternoon it began to rain and darken, forcing the tiny schooner to work its way into Young's Bay and set anchor.

In the gloaming, a canoe was sent from the fort to aid the dignitaries. Although the canoe party failed to find the *Dolly,* they came upon three men on the beach and brought them back to the fort. A second party finally located the *Dolly* and landed the officers at Point George, about two miles from the fort. Scrambling over slippery rocks in the pitch black, Captain Black, Clarke, and Stuart stumbled into the fort at 11 P.M., cold, wet, and peeved. Henry's hot toddy may have restored their humor, but the crew of the *Dolly* stayed aboard the open boat and finally anchored in front of the fort just after daybreak.

The seven-gun salute fired at eight in the morning may not have eased Captain Black's throbbing head, but it salved his ego. By ten the rain had stopped and the sun broke out. All donned their dress uniforms or best greatcoats, combed their hair, and loaded their weapons. At mid-afternoon, three guns were fired as a signal to the *Racoon*, and preparations made for the ceremony. With the four marines arrayed in dress uniforms, the sailors attending the four-pounder, and all the gentlemen at attention, Captain Black ordered the Union Jack raised, broke a bottle of Madeira wine over the flagpole, and took possession of the country in the name of His Britannic Majesty and, in his honor, renamed the place Fort George.

This was followed by three cheers, and a firing of the muskets in which one of the marines almost shot himself in the face. The sailors, however, managed the four-pounder without incident, firing it off eleven times in honor of the occasion. The rest of the day was given to drinking and merriment.[41] In a few years this stumbling, bumbling affair would have serious international repercussions.

A few days after the ceremony, Captain Black assigned three officers, a midshipman, and six seamen the task of charting the mouth of the Columbia River from Cape Disappointment to Fort George by taking and recording soundings of the wide river to find a channel. After traveling across the continent in a bark canoe, partner Alexander Henry was critical that it took British seamen seven hours to row from the ship at Baker Bay to Fort George, arriving well intoxicated with grog. After the second day's sounding of the river, their assignment was completed but the ebb tide prevented their returning to the ship. Henry grumbled that those "fine famous fellows for grog" stayed a second night at the fort.[42] Next morning, after breakfast, the upper sails of the ship were seen hanging loose, a signal the men were aboard the *Racoon* now and ready for sailing. Some parting provisions were sent down with the survey crew, along with four Hawaiian workmen returning home after the end of their contract.

The winter season was not the time for crossing the dangerous bar and entering the ocean.[43] Luckily, on the eighteenth day of the month, the wind calmed, the rain stopped, and the roaring breakers across the bar moderated, conditions that might not occur again for another six weeks. They waited for the beginning of the ebb tide. As that began, Captain Black discovered he had misplaced Broughton's papers, the only notes and chart describing the safe way to exit Baker Bay and cross the bar into the Pacific Ocean. He could not leave without them.

---

41 Hussey, ed., *Voyage of the Racoon*, 622. Another, more truncated version is given in Franchère, *Journal of a Voyage*, 133-34.

42 Gough, ed., *Alexander Henry*, 2:624-65.

43 At the Columbia bar the river's current and the incoming tide can meet with tremendous force. The list of vessels lost there over the years is long and those waters are still used by the United States Coast Guard to train small boat rescue crews how to handle heavy water.

Remembering that he had placed that document in the copy of George Vancouver's *A Voyage of Discovery* given the Nor'Westers at Fort George, Black ordered the ship's master and his clerk to take the pinnace to Fort George and recover the critical document. Then the weather turned with high winds, rain, and mid-channel breakers in the river. Crews made three attempts to go to the fort but were forced to turn around or find themselves awash in the breaking waves. When the precious document was finally retrieved it was too late "to get clear of such a outlandish and uncivilized Place."[44]

Under marginal conditions, the crew of the HMS *Racoon* finally weighed anchor and set sail on December 31, braving the tremendous waves breaking over the bar. For a time, the ship would not answer the helm and the situation appeared critical as she twice struck very hard, damaging the keel.[45] After getting into open water, it was discovered the ship had sprung a leak and was taking on water at an alarming rate. With constant pumping, however, she was able to sail to San Francisco Bay and put in for repairs. The keystone cops conquest of the Columbia was complete.

Finally recovered from his mid-voyage singeing, John McDonald now landed ashore at Fort George, ready to exercise authority as senior partner. Initiative seemed rampant when he overstepped by offering Duncan McDougall a partnership in the North West Company. Admitting a partner into the concern required the approval of the other partners while meeting at the annual summer rendezvous at Fort William, but John McDonald was as much an eccentric as McTavish had been an opportunist.[46]

On Christmas Day 1813, McDougall, the past Pacific Fur Company proprietor in charge at Fort Astoria, accepted John McDonald's offer for reinstatement in the North West Company—which Mr. Astor and his hired scribe, Washington Irving, later took as emblematic of McDougall's disloyalty and duplicitous behavior. The clerk Alfred Seton mistakenly

44 Hussey, ed., *Voyage of the Racoon*, 6-8, 14. Henry noted their arrival in his journal and, again, commented on their intoxication. *See* Gough, *Alexander Henry*, 2:625-26.

45 Hussey, ed., *Voyage of the Racoon*, 14.

46 Wallace, ed., *Documents Relating to the North West Company*, 123.

asserted that McDougall "had been a secret proprietor of the NW Co since December last."[47]

The arrangement entered into by McDougall, however, could hardly have been secret or even quiet, as a party was given in which thirteen guests sat partaking in a hearty meal and with plenty of porter for all. Six places at the table would have been reserved for past and present partners, and the remaining seven places must have been filled by clerks.[48]

One of the rituals among Nor'Westers of all ranks was the avid and usually intoxicating celebration of the New Year. Engagés had few occasions when they were given a day off to sing and dance, drink and argue, gamble and fight. New Year's Day 1814 at Fort George, Columbia River, could not live up to tradition because provisions were short and there was little liquor available to the combined work force of the two companies. Sixty-two workmen, more than twice those needed at Fort George, made do with a little rice, salt beef, some boiled swan, and about one pitiful dram of liquor each. The partners and clerks fared better, with rice, soup, roast wild fowl, roast pork, potatoes, rice pudding, wild fruit pie, cranberries tart, and cheese biscuits. All this they washed down with porter spirits and Madeira wine. At the end of the day, as Henry worked on his journal entry, he reflected a "very pleasant day throughout."[49]

Finally free of distractions, the proprietors at the fort returned to the business of the fur trade. The *Isaac Todd* and senior partner Donald McTavish still had not appeared, requiring a winter express be sent to Fort William to resolve the possibility of a disaster. On January 3, 1814, the clerks Alexander Stuart and James Keith took two canoes with fifteen men, thirty-four packs of trade goods, and a dispatch pouch. Stuart would break off with the packs to assume command at Spokane House; Keith would continue with the dispatches to Kootenae House where

47 Porter, *John Jacob Astor*, 1:231-234; Haeger, *John Jacob Astor*, 167; Jones, ed., *Astorian Adventure*, 149. Picking up on Seton's opinion, Washington Irving publicized the aspersion on McDougall's character that he had entered into a "secret" agreement with the North West Company while pretending to act in the interests of the Pacific Fur Company. In the most recent narrative of Astoria's saga, James Ronda modifies the "secret" into "quiet" arrangements.

48 Gough, ed., *Alexander Henry*, 2:629. The missing three included the former PFC proprietors Donald McKenzie and David Stuart, who had not yet come down from Kamloops, and the Nor'wester John Stuart, who had not yet returned from inventorying goods in the interior.

49 Gough, ed., *Alexander Henry*, 2:632.

four men would carry the mail pouch over the mountains to Fort Augustus on the Saskatchewan River.[50]

Another party was already on the river. After taking an inventory of remaining stocks and delivering a supply of goods to Okanogan and Spokane, Donald McKenzie and John Stuart were returning in a record snowfall.[51] Indians who had been troublesome when the party went up in October were still threatening, but a few musket shots into the woods deterred further harassment and the brigade passed the Cascades the next day.[52] Leaving David Stuart to portage four loaded canoes around the Cascades, John Stuart and McKenzie arrived at Fort George and related the assaults to the other partners.[53]

Concern for the safety of the express led to the dispatch on January 6 of Gabriel Franchère, a guide, and six to ten men to catch up with and reinforce the express. Despite paddling steadily for two days and a night, the relief party was too late. In the dark, early morning hours of January 8, they came upon a canoe containing a wounded Alexander Stuart and survivors of an attack at the Cascades. Trying to deter some pilfering, Stuart was wounded by an arrow that penetrated his chest cavity, just missing his heart. After two Indians were killed, Keith made a quick decision to abandon all the goods and paddle as fast as possible back to Fort George.[54]

It had never occurred to the fur traders that the Cascade Indians expected a gift for their proprietary passage across the portage, something experienced traders should have expected. Rather than treating the demand as a legitimate business expense, the officers characterized the

---

50 Gough, ed., *Alexander Henry*, 2:632-33.

51 Detailed inventories for Astoria, Spokane House, and Okanogan can be found in House Document 45, pp. 20-63. The encounter with the Cascade Indians is described in Cox, *Columbia River*, 122-27.

52 Franchère, *Journal of a Voyage*, 137 mentions the brigade was made up of forty men. Alexander Henry lists the clerks, all former Astorians, as Alexander Ross, Russell Franham, Donald McGillis, François B. Pillet (or Payette), and W. W. Mathews. *See* Gough, ed., *Alexander Henry*, 2:635-36. Alexander Ross claimed to have warned the upward bound express party of the possibility of attack at the Cascades. *See* Ross, *Adventures*, 284-85.

53 Henry got his Stuarts mixed up and has David Stuart accompanying McKenzie in the first canoe when it was actually John Stuart who accompanied the loaded canoes that arrived at Fort George on January 7.

54 A hunter (J. B. Saganakie) hid in the woods and was not relocated before they embarked. Although the resourceful Nipissing was given up for dead, he eventually made his way back to Fort George.

Cascade Indians as "bold Barbarians, villains," and even by a contemporary historian as "native highwaymen."[55] Had they recognized and acknowledged the traditional native right to exact a toll at the Cascades, the fur traders would have served their own long-term interests by insuring a safe passage through a key link in their communication system. Instead, pride, effrontery, and superciliousness prevented them from recognizing that the Natives were the aggrieved party.

Alexander Henry had another telling insight into what lay behind these attacks when he wrote "These villains, we are told, are fully bent on taking revenge upon us for having furnished firearms to their enemies above, and this is one reason why they are collected along the River &c." He recalled the Piikani reaction to Thompson's previous sale of arms to the Salish and Nez Perce.[56] Chinookan Cascades Indians were ethnically unrelated to those Sahaptins who sometimes traded at The Dalles, and sometimes victimized them. Their realization that traders were providing guns to their Nez Perce and Cayuse enemies, while they had none, was true. Guns and ammunition had been a part of both the Astorian and North West Company upstream trade. Fifty guns left with the abandoned outfit had been destined for the Spokane trade.

The Fort George response was a punitive expedition consisting of an armada of four canoes, two large boats, and sixty-two whites.[57] Among the things the fur traders learned from the wife of the Clatsop chief Coalpo, who accompanied them, was that the death of the two Indians must be compensated. However, Indian law provided for a kind of modified Code of Hammurabi that did not require "an eye for an eye" but, rather, allowed for "an eye for something deemed of equal value." Henry, and presumably some of the other partners as well, realized that insuring a safe portage at the Cascades was the ultimate objective and avoided more killings. Although armed with the fort's four-pounder, the idea was not to subdue anyone, but to present a show of force deterring potential future violence.

---

55 Franchère, *Journal of a Voyage*, 137; Gough, ed., *Alexander Henry*, 2:634; James P. Ronda, *Lewis and Clark among the Indians* (Lincoln: University of Nebraska Press, 1984), 217.

56 Gough, ed., *Alexander Henry*, 2:634.

57 Gough, ed., *Alexander Henry*, 2:638-56, has the most detail about the punitive expedition. For a full treatment of Indian law as it applies to this incident, see Reid, *Patterns of Vengeance*, 153-67.

In mid-January conciliatory negotiations between the traders and Indians moved slowly from village to village recovering some goods. On the seventeenth, the fur traders seized a minor Cascade leader but not the most influential, Canook, who refused to be lured into their tents. As it turned out, the Lady Coalpo was related to many of the Upper Chinookans involved in the attack and was a valuable advisor regarding the customary payment for anyone killed.[58] Henry grudgingly conceded, after listening to her advice, remarking "they seem to have some principles of honor among themselves."[59]

Eventually, recovered trade goods included thirty-three of the fifty guns.[60] Many recovered guns were loaded and primed, indicating that the Indians knew how to use them. Unrecovered goods could be viewed as compensation for the deaths of the two Indians, but obscured in the lists of what was sent and what was later recovered was the loss of seventeen guns, as well as 152 pounds of ball and 134½ pounds of powder. If the people of the Cascades had been willing to harass large brigades armed with bows, what might they do with firearms?

In his coverage of the events occurring at the Cascades in early 1814, Alexander Henry continued to avoid mentioning the name of J. G. McTavish. However Alexander Ross and Franchère maintained that command at Fort George devolved onto J. G. McTavish, and failed to mention Henry. Writing the record by omission reflects the ongoing animosity between the two, but until the arrival of Donald McTavish, there was no clearly appointed partner to assume responsibility.

This disharmony became overt toward the end of January 1814, when other officers were away and John McDonald assumed the management of Fort George. Among the changes he imposed was a platform in front

58 Gough, ed., *Alexander Henry*, 2:639-40.

59 Gough, ed., *Alexander Henry*, 2:640.

60 Alexander Henry's list of the property forwarded on January 4 alongside a list of the goods recovered belies the criticism of Alexander Ross who wrote, "They therefore, without recovering the property, firing a gun, or securing a single prisoner, sounded the retreat and returned home...This warlike expedition was turned into ridicule by the Cathleyacheyachs and had a very bad effect on the Indians generally; but the best of it was, on their way back some turned off towards the Wallamitte to hide their disgrace, others remained for some days at the Cowlitz, and McTavish himself reached Fort George in the night." Ross, *Adventures*, 291-92.

of the fort to mount the four-pound cannon.[61] After all the partners returned to Fort George, dissension focused on McDonald's unilateral decision of becoming the dominant partner among equals.

Those objecting included old hands like Henry and John Stuart as well as the recently promoted J. G. McTavish. Disputes about McDonald's presumption became so heated that the disputants resorted to writing letters or notes although they were within shouting distance of one another. Henry had the last word in his journal, "A long altercation took place this evening between the parties concerned, which terminated to the satisfaction of none present."[62] The rancor continued on through the next day.

Gentlemen tried to keep their differences private, but in a confined place like Fort George, the plank walls leaked venom. The recollections of the clerks may have been the origin of the persistent memory that the Columbia department was ruined by "shameful mismanagement and the most unfortunate dissention."[63] On January 29, 1814, an insulted John McDonald declined having anything more to do with the affairs of the Columbia. Despite the fact that his opponents had two letters in their possession appointing McDonald until Donald McTavish appeared, he surrendered the management to the last holdout, J. G. McTavish. Next day, Henry noted that McDonald "agrees to continue the management of affairs here on the strength of our Letter to him on the 28th Inst." without mentioning McTavish's reaction.[64]

Another ongoing matter concerned the fort itself. John McDonald and others were dissatisfied with its location, as it was difficult to access from the river because of the steep hillside. Also, the soil produced a poor garden, and defense from American warships would be difficult with their inadequate arsenal. On the last day of January 1814 the partners decided to rebuild at a better site upstream, near the mouth of the Willamette River. Twenty-seven men in two wooden canoes loaded with building tools were sent under the supervision of Keith, Mathews, and Franchère.

61 Gough, ed., *Alexander Henry*, 2:666. Pictures of the post and gun installation can be found in Franchère, *Journal of a Voyage*, between 130-31; and in Gough, ed., *Alexander Henry*, between 2:614-15.

62 Gough, ed., *Alexander Henry*, 670.

63 Lacking firsthand experience, HBC Governor George Simpson must have based this judgment on what he heard later from McTavish.

64 Gough, ed., *Alexander Henry*, 2:670-71.

Alexander Henry, John Stuart, and ten additional men followed the next day to examine the site for building, but were disappointed to find it subject to springtime flooding.

They searched three weeks in heavy rains and adverse winds for another location, until at the end of February, the exasperated McDonald decided Tongue Point was the most eligible location for building. That peninsula, only two to three miles from the existing fort, was just as subject to naval bombardment and Henry argued that the ruggedness of the land, the lack of river access, and limited water made it unsuitable. Nevertheless, a clerk and twenty men were sent to begin clearing land where they remained for an undetermined length of time. A new fort was never built. Instead, the old fort was expanded and reinforced, making it more suitable as the headquarters of the NWC Adventure to the Columbia.[65]

On the last day of February a ship appeared off the bar of the Columbia, but adverse weather kept it from entering the river for two days. NWC expectations of the arrival of the *Isaac Todd* were disappointed when it turned out to be the brig *Pedler*. After crossing the bar, the ship by-passed Baker Bay and anchored abreast Chinook Point, on the bank opposite and about two miles downstream from Fort George. When Mr. Astor's Pacific Fur Company agent, Wilson Price Hunt, came ashore, he was informed of the sale of Astoria to the North West Company.

Hunt had left the Columbia aboard the *Beaver* on August 26, 1813, knowing that the other Pacific Fur Company partners had decided to abandon the country. After securing a ship to convey two years' fur returns to China, Hunt was disappointed to find those furs, and the company, had been sold. The last article of the agreement specified the value to be placed on the various furs and items of property belonging to the PFC, but bickering and controversy over prices continued until March 12, 1814. When the differences were finally worked out, Hunt added his name to the contract and accepted several bills and drafts totaling $58,291.02. Those documents were consigned to Donald McKenzie to deliver to John Astor in New York.[66] The *Pedler* lay at anchor in Baker Bay for three weeks until weather permitted her to cross the bar on April 3, bound for

65 The plan of Fort George provided by Elliott in "The Surrender at Astoria in 1818," 271-82, shows clearly the original size of the fort and the extent of its expansion. In 1816 the *Colonel Allan* landed two eighteen-pounders to augment the armory.

66 HBCA, F.61, fos. 9-9d, Account Current with John Jacob Astor; Gough, ed., *Alexander Henry*, 2:698.

Sitka, where Hunt hoped to find a way to dispose of the ship or maybe connect with another vessel of Astor's.[67]

The agreed value given to beaver pelts, the single most important item in the entire inventory, was ten shillings a pound or about two American dollars.[68] From the advantage of hindsight when Alexander Ross wrote years later, he thought beaver sold for thirty shillings in Canton.[69] John Jacob Astor, who should have known better, asserted the furs to have been worth twenty-five to thirty shillings or five to six dollars each.[70] By the time those furs reached the Canton market, they averaged three dollars and ninety cents or nineteen shillings per pelt.[71] The Nor'Westers made nine shillings per pelt on their purchase, not an extravagant profit margin considering the war conditions and the uncertainty of the market, but a credit to McTavish's deal.

At Fort George the simmering feud between J. G. McTavish and the other partners continued from the last day of January to the first part of April. During the entire time Hunt was negotiating the remaining details of the sale of the Pacific Fur Company, Alexander Henry made no mention of McTavish, despite his participation in the negotiations, and continued to insert the fictitious name "Thompson" in lieu of McTavish.[72]

The tension hanging so heavily over headquarters evaporated on April 4, 1814, when the brigade for Canada embarked John McDonald and Donald McKenzie in the first canoe. McDonald had the satisfaction of having seen the advance westward across the Rocky Mountains and down the Pacific Slope, but his voyage aboard the HMS *Racoon* had seared that sense of accomplishment. He intended to return to Montreal and retire from the concern. J. G. McTavish and family came along in another, expecting to return from Fort William to manage the interior trade from Spokane House.

---

67 Jones, ed., *Astoria Adventure*, 155.

68 Elliott, "Sale of Astoria, 1813," 49. This can also be found in U.S. Congress, *Message from the President communicating the Letter of Mr. Prevost and other Documents Relating to an Establishment made at the Mouth of the Columbia River*, 17th Cong. 2 sess. H. doc 45, (Washington, D.C.: Gales and Seaton, 1823), 18. A currency conversion table is provided in Appendix B of this work.

69 Ross, *Fur Hunters*, 134.

70 Ronda, *Astoria and Empire*, 291.

71 LAC, Selkirk Papers, MG 19- E1 [new ref. R9790-0-8-E], vol. 31, pp. 9209-10.

72 Gough, ed., *Alexander Henry*, 2:616, 617, 695, and 705.

Because most of the former Astorians were in other boats, Alexander Henry was left as the only NWC partner remaining at Fort George. Although Duncan McDougall remained at Fort George assisting Henry, his status would remain ambiguous until the wintering partners passed on McDonald's status.[73] But when McTavish delivered a report of his actions at Astoria/Fort George to the partners at Fort William, other wintering partners were outraged at the presumptuousness of this upstart. Director William McGillivray felt it incumbent upon himself to mildly rebuke McTavish, in writing.

> The large sum to which your purchase from the American Company amounts very naturally startled people & the Bargain having been entered into without due authority on your part gave alarm lest you might, acting on any other occasion in the same manner involve the Concern—without the cooperation of the other Partners. You were taxed with an arbitrary overbearing conduct &c &c and those who never liked this Business were glad of any opportunity to crying it down—with everything connected with it.[74]

Stipulations found in Article Two of the sale contract revealed that McTavish had agreed the North West Company would render payment in three installments, one due October 25, 1814, a second due November 25, 1814, and the third due December 25, 1814, all payable at Montreal. This costly and extremely inconvenient arrangement created a cash flow problem in Montreal and a loss of interest on funds because the items they purchased would not bring a return for at least two years. The concern lost money in the difference between the rate of exchange in Montreal and that of London, and McGillivray was more severe in his rebuke:

> It has been made extremely inconvenient to the House from your not fixing a more distant Period of the Payments. This was your fault and the Concern will suffer a loss in Interest before the Articles purchased can be turned into cash—but the worst of all is the manner in which the Bills were drawn.[75]

73 HBCA, F.3/2, fos. 117-118d, letter from William McGillivray to J. G. McTavish dated Fort William, July 17, 1814. The promise of a partnership in the company could not become official until a share became available by the retirement of his uncle Alexander McDougall or Angus Shaw.

74 William McGillivray to J. G. McTavish, Fort William, July 17, 1814, HBCA, F.3/2, fos. 117-118d.

75 McGillivray to McTavish, July 17, 1814.

Even here, McGillivray tried to remove some of the onus from McTavish by deflecting it onto others. He ascribed truth to the rumor that

> the manner [of the drawing of the bills] appears to have been exclusively the act of Mr Henry or Mr McDonald or both—and certainly betrays great ignorance to say no worse of it. Mr (Alexander) Stuart says that Mr Henry determined it (for there appears to have been some consultation on the subject) by saying that it would be more convenient to draw on Montreal *as Mr Astor would be paid in muskrats*—which *wise* remark was conclusive.[76]

McGillivray erred when he tried to shift responsibility to Henry or McDonald instead of the newest partner. McGillivray had been grooming McTavish and Angus Bethune "to introduce organization and economy" to the Columbia department.[77] And he conveniently forgot that it was the responsibility of the downstream agency to assure the arrival of the tardy *Isaac Todd.* Under the plea of necessity, the agreement was ultimately accepted by the partners and agents at the July inland meeting.

Alexander Henry inherited sole command of Fort George, but as soon as the others departed he began to fret "Here we are left the Sport of Fortune and at the mercy of chance, on a Barbarous Coast." Lacking any clear indication of hostile intentions, Henry worried that the "natives were inclined to murder us for the sake of our property."[78] Although fifteen of his men were incapacitated by venereal disease, thirty-five others were healthy and capable of defending the depot.[79] Meanwhile the Fort George complement continued to watch for a sail across the breaking waves of that dangerous bar.

---

76 McGillivray to McTavish, July 17, 1814.

77 The paperwork was completed on October 16, 1813. Henry had arrived on November 15, 1813, and McDonald two weeks later.

78 Gough, ed., *Alexander Henry*, 2:712.

79 Gough, ed., *Alexander Henry*, 715. Indian relations remained peaceful and trade continued as usual. The only battle during this time was a skirmish between the Cowlitz and Casino's Multnomah Chinooks.

Chapter Seven

The Early "Adventures to China"

After the brigade going to Fort William disappeared to the west around Tongue Point, Alexander Henry was left at Fort George with his thoughts. When he started trading in the NWC Lower Red River department thirteen years earlier, a log hovel or skin tent was good enough. He spent most of those years at Pembina on the Red River except for an 1806 visit to the Mandan villages on the Missouri River. He had seen the flags that the American captains Lewis and Clark had presented to the Mandan chiefs, and thought the "taking possession" ceremony at Fort George was appropriate. It included giving Captain Black a tour of Fort Clatsop, the site where those Americans spent the winter 1806–07. Not much was left of their post—the Clatsop Indians had since dismantled what was left of it for their own use. Over the years, willow shoots had sprouted twenty-five feet high where the place once stood.[1] Henry mused that the fur trade left many rotting places like that as business moved inland. Now he was left on a distant shore helping rescue an endeavor in which he had little confidence.[2]

His career began when his uncle, Alexander Henry Esq., had offered him an opportunity, even buying a share of the North West Company to give him a start. His mentor convinced his callow nephew to enter the fur trade as a NWC clerk. Although he was an American-born British loyalist, and most NWC managers and field officers came from a clannish Scottish country background that had neither forgotten nor forgiven

1 Barry Gough, "Alexander Henry (the younger)," *DCB* 5 (1983), accessed June 8, 2014.

2 Despite the authors' faulting Ross for the invention of conversations, allowing Alexander Henry to describe his recollections is based on his relationship with his Uncle Alexander Henry and his own previously expressed belief that the shipping scheme was already an expensive failure. This supposition also incorporates Gough's analysis of Henry's personality from his *Journal of Alexander Henry*, lxvi.

battles in the heather, they could not conduct business or command crews using English or Gaelic. If highlanders had to speak French to communicate with their Francophone and devotedly Catholic boatmen, so could a Jersey boy far from home. Despite what Uncle Alexander told him about riding thousands of miles in a fragile birch bark canoe, a career in the fur trade had seemed appealing.

During visits the clerk made to the annual rendezvous, Henry heard wintering partners arguing over old Simon McTavish's plans to open a maritime trade to China.[3] Now as the wintering partner in command of Fort George on the far side of the fur trade, an older and wiser interest holder recalled those shipping experiments and understood that endeavors like that don't always turn out as planned.

His insights about opening trade with China were initiated when his uncle, an experienced northern trader, was associated with Simon McTavish and became involved in experiments to open business with the China market. Canoe-habituated traders were fixed on finding a water route to the Pacific Ocean. While wintering in the north Peter Pond imagined a northern outlet which the ambitious young clerk Alexander Mackenzie tried to find in two explorations. His first exploration turned out to be a dead end, and the second followed a river too dangerous to descend.[4]

Worse, as far as exploration counted, Mackenzie had been a year too late. On May 12, 1792, the Boston coastal trading ship *Columbia Rediviva* entered an unexplored coastal river and according to the old tradition of discovery, sea-otter trader Captain Robert Gray claimed all the drainage of the Columbia River for the United States.[5] Henry could not forgive J. B. McTavish for spending over £50,000 buying it back from the Astorians. Some of that money was Henry's life savings.

As the distance to sources of the Indian trade stretched ever farther north, beaver became the only fur that repaid the costs of acquisition and transportation. Foremost among downstream *hommes d'affaires* was Uncle Henry's associate, Simon McTavish. Both of them made voyages to London to market furs to English or European buyers. Those voyages

3 Before his sons were old enough, Alexander Henry the Elder (Esq.) took his namesake nephew into the fur trade. David A. Armour, "Alexander Henry (the elder)," *DCB* 6 (1987), accessed June 8, 2014.

4 Today's Fraser River.

5 *See* note 4 of the Introduction regarding Priority of Discovery.

opened Mr. McTavish's and Uncle Alexander's minds to other possibilities. Because he was familiar with shipping, McTavish was particularly suited to act as the downstream agent of the North West Company, whose partners knew him as "the Marquis" for his overbearing manner and taste for the good life.[6]

During the American Revolution, Russians had imported more than 100,000 North American beaver skins from England to St. Petersburg and then across Siberia, a distance of some 4,331 miles, to resell to Chinese buyers at Kyakhta on the Siberian-Mongolian border. In 1791 the cumbersome Russian/northern China trade collapsed when a Chinese ban on Russian imports closed that long route.[7]

One-quarter of the NWC furs sold in London had been sent on to St. Petersburg and the North West Company faced the alarming prospect of having almost half of their markets closed to them.[8] A beaver pelt purchased on the London market by Russian buyers would have traveled almost around the world before it graced an Asian neck. If direct access to Chinese markets could be made, and the Russian middlemen eliminated, the agents of the North West Company believed they could expect a tremendous return on investment. That potential had been appealing to a profit-minded management already feeling the pinch of expensive but inescapable transportation costs.

Even a young clerk out of the flow of entrepreneurial calculations soon realized that other Nor'westers were less familiar with the intricacies of maritime commerce. There was an already well-established trade in luxurious sea otter pelts carried to Canton, China, but not a large market for land furs. His uncle Henry admitted that to make a profitable voyage, after the furs were sold the modest gain had to be reinvested in China goods to be carried on the return trip and sold to western markets.

Now years later, the agents of the North West Company still thought that they might enjoy enormous profits. But the East India Company of London had a chartered monopoly for the China trade, just like the Hudson's Bay Company's royal charter to Rupert's Land.[9] The only Chinese

6 MacKay, *The Honourable Company*, 110.

7 Tikhmenev, *Russian-American Company*.

8 HBCA, A.7/1, fo. 27; Rich, *Hudson's Bay Company*, 2:190; Sladkovskii, *Economic Relations between Russia and China*, 25-28, 31-36, 43-55.

9 Morison, *Maritime History of Massachusetts*, 44-45; Lee, "The Magee Family", 81:105; Haeger, *John Jacob Astor*, 58.

seaport open to foreign trade was Canton on the south China coast. If the NWC wanted to do business there, they had to purchase a costly and difficult to procure license. Further, they were prohibited from shipping China goods out of Canton on their own account, or from purchasing specie (silver) with the proceeds from their trade to take advantage of the difference in price of precious metals in Canton and London.[10]

Some British firms endured those constraints in order to trade at Canton but not the Nor'westers, although they were not averse to doing business with those who did. As the principal partner in the North West Company's Montreal agency, Simon McTavish's strong suit had been extensive international financial connections and an acute awareness of British and foreign markets.

Traveling to London in 1791, McTavish had joined his cousin John Fraser to form McTavish, Fraser and Company, as commission agents for purchasing trade goods and selling the returns of the North West Company. Doing the detail work of raising capital or obtaining credit, purchasing goods, and arranging for sales, Fraser became acquainted with the principals of several London exporting firms with China connections. Henry had heard gossip that Fraser told the suggestible Simon McTavish that fine large skins were always saleable in Canton, but not that those skins had to be sea otter pelts. Other kinds of fur were of marginal value to the buyers.[11]

Fraser felt a profit could be made by purchasing North West Company furs at London prices and reselling them for more in Canton.[12] Together with his Montreal associate, Uncle Alexander Henry Esq., McTavish had entered the China trade on two fronts. Soon nearly 39,000 beaver skins that they sent to London were sold by McTavish, Fraser and Company to be reshipped to China under a contract with another British firm holding an East India Company license to export furs to Canton.[13]

10 As an example see the license of the *Isaac Todd.*

11 HBCA, F.3/1, fo. 56.

12 Fifteen shillings, six pence for fine and twelve shillings, six pence for cloudy beaver in London.

13 HBCA, F.3/1, fo. 106, 117. The lure of a profitable China trade had been set a year earlier when the commission merchants, Brickwood, Pattle and Company wrote McTavish "The trade with Russia is not yet open but late advices from China by our own Ships are very favorable." HBCA, F.3/1, fos. 3-4. *See* Duckworth "British Capital in the Fur Trade," 39-56.

In December 1792 McTavish, Frobisher and Company had informed London commission merchants with China connections to have their agents in Canton purchase £24,689 worth of China goods, to be paid for with the returns from beaver pelts. Two American ships carried the peltry to China and shipped the return cargo to New York.[14] When Uncle Alexander explained the plan to his namesake nephew, that had seemed to be keeping the skin game in the family.

While Fraser established licit trade connections with China, Simon McTavish intended to avoid the East India Company constraints by forming liaisons with Americans, including the New York fur buyer, John Jacob Astor. In 1792 North West Company capital (or credit) merged with American shipping to launch the Canadians' first "Adventure to China," through American ports.[15]

Taking advantage of Astor's friendly association with Alexander Henry Esq., McTavish negotiated the connections that soon united Canadian and American interests in a joint venture to China in which McTavish, Frobisher, and Alexander Henry held a fifty percent interest while Astor and his American business associate, William Edgar, held the other fifty percent. The Americans' share of the profits came out of the sale of the return cargo in the United States.[16]

Transporting Canadian furs to an American port in the face of British trade restrictions was not a problem. Old hands in the skin game just smuggled them across the thinly guarded northern border, evading or bribing customs agents in Plattsburg and Champlain, New York.[17] At the end of December 1792, the two ships had sailed for Canton.[18]

Because the purchase of a return cargo required separate and discreet arrangements, McTavish and Fraser engaged a London firm which

14 HBCA, A.7/1, fo. 37d; F.3/1, fos. 106, 118.

15 The phrase "Adventure to China" appeared regularly in the North West Company's accounts to identify their speculative investments in the China market.

16 Haeger, *John Jacob Astor*, 59-60, points out that William Edgar became acquainted with Alexander Henry Esq. while trading at Detroit in the 1760s and 1770s. It was probably through Henry that Edgar met Astor. *See* Wallace, ed., *Documents Relating to the North West Company*, 47-62.

17 Rich, *Hudson's Bay Company*, 2:206; Haeger, *John Jacob Astor*, 60. Henry's connections in Albany, New York, began during the British conquest of New France and remained active until his death. Smuggling over that route had been a common practice during the early French regime and later.

18 HBCA, F.3/1, fo. 117.

had Canton agents to transact their business.[19] Passing themselves off as representatives of the Danish Government, the agents occupied a *hong*, or factory, separate from that of the East India Company. Although the ruse was transparent to East India Company managers, over 6,200 pieces of freight, consisting of dry goods, tea, and chinaware were purchased in Canton for the return cargo, half of which was carried in each of two ships to reduce risk in case of loss.[20]

The *America* and the *Washington* arrived at New York harbor in late July or early August 1794. Much to the chagrin of Astor, who had been led by Henry to expect he would be given the consignment of the North West Company property himself, the goods were consigned to New York merchant John Murray.[21] By August, sufficient sales had taken place to suggest "the profit will not be great…being loaded with so many heavy charges."[22] Sales from this cargo had enabled them to meet some of their most pressing obligations, but the benefit of receiving cash for their share from the sales of the cargo of the two ships was short-lived. McTavish, Frobisher and Company and Alexander Henry Esq. owed some £13,454.13.7¼ on their investment.[23]

Seeing his uncle lose on the first cast of the dice was a lesson Alexander Henry had never forgotten. If experienced merchants like Uncle Alexander and Simon McTavish had to learn the problems of world commerce the hard way, twenty years later the McGillivray brother's plans for the *Isaac Todd* still failed to consider the limited demand in China for furs and that financial success depended on the profitable sale of the return cargo.

Uncle Alexander had admitted to his nephew that the first two voyages were likely to lose a total of some £15,000 and the outlook for the third voyage was even more dismal. The warehouses in Canton were holding some 67,000 beaver skins that could not be sold even at three dollars a skin and the Canton agents begged the NWC to send no more

19 HBCA, F.3/1, fos. 66d-67. It was Andrew Reid who informed Fraser of the lucrative prices furs commanded in Canton, and their apparently successful experience in China provided the basis for McTavish, Fraser and Company to seek them out.

20 Dermigny, *La Chine et l'occident*, 1084, 1153, 1236. We are indebted to Professor Harry Duckworth for bringing this source to our attention; HBCA, F.3/1, fos. 117, 118.

21 HBCA, F.3/1, fos. 118, 185.

22 HBCA, F.3/1, fo. 185.

23 HBCA, F.3/1, fo. 217.

furs that year, breaking existing contracts, if necessary, on any terms, to avoid a further saturation of the market.[24] Business was thicker than blood and next year Uncle Alexander sold his share, leaving his nephew on his own.[25] Henry had to wait until 1801 to gain a partnership at the Grand Portage rendezvous, and over those years he came to doubt the promises of downstream agents with flawed business plans.

Despite the initial loss, Simon McTavish had still believed a profit could be made in creating a more promising arrangement with different American partners. Canton agents stoked the embers by suggesting the China trade "might still become profitable if an 800-ton ship was sent from New York with 40,000 beaver pelts and carrying $50,000 in silver to Bombay to buy Indian raw cotton and opium for the Canton market."[26] Instead J. J. Astor proposed a more modest adventure: a 300-ton vessel to carry $40,000 in specie and a reduced allotment of beaver pelts.

Knowing that the Canadian shippers were in need of an American connection, Astor proposed becoming a share-holding partner in the North West Company so the China and European trade would run through New York. Confident that Alexander Henry Esq. would encourage acceptance of it, Astor traveled to Europe to talk with John Fraser about establishing potential continental business contacts for the proposed next adventure to China.[27] But "the Marquis" resented Astor's manipulation, and the North West Company rejected his proposal and contracted with another New York firm to act as their American shippers.

Four months later, the Canton agency reported that the Canton market was swamped with over 67,000 unsold skins which could not be sold

24 HBCA, F.3/1, fos. 213, 213, 230. The first letter warning of these unpropitious circumstances was addressed to D. Scott and Company and not to any of the agencies involved in the North West Company's furs.

25 Armour, "Alexander Henry the Elder," *DCB* 6, accessed June 28, 2014; Gough, ed., *Alexander Henry*, xv-xxix.

26 HBCA, F.3/1, fos. 165d, 185; Morris, "Some Letters," 42:54-55. The size of the vessel recommended by Hamilton and Reid suggests cotton was the intended cargo. A 1786 famine in south China resulted in the Chinese converting cotton fields to food production and increased demand for imported cotton. *See* Bulley, *Bombay Country Ships*, 101-05.

27 Morris, "Some Letters," 48-87; Rich, *Hudson's Bay Company*, 2:210; Haeger, *John Jacob Astor*, 71.

at a profit and they saw "no possibility of disposing of Furs but for tea."[28] Their warning arrived too late to prevent shipment in 1795.

McTavish, Frobisher and Company's New York connection in spring 1795 was with a relatively new mercantile firm, Seton, Maitland and Company.[29] The Canadians would supply the furs and at least part of the capital, while Seton, Maitland, whose London partners held a one-half interest in the NWC's 1795 Adventure to China, arranged for some of the outgoing cargo and assisted in shipping arrangements to the Canton agency.[30]

Another innovation had involved the establishment in New York of an agency similar in purpose to McTavish, Fraser and Company in London, which would include J. J. Astor. At least he had the competence and experience necessary to transact the overseas business, but sentiments within the Montreal agency against him blinded the Nor'Westers. The NWC had decided to either charter or purchase their own vessel to ship their cargo. Including the costs of the ship, wages and provisions for the crew, fees, insurance and commissions, and some 230 tons of China goods as return freight, the total investment for the proposed fifteen-month voyage would amount to $279,894.[31] The 316-ton *Asia*, leased to McTavish, Frobisher and Company, sailed from New York on May 4, 1795.[32]

If involving Astor wasn't enough, at the 1795 Grand Portage meetings the clerk Henry heard wintering partners grousing about bringing Alexander Mackenzie into the Montreal agency. But the abrasiveness that developed between Mackenzie and Simon McTavish probably involved

---

28 Rich, *Hudson's Bay Company*, 2:207; HBCA, F.3/1, fo. 213.

29 William Seton, like McTavish an immigrant Scot, arrived in New York in 1763 and, by 1784, became the chief executive officer of the Bank of New York. Ten years later he left the bank to go into business for himself as Seton, Maitland and Company. Jones, ed., *Astorian Adventure*, 2.

30 HBCA, F.3/1, fos. 221-222; 223-224; 231-232d; 233-234; 235; 237-238; 239-239d; 257d. Adventure 1795 may have been the first significant financial investment Reid, Lennox and Company made in McTavish's China adventures.

31 Taking their lead, perhaps, from Campbell, *The North West Company*, 91, both Gough, "The North West Company's 'Adventure to China,'" and Haeger, *John Jacob Astor*, 60, give this figure as £279894. However, a careful reading of the document will reveal that the computations are in dollars. It would have been unprecedented to invest over a quarter of a billion *pounds* in a single adventure. The actual conversion would be £62,976.

32 HBCA, F.3/1, fos. 221-222, 235; HBCA, F.3/1, fo. 257d; Morris, "Some Letters," 57-58.

the younger man's criticisms of McTavish's management of the agency, a disapproval supported by many wintering partners.[33] Plans for a 1796 adventure from New York to China were abandoned.[34]

Over the next years, maritime operations went badly. Simon McTavish returned the North West Company to the China trade by way of New York, buying the ship *Nancy* that was lost on its return voyage from Canton with goods invoiced at $72,427.[35] Given the responsibility of arranging another voyage to China, Mackenzie arrived in New York City in January 27, 1798, and was frustrated by the details in arranging chartering or purchasing a vessel, hiring a captain and crew, amassing specie, and collecting together the furs to be sent to Canton as cargo.

In early March Mackenzie went to Philadelphia and found the ship the *Northern Liberties*, 335 tons, eleven guns and swivels, and carrying a crew of thirty-five, the only ship available in American ports at the time.[36] The purchase price was $17,500 and outfitting it for the China voyage required another ten to twelve thousand dollars.[37] The outgoing cargo of the *Northern Liberties* was insured for $42,000 in furs and $46,000 in specie.[38] The ship arrived safely in Canton in September 1798 at the unusual moment when the prices received for beaver were among the highest of any North West Company adventure to China, realizing an average of $5.50 per skin. Although otters also did well at $8.00 each, John Fraser warned McTavish that unsettled conditions in the United States rendered it advisable for the NWC to decline any China adventure for

33 Rich, *Hudson's Bay Company*, 210. Not all historians agree with Rich that this was the reason Mackenzie was sent to New York in January of 1798. W. Kaye Lamb, for one, pointed out that "evidence on the point seems to be lacking." *See* Lamb, *Journals and Letters of Mackenzie*, 27-28.

34 Lamb, *Journals and Letters of Mackenzie*, 83. When Mackenzie wrote there was no shipment to China in 1796 he must not have been aware McTavish, Fraser and Company of London sold nearly 26,000 beaver skins to David Scott and Company that year under contract to export them to Canton on behalf of the North West Company. Mackenzie was speaking of the American arrangements and not those taking place in London. *See* HBCA, A.7/1, fo. 38.

35 HBCA, F.3/1, fos. 282-282d; Morris, "Some Letters," 74.

36 Ten letters survive from Alexander Mackenzie dealing all or in part with the adventure of this year, eleven letters survive from the pen of James Hallowell, five from John Fraser, and one from Andrew Reid.

37 HBCA, F.3/1, fos. 273, 275d-276, 280, 281, 295-295d. Part of the expense for outfitting a China voyage was the copper sheeting of the hull to prevent the growth of barnacles or penetration of maritime worms.

38 HBCA, F.3/1, fos. 281-281d, 295-295d.

the ensuing year.[39] But McTavish went ahead with another risky financial investment by sending an unspecified amount of specie to New York.

Arrangements for the next voyage to China were assumed by William McGillivray, who traveled to New York in early January 1799 before the *Northern Liberties* had returned. Outfitting the ship *Jean* required moving cargo from New York to Philadelphia where it was moored. Obviously, the teas, nankeens, and silks being loaded were not intended for the China market because an illicit stop must have been planned at some intermediate port of call where those goods were exchanged for either specie or goods appropriate to sell in Canton.[40] The loaded *Jean* sailed about the first of June 1800 and the outcome of the 1800 voyage was clouded in uncertainty.[41] Judging from the discontinuation of any subsequent China voyages, it too lost money. With that transaction the Nor'Westers abandoned direct investment in any adventures to China.

Later, William McGillivray was recalled from New York so he could accompany the troublesome Alexander Mackenzie to Grand Portage. They didn't get along. Eventually the explorer helped form a rival Montreal syndicate, the XY Company which later took the designation, "Sir Alexander Mackenzie & Company."[42]

When Mackenzie's *Voyages from Montreal* was published in 1802, copies were carried to the inland rendezvous where his former associates sniffed that he was knighted for his explorations of two dead-end rivers and a coastal trade already spoiled by ship traders in search of sea otter pelts. In his book Mackenzie proposed that the British government assist the merchants from Canada in extending fur trade routes to the shores of the Pacific Ocean and establishing depots at the mouth of the Columbia River or at Cook's Inlet for the transshipment of peltry to the markets of China. It would be to the advantage of British hegemony in North America, he asserted, if Montreal merchants were to unite with the Hudson's Bay Company but, short of that, some way had to be found to allow Canadians the right of passage from the west shore of Hudson Bay to the

39 John Fraser to Simon McTavish, London, Dec 14, 1799, HBCA, F.3/1, fo. 344.

40 HBCA, F.3/1, fos. 312d, 338; F.3/2, fo. 20. John Murray had been enlisted to assist in the purchase of a ship. Finally, by May 19 the *Jean* had been chartered or purchased—it is not clear which. *See* HBCA, F.3/2, fo. 20, 28; Morris 1941, 86.

41 HBCA, F.3/2, fos. 28, 30–30d, 32–32d, 34; Morris, "Some Letters," 86–87.

42 *See* chapter one, p. 10.

Columbia River and its tributary waters. Between 1801 and 1808, 20,000 to 25,000 North West Company beaver pelts were sold at New York for reshipment to China.[43]

Clerk Alexander Henry was finally made a partner in 1801 and promised a forty-sixth share of profits.[44] Now thirteen years later he found himself in a crude building on an alien shore waiting for the *Isaac Todd* to arrive. Instead of attending the 1808 meeting at Fort William, he had been abruptly sent up the Saskatchewan River to take charge of the Lower Fort des Prairies department. His expressions about the Columbia Adventure led to "ungenerous & unfriendly conjectures…at the 1809 'Grand Divan'" at Bas de la Riviere Winnipeg where those nabobs reproved him for coming down from Fort Vermillion in a light canoe. His answer was to hurry the outfit the Columbia Adventure needed now that the Astorians were eliminated, but he failed to get an explanation why his previous dispatches had been thrown aside and his letters kept back.[45] That was not how a partner who had been in the skin games for twenty-two years should be treated.

Henry had already expressed his concerns to the HBC Edmonton House Master James Bird as he came west. The Nor'westers had a hundred men including officers for the Columbia venture and expected to take possession of the American settlements. But that had already run up a cost of £50,000. Recalling previous disappointments, he did not believe it could be profitable, "notwithstanding the high opinion their agents have formed of it, and the opinion entertained by some that they would be able to carry on their Athabaska Trade by that quarter."

In his mind Alexander Henry felt he had been left with command of another madhouse Bedlam while the fools were running around loose. And what could one clear thinker, marooned on a lonely shore, do to guide the business where others had failed?

43 HBCA, A.7/1, p. 38; F.3/2, fos. 30-30d.
44 Wallace, ed., *Documents of NWC*, 173.
45 Selkirk Correspondence, NAC, MGA, E1, vol. 29 (reel 8, p. 128, 8835).

Whampoa in China. "View from Dane's Island (Changzhou island) of East Indiamen, sampans, and junks at the Whampoa anchorage in the Pearl River in Guangzhou (Canton), midway to Macao." Oil on canvas; 1835, William John Huggins. *Peabody Essex Museum.*

Chapter Eight

Canton and Return, 1814-1815

The log of the *Racoon* records the arrival of the *Isaac Todd* at Monterey, Alta California, sometime in January 1814, where it lay at anchor as late as February 21.[1] The ship moved to San Francisco Bay on March 2 to assist in careening and repairing the damaged *HMS Racoon.* Anticipating a shortage of provisions at Fort George, Donald McTavish purchased corn, tallow, and flour valued at £550, as well as two young bulls, two cows, and poultry for use in the Columbia department.[2]

After a month in San Francisco Bay, the NWC ship departed on the first of April. A three week voyage brought them off the mouth of the Columbia, where the *Isaac Todd* fired three cannons to alert the men at the trading post of their presence. Because of the war with the United States, tensions ran high among the British subjects who had no way of knowing whether the gunfire announced the arrival of friend or foe.

During the recent Christmas revels, the erstwhile Astorian Duncan McDougall had joined the ranks of the North West Company but was still regarded as expendable. After ordering three boats be readied with goods and supplies in order to flee should the ship prove to be American, McDougall crossed the river to an open place that allowed him to learn the new arrival's identity. But two anxious days passed before Fort George learned it was the *Isaac Todd.* Initially anchored along the north shore in Baker Bay, the crew cautiously inched the ship farther upriver and anchored along the north shore, opposite the fort.

1 The January 1814 date is given in Eldredge, *The Beginnings of San Francisco*, 1:246. The February 21 date is mentioned in Davis, *Seventy-five Years in California*, 268. News of the *Isaac Todd*'s presence in Monterey under the date March 1 can be found in Hussey, ed., *Voyage of the Racoon*, 19.

2 Memoranda Book, 33, James Keith Papers, LAC; Gough, ed., *Alexander Henry*, 2:729, 731.

Donald McTavish, who had been appointed two years previously to command the "Adventure to the Columbia," finally went ashore on April 24, 1814.[3] He was surprised to find Alexander Henry in charge. Henry related that John McDonald, J. G. McTavish, and many former Astorians had left twenty days ago with a brigade of ten boats. In order to inform anxious agents and proprietors that the overdue *Isaac Todd* had finally appeared, another express canoe needed to follow. After a week of catching up on what had occurred since the 1812 meeting at Fort William, the two proprietors put Duncan McDougall in charge of two canoes only going as far as Spokane House. From there, James Keith would conduct the express on to Fort William and McDougall could return to Fort George.[4] As matters turned out, Keith delivered the good news about the *Isaac Todd* and returned to the Columbia with instructions advising J. G. McTavish that Donald McTavish should have the superintendence "spiritually necessary for the settlement of matters on the Columbia."[5]

That was optimistic because Captain Frazer Smith of the *Isaac Todd* had found it impossible to get along with Donald McTavish. Whatever the circumstances may have been, Alexander Henry observed in his journal that Captain Smith was eager to rid himself of McTavish.[6]

Or maybe it was Smith who was difficult, as he soon displayed a peevish unwillingness to cooperate with the Nor'Westers. Refusing to moor alongside the newly repaired wharf at Fort George, he argued the channel was too shoal and narrow for his heavily laden ship. Although the PFC ships *Tonquin* and *Beaver* lay there successfully, a vessel the size of the *Isaac Todd* had not tested the south-side channel before. Smith insisted on sounding the channel anew, both above and below Fort George.[7] His obstinance required the Nor'Westers to use their river schooner, *Dolly*, as

3 Hussey, ed., *Voyage of the Racoon*, xxi-xxii; 19-20, 27. *See* Gough,ed., *Alexander Henry*, 2:724-26, for an account of the arrival of the *Isaac Todd* at the mouth of the Columbia, or James Keith Papers, Memoranda Book, 25, LAC.

4 At the time, Keith was still a clerk, but at the meeting he would be made a partner in the concern.

5 HBCA, F.3/2, fo. 119.

6 Gough, ed., *Alexander Henry*, 2:730-31; 736. Exactly when the rancor started is hard to determine, but Alexander Henry initially attributed the cause to a quarrel between the captain and the first mate.

7 Gough, ed., *Alexander Henry*, 2:733, 737, 744. Captain Smith's sounding of the upper channel did not substantiate the earlier work done by the *Racoon*, and he proved warranted in his caution.

well as the ship's boats, to ferry the precious cargo across the river, taking over half an hour each way and only when the weather permitted.[8]

The invoice of goods shipped aboard the *Isaac Todd* has not survived, but the value of the cargo finally landed at Fort George amounted to nearly £20,000 and hints taken from other records referred to silk, glass, and coats.[9] In September 1813 eighty-seven bales of munitions and trade goods, as well as three casks of beef stowed aboard the *Isaac Todd*, had been transferred to the *Racoon*, in anticipation of it arriving at the Columbia River first. Henry mentioned a lading of calico, hides, guns, bacon, weights, coals, six six-pound cannons, and a load of "Hessens" (Hessians), a strong, coarse cloth made of a mixture of jute and hemp, employed to make sails.[10] To this amount should be added the £796.4.5 in "sundry goods" sold to the officers of the *Racoon* at San Francisco in March, as well as the value of the livestock and supplies purchased from the Spanish authorities in California.[11]

Few leaders escape untarnished from the recollections of subordinates, but it was soon Henry who recorded differences between him and Donald McTavish. Both gentleman were interested in the "protection" of John McDonald's contracted seamstress, Jane Barnes. As the first Englishwoman to grace Fort George, she was a "plum" neither was willing to surrender. Henry's description of the negotiations is a model of discretion because the matter was resolved in his favor.

The difficult chore of unloading the vessel was not completed until May 20. Two days later, on Sunday morning, McTavish, Henry, and five sailors set out to cross the river in a small open boat and argue with the

8 Although inconvenient, there was sufficient time to off-load the supplies and provisions and to load the outgoing cargo by the planned departure date of August 1. Gough, ed., *Alexander Henry*, 2:730.

9 The account clearly states "...amount of Inventories remaining on hand at...Fort George landed from *Isaac Todd*" totaling £19,888.2.2. HBCA, F.4/4, pp. 28, 30; In a letter dated Montreal, May 9, 1813, to J. G. McTavish, agent William McGillivray claimed "the ships outfit has cost £40,000 S[tg]—equal to *one-third* of all the N W outfits of the year." HBCA, F.3/2, fo. 115. Regarding the cargo, *see also* HBCA, F.4/4, p. 28. Payette, ed., *Oregon Country*, xi; Coues, *New Light*, 763. The trade goods included blankets, strouds, tobacco, kettles, shirts, flints, and beads.

10 Gough, ed., *Alexander Henry*, 2:731, 736, 739; *Oxford English Dictionary*, 2nd ed., s. v. "Hessian"; S. F. A. Caulfield and Blanche C. Saward, *The Dictionary of Needlework* (London: L. Upcott Gill, 1882), 252; F. W. Howay, "A Yankee Trader on the Northwest Coast, 1791-1795," *Washington Historical Quarterly*, 21:2 (April, 1930): 89-91.

11 HBCA, F.4/4, p. 32; Gough, ed., *Alexander Henry*, 2:732.

pigheaded Captain Smith about moving the ship to the other side. The Columbia had already displayed its cannibal appetite for mariners. As they were crossing, a sudden squall came up in mid-river, swamping and capsizing the boat. As everyone struggled in the paralyzing cold seawater, it is possible to imagine the strangulating partners trying to help each other. Six of the seven men, including Donald McTavish and Alexander Henry, drowned. The survivor, only known as John, clung to a driftwood stump until passing Clatsop paddlers came in a canoe to rescue him.[12]

The deaths of Donald McTavish and Alexander Henry made Angus Bethune the most senior clerk at Fort George. Slated for a partnership the following summer, Bethune had been appointed to serve aboard the *Isaac Todd* as supercargo.[13] He immediately sent a message to Spokane House that brought J. G. McTavish to the mouth of the Columbia by July 8, 1814, just in time to address the arrival of a second NWC ship, the *Columbia*, Captain Anthony Robson, which anchored alongside the *Isaac Todd*.[14]

It would be over a year before the Montreal agents were made aware of the tragedy. The rumor came from, of all people, their former rival, John Jacob Astor. In a letter to J. G. McTavish, William McGillivray wrote:

> In a letter I received from Mr Astor about five weeks ago—he mentioned a report which some of the Coast vessels brought to China, that a Mr McTavish & Mr Henry had been drowned by the upsetting of a Boat last September in the Columbia—altho' I care to not give credit to this Account I was much shocked at it—but as no express has yet come down—(which I think to suppose would be the case had there been any truth in the report) my apprehensions are weaning off.[15]

Apparently captured as a prize of war from the Americans during the War of 1812, the *Columbia* had been purchased by their London agencies for the North West Company. Initially rigged as a 185-ton schooner, the

12 Henry's body was never found. McTavish's remains drifted ashore near Cape Disappointment and were buried there. He was not re-interred at Fort George until the following October when Captain Anthony Robson read the burial service. Corney, *Early Voyages*, 105, 117-18.

13 HBCA, F.3/2, fos. 115-116, letter from William McGillivray to J. G. McTavish dated Montreal, May 9, 1813.

14 Corney, *Early Voyages*, 113.

15 HBCA, F.3/2, fos. 121d-122. Eleven days earlier, in a previous letter to McTavish, McGillivray repeated that unpleasant story he heard about two months ago—by way of New York. HBCA, F.3/2, fo. 123.

ship carried a crew of twenty-five and was armed with ten nine-pounders. Although smaller than the *Isaac Todd*, the *Columbia* sailed faster, requiring a little more than eleven months to complete the voyage from London to Fort George.[16] The shallower draft *Columbia* was able to cross over the river and anchor close to Fort George.

The *Isaac Todd* was already loading furs, those acquired in the purchase of Astor's Pacific Fur Company and those traded by their own posts. Surviving records do not provide a precise account, but it is known the Nor'Westers purchased 17,705 pounds of parchment beaver, and an additional 465 pounds of beaver coating together with an array of other peltry valued at $39,173.66½.[17] These pelts represented the returns for the two years the Pacific Fur Company traders were in the field.

Added to these furs were packs obtained by North West Company traders during the 1813–14 season containing 3,570 pounds of large and small beaver, another 260 pounds of beaver coating, and a miscellaneous array of other peltry valued at $15,277.20 in American dollars.[18] Because North West Company accounts are not complete, it cannot be said in confidence that these packs represented their total returns. Because of the anticipated arrival of the *Isaac Todd*, those furs were probably held in storage and shipped out at the same time as the returns of Outfit 1813–14.[19]

On July 22, when the *Isaac Todd* was fully loaded and ready for sea, Angus Bethune came aboard and the ship dropped down below Chinook Point. Finding conditions hazardous for crossing the bar, Captain Smith anchored in Baker Bay to await better weather and remained there for more than two months, until conditions allowed him to cross the bar in safety.[20]

Captain Frazer Smith was finally free of fur traders, and all he had to contend with, after setting the course, was putting up with their

16 Corney, *Early Voyages*, 105-06.

17 Anon., *Message from the President communicating the Letter of Mr. Prevost and other Documents Relating to an Establishment made at the Mouth of the Columbia River*, 59-60. The North West Company valued the American furs at 10 shillings a pound whereas they valued their own furs at 15 shillings. *See* HBCA, F.3/2, fo.123. On prices, *see* Irving, *Astoria*, 317-318.

18 HBCA, F.4/4, p. 10. United States values totaling $54,450.86½ have been cited for comparison.

19 William McGillivray to J. G. McTavish, June 19, 1815, HBCA, F.3/2, fo. 123.

20 The ship cleared on September 26. Corney, *Early Voyages*, 113-17.

landlubber supercargo, Bethune. No log of the *Isaac Todd*'s voyage from the Columbia to China has been found, but other sources show that the ship called at the Sandwich Islands (Hawaii) for water and provisions and returned some Islanders previously employed on the Columbia.[21]

While at Oahu, Captain Smith acquired a most interesting passenger. John Jennings, the erstwhile captain of the brig *Forester*, requested passage aboard the *Isaac Todd* as far as China. After being disposed by a mutiny of his crew, Jennings was attempting to make his way home or to find another berth.[22] Smith agreed to transport him to Whampoa.

Arriving at Macao Roads on the Pearl River sometime in late November or early December 1814, the captain and the supercargo immediately encountered a bewildering display of Chinese bureaucracy. To strictly regulate foreign trade the Chinese imperial government limited all commerce to the southern city of Canton. Official tariffs were set in Peking, but actual application of import and export duties resided in the hands of a local custom official called the *Hoppo*. Individuals purchased this position at high cost and for short terms, so self-interest dictated they augment imperial tariffs during their tenure in office to provide for their own financial future. As a result, import and export duties could fluctuate in seemingly inexplicable ways, according to the whims of a particular Hoppo and much to the exasperation of western shippers.[23]

While the Hoppo set tariff policy, the actual business of trade with foreigners was monopolized by a guild of thirteen or so merchants called the *Co-hong*. On arrival at Macao, a merchant vessel would hire a pilot and acquire a *chop*, or permit, allowing the ship to proceed up the Pearl River to the height of navigation on the river at Whampoa. Once there, one of the Co-hong merchants assumed responsibility for all financial

21 The terms of agreement in the sale of the Pacific Fur Company to the Nor'Westers required the return to their homes of Hawaiian laborers whose contracts were not renewed. An unknown number of Hawaiians were aboard the *Isaac Todd*. More on them is in Barman and Watson, *Leaving Paradise*, 55-56.

22 J. J. Astor sent the *Forester*, while flying British colors, on a clandestine voyage to re-supply and protect Astoria. On finding American vessels in Hawaii, the crew rebelled and threatened the captain. Jennings escaped and made his way to Oahu where he eventually met the *Isaac Todd*. *See* Corney, *Early Voyages*, 124-27.

23 A few years later, James Keith noted that duties exacted on the schooner *Columbia*'s first visit to China (including "Hopoo Fees") amounted to $3246 while, on the second voyage, it was charged an additional $30 or $40. He commented, "So much for Chinese regularity & Honesty." James Keith Papers, Memoranda Book, 18, LAC.

transactions concerning the ship, including payment of pilotage, import and export duties, and the fee for ship clearance (which was the permission to sail from Macao to Whampoa). All required Chinese labor including a linguist, a "tidewaiter" who watched the ship to prevent smuggling, and a comprador, or ship chandler, for the unloading and sales of the cargo, and the purchase of a return cargo.

Fees were charged for wharfage, for transportation to and from Whampoa, and for *cumsha* (bribes and presents for Chinese officials). On arrival at Whampoa, the Hoppo measured the ship (length x breadth ÷ 10) to determine the import duty owed. A sum for a vessel the size of the *Isaac Todd* could amount to £900, to which the Hoppo added an additional £682 for cumsha as well as the myriad of fees charged for labor and services while in port.[24]

Angus Bethune's previous experience had been in the inland trade. Now he was getting a crash course in international commerce. Prohibited from venturing inside the walls of Canton, visiting merchants were further required to vacate even the factories during the off-season between April and October. At the factories, Westerners were not allowed to go upon the river or even to walk its banks without a Chinese escort. Time and place ashore for the crew of foreign vessels were strictly limited to certain hours of the day, all in the interest of preventing misconduct. For instance, between January 1 and March 13, 1815, the crew of the *Isaac Todd* received only two days of shore leave.[25] Nor were the officers and crew of foreign vessels allowed to learn Chinese.

Weapons of any description were not permitted ashore and no direct communication was allowed with the Hoppo or other officials; foreign traders could speak directly only with the Co-hong. Yet despite the frustrations encountered through exorbitant expenditures and social restrictions, relations between foreign traders and Co-hong merchants were generally friendly and honest.[26]

---

24 Dernberger et al., eds. *The Chinese*, 515-16; Clyde and Beers, *The Far East*, 67-70; Russell, "Chinese Voyages," 22-27. For a clear and thorough description of the Canton System, *see* Gibson, *Otter Skins*, 50-53, 86-94.

25 Asia, Pacific and Africa Collections, *Isaac Todd* 1815 Journal, L/MAR/B/186A, British Library.

26 Clyde, *Far East*, 71; Gibson, *Otter Skins*, 90. Among the friendly Co-hong merchants was one Wu Ping-ch'ien, known to traders as Houqua. The last vessel transporting North West Company furs to China was named in his honor.

American shippers, such as J. J. Astor, had already learned that the real profit from the China trade lay in the return cargo, made on the sale of China goods in America (or Europe).[27] To maximize profit through purchasing the greatest quantity of goods, they augmented their trade of furs with ginseng and specie, a flexibility the license denied to the Nor'Westers. The license also proscribed the fur traders from purchasing China goods in any amount on their own account (although Captain Smith seems to have been allowed a private trade).[28]

The complex web of Chinese bureaucracy was not the only barrier faced by the Nor'Westers. Restrictions placed in the East India Company license made it impossible for them to make a profit from their transactions in China. Because the *Isaac Todd* was under license of the East India Company, that concern's resident agent handled all business matters and communication between Captain Smith, the supercargo Bethune, and the Co-hong merchant.

Angus Bethune ostensibly handled all financial transactions regarding the sale of the cargo. However, because this responsibility was co-opted by the East India Company agent, Bethune's role reverted to that of an auditor, making his presence in China essentially superfluous. The North West Company furs were purchased on their behalf by the East India Company agent who gave Captain Smith a bill of exchange for the proceeds. Normally, Bethune would also have been responsible for the purchase of return goods, but because the license required him to accept only a bill of exchange for the proceeds derived from the sale of the furs, the return cargo was the property of the East India Company and this duty fell to the East India Company agent. The license required the *Isaac Todd* to transport a cargo of Bohea tea, Congo tea, Hyson skin tea, and nankeens for the East India Company to London, for which they would receive cartage.[29]

This meant that the only source of revenue from this adventure was the bill of exchange drawn on the East India Company and some income from the payment for freightage, earned at the rate of sixteen guineas per

---

27 Haeger, *John Jacob Astor*, 60, 78-92.

28 *Isaac Todd* 1815 Journal, 16 February, British Library.

29 For stipulations of the license, *see* LAC, Ellice Papers, A-19, Acc. 1993, 1st Inst., Bundle 54, especially Article 8 and the sections following Article 22. For a description of the cargo loaded aboard the *Isaac Todd* at Whampoa, *see* the *Isaac Todd* Journal, 1815, 30 January, 2, 13, 27 February, 8 March, British Library.

ton. The three hundred tons of East India Company freight eventually earned the North West Company £5,040.[30]

On March 13, 1815, the *Isaac Todd* was measured once more to determine export duty, and, after receiving her "grand *chop*" or departure permit, sailed from Whampoa. Left behind were Angus Bethune and sixteen Sandwich Islanders awaiting the arrival of the next North West Company ship, the *Columbia*.[31] Except for the ship itself and the delivery of the bill of exchange, the affairs of the North West Company were at an end aboard the *Isaac Todd*.

Two days later Captain Smith anchored close in to Macao where he found the schooner *Columbia* awaiting a pilot for Whampoa. On March 17 the *Columbia* sailed for Whampoa where Captain Anthony Robson found Bethune and the Sandwich Islanders awaiting him.[32] For unknown reasons, Bethune replaced Robson with John Jennings as captain of the *Columbia*. (The succeeding chapter details the *Columbia*'s voyages in 1814-1817.)

Unaware that the War of 1812 had ended, the *Isaac Todd* left, in company with the East India Company ships *Cambridge* and *Surrey*. The pirate-infested waters in the Strait of Malacca were poorly protected by a British naval station at distant Singapore, so most merchant shipping sailed south through the Sunda Strait between Sumatra and Java. With British forces in Batavia (present-day Jakarta), the Sunda Strait route was relatively safe but pirates, as well as American warships or privateers, could still be lurking to prey on merchant ships.

The *Isaac Todd* required only seventy-one days to cross the Indian Ocean and call at the Cape of Good Hope on the southern tip of Africa. Previously maligned as a "slow sailer," the *Isaac Todd* sailed a steady 6 to 8 knots an hour and had no trouble keeping up with the Indiamen in the convoy.[33] After being battered about for nearly two weeks trying to enter

30 James Keith Papers, A-676, A-2, Memorandum Book, p. 48, LAC.

31 Because the actual number of Hawaiians sent home on the *Isaac Todd* is uncertain, the sixteen may have been new hires at Oahu expecting transport back to the Columbia River.

32 Corney, *Early Voyages*, 123-24.

33 During the 1790s, Dutch East India Company ships averaged 89 days between Batavia and Cape of Good Hope and another 117 days between Cape of Good Hope and Holland. By comparison, the *Isaac Todd* took 71 days between Angier Bay and Cape of Good Hope and 83 days between the Cape and London. J. R. Bruijn et al., eds., *Dutch-Asiatic Shipping in the 17th and 18th Centuries* (The Hague: Martinus Nijhoff, 1987), tables 6, 11, 15, 20; quoted in Dean King, *Harbors and High Seas: An Atlas and Geographical Guide to the Complete Aubrey-Maturin Novels of Patrick O'Brian*, 3rd ed. (New York: Henry Holt and Company, 2000), 22.

the Royal Naval anchorage at the Cape of Good Hope, the small convoy stayed for nearly two weeks, making necessary repairs to rigging and taking on water and provisions. In June they learned that the war between the United States and Britain was over. No longer relying on East India Company ships for mutual protection, the *Isaac Todd* sailed alone to St. Helena in the south Atlantic.

At St. Helena on August 24, 1815, Captain Smith received tardy news of the surrender of Napoleon, ending twenty-two years of warfare. Then, somewhere west of the Azores, the *Isaac Todd* and the HMS *Northumberland* crossed paths, the merchantman bound for London only four weeks short of completing a two-and-a-half year circumnavigation of the globe, and the warship sailing southward toward St. Helena with the exiled Napoleon Bonaparte aboard.

At twelve noon on September 20, 1815, the *Isaac Todd* anchored abreast the East India Company Docks in London, ending the North West Company's largest investment in maritime shipping. Captain Frazer Smith arrived with a ship valued at £5,000 and a bill of exchange in his pocket for £25,289, unredeemable for another year.[34] At the Canton sales in 1815, beaver sold for between $3.80 and 3.90 per pound, a figure far below what was anticipated and needed to bring a profit.[35] At this price, costs exceeded profits and as early as June 19, 1815, William McGillivray, chief agent for the North West Company, had already conceded that the Adventure of the *Isaac Todd* would lose nearly £15,000. He could only hope freight-money and the remaining unsold furs might help defray some of the loss.[36]

The Nor'Westers operated under the constraints of slow ships, great distances, and the obligation to keep the maritime project moving forward. Even before they learned the potential loss, the North West Company had purchased two additional vessels, the 185-ton brig *Columbia*, and the 310-ton brig *Colonel Allan*. Except for an investment in the cargo of a brig owned by Anthony Robson, all future shipping to the Columbia would be placed in the hands of an American firm, J. and T. H. Perkins

34 Selkirk Papers, 9209-9210, LAC.

35 Selkirk Papers, Red River Settlement, MG19/E. vol. 31, 9209-10, LAC.

36 HBCA, F.3/2, fos. 123-123d. Bethune must have written McGillivray on January 17 revealing the sluggish sales in Canton and sending the letter on an Indiaman then sailing from China for England from whence it was forwarded to Montreal and arrived sometime before June 19.

and Company of Boston. As McGillivray explained, "The Expense attending the sending our own vessels to China is too heavy—and the Partners of the North West Company do not understand the management of ships or Captains; soliciting and trading skins is their real business."[37]

The ship *Isaac Todd* was sold to an unknown buyer for £2,270 sterling and was still in service in fall 1819. It ended its days in 1821 when it wrecked off the Gaspé Peninsula in the Gulf of St. Lawrence.

---

37 William McGillivray to J. G. McTavish, Montreal, April 28, 1816, HBCA, F.3/2, fos. 129-129d; Inglis, Ellice and Company to Sir Alexander Mackenzie and Company, London, November 5, 1817, Université de Montréal, Division des archives historiques, Montréal, François-Louis-Georges Baby Collection, u/5943, Université de Montréal (hereafter Baby Collection, UM).

Chapter Nine

Maritime and Marital Activities of the "other" *Columbia*

THE BOSTON SHIP *Columbia Rediviva*, Captain Robert Gray, gave the great western river a name.[1] The second *Columbia* to arrive on the Northwest coast was Baltimore sharp-built and rigged as a clipper schooner when it was captured during the War of 1812.[2] The London agents of the North West Company purchased the 185-ton schooner for its Columbia Department trade only eight months after the departure of the *Isaac Todd*. Little more than half the size of the *Isaac Todd*, the *Columbia* was small by the standards of the Northwest Coast, and its cargo may have been intended to supplement the previously shipped first year's trade goods and provisions.

A second East India Company license was purchased for the *Columbia*, but on more liberal terms than that of the *Isaac Todd*, and good for more than one voyage. Changes allowed Chinese goods to be shipped at least to the North American coast if not to Europe.[3] But it was still war time and should it be attacked, the *Columbia* mounted ten nine-pound guns that a crew of seventeen officers and men would have been unable to adequately serve. The captain was Anthony Robson and the first mate Peter Corney.[4]

Sailing from England in convoy with the Brazil fleet, the *Columbia* reached Rio de Janeiro on February 10, 1814, where several of the crew

1 A definitive account of this *Columbia*'s two visits to the coast of Northwest America is found in Howay, ed., *Voyages of the "Columbia."*

2 Sharp-built meant a narrow or wedge-shaped bottom designed for speed.

3 The only evidence of this license is indirect as no copy has been found. Inglis, Ellice and Company to Sir Alexander Mackenzie and Company, London, November 5, 1817, Baby Collection, UM, u/5943.

4 Corney, *Early Voyages*, 36-37.

deserted and replacements were picked up with some difficulty. Before attempting to double Cape Horn in mid-March, Captain Robson refitted at the Falkland Islands. By April the *Columbia* was sailing north along the South American coast, an astonishing feat considering the late season and the storms they must have encountered.

On their way northward the *Columbia* did not call at any of the ports along the South and North American coasts, nor in Hawaii. Being so long at sea was too much for four disgruntled crew members who, off Cape Blanco on the Oregon coast, plotted a mutiny. When their intent was discovered, they were put in irons. After crossing the Columbia bar on July 7, 1814, and anchoring in Baker Bay, the crew was startled by the approach of thirty or more cedar canoes full of men, women, and children.

Next day, the schooner ran up the river where the *Isaac Todd* was still loading furs. Captain Smith's recent refusal to move the *Isaac Todd* across to Fort George had been an indirect cause of the deaths of two proprietors, but a shallow draft schooner might anchor closer to the fort. First mate Corney recorded that they found three and a half fathoms crossing the river and six of excellent holding ground once there. However, a nautical chart, which Corney probably had a hand in drawing, shows only two fathoms and at most five fathoms in the south channel.[5] Captain Robson was willing to risk it and moved the schooner to an anchorage abreast Fort George on July 9.

With two ships to unload and reload, the depot was bustling. J. G. McTavish and Robson discussed details concerning the future of the *Columbia*. They decided to keep the ship as a trading vessel sailing between the Columbia, Spanish California to the south, Russian America in the far north, the Sandwich Islands (Hawaii), and Canton. That schedule would keep the *Columbia* in the Pacific for nearly four years and prove the Columbia Department was exploring alternative opportunities beyond the fur trade.

For the initial run north, the *Columbia* took on a cargo of bar-iron, rum, powder, and ball valued at £450, to be carried to the Russian settlement at Norfolk Sound. James Chisholm McTavish and the former

5 Corney, *Early Voyages*, 113; "Chart of Columbia River Copied from that of Captain A. Robson taken in 1815," Pacific Northwest Collection, N979.796.A153j, University of Washington Libraries, Seattle.

Astorian Donald McLennan accompanied the ship as supercargo and clerk.[6] By mid-August 1814 the *Columbia* was sailing toward the Russian settlement of New Archangel (Sitka). In addition to alcohol, ironware, and munitions, the *Columbia* traded Chinese goods such as nankeens, a durable cotton fabric of Chinese manufacture, in return for an unspecified number of large and small seal skins valued between 82½ cents and a dollar each.[7]

Robson and his crew returned to the Columbia River in October 1814 and lay at anchor for a month while taking on peltry not embarked on the *Isaac Todd.* In addition, an assortment of goods for the Spanish colony at Monterey was stowed aboard the ship with Duncan McDougall serving as supercargo. Early in November the belongings of Jane Barnes were brought aboard the ship. The disruptive seamstress was still creating problems in the fort and J. G. McTavish convinced Robson to accept the responsibility of arranging her transportation back to England.

That should have been a brief postscript to the romantic escapades of a lost woman from the dregs of Portsmouth, England, whose mildly licentious interlude is still perpetuated by the bawdy and historic-minded barmaids of Astoria, Oregon.[8] John McDonald had already departed with the spring brigade, and the passions of Donald McTavish and Alexander Henry ended with their deaths. Management of the Columbia Department had returned to John George McTavish, who already had a docile Chinook country wife and apprehended what trouble a fallen white woman among the Chinook neighbors might cause. The usual procedure for ending fur trade unions was known as "putting off," but Ms. Barnes had a legitimate NWC contract guaranteeing her return to the place of her "enlistment."[9] Captain Robson gallantly agreed to take "Mrs." Barnes to California and arrange for a ship to take her home to England.

At Monterey the *Columbia* received a cool reception from Lieutenant José Maria Estudillo, commander of the presidio, or fort. Californians

6 Corney, *Early Voyages*, 114.

7 Invoices for goods destined to Norfolk Sound can be found in HBCA, F.4/7, p. 44; 73-78; 79-80. The value of the goods traded to the Russians ranged between $1,584 and $9,177. Values for the goods shipped to Norfolk Sound as well as for the seal skins appear in James Keith Papers, Memoranda Book, p. 33, LAC.

8 Astoria barmaids still compete to see which of them can sell the most drinks and the winner receives the title Jane Barnes.

9 LAC, MG 19, A-17, fos. 1365-1373; Payette, "McDonald's Journal," v; Gough, ed., *Alexander Henry*, 2:725.

were not allowed to trade in furs there, but McDougall could offer his trade goods in exchange for provisions such as beef, flour, and peas.[10] The value of the trade was small, only £350, but could provide the groundwork for more profitable trade in the future. Because the provisions required for the barter were not immediately available, McDougall requested permission to remain at Monterey to collect food for Fort George to be shipped on some future visit. Although McDougall was denied permission to debark at Monterey, he did receive permission to leave a cooper behind to supervise the curing of the beef they would acquire.

During the month the *Columbia* remained in Monterey, eight men from a crew of twenty-five deserted. Who could blame them? California was a paradise compared to life aboard a sailing ship. Losing a third of the crew to desertion would have a significant impact on management of the ship, but First Mate Corney made no mention of difficulties as they weighed anchor and sailed north on December 21, 1814.[11]

A one-day visit to the Russian establishment at Fort Ross, north of San Francisco, also resulted in a polite but succinct refusal to allow McDougall or "Mrs." Barnes to stay ashore while the schooner made its voyage to China and returned. Instead, both were forced to continue the voyage aboard the *Columbia* as far as the Sandwich Islands. There, King Kamehameha granted permission for McDougall, his clerk, Donald McLennan, and a servant boy to remain ashore until the schooner should return.

After only two days in paradise, Robson set sail for China, taking along Jane Barnes, like Coleridge's albatross, as his burden. After an unremarkable voyage of seven weeks they anchored in Macao Roads on March 10, 1815. Upon arrival at Macao, "Captain Robson…took the young woman on shore, the Chinese not allowing her to proceed to Canton in the schooner."[12] Because foreign women were not allowed to land on Chinese soil, Robson was now obliged to provide lodging for her at the Portuguese colony before proceeding to Whampoa.

10 NAC, James Keith Papers, Memoranda Book, p. 33; Corney, *Early Voyages*, 119. In his *History of California*, Hubert Howe Bancroft blended this visit of the *Columbia* with its 1815 voyage the following August. *See* Bancroft, *History of California*, 2:273-74 for his confused and unreliable account.

11 Corney, *Early Voyages*, 119.

12 Corney, *Early Voyages*, 123.

At Whampoa, Robson found Angus Bethune, sixteen Sandwich Islanders, and a stranger named John Jennings awaiting his arrival. Jennings had been captain of the British-registered brig *Forester*, the property of John J. Astor who employed the British ship as a ruse in wartime to supply his trading post on the Columbia. As a result of a mutiny, Jennings had lost command of his ship and found himself cast ashore in the Sandwich Islands. When the *Isaac Todd* was there, he had asked for and received permission to come aboard, hoping to get back to England.

During the time Bethune spent with Jennings at Whampoa, he appears to have formed a favorable opinion of him. When Captain Robson brought the *Columbia* to Whampoa, he, Bethune, and Jennings spent eight days discussing the affairs of the North West Company. Bethune's already hostile attitude toward Robson may have hardened, as Corney wrote that Robson grew "quite tired of the northwest coast of America" and was paid the sum of $2,000 in wages to give up command of the *Columbia*.[13]

With cash in his pocket and free of responsibility, Robson was beginning to regret his agreement to see Mrs. Barnes returned to England. She was expensive. Making his way back to Macao, Robson arranged for his and Barnes's transportation back to England. At Macao Roads, landing fees, boat hire, clothing, and three weeks of the woman's board and room added up to £126.15.7.[14] By the time Barnes was returned to England and her bills were presented, just the cost of her transportation alone, from the Columbia River to London by way of China, would amount to £717.12/, a figure nearly the equivalent of a partner's annual income from holding two shares in the company.

No surprise then, that to spare his purse and settle expenses Captain Robson doctored the invoice. When he paid her board, on May 2, Robson billed it to the North West Company.[15] In what suspiciously looked like an attempt at a cover up, the account book credits the expense of the stay at Macao as follows:

---

13 Robson later complained to the London agents of ill-treatment on the Coast of China. Letter from Ingles, Ellice & Company to Sir Alexander Mackenzie and Company, London, May 18, 1816; Baby Collection, u 5932.

14 North West Company Account Books, 1815-1817, HBCA, F.4/7, p. 3.

15 North West Company, Adventure to the Columbia 1814, HBCA, F.4/7, pp. 2-3.

	To Cash on Acct. of *James* Barnes viz[t]	
Ap[r] 11	To duty paid for landing *him* at Macoa	$9.00
	To Sundries P[r] Capt Robson (Cloathing &c)	75.00
	To Board for 24 Days	110.00
	To Boat hire for Capt[n] from Canton to Macoa	71.00
May 2	To paid his Board &c as P[r] draft from Capt[n] Robson	95.50
		360.50
	Exchange 20 P[r] C[t]	72.10
		$422.60[16]

After refitting the schooner at the shop of the American chandler W. F. Megee (or Magee) to the amount of £288, Captain Jennings and the crew of the *Columbia* sailed from Macao Roads on May 2, 1815. They had Angus Bethune and sixteen Sandwich Islanders aboard, several of whom died on the return voyage, along with Joseph Ashton, who reportedly jumped overboard in a fit of madness.[17] Completing their first circuit of the Pacific Rim, the schooner and its human cargo arrived at Fort George on July 1.[18]

From there the ship sailed to Monterey to pick up the cooper left there the previous December and load provisions. Jennings must have been a man hunter, as he also recovered the eight deserters from his previous trip, along with four others who had deserted from the *Isaac Todd*.[19] Acting as supercargo, Angus Bethune attempted to trade £333 worth of Chinese goods and English goods valued at £580, but neither sold well.[20]

Although Don Maria (José Maria Estudillo), the *commandante* of the presidio at Monterey, ordered goods in 1815 and again in 1816, the trade was not profitable.[21] Local authorities were not allowed to exchange sea otters for Chinese and European goods and were restricted to offering the Nor'Westers provisions for the ship, depot, and inland posts in a

16 North West Company, Adventure to the Columbia 1814, HBCA, F.4/7, p. 3. The account is a clerk's copy but "James" is not a transcription error, for the next line refers to "him" and juggling expense accounts is nothing new. Emphasis on the name "James" added.

17 Corney, *Early Voyages*, 127. For Ashton, *see* Jones, ed., *Annals of Astoria*, 212.

18 For fitting out the ship, *see* HBCA, F.4/7, pp. 11-15, North West Company Account Book, 1815. The American firm is mentioned in Morse, *Chronicles of the East India Company*, 3:236.

19 Corney, *Early Voyages*, 129.

20 NAC, James Keith Papers, Memoranda Book, p. 33.

21 HBCA, F.4/7, pp. 9-10 and 42-43. While his men had not been paid in years, Estudillo nevertheless was able to purchase artificial flowers, silk stockings, and flowered ribbon among the goods ordered from China.

barter trade. Trading with cash or silver coin was out of the question because of the Hidalgo Revolt, and subsequent disorders in New Spain (1810-1817) created shortages at Monterey, such as the failure to pay the garrisons for several years.[22] After trading all they could, the Nor'Westers sailed back to the Columbia River.

Losing little time between voyages, a cargo about the same size as that taken to California was loaded to go to the Russian settlement New Archangel. The *Columbia* sailed north for that port in mid-September 1815, and in Norfolk Sound anchored alongside a number of American vessels, including Wilson P. Hunt's *Pedler*. Contrary to Russian policy, it tried trading gun powder to the Tlingits and was seized by the Russians. Columbia supercargo Bethune traded both Chinese and European goods in return for fur seal pelts, although those sold for only one to one and a half dollars each in Canton. Because the fur seals brought in some revenue, the NWC made five trips to Norfolk Sound between 1814 and 1817 and three trips to California, not including an additional voyage to pick up goods traded in a previous visit.[23]

After returning to the Columbia River with the seal furs, the *Columbia* made a four-week voyage to the Sandwich Islands where tanned and smiling Duncan McDougall and Donald McLennan came on board.[24] Corney did not mention what, if any, arrangements McDougall and McLennan enjoyed for female companionship, but judging from the hospitality provided the crew of the *Columbia* during the three weeks spent on Oahu repairing the ship's rigging, it must have been pleasant. "At sunrise," the worldly Corney wrote, "we fired two muskets and sent the women out of the ship and at sundown did the same as a signal for them to come on board."[25]

Writing little about the last voyages of the *Columbia* to China, Corney did not mention what the cargo carried and what it bought in terms of trade goods.[26] However, invoices in the Hudson's Bay Company archives reveal Jennings spent $2,714 refitting the ship, probably with a Chinese

22 Gary S. Breschini, "Monterey's First Years: The Royal Presidio of San Carlos de Monterey," Monterey Historical Society, www.mchsmuseum.com/presido.html, accessed May 21, 2007.

23 Memoranda Book, p. 33, James Keith Papers, LAC.

24 Corney, *Early Voyages*, 133.

25 Corney, *Early Voyages*, 135.

26 Corney, *Early Voyages*, 135.

comprador, a Chinese agent working for the ship rather than the American chandler, and expended a further amount of $692 for fresh provisions while at Whampoa between February and April 1816, as well as another $1,056 for sea stores. These costs came to $4,462 for supplies and maintenance, not including port fees, which the previous year amounted to $2,748.[27] Port fees tended to increase each year so that costs probably exceeded $7,500 for the *Columbia*'s 1816 adventure to China.

The return cargo from Canton consisted of $3,122 in goods ordered by the Spanish in California or $9,177 by the Russians at New Archangel. Only a small assortment of mostly beads and nankeens worth $650 were intended for trade at Fort George.[28] No profit could be expected from the Spanish goods because they could only be traded for provisions used at the Columbia post. Governor Baranov would only accept the Russian goods the *Columbia* delivered at 80 percent of original cost, traded for low value seal furs.[29]

The hard working *Columbia* returned to Fort George in August 1816 for a five-month layover while sails and seams were repaired. It had been decided (by whom is not known) to convert the rigging from a fore-and-aft sloop to a square-rigged brigantine. For this overhaul, the vessel was careened ashore while the crew lived nearby in tents. The consignment of Canton goods on board that would go to California and an additional assortment in inventory at the fort was stowed aboard the brig *Colonel Allan*, which had arrived on the river in June and would make a voyage while the *Columbia* was incapacitated. Duncan McDougall was assigned as supercargo on the brig and returned to sea almost as soon as he arrived on shore.

During the time the officers and crew of the *Columbia* remained at Fort George, they witnessed significant changes in the organization of the North West Company. In spring 1816 James Keith replaced J. G. McTavish as proprietor in charge of the Columbia Department. The purchaser of Astoria left on April 16, never to return west of the mountains, but Keith would have only six months to settle into management of the Columbia Department before Donald McKenzie returned in September

27 North West Company Account Book, 1816, HBCA, F.4/7, pp. 35-41.

28 HBCA, F.4/7, pp. 42-44, North West Company Account Book, 1816. Among the items for Fort George were two hats valued at $5.25 for James Keith.

29 NAC, James Keith Papers, memoranda book, p. 33.

displaying a three-year special contract with McTavish, McGillivray & Company to conduct the trade in the interior. In another alteration of duties, Angus Bethune exchanged his sea-legs for a cramped seat conducting express brigades between Fort George and Fort William.

Now rigged as a brig, the *Columbia* crossed the bar on January 10, 1817, and set course for the Sandwich Islands. While in the islands, the brig was refitted again, Hawaiians recruited for the Columbia, and about one hundred barrels of pork cured for trade with the Russians at Norfolk Sound.[30] With the expectation that developing the Pacific coastal trade could lead to profit, the pork intended for Russia was augmented with an additional assortment of goods and a thousand dollars in specie to trade either at the Sandwich Islands or New Archangel. Nothing sold well at either place and, after a voyage of five months, the ship returned to the Columbia.[31] In one last attempt at finding success in the coastal trade, an assortment of goods was taken aboard and the brig sailed along the coast as far south as the Farallone Islands, hoping to discover a market somewhere. After three months of little success, Captain Jennings gave up the effort and returned to the Columbia River.[32]

Considering the difficulty in managing business from long distance, it is not surprising William McGillivray advised Keith that "we cannot well see how you can continue Trade with the Russians—it cannot be done without your sending a vessel to Canton which will subject the Concern to heavy charges in that Part, which was one cause for our entering into arrangements with an American House." McGillivray's letter continued, diplomatically, but Keith must have realized that the distant management was beginning to recognize that the coastal trade, like the NWC's China adventure, was at risk:

> We would not wish to restrict you in any thing in which your judgement was satisfied that there was a probable chance of advantage to be desired—because being on the spot you must be better acquainted with circumstances to guide your decisions that we can possibly be—for this reason we left it to your discretion whether or not to keep the Schooner *Columbia* on the coast for a twelvemonth after the plan of employing vessels of the Companys was given up & we are still disposed to leave

30 Corney, *Early Voyages*, 158-59.

31 NAC, James Keith Papers, Memoranda Book, p. 33; HBCA, F.4/7, pp. 73-80, North West Company Account Book; Corney, *Early Voyages*, 162.

32 Corney, *Early Voyages*, 162-73.

> you the same discretion as long as she can be employed to advantage… We are not aware of any difficulty that can arise from your disposing of the Schooner to the Russians and certainly it will be much the best Plan for in England she will bring very little and the Expense of sending her hither unless some Freight could be procured for her—would be considerable.[33]

By the time Keith received this letter, he had already decided to sell the *Columbia* to King Kamehameha in the Sandwich Islands or failing that, to Baranov at New Archangel.[34] To make the sale more attractive, Keith ordered six long twelve-pound cannon together with powder and shot loaded aboard the ship and included in the price. On December 6, 1817, the brig *Columbia* arrived at the island of Owhyhee (Hawaii) and two weeks later, a price of 3,700 piculs of sandalwood for the ship and its accouterments was agreed to between Jennings and the Hawaiian king.[35] One of the Montreal agents, thinking of the insurance on the vessel, wrote "It would have saved the Concern several thousand Pounds, if the Old *Columbia* had been burnt, when she loaded her Cargo."[36]

Between mid-June and the end of July 1818 a third ship named *Columbia* made its appearance on the namesake river.[37] This vessel has mystified historians from F. W. Howay to Glen Adams, in part because of its similarity to the North West Company brig also called *Columbia*, sold in Hawaii six months earlier. Both ships were commanded at one time by Anthony Robson. The mystery was discovered to be a ruse employed by the London agents to avoid the cost of obtaining another East India Company license.[38]

---

33 William McGillivray and Henry MacKenzie, Fort William, to James Keith, July 26, 1817, James Keith Papers, University of Aberdeen (hereafter UA).

34 Pierce, *Hawaiian Adventure*, 89; Corney, *Early Voyages*, 175.

35 A picul equaled 133⅓ pounds. *See* Morse, *East India Company*, viii. For the voyage and sales agreement, *see* Corney, *Early Voyages*, 178-86. The figure 3,700 piculs is given in NAC, James Keith Papers, Memoranda Book, p. 33.

36 Thomas Thain, Montreal, to James Keith, June 7, 1819, James Keith Papers, UA.

37 Reference to this vessel can be found in Baby Collection, UM, u/5943, letter dated London, 5 November 1817, from Inglis, Ellice and Company to Sir Alexander Mackenzie and Company; HBCA, F.3/2, fos. 194-195d, letter dated Fort George, 31 March 1819, from Alexander McKenzie to J. G. McTavish.

38 Howay, *List of Trading Vessels*, 124-25; Corney, *Early Voyages*, 36-37. The ruse is revealed in Baby Collection, u/5943, UM, letter dated London, 5 November 1817.

In spite of their losses in the Canton trade using their own vessels, the North West Company purchased an interest in the cargo carried by this reinvented *Columbia.* In the spring of 1816 Captain Anthony Robson had returned to England from China and purchased a vessel of about 180-tons burden. Outfitted for a voyage to the Pacific, Inglis, Ellice & Company loaded him with goods that nearly filled his ship and paid him £2,000.[39]

Robson also took goods of his own to sell to the Spanish in California without realizing that cash was almost nonexistent in California. He also anticipated selling his vessel to the Nor'Westers, if they had need of it, or to "the contending parties to the southward" if they did not.[40] On that possibility the London agents suggested to Robson that he name his brig *Columbia* in case it was chartered or sold to the Nor'Westers. Their East India Company license for the previous *Columbia* could be surreptitiously assigned to his ship because they were both about the same size and rigged as brigs. This clandestine act would save the necessity and costs of obtaining a license.[41]

Jane Barnes, having once escaped the wretchedness of her life in Portsmouth, England, only to be exiled from Astoria in Captain Robson's care, would now return to the mouth of the Columbia. Her long voyage home with a deadheading and bored Captain Robson must have resulted in a shipboard romance, as she was now Mrs. Jane Robson, the respectable wife of the captain and already the mother of two children. Perhaps, too, knowledgeable of the foible of mariners, she chose to accompany him on his adventures to the Northwest Coast.

Early in November 1817, the Robson family embarked from London on the *Columbia* and arrived at Fort George eight months later on June 19, 1818. The brigade going into the interior had not yet departed and the brig's propitious arrival allowed the inland traders to augment their supplies with "a fine assortment of goods."[42] According to his intention,

39 For Robson's date of arrival in England, *see* letter, Inglis, Ellice & Company, London, to Sir Alexander Mackenzie & Company, May 18, 1816, Baby Collection, u/5932, UM.

40 Letter, Inglis, Ellice and Company, London, to Sir Alexander Mackenzie and Company, November 5, 1817, Baby Collection, u/5943, UM.

41 Letter, Inglis, Ellice and Company, London, to Sir Alexander Mackenzie and Company, November 5, 1817, Baby Collection, u/5943, UM.

42 HBCA, F.3/2, fos. 194-195d, North West Company Correspondence, etc. 1800-1827, letter dated Fort George, March 31, 1819 from Alexander McKenzie to J. G. McTavish.

Robson called next upon the Spanish at Monterey hoping to engage in a trade with them. Historian H. H. Bancroft wrote that "an English craft came [to Monterey] from the Columbia River" on September 22, 1818, which could only have been Robson's *Columbia*.[43]

The governor of Alta California, Pablo de Sola, insisted on restricting trade to the provisioning of foreign ships, and the success of Robson's California adventure must therefore have been very limited. After the Nor'Westers declined his offer to charter or purchase his vessel, Robson disappeared from the historical record.

The Spokane House trader Finnan McDonald, who had a country wife he cherished, seems an unlikely arbiter of social behavior when he could not resist writing to J. G. McTavish in spring 1819:

> I have to tel you that we got fright last summer at Fort George no Goods nor Vasil radey to start the next Day with nothing when Vasil *Columbia* made aperience in the in side of the Bar[44] in grate joy it rise hour harts and Give Blessing to the Day—This Captin was your Old Frind Cap[t] Robson with Misteris Robson in Former days you re] Cal Mis Jen which we had the honner to sey [see] her Eateing at the same table with [us] at Fort George in the Plase of eateing on the flour [floor][45]

43 Bancroft, *History of California*, 2:383; Baby Collection, g1/146 and g1/147, UM.

44 The ship arrived on June 19, 1818.

45 Finnan McDonald to J. G. McTavish, Spokane House, April 9, 1819. Mrs. Robson went from being a mistress relegated to eating apart from the men, as their Indian wives did, to becoming the wife of a ship captain entitled to dine at the table with the gentlemen.

Chapter Ten

Final Attempts at Shipping

The Voyage of the *Colonel Allan*, 1815-1817

After sending out the *Isaac Todd* and the *Columbia*, the North West Company gave over transporting their returns to Canton to American shippers who did not have to purchase licenses from the East India Company. Prior to that arrangement in 1816, the last North West Company ship engaged in the Columbia Adventure was the *Colonel Allan*. It had been two years since the North West Company had begun considering a plan to address the uncertainty and high costs involved in sending their own ships to supply the Columbia River and carry peltry returns to the Canton market. After full discussion among the wintering partners and their Montreal agents, it was agreed, "If a favourable connection could be made with an American house...it should be adopted for facilitating the Business in China."[1]

The company's agent in Montreal, Simon McGillivray, was given responsibility for negotiating with an American shipper. He settled upon a Boston firm, J. and T. H. Perkins & Company. They agreed to deliver North West Company trade goods and provisions at the mouth of the Columbia River and to market NWC furs in Canton in return for one-fourth of the net proceeds. However, this arrangement was made too late to cover requirements for the 1816 season, and thus a third company ship was needed rather quickly. This ship would be the *Colonel Allan,* and a close look at its history shows how control of the Columbia River fur trade had already begun slipping away from the North West Company.

Early in the spring of 1815, Edward Ellice, one of the North West Company's agents in London, purchased the *Colonel Allan* for £1,500.

1 Wallace, ed., *Documents Relating to the North West Company*, 283.

Ellice considered the ship a superior vessel to either of the company's previous ships. She was French-built, of Italian oak, about three to four years old, and at 310 tons, capable of carrying stores for a four to five year voyage.[2] But four years of service and a likely renaming meant it would require an extensive overhaul and outfitting. Ellice admitted this would run the total cost of the ship to somewhere in the neighborhood of £8,000 to £10,000. The invoice value of the trade goods loaded aboard for the first voyage amounted to £14,057.17.8, of which £300.10.10 was intended for trade in the Sandwich Islands.[3] "However," Ellice assured the Montreal partnership, "all possible economy shall be used & she will get away by 1 July."[4]

The bulk of the cargo sent on the *Colonel Allan* when it departed in 1815 was the private £14,057.17.8 venture of Inglis, Ellice & Company, carrying the mark "IEC."[5] Apparently, it remained optional with the North West Company whether these goods should apply to their account or remain as a separate adventure of the London agency.[6] Some of the cargo must have been traded on the voyage as James Keith, the NWC partner in charge at Fort George, would record in his Memoranda Book that according to the invoice from the *Colonel Allan,* the Columbia Department was charged £13,023. While a portion of the cargo consisted of provisions and trade goods intended for the Columbia Department, it is clear that the partnership participated in a separate adventure arranged by Edward Ellice. James Keith listed £4,840 in goods charged to the Columbia Department "assumed" from IEC.[7]

Ellice's actions were not unilateral. Representing the Montreal agency of McTavish, McGillivray & Company, Simon McGillivray and the new partner, Thomas Thain, had arrived in London in November 1814 to arrange the outfitting of a 1816–17 adventure to the Columbia. While

2 Davidson, *North West Company*, 166; Baby Collection, u/3988; u/5929, UM.

3 Baby Collection, u/5929, UM.

4 James Keith Papers, Memoranda Book, 31, NAC. It should not be overlooked that the London agency of Inglis, Ellice & Company was tinkering with matters beyond their responsibility as representatives of a Montreal fur trade business.

5 Two London firms, McTavish, Fraser & Company and Inglis, Ellice & Company, were acting as agents for the North West Company. The former firm had been associated with the North West Company from its inception and the latter became involved when the North West Company merged with Sir Alexander Mackenzie & Company in 1804.

6 Baby Collection, u/5929, UM.

7 James Keith Papers, Memoranda Book, 31, NAC.

Ellice, McGillivray, and Thain began laying the foundations for the voyage of the *Colonel Allan* over the winter of 1814–15, the Treaty of Ghent ended hostilities between the United States and Great Britain. At Fort George, the NWC remained armed and ready for the possibility of being subjected to attack.

Early in the spring of 1815 Thain returned to Montreal to resume his duties and Simon McGillivray went to the United States to search for an American company by which it was hoped an economically sound agreement might be arrived at to transport company furs from the Columbia River to the Canton market. Then in July, another treaty between the two countries was signed which liberalized commerce. This commercial "reciprocity" treaty provided for "a most favored nation" status between "His Britannic Majesty's territories in Europe" and the United States. One section read:

> The inhabitants of the two countries respectively shall have liberty, freely and securely to come with their ships and cargoes to all such places, ports, and rivers in the territories aforesaid, to which other foreigners are permitted to come.[8]

The treaty also provided that no higher or other duties were to be imposed by either nation on the other's commerce that were not also imposed on other foreign nations. But as it said nothing about liberalizing trade between the United States and Canada, the intent was to remove transatlantic barriers to trade that had arisen during the late war and earlier, but not to promote transcontinental trade within North America. Ellice foresaw that this "most favored nation" convention might act contrary to the North West Company's larger economic interests because the protective tariffs making it profitable to dispose of North American beaver on the London market would be withdrawn. For these and other reasons, the Montreal agents remained cautious about the outcome of the Treaty of Ghent and distrustful of the American government.

In August 1815 Simon McGillivray was in New York with his ear tuned to the city's gossip when he warned Ellice that "violent proceeding against remote Fort George might have already been taken either by the

8 Treaties and Agreements Affecting Canada in force between His Majesty and the United States of America 1814-1925 (Ottawa: F. A. Acland, 1927), 9-12.

American Government or American speculators."[9] The implication: Mr. Astor was still dangerous.

The tense international situation, and the war-like American posturing with regard to the reoccupation of the Columbia River that had McGillivray on edge, left Edward Ellice with the impression that it was prudent to provide for the possibility of American aggression against the company's small post. As far as those distant managers knew, by the time Captain Daniel McLellan and the *Colonel Allan* arrived there the North West Company's people might already have been "moved off by the Americans." Consequently, two eighteen-pound cannon, weighing some two tons each, were ordered shipped from London to Fort George, along with an unspecified number of twelve-pound cannon and eight hundred pounds of powder. All these added over 4,800 pounds to the *Colonel Allan* cargo.[10]

Captain McLellan, master of the *Colonel Allan,* was so familiar with Ellice that the shipmaster was allowed to sail without a supercargo.[11] To diversify their investment, the North West Company cargo also included 1,000 muskets and 100 barrels of powder that would allow Captain McLellan to take advantage of "the peculiar circumstances [then] agitating South America."[12] Selling arms to revolutionaries, it must be noted, stepped quite a bit beyond the previous sale of guns and ammunition to Columbia River Indians.

Besides armaments, a wide array of piece goods that a London agent might select, such as wearing apparel and similar items suitable for the South American market, were also stowed in the ship's hold.[13] Among these articles were fine hosiery, corduroy jackets and trousers, gingham and silk umbrellas, and military boots. As Ellice complacently stated, "altogether, the ship will have a full load."[14]

9 Baby Collection, u /5929, UM.

10 Ellice was left with the responsibility of finding gunners competent with such weaponry, to which end he used his contacts in the British army to procure two men with appropriate experience who could double as clerks while assigned to Fort George. See Baby Collection, u/3990; u/3989, UM.

11 Baby Collection, u/3989; u/3990; u/5929, UM.

12 Baby Collection, u/5929, UM.

13 While a complete manifest has not been found, a partial inventory of goods remaining at Fort George from the original invoice of the Colonel Allan can be found in HBCA, F.1/7, pp. 45-54.

14 Baby Collection, u/3989, u/5929, UM.

The *Colonel Allan* sailed from the Downs past Gravesend on August 5, 1815, without planning to put into port anywhere except to resupply water.[15] Even so, Ellice wrote, "McLellan thinks of trying Lima with his goods on his way up the Coast."[16] In fact, at least part of the cargo of muskets and powder was traded in Peru for specie.[17] In Lima, McLellan purchased supplies of coffee, sugar, tobacco, and rum for use at Fort George at a price cheaper than they would have cost in London.[18] Life at the end of the world was getting downright luxurious.

At Fort George, Alexander Ross, who was serving as Keith's clerk, reported the arrival of the *Colonel Allan* a few days after the June 7 appearance of the 1816 spring brigade.[19] Over the winter 1815–16 Ross had been replaced at Okanogan by fellow clerk Ross Cox who would oversee the rebuilding of that depot. Alexander Ross should have been in a position to provide reliable and detailed information, but he was remarkably vague and only devoted a page to the arrival of the ship. Captain McLellan had been asked by Ellice to make a survey of the bar of the Columbia and channel to Fort George which took three weeks to complete. He was assisted by the increasingly disparaging Ross, who was also finding fault with his superior Keith and the distant owners of the cargo.[20]

Although James Keith made a careful record of the survey, he was not pleased to have unusual, distracting activities going on. As the proprietor in charge at Fort George, Keith had been led to understand that he was responsible for the Pacific maritime business of the North West Company. Before leaving London, Captain McLellan had been provided with a letter extending to him an unusual degree of prerogative with regard to the mission of his voyage, including acting as both ship's master and supercargo.

Like his predecessor Alexander Henry, Keith could be testy and resented the usurpation of his authority to assign the men who would serve on the ship. McGillivray was later obligated to point out distinctions in command duties. At the time of the *Colonel Allan*'s departure

15 Baby Collection, u/5929, UM.
16 Baby Collection, u/3989, UM.
17 Ross, Fur Hunters, 59.
18 Memoranda Book, n.p., James Keith Papers, NAC.
19 Ross, *Fur Hunters*, 59.
20 Ross, *Fur Hunters*, 61-64. That survey, together with maps and drawings, is not known to have survived.

from England, it had not been known which partner would be managing the company's affairs at Fort George, and McGillivray had to assure Keith that, in providing McLellan with his broad instructions, there was no intent to impugn the abilities of any individual.[21]

Clerk Ross did include a line in his account confirming that "the *Colonel Allen* after a short stay at Fort George sailed for California and South America on a speculating trip, and returned again with a considerable quantity of specie and other valuable commodities consigned to some of the London merchants."[22] While at Monterey in late August and into the autumn, the ship traded with the Spanish missions for flour and fresh produce to provision Fort George. That is confirmed by historian Marian O'Neil, who found Spanish records revealing "the arrival on August 29, 1816 [at Monterey], of the 'Allan,' Captain Mr Danial [McLellan], supercargo Dunc McDougall" and her "departure on October 12."[23]

After arranging purchases Duncan McDougall must have returned north with the ship, as by November 1816 the *Colonel Allan* was back at Fort George and ready to embark for England.[24] In addition to the specie obtained in Monterey and the arms Ellice previously suggested might be sold "in the Brazils and the Cape of Good Hope," the ship's cargo now included 6,403 beaver skins, 10,993 muskrat, 17 bear, 62 marten, 345 mink, 80 fisher, 26 fox, and 12 swan skins loaded at Fort George.[25]

In addition, Keith shipped for sale from the Columbia £3,068.9.4½ in weaponry (including four four-pound brass guns and fifteen cases of muskets) and £501.9.9 in liquors.[26] Marked "CR (Columbia River)" they were not part of the Inglis, Ellice and Company stock "consigned for sale and returns for account of the North West Company." Whatever goods were acquired from the three hundred consigned to the Sandwich

21 William McGillivray and Henry McKenzie, Agents for the North West Company to James Keith, Fort William 26th July 1817, Keith Papers, University of Aberdeen (MSS Davidson & Garden) 2769/I/57/4.

22 Ross, *Fur Hunters*, 59.

23 O'Neil, "Maritime Activities of the North West Company," 264.

24 Brown, "Duncan McDougall," 526. McDougall later accompanied Angus Bethune, Ross Cox, and others in the spring brigade that left Fort George on April 16, 1817, to go to Fort William.

25 Baby Collection, g1/146; g1/147, UM. Keith reported only 6,110 P[archment] beaver and 11,000 muskrats. See Memoranda Book, 32, James Keith Papers, NAC.

26 HBCA, F.4/7, 62-64.

Island trade is unknown, as are the proceeds from the "private adventure" referred to in a letter from McGillivray to Keith, dated July 26, 1817.[27]

Although the goods aboard the *Colonel Allan* were the private adventure of the London agencies, the NWC was also sending furs to test the London market. James Keith had the option of assuming any risk or profit on the part of the North West Company, which was approved later.[28] "The arrangement with Captain McLennan and your assuming for the North West Company the remaining goods of the private adventure by the *Colonel Allan*—we approve of as well as your shipment of goods by that vessel which has enabled you to get rid of so many superfluous articles." Those "superfluous articles" may have included the items traded to the Spanish for "flour and produce" in the fall of 1816.[29]

Keith assumed risk on goods valued at £4,840 sterling carrying the IEC mark, and kept some goods valued at a little over £1,000 for his stores at Fort George.[30] The remainder stayed aboard the *Colonel Allan* as she departed for London in November 1816. Including cutlery, drapery, and an assortment of dry goods such as "corded shawls, vandyke hose, olive velveteens, and warped lace" worth some £3,771.0.9½, those items were intended for sale on the voyage home. Whether that would have been in the Brazils or at the Cape of Good Hope depended on what route Captain McLellan chose. After so many years the proud Montreal traders finally deserved the derogatory name "pedlars."

Somewhere nestled among the bales of fur and other goods were even more unusual items. Like other European visitors, James Keith was not above robbing native graves to obtain the flattened skulls of the Chinooks. Simon McGillivray wrote to Keith in July 1818, begging him "to accept my best thanks for the curiosities you had the kindness to send me

27 William McGillivray to James Keith, Fort William, July 26, 1817, James Keith Papers, James Keith Papers, University of Aberdeen; HBCA, F.4/7, 55-61.

28 Revealed in McGillivray's July letter to James Keith, noted above, which would not have been delivered to Keith until the Fort William express returned.

29 The legacy of this adventure of the brig *Colonel Allan* survived at Fort George until an inventory was taken by the Hudson's Bay Company in 1821. That revealed an assortment of goods carrying the IEC logo such as table forks and, of course, the two eighteen-pound cannon with 120 rounds of shot and 120 rounds of canister shot. Perhaps the suit of mail armor found in the same inventory, and so much ridiculed by servants of the Hudson's Bay Company, was part of this consignment. HBCA, F.4/39, 191, 209-234, and F.4/55, 1-55).

30 Memoranda Book, 31, James Keith Papers, NAC.

by the *Col'l Allan*."[31] Keith also found occasion to extend similar "kindnesses" to Colonel Perkins of Boston, John Richardson of Montreal, and other friends in Great Britain as well as the Royal Colleges of Surgeons in London and Edinburgh, and Marischal College in Aberdeen.[32] Perhaps he felt he was advancing the frontiers of medical knowledge as well as providing some intriguing amusement for his friends.[33]

Keith may have known that Simon McGillivray had previously negotiated an arrangement in New York with J. and T. H. Perkins & Company of Boston. Perkins would ship up to a hundred tons of supplies per vessel, delivered to them at Boston, to the northwest coast and market fur returns from Fort George in Canton. Further, they would use the proceeds from that sale to purchase Chinese goods such as teas, nankeens, and silks to be sold in Boston with the North West Company receiving a portion of the profits. For this, the Perkins concern would receive one-fourth of the net proceeds to defray expenses of their ship. It was understood that the North West Company would not ship any skins collected from the trade of the Columbia River except by vessels belonging to the Americans.[34]

With no Perkins ship contracted for the 1816–17 season, and with an opportunity to ship lower-grade skins to London where the market was presumed better, Keith saw an opportunity to advance the interests of the company by sending lower quality Columbia beaver to the London fur auctions.[35] William McGillivray appreciated that Keith's decision "made a better assortment for the Canton market," but worried that Perkins & Company might see this as an abridgment of their agreement. He

31 Simon McGillivray to James Keith, Fort William, July 20, 1818, James Keith Papers, NAC.

32 James Keith to Colonel Perkins, Fort George, April 13, 1821, James Keith Papers, UA; James Keith to Thomas H. Perkins, Fort George Columbia River, June 12, 1817, James Keith Papers, NAC.; T. H. Perkins to James Keith, Boston, November 22, 1821, James Keith Papers, UA.

33 James Keith to the Board of Curators of the Royal College of Surgeons and to the President and in his absence to the Secretary of the Royal College of Surgeons Edinburgh and to the Principal of Marischall College, Aberdeen. London, May 1822.

34 William McGillivray to James Keith, Fort William, July 26, 1817, James Keith Papers, UA.

35 As an example of the prices for various furs on the Canton market, see the letter from Perkins and Company of Canton to J. and T. H. Perkins and Company of Boston, February 28, 1821, in the Russell Company Papers, Perkins Letter Book, vol. 19, 79-3734, Pos. C9 box 49 #4, Baker Library, Harvard Business School, Harvard University, Cambridge, MA.

warned Keith "if they claim some advantages from the skins shipped, we conceive they have a right."[36] Such concern proved unnecessary as the American firm did not get a ship to the North Pacific Coast until June 1817 when their first vessel, the *Alexander*, arrived a few days after the appearance of the annual brigade from the interior and more than six months after the departure of the *Colonel Allan*.

Unlike its voyage out to the Pacific, the *Colonel Allan* made a speedy return to London, a trip of some seven months, and arrived on May 28, 1817. The North West Company imported furs valued at £1,458.5.8 from the Columbia River, but this figure reflects the amount upon which duty was paid and not the actual market value. A Customs House document noted that the most valuable item was six hundred and forty beaver skins valued at £1,121.15.0.[37] A careless clerk apparently dropped the last number of the actual amount of 6,403 beaver skins. James Keith gave an invoice value to the cargo of the *Colonel Allan* as £9,407, reflecting perhaps the difference between what was told to the insurance company and what was declared to the customs agent and charged £347.15.0 in duties.[38] Unaccountably, the accounts signed by Inglis, Ellice and Company stated that 103 bales of furs carrying the mark "15/NW" were charged only £315.8.0 for duty.

The average prices received in London were roughly equivalent to the prices beaver skins sold for in Canton. In London, they received an average of about eighteen shillings and at Canton, in the neighborhood of seventeen shillings per pelt. The change in markets, despite Keith's hope, did little good but the idea of trading lower quality beaver in London and reserving finer beaver for other markets was sound as a marketing strategy.

The problem was that the London market had not yet recovered sufficiently from the unsettling times of the Continental and American wars. The Nor'wester's timing was off and they entered into the London market when the prices paid for beaver were low. In addition, because of the convention of commerce entered into with the Americans in the 1815

36 William McGillivray to James Keith, Fort William, July 26, 1817, James Keith Papers, UA.

37 Davidson, *The North West Company*. Davidson's source must have dropped a three, for the North West Company accounts show 6,403 beaver skins were brought in by the *Colonel Allan*.

38 Memoranda Book, 32, James Keith Papers, NAC.

treaty, the NWC partners and their agents were worried that an increase in supply with no increase in demand would further degrade their weakening trading advantage.

Changes were coming, but the year 1817 was too early to know what the impact of this agreement would have on future trade. Had they persisted, the Nor'Westers might have eventually succeeded in expanding their markets because the distrustful and unsettling residue left over from the war with the United States soon dissipated, and increased American access to British markets proved of little consequence. Unfortunately for the NWC, by the time the *Colonel Allan* reached London, the new agreement with J. and T. H. Perkins & Company of Boston committed the NWC to supplying the Canton market by way of American shippers. They locked into a losing proposition because the Chinese were already oversupplied with less valuable Columbia beaver.

Looking back in a July 20, 1818, letter to Keith, William McGillivray confirmed, "The purchase was certainly the cheapest ever made by the North West Company but it will not be regretted by the shippers considering who the purchasers were, more particularly as much handsome profits had been made by the sale of other goods." Those "other goods" may very well have been the muskets and powder sold in South America.

It is impossible to say, with any precision, what the final figure of profit or loss was on the adventure of the *Colonel Allan,* but there was no question that investors considered the voyage a total loss, probably in excess of £6,500.[39] After their experience with the *Colonel Allan*, the North West Company declined becoming involved in the purchase of another ship.

McTavish, McGillivray & Company in Montreal also realized the lesson of the *Colonel Allan* and in their desperation made a new arrangement that by fall 1816 would return former Astorian Donald McKenzie to the Fort George wharf, charged to reform the inland trade.

39 HBCA, F.4/33, fo. 101.

Chapter Eleven

"A Place so Dull and Dreary"
The Interior Fur Trade

The War of 1812 had been an unpleasant interruption that provided the Nor'westers on the Columbia River with an unanticipated but hastily improvised opportunity to buy out the timid Astorians and secure a monopoly on the western fur trade. No matter what many secondary accounts say, Astoria was not the center of the new country. As a shipping point Fort George was on the leading edge of the North West Company Columbia Adventure, but it was soon apparent that the same difficulties that initially defeated early experimentation in a China trade would still inhibit McTavish, McGillivray & Company's misadventures in maritime shipping from the Columbia.

The fishing tribes of the rivers and lakes must have marveled at the antics of the trappers willing to travel far in search of beaver, but only taking the skins of those delectable animals. Shipping lists revealed the diversity of peltry being carried from the Columbia: beaver, muskrat, fox, mink, martens, fishers swan, lynx, wolf, and bear—an assortment showing that native peoples, despite the scarcity of steel traps, were participating in the interior trade by catching "small furs" in deadfalls and snares. No matter the variety or numbers of other skins, beaver remained the only fur that paid the costs of transport, and tribal hunters were willing to ditch and tear the roofs off beaver lodges to get at them.

At the end of a war fought to a draw in the east, the treaty of peace between the United States and Britain returned the Pacific Northwest and the Columbia River drainage to the Americans. The only British representation was a private business partnership left in sole possession of a shipping port on foreign soil as "tenants at will" of an unfriendly

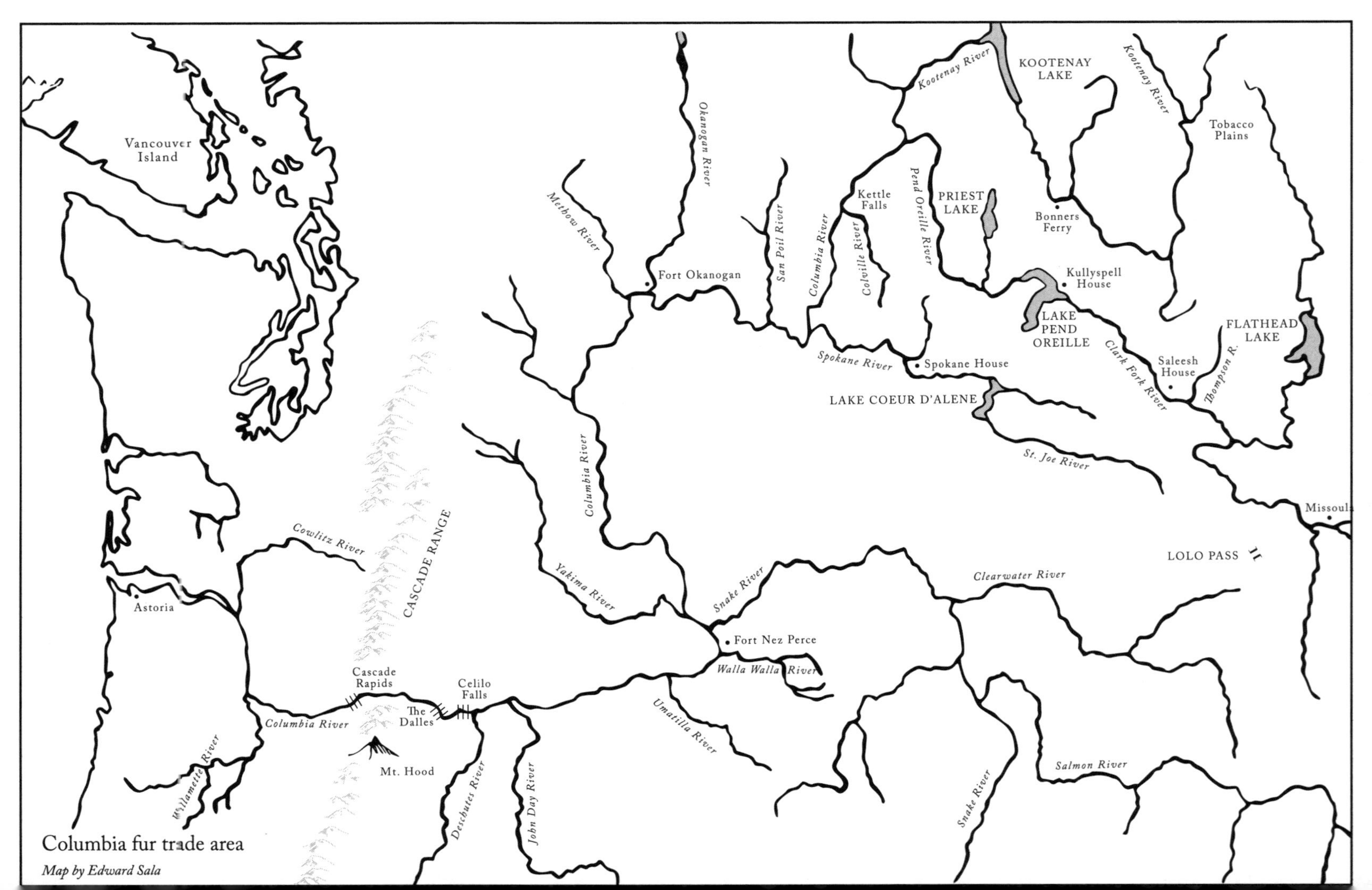

Columbia fur trade area

Map by Edward Sala

power. If the fur trade west of the Rocky Mountains was to prevail, the success of the Columbia Adventure depended less on the acts of "great men" and more on the actions of clerks and engages who were already in the country. During the preceding seven years they had learned how to exploit the skill and strength of *les louers de canots, portageurs, et le cheval et ces fichues fourrures* (boatmen, portagers, and packers of horses carrying furs). Their backcountry French became the operative language of the western fur trade.[1]

It was *Canadiens* who gave the western tribes the French names by which they are still known: *Tetes Plattes* (flatheads), *Nez Perce* (pierced noses), *Pend d'Oreille* (hanging from ear), and *Coeur d'Alene* (pointed hearts). They named geographic features that are part of our vocabulary; landmarks we still know as the *Platte* River, the *Grand Tetons*, the *Deschutes*, *les Dalles*, and *les Cascades*.

Meanwhile the operative fur trade was scattered in rough-hewn posts sagging on the great river's tributaries. Getting to them relied on the strong arms of Iroquois or Kanaka paddlers or on the limited patience of transplanted Canadian packers whose engagé French echoed through the pines. Driving a canoe against a continental river tested the perseverance of Nor'wester boatmen. Whether an *avant, milieu,* or *gouvernail* of a canoe, *un portier*, or a horse-bit leader of an untrustworthy *bête de somme*, being *un engagé* or *un marchand de fourrures* was rigorous work under the worst conditions. No matter that Scots officers spoke English or Gaelic between themselves, French was the working language of the Columbia Adventure and little was likely to move on Columbia or New Caledonian waters unless orders were understood by the transcontinental *voyageurs.*[2] The fur trade was a hard life, but at least it could sing.

After the shabby fort at the wide, gray mouth of the Columbia passed into the possession of the British company, furs still had to be collected inland and moved downstream to the shipping port: goods offloaded from ships had to be paddled, rowed, poled, towed, or packed hundreds

1 It may seem presumptuous to impose a few words of the operational language of the North West Company on the Pacific Slope during the two decades of its operation. It is a way of reminding the reader that French was the language echoing behind most events.

2 Wallace, ed., *Documents of North West Company*, 256. At the 1808 NWC Fort William annual meeting, a fund was proposed for "the unfortunate Case of many Old Voyageurs lately discharged from the Companys Service, who have no means of Support being too Old and Infirm to work in Lower Canada."

of miles upstream to posts in the Salish and Kutenai heartland or as far north as distant New Caledonia. The Columbia was not the river we know today, tamed by long ponds of slack water between the dams. Gathering its power from the tributary waters of the Pacific Northwest, it was a wild, vigorous force, subject to spring freshets and fall lows. Boat drivers were never certain of what challenge they would meet around the next bend of the river.

The romantic careers of some boatmen began in the Montreal and Trois Riviers hiring halls and became very real when they skirted the steep, rocky cliffs along the north side of Lake Superior. When a storm came up there was no place to land a thirty-six foot long Montreal cargo canoe. Across the Rocky Mountains, *voyageurs* found the pinched, dark cleft of the Columbia River gorge just as intimidating when they were forced pass the plunging channels of *Les Dalles* and frothing *Cascades.*

Returning upriver with laden canoes, the terrain changed from thick forests lining the deep gorge to arid sagebrush desert. The Long Narrows was a five mile stretch of fast water 194 river miles from Fort George, but boatmen didn't start counting paddle strokes until the boat brigades passed the mouths of the Umatilla, Walla Walla, and Snake rivers where local tribes could be aggressive. Paddling under the landmark White Bluffs north of present Tri-Cities and stemming the Priest Rapids, canoes entered the ancient channel where the river cut deep through the Columbia plateau basalts. Paddlers sweating against the current in that bake oven beneath the cliffs between present Vantage to Wenatchee must have welcomed any shade. Feeling oppressed, they sang their familiar boat songs, like sailor's sea shanties that echoed in French from the rocks. Somehow they lined up the *Petit Dalles* by pulling the boat with tracking lines. Beyond, the dangerous *Dalles des Mort* would account for several deaths until only light express canoes went as far upstream as the Boat Encampment.

The water craft used on the Columbia River appear to have evolved from David Thompson's innovative cedar plank canoe. Initially disappointed by Jaco Finlay's failure to build a canoe large enough for use on the upper river, he soon found that birch bark used east of the mountains didn't grow on the west slope. Although the Lower Lake Kutenai and others found enough bark to make their peculiar sturgeon-nosed craft, those fragile boats were unsuited to voyaging on an unknown river.[3]

Searching for suitable birch bark led to extremes. "[T]o guard against a failure in this fanciful article, a stock of it was shipped at Montreal for London, and from thence conveyed around Cape Horn for their establishment at Fort George."[4] Due to the lack of material, Thompson and his boat builders learned to lash together a traditional canoe frame. But instead of a bark skin, they split out thin boards of cedar, dressed them with a curved knife, and laced them together with spruce roots. The inevitable cracks were filled with tree gum (pitch) and grease, and often repaired.

The Astorians had purchased an Indian carved cedar canoe to follow Thompson up the Columbia. Later they switched to planked boats like his, or sometimes ingloriously described heavy barges made from sawn timber.[5] Those larger, more substantial *bateaux* could be paddled, but were stiff enough to be rowed. Astorian John Clarke took a barge inland and left it at the mouth of the Snake where local tribesmen broke it up for the nails. On April 4, 1814, when returning Astorians accompanied the upriver supply brigade, Alexander Henry carefully distinguished between four bark and six wooden canoes. Four years later Alexander Ross, who used the term "boats," also mentioned a barge at Fort Nez Perces.

Truth is, those craft became so much a part of trader's lives that they were rarely described in detail, while the dramatic folklore of the many unforgiving rapids was often repeated. Some voyageurs, like Ignace the Iroquois, never learned to swim. He was lucky when a whirlpool cast him out of the rapids, to be saved by his companions. Choke points had to be portaged barefoot through cactus and deadly rattlesnakes, while unarmed paddlers worried about sullen natives who could explode in unforeseen violence.

The inland business of the North West Company, conducted on the main stream of a great continental river, remained a demanding test of human endurance for years. It was not distance but altitude that tried

3 Journal of the Rocky Mountain House Occurences, 1806–07, October 11, 1806–July 26, 1807, by David Thompson [also Kootenai House B.C. penciled in by someone else], MS, Microreel 2, Series I, Vol 8, DT Book 18 &19; Royal Commonwealth Library recopied version; Thompson notebook 27, in Nisbet, *Mapmaker's Eye*, 91-92.

4 Ross, *Fur Hunters*, 55.

5 Ross, *Fur Hunters*, 111.

voyageurs. Driving boats upstream was a matter of brute strength against 2,200 feet of river rise to reach Thompson's boat encampment. The altitude was only 1,617 feet at Kettle Falls, which was as high as heavily laden boats were rowed. Only lightly laden express canoes carried expresses to the foot of the Athabaska Pass, and Columbia River traffic continued for another decade.

> The brigade of porters of the north arrived at Vancouver on the 6th of June 1839 conducting nine bateaux loaded with merchandise. It came from the different posts in the north located on the Fraser River, tributary of the Thompson River [although in fact the reverse is true]. The number of porters was about fifty-seven, and a good number of them had been left to guard the posts. For the most part they are married according to the fashion of the country, and have their families distributed in the forts of which mention has just been made. That class of men is very dissolute, and the missionaries greatly dread their presence in the midst of the growing Christianity of Vancouver.[6]

The men who drove those heavily laden boats were experienced French Canadians or transplanted Iroquois whose past experience made them capable of navigating the dangerous waters of the Columbia River and its tributaries. Steersmen might use a nine-foot-long paddle to lever a weighty boat past hungry rocks, and the bowman poised another oversize paddle to help pull the bow around, fend off rocks, or pry loose from unforgiving water pressure. Middlemen provided the power and momentum while putting their faith in the skill of the master voyageurs.

Most NWC engagés had been the sons of habitant families living on long, narrow concessions (most with water frontage) along the lower St. Lawrence River. Following the example of fathers, brothers, or neighbors, they engaged to paddle the voyageur mainline and the long climb up the Saskatchewan River. Having already crossed the continent in a series of contracts renewed ever farther from their homes, most never went back.

Although many Astorians were also drawn from the same Canadian background, it had taken them eighteen months by way of the Missouri and Snake Rivers to get to the mouth of the Columbia. In the combined list of 176 persons on the Columbia during 1813–14, the Pacific Fur Company log recorded 110 boatmen to 60 proprietors, clerks, interpreters,

---

6 Landerholm, ed., *Notices & Voyages of the Famed Quebec Mission*, 10, 28.

tradesmen, a boy, and a fool.[7] Sixty-six of those boatmen were Nor'westers; forty-four were Astorians willing to stay on to stem *les Cascades et les Dalles* and earn the right to call themselves voyageurs.

There were also contracted Hawaiians known in the northwest as Kanakas, hired as laborers or boatmen in their island homeland and shipped to the Columbia by the Pacific Fur Company or North West Company. They were voyagers of another kind whose ancestors navigated the vast, empty Pacific Ocean on sailing rafts to populate widely dispersed volcanic islands. Their bodies were acclimated to warm waters and easy living. The only snow they knew was on the top of a volcano. They must have been shocked to come ashore in a cold, driving northwest rain. Natural paddlers and good workmen, they were rarely mentioned as beaver trappers.

Despite the focus to this point on transport and transporters, the fur trade west of the Rocky Mountains began as a sedentary operation reflecting old habits that expected tribal hunters to come to a post. David Thompson located Kootenae House on a headwaters lake of the Columbia which was left behind when operations moved south to a more promising area to trade along the Clark Fork of the great river. Kullyspell and Saleesh Houses lasted longer as outposts to what became Spokane House. Rehired to build it, Jaco Finlay astutely selected a nice meadow on a peninsula formed by the confluence of the Spokane and Little Spokane Rivers a few miles below Spokane Falls where salmon swarmed and tribes came long distances to take them. A deep and dangerous gorge denied boats, but the focus at that time was the triangular connection to the Clark Fork, Spokane, and the Kettle Falls. Two years later John Clarke led a large party of Astorians to locate nearby and compete with the NWC and its dependencies, the Flatheads and Kutenai posts.

Spokane soon developed a reputation as the gem of the inland trade empire. To escape the boils around Fort George, J. G. McTavish usually returned upriver. Cox described spending a pleasant summer there, where "in addition to a fine crop of potatoes, we reared a quantity of excellent esculents. The soil was deep and rich: a few melons and cucumbers, which we had put down, throve admirably." The kitchen garden so

---

7 Jones, ed., *Annals of Astoria*, 226-37. Significantly, only thirteen men were designated as hunters, and some of those were also available as boatmen. The fool was a deranged American who had been lost and lived among tribesmen before showing up at Astoria.

impressed local Indians that a guard had to be posted at night to discourage visits that might "prevent their women from collecting their own country fruits and roots in the autumn, and thereby render them lazy."[8]

Alexander Ross, who already had an Okanogan wife, appears to have only visited Spokane House once, and returned impressed when he wrote, "There was a ballroom, and no females in the land so fair to look upon as the nymphs of Spokane. No damsels could dance so gracefully as they; none so attractive. But Spokane House was not celebrated for fine women only, there were fine horses also."[9]

After the PFC was eliminated, outfits going from Okanogan to Spokane were packed on horses and carried overland. That pack trail left the south side of the Columbia across from the mouth of the Okanogan River and ran east through a rocky and barren country approximately 136 miles (Alexander Ross thought the distance was 150 or 160 miles) to Spokane House.[10] The trail from Okanogan to Spokane followed Foster Creek to a descent by way of Barker Canyon into the steep basalt gash of the Upper Grand Coulee. Dropping down two or three hundred feet brought the pack trains to a mile-wide bottom studded with curious rocky islands carved by ancient floods. The laboring horses ascended what is now named Northrupt Canyon to an elevated plain desolate of wood and water, and lashed by snowstorms in winter. From the first sheltering clump of trees it was still a seven day march to the trading post located on the Little Spokane River.

Ross Cox's attention to dates of departure and arrival provide a schedule of inland business operations and a sense of what was required of struggling packers. He and Russell Farnham built their 1812 winter house on the Clark Fork about twenty miles upstream from the present Idaho/Montana boundary, but still forty miles short of old Saleesh House where Finnan McDonald traded.[11] By July 1813 Cox had become a Nor'wester and Joseph LaRocque sent him to James McMillan at the

8 Cox, *Columbia River*, 213.

9 Ross, *Fur Hunters*, 96. Every writer since seems to have fastened on and repeated those lines.

10 Ross, *First Settlers*, 217.

11 Cox, *Columbia River*, 130-31. That would have been near where road 56 joins highway 200, but their reason for stopping there isn't explained.

Flatheads post with the warning that "if they were reduced to eating horses, those chosen ought to be the worst."[12]

In fall 1814 Alexander Ross and Cox made a horse buying expedition to the Yakama country and they obtained twenty-five horses, part of a herd of fifty-five that Cox drove overland to Spokane. Those that escaped being eaten during the winter would carry returns back to the shipping point. The journalist described the packtrain leaving from Okanogan on December 13:

> The party consisted, besides, of Messrs [Alexander] Stewart, M'Tavish, M'Millan and Montour; with twenty one Canadians, and four Sandwich Islanders. We had twenty-six loaded horses; and in addition to our ordinary stock of provisions, we purchased forty dogs from the natives at Okanogan, which were killed, after we had crossed the river, and formed part of the loading. The cold was intense, and the ground covered with ten to twelve inches of snow. This necessarily impeded our progress, and prevented us from advancing more than twelve miles a day.[13]

On the evening of December 16, as they neared their destination, a heavy storm struck, obscuring the trail. In the bitter cold the pack train scattered. Cox and McTavish dug a snow cave and survived the night, although one horse froze to death and two Sandwich Islanders were frost bitten. When they caught up to the train, the two men found the rest of the party cozily camped in the sheltering pines and teasing Stewart that they had eaten his pet dog.

Cox continued from Spokane with eight men and twelve loaded horses, following the thickly wooded trail and losing two horses due to exhaustion from the depth of snow. They arrived at Saleesh House just in time to spend Christmas with James McMillan and his family. But when Nicholas Montour received an outfit for the Kutenai trade, he still faced a cold return to his post located a bit above where Fisher Creek came into what is now labeled the Kootenay River. After a previous duel with his PFC opponent Benjamin Pillet, Montour may have been unopposed.

12 Perhaps that was banter between clerks rather than an order. Or maybe literary exageration, as there was a market for books. Franchère published in 1820 and then an English translation in 1840. Cox published next, in 1831, followed by a New York edition the next year. Alexander Ross brought out *First Settlers* in 1844, followed by his *Fur Hunters* in 1855. All those authors had plenty of time to improve on a good story.

13 Cox, *Columbia River*, 206.

Astorians trailing David Thompson reached the mouth of the Okanogan River where they left the clerk Alexander Ross and his dog, before going on to Kamloops. Ross found Okanogan, surrounded by high barren hills that cut off the view, a dreary and claustrophobic place. Ross was not alone in that sentiment. Clerk Joseph LaRocque stationed there during the 1813–14 winter found it a horribly dull place where half of his men were Canadians and half Sandwich Islanders. The library was wretched and there was no chance to have his own books until the next year, and unless his friends at Spokane sent a few volumes, "I shall absolutely die of *ennui*."

> The Indians here are incontestably the most indolent rascals, I ever met: and I assure you it requires no small degree of authority, with the few men I have, to keep them in order. Montignier left me on the 23rd of December to proceed to Mr. McDonald at Kamloops. On his way he was attacked by the Indians at Okanogan Lake, and robbed of a number of horses…I have not made a pack of beaver. The lazy Indians won't work; and as for the [Hawaiians], they know as much about trapping as the monks of *La Trappe*.[14]

To command, control, and exploit the Columbia as an outlet to a trade in China, the North West Company stitched together a complex transport system from the Fraser River through Kamloops to Okanogan. "The lifeline of the Oregon Country [was] a minimal construction of nodes and circuits intended to facilitate trade in an isolated corner of the world and to make connections to distant managers and markets."[15]

However disappointing the local trade may have been, Okanogan became the riverside transfer point where cargoes from northern trading posts were melded with those coming down from the Clark Fork.[16] Traveling from Spokane to Okanogan at the end of May 1814, the packers met parties from Kamloops and the Fraser River. Their relatively short trip to and from Spokane was easy compared to what faced packers and horses on the trail to Kamloops. In 1813, after taking the first steps toward buying out the competition, J. G. McTavish had sent the clerk Joseph

14 La Rocque to Cox, Okanogan, February 1814 as cited in Cox, *Columbia River*, 145.

15 Gibson, *The Lifeline of the Oregon Country*, quoting R. C. Harris and H. R. Hatfield, *Old Pack Trails in the Cascade Wilderness* (Summerland, B.C.: Okanogan Similkameen Parks Society, 1982).

16 Taken from Gibson, *Lifeline of the Oregon Country*; Cox, *Columbia River*, and the two books of Alexander Ross.

LaRocque and two Fraser River men from Spokane on a long detour in the hope they would catch the winter express going east to headquarters and then swing back to Spokane by way of the Fraser River. They made it to Stuart Lake by early November 1813, and after wintering in New Caledonia, started with letters to the Columbia.[17] LaRocque retraced the combination horseback and water trail that John Stuart had recently laid out to Okanogan, where he met Finnan McDonald and family who had been reassigned to Kamloops on the Thompson River.

But the transportation network of the Northwest was a challenge to a rain-soaked packer after a load turned under the belly of an emaciated horse, whose rock-worn hoof was planted on the toe of his moccasin. Clerks amused themselves assigning descriptive names to the half-broken ponies they rode; *Le gris le Galeux, La Guele de travers, La Crême de la petite Chienne.* Packers named their animals with oaths and refrained from becoming too close to a horse they might have to eat.

New Caledonia's supply brigades followed the intricate route first traversed by Nor'wester John Stuart. Going north to the end of navigation on the Okanogan River, the New Caledonia boats off-loaded cargo to horses. Although the numbers varied from year to year, normally twenty horses were needed for the relatively short trip to Kamloops, and eighty to one hundred horses for the longer New Caledonia haul.[18] Many animals were purchased from Yakama, Nez Perce, or Cayuse herds and driven overland to Okanogan.[19] Finnan McDonald described the difficulties of buying animals:

> The Day we arrived At M^r [Alexander] Ross is [Ross's] fort he Left it the Morning the Nex Day Mr Ross start Horse Back with M^r [Ross] Cox and part of the Men to trade Horses M^r [Joseph] La Roque and sef and the rest of the Men start with Canoes to Overtake Mr Ross which we Camp in the Evening togather and Next Morning [he] Cut of [off] troe [through] the Mountain to the Yakama River—We war 19 Days on our Voyage and onley the Half of the Number of Horses that We exspect to trade not so Luckley is [as] we exspect to be—[20]

17 Lamb, ed., *Sixteen Years in the Indian Country*, 165-66.

18 Gibson, *Lifeline of the Oregon Country*, 172; Merk, ed., *Fur Trade and Empire*, 255-56.

19 Gibson, *Lifeline of the Oregon Country*, 171-72.

20 Finnan McDonald to unknown—probably J. G. McTavish, Kamloops, September 12, 1815, HBCA, F.3/2, fos. 125-26.

The inability to obtain horses from several tribes had frustrated the Pacific Fur Company plan to evacuate Astoria and pack the property overland to St. Louis. Later the North West Company had better success obtaining unshod horses from the herds of those standoffish breeders. Many animals were driven approximately 150 miles across the rocky plateau country and often arrived too jaded or footsore to continue through Kamloops to Fort Alexandria on the Fraser River. Others, too wild for packing, were gelded to tone them down and needed time to recover from the operation.[21]

An oversupply of horses was required each year because many died from the harsh northern winter, or from severe overuse on the trail. Driven too hard over the rocky and steep trail between Okanogan and Kamloops, "knocked up" animals were left along the trail to recover or soon die from over-exertion or predators. Those that survived the trip were "a most miserable plight, lean, dreadfully wounded and bruised, and [having] lost their hoofs, are quite lame."[22]

The considerable amount of leather needed for packing and harness gear (called *agrés* by the fur traders) was not available west of the Rockies. Leather and hides were imported from the east side of the mountains and stored at Okanogan. *Apishamores*, or pack-saddle cushions of buffalo hides, were another necessity.[23] Later shipments might require as many as sixty-five elk skins, one skin lodge, and five hundred fathoms of pack cord for use of the New Caledonia and Thompson River brigades.[24] For one season, that might add up to five hundred dressed moose (elk) and deerskins as well as two thousand fathoms of pack cords.[25] Not all of the leather supplies were stored at Okanogan because *agrés* and *apishamores* were needed at the other end of the line (Fort Alexandria) as well.[26]

In the summer two years later, Ross Cox caught a break from constant traveling and stayed at Okanogan to rebuild the post into a fortified place protected by fifteen-foot high palisades and bastions on two corners. Spending a cold winter with snow piled two to three feet deep,

21 Gibson, *Lifeline of the Oregon Country*, 172-75.

22 Thompson's River Post 1841-43, HBCA, E.243/7a, p. 18.

23 Derived from an Algonquian word meaning a skin to sit upon.

24 HBCA, B.97/a/2, fo. 8. Lines were cut from hide to be used to tie pack loads.

25 William Connolly to Chief Factors and Chief Traders of the Northern Department, February 4, 1826, Stuart's Lake Correspondence Book Inwards, 1824-1826, HBCA, D. 4/119, fos. 34d-35.

26 Gibson, *Lifeline of the Oregon Country*, 26-29.

he had little to do except hole up by the fireplace, stare at the snow blocking the parchment-covered windows, and complain.[27] Lonely clerks in "a horribly dull place" without companionship resorted to writing letters, keeping diaries, or counting the days until the arrival of the mail expresses or annual brigades. Their notes, published later, provide much of the data for this reconstruction of the trader's life.

Beyond the palisades, the native people in and about Fort Okanogan lived well. The varieties of food were not only adequate but delicious. Salmon, both fresh and dried, supplied the yearly staple, supplemented with sturgeon, suckers, eels, trout, and roe. The fishery was augmented with various nutritious root crops. In the fall women harvested a variety of berries which, mixed with dried salmon, made tasty winter pemmican, and during the fall and winter added deer meat or an occasional elk to the diet. On special occasions, a mountain goat might go into the always bubbling pot. But now, instead of cooking with heated stones dropped into a tight woven basket, women used trade utensils to prepare meals.

Indian men had to be encouraged to trap or snipe unwary animals or laboriously dig beaver families out of their tangled stick and mud dens. Native hunters were rarely willing to endure that cold, hard chore in order to get the few trade items they desired. Incorporated into a new trading system, tribes found just as rewarding markets for dried fish, meat, and horses.

Each season brought something new, keeping the cycle of the annual tribal round filled with purposeful activity. Natives remembered and took pleasure and meaning through their games and oral recitals. Those memories were recovered from knotted strings and repeated around the winter fires. With plenty to do in the routines of daily existence, and with extensive kinship ties to surrounding villages, an elaborate web of social exchanges filled the year and preserved their traditions.[28]

Because of the negative impression left on many a sojourning fur trader, it is surprising to realize that Fort Okanogan was the longest continuously occupied location on the main stem of the Columbia, serving the fur trade for nearly half a century. Longevity was due to its importance as a key site for facilitating communications and trans-shipping cargoes.

---

27 Ross, *Adventures*, 152; Cox, *Columbia River* (1957), 145; McDonald, *Fur Trade Letters*, 74.

28 An excellent description of the various Salishan peoples surrounding Fort Okanogan is in Jay Miller, "Middle Columbia River Salishans," in *Handbook of North American Indians*, vol. 12, Plateau (Washington, 1998), 253-70.

Okanogan became the anchor of the "Lifeline of the Oregon Country," a now-essential horse brigade trail and boat system carrying returns to the sea.

Life at Kamloops, on the north end of the connection to Okanogan, was another matter. After buying Yakama ponies, the Finnan McDonald family proceeded to Kamloops where they passed two winters. In spring 1815 McDonald wrote a letter to J. G. McTavish:

> Montagney just arived from the upper Part of Frasure River that they Call Quisnil is [Quesnel's] River[29] his trade not neare so grate as we Exspect it to Be—I was whole Mont a way [whole month away] this Summer Made onley 40 od Skins with fue Salmon and Lost 17 Skins on My trip[30] those nasion [nation] they the porest set that Even I Had seane sence I Came in the Cuntre [country] hardley aney to Cover ther Bodey start [stark] nakit Seames to be the Slaves of all nasion and the fue skins they had they Exspect to gate [get] the Divel [devil] and all it [of them] torable [tolerable] found [fond] of Smokeing.[31]

Finnan did not respond well to the Thompson and Fraser River tribes, whose language he didn't understand and whose activities he mistrusted.

> [O]n this [trip] we got one of our Horses stold which we got Back the Horse and the Scoundril got good Beating for his Plasure rideing which we resived the Nouse [news] that those Indians is to Steale our Horse's and to kill our selves which they ar raskils anouf to doe all that—

New Caledonian provisions failed to satisfy those accustomed to a diet of dried buffalo meat and with occasional imported delicacies. Kamloops was salmon country, where jaded traders complained about having to eat dried split "shingles." The disappointing salmon run of 1813–14 was noticeably improved when McDonald recorded:

---

29 The Quesnel River is a good 250 miles from Kamloops, but traders were stationed even higher. Lamb, ed., *Sixteen Years*, 174.

30 Ross returned to his post among the She-whaps in August 1815 but does not mention McDonald. Charette, the summer master who went six days up the Fraser from Kamloops, had been murdered during Ross's absence, but McDonald made no mention of that. Ross, *Fur Hunters*, 48.

31 Using Finnan's letters as a base line seems risky in the face of the two usually accepted sources; Alexander Ross and Ross Cox. However Finnan was writing in the moment with no reason to color his letter to J. G. McTavish, while Ross and Cox wrote from memory some years after the fact.

> I am to Start to Morough Morning up the Nort Branch[32] for Salmon I Exspect to Be Back in in three Days—his is profitable year to the Indians for salmon Sin [Since] 5 years ago there was not somaney [so many] salmon here the river is alived with salmon which Exspect Plenty Salmon round about here without going to Frasure river for they ar grate rocks which will Make them More frindley another year - We got Made Store of 40 feet Long & 20 Brode [broad] & House 26 By 20 as much is [as] the Men Could Doe By voyageing and Makeing Canoes Labloe [Labor] Lost the Whole Summer Makeing 2 Canoes which will Be radey in the Course of 4 or 5 Days[33] he Lost good Deale of time rise-ing Burch Rind By the Hight of the Water in the Lac Grounds

Writing in fall 1815, Finnan expressed his frustration

> I am Vary Sorey that I am not going down to the Sey [sea] this Fall rather then Stay here... I have a nosion [notion] in My heade to Leave this Part of the Cuntre I am triard of Eating Rottin Salmon Sence 4 years agoe that I am in this Cursed part of the Cuntre Be sides other things that is Laying on me which M^r [James] McMillin will tel you I may say that I am averey one is [everyone's] foot Bole...I wood Be varey happy if you Could take me out of this Bad Place.[34]

However, Finnan had to spend another winter at Kamloops before he took his family to Spokane House where his wife Peggy would be nearer her Pend Oreille relatives.

Over those years while Montreal managers struggled with a mis-guided business plan and money-losing ships sailing the Pacific, an experienced cadre of clerk/traders, engagés, and freemen conducted the fur trade. Many developed good connections to tribesmen because they had married their daughters *a la façon du pays*. The downstream gentlemen who came to the Fort William summer gathering tried to discourage those arrangements, not from moral high ground but because the addition of women and inevitable offspring were seen as a burden on business.

Partners were exempted from this restriction. David Thompson and one of his men initially brought their wives and children west of the mountains. But after the first hungry winter at Kootenae House,

32 The north branch of the Thompson River.

33 No one whose name approximates Labloe can be found on the roster of 1813–14. HBCA, F.4/61, fos. 3-7d.

34 Finnan McDonald to unknown—probably J. G. McTavish, Kamloops, 12th Sep^t 1815, HBCA, F.3/2, fos. 125-26.

Thompson returned his mixed-blood wife, Charlotte Small, to the care of her brother at Boggy Hall below Rocky Mountain House. Thompson's clerk, James McMillan, joined the NWC in 1803–04 and had a child born on the Saskatchewan and two children born in the Columbia Department when he was made a Chief Trader in 1821.[35] J. G. McTavish acquired a consort at Spokane House who may have been a daughter of Jaco Finlay and later brought her to Fort George.[36] Sent west of the mountains, Peter Skene Ogden left a country consort at Isle a la Cross who came to Edmonton House looking for him after he married another daughter of the country at Spokane House.

When Alexander Henry was transferred to Fort Vermillion, he brought his Pembina Ojibwa wife and children. In the 1809 list of those living at the post, only his clerk lived alone; twenty-seven of the thirty-nine workmen were married and had sixty-seven children living in ten houses and three tents at the fort. Later, before leaving for the Columbia Department, his family was left under the care of another officer and whether he intended to bring them later cannot be determined. At Fort George, he was disgusted with the exorbitant bride price Duncan McDougall contracted sometime prior to 1814, but was unable to fully pay off until the *Isaac Todd* unloaded goods.[37]

Those were the prerogative of gentleman officers who could afford comforts. But workmen, denied formal relationships, had to find other consolation. Henry's list of those who remained at Fort George that year totaled fifty men, of whom twenty were hospitalized with varying degrees of venereal disease, the consequence of their sexual activity with already infected Chinook women. To avoid infection, officers like the clerks Alexander McKenzie, Angus Bethune, and the unfortunately named Benjamin Clapp, took very young Indian girls.[38] Despite Henry's apparent loyalty to a wife left on the Saskatchewan, he and Donald McTavish had differences over which gentleman was going to "protect" Miss Jane Barnes.

35 Gregory Thomas, "James McMillan," *DCB* 8 (accessed 7/28/2014).
36 Gough, ed., *Alexander Henry*, 2:743-44.
37 Gough, ed., *Alexander Henry*, 2:407-08, 710-11, 732. There was no mention of his family at Fort George, so Henry must have left them on the Saskatchewan.
38 VanKirk, *Many Tender Ties*, 30, 36.

Consorts might be abandoned when the men were transferred to a new duty station; it was "the custom of the country." By winter 1814–15 the Nor'westers had been west of the mountains for seven years. Although Ross Cox skipped over any relationship he might have arranged, he did note that "none of the Columbian [girls] were of a sufficiently mature age." He described the marital arrangements between a young mixed-blood, Pierre Michel, and a seventeen-year-old Spokane girl. Unfortunately for Michel, the bride already had a tribal husband and the release price he was required to pay for her proved expensive.[39]

Brides were taken at a very young age, fourteen or so, to avoid venereal disease, but old enough to have learned women's skills in camp or on the trail that made a husband comfortable. Young Indian girls were called upon to make themselves useful lacing snowshoes or pulling down dead tree branches to fuel the campfire. The food-gathering knowledge their mothers taught them enabled the collection of natural plants for the cooking pot to relieve the monotonous meals of smoked salmon or dried meat. Women on the trail knew how to wrestle a heavy skin lodge up on the back of a pack horse and lash their children on top of it. Babies might be packed, swinging in a basket, from the mother's saddle horn.[40]

The custom of officers putting off a companion when they left the region seems cruel, but that was more of a dilemma for workmen being transferred to another station or discharged. Just as officers found some subordinate to take over support of his "girl," a laborer had to find an associate to assume responsibility of his country wife. The family lineages generated by those arrangements are at times very complex. As an example, the death of clerk Nicholas Montour who crossed the Rocky Mountains before David Thompson seemed to end that name. But the careful Flathead Valley tribal genealogist Gene Felsman discovered that Montour's daughter married two brothers of the large Finlay family and left family associations to 567 descendants.[41] While eastern agents were

39 Cox, *Columbia River*, 142, 194-99, 209-11. No clerk or interpreter of that name appears on the list of the combined companies. Cox, like his contemporary Alexander Ross, may have repeated a good yarn.

40 Juliet Pollard, "The making of the Métis in the Pacific Northwest: Fur Trade Children: Race, Class and Gender," doctoral diss., University of British Columbia, 1990, circle.ubc.ca/handle/2429/30632, accessed Nov. 1, 2012.

41 Personal interview July 5, 2011.

tinkering with long-distance management decisions to increase production of beaver, their western officers and workmen were generating a new community of mixed-blood marriages and Métis children. The future of the Columbia Adventure hinged on the efforts of dedicated clerks who left accounts of their experiences and on the workforce that was absolutely essential to operations then, but is mostly anonymous today.

With competition muffled and inland posts established in strategic locations, Columbia River traffic could expect to run on a schedule. The inland traders and sixty-four men returning upriver on August 5, 1814, found that the punitive expedition of the previous year had failed to pacify the river tribes. Boatmen were not warriors and few were actually armed, which may explain why officers are the ones who usually figure in heroics.

If Cox's highly colored version is believed, a confrontation took place when local Indians intercepted the brigade near the Walla Walla River. On the first of December James Keith, ten clerks, and fifty-four boatmen, including six Sandwich Islanders, found they were facing 180 pugnacious "Chimnapum, Yackaman, Sokulk and Wallah Wallah." A tribesman who attempted to loot Finnan McDonald's canoe was shot and two others were wounded. Keith, who stood firm and negotiated condolence and passage gifts, managed to placate their outraged demands for McDonald's red scalp.[42] Twelve days later the boat brigade reached Okanogan, where McDonald dropped off to return to Kamloops and Keith went on carrying dispatches east.

The downstream boat brigade to Fort George was held until October 24, 1815, awaiting Keith's return from the Fort William meeting. Driving fast in a sluggish river, they reached the depot on November 8 and after just eleven days started back up the Columbia. Mid-November was late in the traveling season and ice stopped Keith's party just above the Cabinet Rapids, miles short of Okanogan. Although hikers were sent on to obtain horses to feed the marooned brigade, the boatmen spent six weeks huddled in a miserable camp until the ice broke in mid-February 1816 and the delayed outfit was finally delivered to Spokane House on March 9.

The Salish country was a dependable source of peltry and the success of the Clark Fork trade continued to depend on the clerks who had helped initiate it. Over the years Finnan McDonald, James McMillan,

42 Cox, *Columbia River*, 194-205.

and Nicholas Montour nurtured mutually profitable relationships with the Spokane, Coeur d'Alene, Pend Oreille, Kalispell, Salish, Lake, and Upper Kutenai Indians. Most of the engages they supervised were "comers and goers," on the move most of the time, traveling up and down the river, bringing up outfits and taking down returns. They wrangled packhorses, ran with dog trains, built boats, and developed more intimate relationships with the tribes by marrying their daughters. Some who were previously treated as half-engagéd men eventually became freemen. That allowed them to trade the peltry they took by self-directed trapping for what they needed to support their families. Few western engages took advantage of the NWC's contractual obligation to transport them to eastern homes that were already receding in memory.

Trapping fur-bearing animals necessitated exploring the tributaries of the Columbia, down to the least rivulet or impounded pond supporting a beaver colony. Pressure on those unsuspecting creatures was intensified because imported eastern Iroquois understood the use steel beaver traps. It is difficult to see why lists of outfits failed to include traps in their inventory. Although David Thompson brought eight guns, he mentions carrying only two traps, valued at twelve skins, in an account of goods he managed to bring from the stranded 1810–11 outfit.[43] Traps were necessary to familiarize native hunters with their use. Thompson mentioned searching for a cache of ice chisels, which suggests that native hunters were still breaking into beaver houses and slaughtering whole families.

Alexander Henry's journal includes a half (pack?) of steel traps in a later list of canoe ladings.[44] The usual chatter about broken traps, iron rings, or snapped chains that characterizes later accounts is missing from early records. Although traps were not among the list of goods the Astorians turned over to the Nor'westers, at some point they had to become an item of the Indian trade. In contrast to necessary business, guns were the hot trade items. Although no traps are invoiced, fifty guns were part of the list of trade items forwarded to the interior in early January 1814.

As the number of trappers increased, most of them were almost-anonymous freemen trappers who answered to no one except themselves, or perhaps to their not-always-submissive Indian wives. By the time the northwest fur trade settled into the pattern it would follow for half a

43 Belyea, ed., *Columbia Journals*, Notes, 255-56.
44 Gough, ed., *Alexander Henry*, 2:668-69, 745, 747.

century, the first mixed-blood children of those unions were getting to be six or seven years old.

Supporting families meant setting traps in the spring creeks along the high mountain side of the Flathead Valley. When easy trapping was exhausted, the hunters looked for willowy places that attracted those fine-furred swimmers, laying scent-baited traps to catch and drown an animal without damaging the fur. In the mornings, if a set was sprung, they carefully peeled off the pelt and ate the naked carcass for breakfast. Their wives scraped and trimmed a skin and lashed it to a circle of bent willow so it would dry into a tradable round. Sometimes a freeman worked with tribal kinsmen to trench, block escape routes, and tear open beaver dens.

Freemen became the unanticipated but essential face of the Columbia Adventure, and, as it would turn out, its critical dependence. Although it is difficult to get much more than a glimpse of individuals who left few written records, recovered details hint that they were more than anonymous background spear carriers to the unfolding fur trade opera. Freemen became the framework upon which more than the Columbia Adventure would be built.

They were also its voice. Supervisors at the posts and clerks in the field, no matter their places of origin, learned to speak French as the operative language in daily operations. Francophone engagés taught their country wives and growing children. Iroquois brought the mission French that they learned in Canada. Used for the first quarter of the nineteenth century in the Pacific Northwest as the functional language, French would persist almost to the present.[45]

As the North West Company matured in the second decade of the nineteenth century, Finnan McDonald, James McMillan, and Nicholas Montour became the old hands in the Salish trade, a life that marked them with a touch of feral that their tribal customers appreciated over the institutional proprieties of corporate gentlemen. Glad to break free of his Kamloops exile, McDonald returned to Spokane House in 1816 and was surprised to be joined by the former Astorian, Donald McKenzie, who had found favor with the Montreal agents.

45 Robert R. Foxcurran and John C. Jackson, "*La Question* Oregon," unpublished monograph.

Chapter Twelve

Reforms and Unconvinced Reformers

No matter what the Montreal and London agents concocted in their downstream offices, the North West Company from the beginning was a partnership of equals, fur traders who spent a good part of their lives traveling hundreds of miles in birch-bark shells and dealing directly with Indian customers. Partnership made them lords of green-log posts and privileged to spending long months in winter darkness, where calculating their financial share of the concern could make them as sullen as hibernating bears. To escape the cost of provisioning their workmen, those parsimonious Scots sent them away, half-engaged, to live with Indians. Traders, engagés, and tribesmen were locked in an inescapable symbiosis.

During a brief week at the annual Fort William rendezvous, the wintering partners were reminded that they were gentlemen with access to a comfortable cluster of accommodations, banquet facilities, and warehouses stocked with imported treats. Those well-deserved regales became less comforting as the uncomplicated old business shifted to complexities of diversification and modern business. A new generation of corporate managers who fancied themselves as executives were making the big decisions in Montreal and leaving the implementation to clerks. Bored journalists recorded the outrageous behavior or colorful foibles of the working class who couldn't read, write, or speak English, who were rarely mentioned in business correspondence. The North West Company interdependent partnership of equals was morphing into a corporation that not all old partners found comfortable.

This was increasingly evident in the distant Pacific Northwest, where the Montreal and London management was months removed from the execution of their expectations. It had taken Alexander Henry four months to arrive at the mouth of the Columbia River from Fort William.[1] And even traveling in a lightly-laden express canoe in spring 1814 only managed to trim a week or so off what was still a six-week canoe voyage from Fort William to Montreal.

The great distance meant the annual Fort William meeting of wintering partners and downstream agents might be their only connection for another year. Returns from shipping and selling a China cargo could drag on for two or more years. The communication gap between the components of the Columbia Adventure forced local proprietors to exercise a good deal of individual initiative. After the takeover of Astoria a number of changes were made somewhat precipitously that had more to do with personalities than with the grubby business of actual trading. The rapid succession of John George McTavish, John McDonald, Alexander Henry, Donald McKenzie, Duncan McDougall, and John George McTavish again, all within a matter of months, suggests an institution that was looking for a cake but cooking an omelet. Moving clerks around to unfamiliar posts during this expansion neglected the proven practice of keeping a trader among the tribesmen who knew and trusted him to deal fairly with them.

Astorians sent to the Columbia had been unfamiliar with the peculiarities of the western tribes, and John Clarke's summary execution of an Indian for an inconsequential theft near the mouth of the Snake River created lasting resentment for brigades moving upstream. Cayuse, Walla Walla, or Nez Perce were horse-people and warriors. Those matters were better left to experienced NWC clerks like Finnan McDonald at Kamloops, James McMillan and Ross Cox at Spokane, and Alexander Ross at Okanogan, all of whom had already learned the delicate art of dissimilation.[2]

It was the downstream managers reviewing shipping profit/loss columns who began seeing cracks in the business plan they had concocted in Montreal. Although the war with the United States was winding down in Lower Canada, and competition with the Hudson's Bay Company was

1 Gough, ed., *Alexander Henry*, 2:609n117.

2 Among the 71 former Pacific Fur Company engagés whose names appear on the "List of People on the Columbia for Winter 1813/14," 25 signed multiple-year contracts with the North West Company while another 11, like Franchère, agreed to serve only until the departure of the brigade the ensuing spring. Five of the eleven of Pacific Fur Company clerks signed contracts with the North West Company. HBCA, F.4/61, fos. 6-7d.

intensifying, the Columbia Adventure was distanced from those distractions. They had effectively mooted the competition with Astorians, but where was the increase in returns that would realize the investment?

If losses were the consequence of disharmony among the partners at Fort George, as some believed, new leadership was needed. Profitability might be restored if beaver, which in theory carried good value, could be increased significantly. But that required finding a more efficient way to extract peltry from the Columbia drainage basin. Although peltry from the Salish country was steady, beaver were not as plentiful as they had been and waiting for unmotivated Indian hunters or undependable free trappers was not meeting NWC needs. Reorganizing the Columbia Department called for the implementation of new strategies in three areas: shipping, productivity, and leadership. For the first concern, management found the man they needed in James Keith.

The brothers James and George Keith came to Montreal early in the century as apprentice clerks for Forsyth, Richardson and Company, one of the participants in the rival New North West Company. James Keith had served in the upper Churchill River district until the 1804 merger with the North West Company. At the Fort William meeting in July 1813 he was sent to the Columbia Department with expectations for advancement a clerk could not refuse. But his country wife, the daughter of the pioneer trader Jean Baptiste Cadot, was pregnant. She and their two-year-old daughter could not accompany him. What that meant to a responsible man like Keith was starkly noted in an entry in his memorandum book marked Private.[3]

> Augt 21st - 1809 Commenced Cohabitation
> Septr 11th - 1811 Helen born
> June 7th - 1813 Discontinued Cohabitat^{n}
> Jany 1st - 1814 Mary born—

Before leaving Fort William, Keith took the example of his traveling companion Alexander Henry and drew up a will. In case of a disaster, his family would be under the care of his brother, George Keith.[4]

3 James Keith Memoranda Book, James Keith Estate Papers, National Archives of Canada, Ottawa, A-676, A3 (NAC James Keith Papers); UM, Baby Collection, u/5929. It is necessary to distinguish between the James Keith Papers kept at the National Archives of Canada (NAC James Keith Papers) and those found in the Special Collections Library of the University of Aberdeen (UA James Keith Papers).

4 Gough, ed., *Alexander Henry*, 1:lxiii-lxv, lxvii-lxxi, 103, 109.

Driving up the lower Saskatchewan with Henry, another clerk Alexander Stewart, and thirteen men in two light canoes, the Nor'westers overtook the HBC's Edmonton master, James Bird. Around the evening campfire, Keith overheard Henry telling the rival trader that the Columbia Adventure now had a hundred men, including officers west of the mountains who expected to take possession of the American settlements there. But that would cost the NWC £50,000 and Henry, as a proprietor, admitted dim expectations "notwithstanding the high opinion their agents had formed of the purchase."[5] Keith realized that his new job would not be easy, but there was no going back when the party arrived at Fort George on November 15.

Riding high on his recent accomplishment of eliminating Astorians, John George McTavish was only four years older than Keith and described him as a "stiff, formal good fellow." Years later, others would characterize Keith as "the most faultless member of the Fur Trade" and a "scrupulously correct, honorable man of serious turn of mind who would not to save life or fortune...do what he considered an improper thing."[6] Keith had the makings of a perfect corporate man, but it would be a mistake to dismiss him as a prissy bookkeeper, just the sort to run a downstream depot while real traders worked in the field. Educated and trained for business, he had already traded a skin and knew how to deal with Indians. Keith made it a habit to keep notes and observations in a private memorandum book that became the insightful, information-crammed log of Fort George.

After the turn of the year 1814, Keith and Stewart were sent east with the express carrying news of the arrival and departure of *HMS Racoon.* Stewart would stay at Spokane and Keith go on to old Kootenae House. From there four men were to be sent across Howse Pass with dispatches in time to catch the winter express to headquarters.[7] The two clerks started out with fifteen men in two canoes carrying, along with other trade goods, fifty new guns to sell to Spokane customers. Along the way two brigades returning downstream warned them to be on guard passing the Cascades. Despite precautions, there was an encounter in

5 Edmonton Journal, HBCA, B60/a/12, fol.1d.

6 D. P. De T. Glazebrook, *The Hargrave Correspondence 1821–1843* (Toronto: The Champlain Society, 1938), 1, as cited in Glydwr Williams, ed., *Hudson's Bay Miscellany, 1670-1870* (Winnipeg: Hudson's Bay Record Society, 1975), 177.

7 Gough, ed., *Alexander Henry*, 2:632, 638,668-69.

which Stewart was seriously wounded by an arrow. Keith bravely rescued another wounded man, but with no hope of continuing or recovering abandoned property, the party fled back downstream.

The incident prompted the Fort George officers to organize a punitive expedition to recover the property. Keith spent the rest of the winter at Oak Point catching sturgeon to feed the large number of men waiting for the *Isaac Todd* to arrive. In spring 1814 the brigade started upriver, carrying returning Astorians with John McDonald and Donald McKenzie riding in the first boat. Keith brought up the rear in a tenth wooden boat carrying a "wheel carriage."[8]

During the voyage Keith had opportunities to become acquainted with the former Astorian McKenzie, with whom his future would intertwined. They were about the same age and similar experience. If Keith formed an opinion that McKenzie was not as principled as he might be, that was something a gentleman properly kept to himself.

The dispatches delivered to the wintering partners and downstream agents meeting at Fort William in July confirmed that even if the price for buying out the Astorians was a steal, the cost gobbled up about a third of NWC operating capital as the management was also facing an expected loss of £15,000 on its *Isaac Todd* adventure to the Columbia River. Because of the setback, McTavish, McGillivray and Company were desperately looking for another way to generate operating funds. Older partners felt that the downstream agents were dabbling in unfamiliar waters. The projected costs of purchasing three vessels, providing for captains and crews, buying sea stores, licenses, import and export duties, fees, and other expenses would not be offset by the value of Russian seal skins or baubles sold to Californians.

It was small comfort that after testing the western fur trade for just one season, the Hudson's Bay Company decided that it wasn't worth the trouble of pursuing. Some NWC partners viewed the beaver hunt as their best hope of expanding into the China market. At the Fort William meeting Simon McGillivray induced the partners to re-appoint "Jno Geo McTavish Chief of the Columbia Department with powers to give him confidence & secure him against cabal" for another year.[9] Just

8 Gough, ed., *Alexander Henry*, 2:747. Henry offers no explanation for this unusual carriage which may have mounted a small canon.

9 Morrison, ed., *The North West Company in Rebellion*, 19, 21, 24, 28, 32; William McGillivray to J. G. McTavish, Montreal, 19 June 1815, HBCA, F.3/2, fos. 123-24.

who made up that cabal is uncertain but James Keith wrote several letters to his friend and mentor, John Richardson, expressing his thoughts on how the business might be improved. It was a whole year later before Richardson replied:

> I have had the pleasure to receive your esteemed favor of 26th March, 30th April & 30th July 1814,[10] with your Memorandum regarding the N.W. Coast &c: all of which I have perused with great satisfaction, as they afford a body of clear and instructive information seldom to be met with—Your observations and reflexions are to my mind convincing—I pretend not to be a proper judge of the best course to be pursued in the Columbia Trade, but as peace with the States was concluded last Decembr at Ghent and ratified at Washington in February, permanent arrangements of some kind, can now be made in greater security—There is nothing in the Treaty of peace about the N.W. Coast or Country beyond the Rocky Mountains, therefore the Trade will be left to be pursued by both Nations.[11]

After venting his concerns to a supportive friend, Keith returned to Fort George with the promise of a partner's share as soon as an opening was available. That could happen sooner than expected. Upon arriving, he learned that five and a half weeks after he left with the express confirming the arrival of the *Isaac Todd*, Alexander Henry and Donald McTavish drowned crossing the lower Columbia. As the only surviving partner, McTavish remained in command of the Columbia Department and delegated Keith to carry the 1815 dispatches as far as Rainy Lake. There the much traveled clerk understood that he would inherit the management of the Columbia next year when McTavish finally returned east.[12]

As the express canoe surged through the water, Keith realized he would inherit an uneasy situation and upon arriving at Fort George, he wrote a clear-headed evaluation of the state of Columbia affairs. William

10 It is likely Keith wrote the first two of these while at Fort George, and the third while attending the summer meetings at Fort William. Keith informed Richardson of the arrival of the *Isaac Todd,* but he left Fort George too early to know of the drowning of Henry and McTavish in the Columbia River on May 22, 1814.

11 John Richardson to James Keith, Montreal, June 1, 1815, James Keith Papers, UA. When Richardson wrote he must have been unaware that Captain Black, of the H.M.S. *Racoon*, had taken possession of the Columbia in the name of the British government.

12 William McGillivray to J. G. McTavish, Montreal, June 19, 1815, HBCA, F.3/2, fos. 123-24.

McGillivray must have been dismayed when he received it, as in his reply, he snorted

> I observe you had in part made up your mind that either the Business of the Columbia was to be given up or an arrangement entered into with M[r] Astor—the latter was immediately attempted after my Brothers return to Mont[l] but without effect—the whole or a part was offered to him but he was too unreasonable—as to giving it up altogether we were loath to do it after sinking so much money, without trying another experiment—and honor the arrangement with M[r] Donald M[c]Kenzie - which combined with the manner in which the Furs will in future be disposed of, I think promises a safe Business, if not a profitable one.[13]

When James Keith replaced McTavish as proprietor in charge of the Columbia Department in spring 1816, he already knew that he would not be acting alone. William McGillivray had already explained to McTavish:

> We have entered in Engagements with M[r] [Donald] M[c]Kenzie for the remainder of the present Concern—by which he holds an Interest in all the Business to be transacted on the Columbia, & we expect chiefly by this means to introduce a system of trapping & hunting by the Companys Engagees & servants, *which will render us independent in a great measure of the natives*—This is an experiment of course, and if in three years it does not succeed we shall have to give up the whole—but anything is better than the old system—[14]

Among McGillivray's complaints was that "the Partners of the North West Company do not understand the management of ships or Captains," but Keith knew that it was the agents who failed to grasp the limitations of the China market which no amount of their own tinkering would solve.[15] The optimistic expectation of a good return after costs failed to grasp the risk of a venture in world trade based on a single, specific commodity. Astor's adventures to China were more successful than were those of the NWC because he sent a diversity of goods that would

13 McGillivray to Keith, Fort William, July 28, 1816, James Keith Papers, UA.

14 McGillivray to J. G. McTavish, Montreal, June 19, 1815, HBCA, F.3/2, fos. 123-24; McTavish, McGillivrays & R. MacKenzie to Keith, Montreal, April 28, 1816, UO, Davidson & Garden mss 2769/I/57/4.

15 William McGillivray to J. G. McTavish, letter dated Montreal April 28, 1816, North West Company Correspondence, 1800-1827, HBCA, F.3/2, fos. 129-130d.

sell in Canton. It should have been obvious to those "Directors" how difficult it would be to market beaver in a place that did not make felt hats.[16]

Keith was just getting settled into his new responsibilities at Fort George in September 1816 when the former Astorian McKenzie returned to the Columbia. It had been two years since he had disappeared into the upper Columbia River mists. After delivering the documents on the sale of Astoria to John Jacob Astor in New York, Donald McKenzie had headed north to see what he could salvage for his own future among the Montreal interests. The arrangement he concocted with McTavish, McGillivray & Company hired McKenzie for three years as their special agent to increase beaver production. The wintering partners had not been consulted and McKenzie would not have the status of a partner. Although he returned to the Columbia with a mandate to take over the conduct of the inland business, he also carried a reputation of meddling with the status quo.

Donald McKenzie came from Scotland at the age of seventeen to join his brothers, Roderick and James, in the service of the North West Company. After spending eight years stalled in the capacity of a clerk, he had considered joining another ambitious Nor'wester, Colin Robertson, in a scheme to lead a rival Hudson's Bay Company party from Montreal to beaver-productive Athabaska. When Robertson's scheme foundered, McKenzie turned his ambition south and accepted a partnership in John Jacob Astor's Pacific Fur Company.

Using an insider's understanding of the Montreal labor pool, McKenzie guided the St. Louis storekeeper Wilson Price Hunt through hiring voyageurs at Montreal and Michilimackinac. After a long overland hike and a disastrous trial of floating the Snake River, the starving expedition disintegrated. McKenzie, fellow partner Robert McClellan, and seven men hiking north toward the Columbia were drawn into the desolate depths of the great canyon of that river (present Hell's Canyon). Finally climbing out to the Little Salmon River, the starving party was fed by indulgent Nez Perce and guided to connections that brought them to Astoria on January 18, 1812.[17]

16 This supposes that after refusing to recognize that pomposity, the wintering partners were still testy.

17 Jones, ed., *Annals of Astoria*, 67-68.

After recovering from the overland ordeal, McKenzie made a brief exploration into the Willamette River Valley as far south as the tributary now bearing his name. His second foray up the Columbia and Snake Rivers reached the place where the Clearwater River came in (near present Lewiston, Idaho) in August 1812. McKenzie intended to establish a provision and horse-buying post, but instead of improving on the good relationship with tribesmen who had recently rescued him from disaster, McKenzie found the Nez Perce indifferent customers and a "rascally tribe."[18]

After building a house to shelter the men and outfit, McKenzie had time for a pre-Christmas visit to fellow Astorian John Clarke at Spokane House. He was still there when news of war between Great Britain and the United States arrived. Astoria had to be warned. Racing back to his Clearwater post, McKenzie hastily had the untraded outfit buried beneath the floorboards, and then burned the house so the ashes would conceal the cache. Although his return downstream to warn his associates seems a bit hysterical, the decision made by Duncan McDougal and McKenzie to abandon Astoria and retreat to the interior was not made in haste. It was twelve days before the bad news of war was entered in the post log. Despite the perceived danger of a British attack, McKenzie and a lightly equipped party did not leave to return to the abandoned Clearwater location until the end of March.

McKenzie arrived at that post expecting to buy packhorses for the PFC evacuation of the lower Columbia to a place beyond the reach of a potentially hostile British navy. Instead he found his caches had been plundered by Nez Perce. The overbearing tactics he used to recover the looted property humiliated Indian leaders and created a sullen resentment in a people who had welcomed and assisted Lewis and Clark, and then the Astorians.

After a prominent role in the sale of the assets and abandonment of Astor's Pacific Fur Company, McKenzie carried the sale contact to New York. The act of delivering the disappointing documents to Astor finished their association, and by March 1815 McKenzie was in Montreal, scheming again with Colin Robertson about leading a competitive Hudson's Bay Company trapping brigade into Athabaska. But when Robertson left for the interior on May 17, 1815, he was accompanied by another

18 Josephy, *Nez Perce Indians*, 46–49.

ex-Astorian, John Clarke, in the role that McKenzie let slip.[19] McKenzie waffled on this move because the capital of his brothers was locked up in the North West Company account books, and going over to "the enemy" might endanger their investment.

Although retired from the skin games, Roderick Mackenzie (Sir Alexander's brother) retained a financial interest in the Montreal agency of the North West Company. He used his influence with William McGillivray to find a place for Donald in a new plan to make the NWC Columbia Adventure profitable.[20] Donald McKenzie was engaged by McTavish, McGillivray and Company for a three-year experiment to increase peltry production with a moving brigade of contracted or debt-obligated trappers. As a special "agent," his rate of pay exceeded what wintering NWC partners might expect to earn from their shares, an arrangement that would inevitably attract objections from other proprietors.

It was still necessary for an Indian, or a freeman, to wade into the icy water and set a beaver trap, drag the carcass out onto the bank and skin it, stretch it to dry on a bent willow hoop, and eventually pass those leathery, furry rounds through the trade shop window to a buyer. East of the Rocky Mountains traders operated in an accustomed symbiosis of Indian hunters and receptive buyers, but in the west, they were disappointed with the fur production of the tribes. As McGillivray's letter to McTavish had indicated, the agents intended to take measures *"which will render us independent in a great measure of the natives."* The experiment had to rely on independent trappers organized into a roving party (brigade) to sweep new beaver streams and ponds.[21]

At the sale of Astoria, the combined manpower of the PFC and NWC lists counted only thirteen engaged, or contracted, hunters of which six may have been half-engaged or freeman provision-hunters killing game in the Willamette Valley to feed the post, and taking an occasional beaver.[22] Organizing an efficient new force required McKenzie to locate and convince an undetermined number of freemen living with various Indian groups to leave their families for long periods and accept a disciplined way of life.

---

19 Rich, ed., *Colin Robertson's Correspondence Book*, xxvii, lxii.
20 Peter Deslauriers, "Roderick Mackenzie," *DCB* 7, 565-67.
21 Rich, ed., *Colin Robertson's Correspondence Book*, 198.
22 Their names are listed in HBCA, F.4/7, p. 31.

During the Montreal agent's discussions with McKenzie, the concept must have seemed so promising that they were willing to send additional trappers west. Before leaving Montreal in 1816, McKenzie enlisted a number of Iroquois accustomed to the use of steel traps. When he left Fort William with two canoes, McKenzie was accompanied by six or seven of the Iroquois recruited around Montreal and he expected around fourteen others to follow the next year.[23] Since the beginning of the beaver trade, Iroquois had traveled to distant places to hunt, so contracting to cross the continent for an indefinite period was not that daunting. Most were dutiful sons or husbands who saw that their enlistment bounty was paid to those they were leaving behind.[24]

As the recently promoted manager of the Fort George depot, James Keith may have thought of his imposed associate McKenzie as an inheritance from the failed Astorians, the same individual who had contributed to Mr. Astor's disappointment. But that had to do with character, and Keith's objection to McKenzie's assignment was in the unusual arrangement of his hiring by the Montreal agents without the approval of the wintering partners. Keith had immediately criticized McKenzie's three-year contract and was rebuked by McGillivray, perhaps in the dispatches McKenzie delivered on arrival.

There were also performance issues. Although he had traversed it from east to west *only once* with the overland Astorians…and almost perished in the attempt, McKenzie convinced the agents that no one knew the Snake River country better than he. And there was a question of how Indian tribes would accept encouragement of direct hunting on a scale not previously employed west of the mountains.

Along the way west, McKenzie looked to his future comfort by pausing at Fort William long enough to contact the widow of Alexander McKay who had taken up with the young partner, Dr. John McLoughlin. She had a daughter Mary McKay and when McKenzie went on he was accompanied by a new country wife. The bride might have been sixteen or so, but having grown up along the lakes and rivers, was not well prepared to be the helpmate of someone planning to lead a horse-borne hunting brigade.

23 According to Keith's Memorandum book, seven came in 1817 and four in 1818.

24 HBCA, F4/7, p. 31.

At this time, the Hudson's Bay Company was also confronting diminished fur returns and throughout the Canadian hinterlands, rival interests were locked in a deadly struggle for supremacy. On June 19, those excesses culminated in a violent battle near the forks of the Red and Assiniboine Rivers where Robert Semple, the HBC Governor of Rupert's Land, and twenty-one of Lord Selkirk's colonists were killed by NWC-inspired Métis. One of the mixed-bloods was Mary's brother, Thomas McKay. McKenzie's party took a long detour to avoid any reaction to the battle, crossed the mountains to the upper Columbia, and rode two canoes downstream to Okanogan, where the postmaster, Ross Cox, gave McKenzie a letter submitting his resignation.

Before the overland party left Montreal, the agents replied to James Keith's criticism of the new plan, and McKenzie's assignment. Upon his arrival at Fort George, McKenzie delivered their letter to Keith:

> Referring you to our general Letter addressed to the Proprietors of the North West Company on the Columbia, we have little to say on the same subject—In the arrangement with Mr Donald M to improve efficiency and project harmony into the Columbia Department. You will point out to Mr McKenzie the most expeditious mode by which he can get on, for it is of the first importance that he should reach Fort George in time to prevent any of the vessels sailing with the Returns of this year."[25]

Keith and Angus Bethune must also have questioned why this new arrangement had been made outside the usual requirement for approval by the wintering partners. It seemed to mean that the new inland superintendent was only answerable to the downstream agency. The Montreal agency was managing complex affairs from long distance when William McGillivray wrote to Keith on July 28, 1816, a terse dismissal of Keith's concern that McKenzie could operate under a contract that overrode any input from the wintering partners, and was insulting to the Fort George factor.

> For reasons which appear to us of weight at the moment we do not think it proper to transmit a Copy of Mr Donald McKenzies agreement

25 This letter has not survived but Ross in *Fur Hunters*, 57-58, 68-70, wrote that it contained important resolutions for improving the trade in the Columbia. The immediate problem was that the number of skins from the winter 1815-16 trade was too small to cover port charges at Canton.

> [to you]. We stated that there was such an agreement and that M^r^ M^c^K-enzie was a Partner and to have a certain management of a part of the Business—which for the time we deemed sufficient—and might suppose that M^r^ M^c^Kenzie would make no scent of the nature of his Agreement—it might be cavilled at and there had already existed too much distention among the Partners.[26]

Keith's friend John Richardson had foreseen this when he wrote to Keith on April 29, 1816:

> The continuance therefore of the Columbia business, as it is, becomes a matter of necessity; but measures are concerting for avoiding the future expense of [licensing to the East India Company] Vessels from England, by getting a Boston House to undertake the conveyance of supplies, and to carry the Returns to Canton, which plan will prevent many heavy advances and risks otherwise indispensable."[27]

A stickler on details like Keith recognized that McKenzie was not a legitimate partner. He was an agent representing the Montreal agency, and McGillivray overstepped the bounds of agreement between the wintering partners and the Montreal agents in asserting that Donald McKenzie "was a Partner."[28] But when he asked for clarification on that point of procedure, McGillivray indignantly responded:

> It was not the business of the Agents to give ground for more—They had a right to act as they did & they certainly conceived that the arrangement was for the Interest of the N W C^o^—The Agreement is founded on the principle of an experiment of which to sustain the result would take three years—at the end of which if unfavorable it was to be given up. Otherwise to be continued to the End of the present concern—M^r^ M^c^Kenzie to hold one Eighth in the Trade of the Columbia—which for the above three years the Agents guaranteed him at £500 P An^m^. —if the business continued after three years then he had his Eighth Share

26 *See* Masson, ed., *Les Bourgeois*, 2:479.

27 John Richardson to James Keith, Montreal, April 29, 1816, James Keith Papers, (MSS Davidson & Garden), 2769/I/57/4, UA. The ships the NWC had in the Pacific were the *Colonel Allan*, destined for London, and the schooner *Columbia*, which, as described earlier, traded between the Columbia River, the Sandwich Islands, Monterey, Canton, and Russian America.

28 Article 18 of the agreement entered into between the Agents and the partners in 1802, and which remained in effect for twenty years, clearly stated "That every person hereafter to be admitted a Partner in this Concern shall be accepted and approved of by the other Partners or their Attornies named and appointed under this agreement."

> whether that yielded profit or loss—but if given up at the End of three years his agreement was at an End—An allowance of £250 was also made him for a part of his Expenses during the winter at Montreal—This Agreement was laid before the Concern last year, and the allowance for part of his winters Expenses was the only part on which any comment was made.[29]

Enter an amanuensis. After spending the 1815–16 winter ranging between Okanogan and Kamloops, Alexander Ross was relieved when Ross Cox arrived from Spokane to rebuild Fort Okanogan. Ross had returned downstream in June to be Keith's second at Fort George during the following winter. So he was present when McKenzie arrived, and years later appropriated the role of McKenzie's chronicler on the excuse that his hero was a poor correspondent.[30]

Perhaps it was loyalty to a former associate that caused Ross to find ways of distorting the sequence of events and keep himself central to important developments. It was unlikely that clerks were permitted to be present at the Fort George Council discussions between the proprietors, particularly if those conversations were acrimonious, and Ross was not mentioned in the notes of the September 30, 1816, Fort George council meeting that included Keith, Bethune, and McKenzie. His version of their conversations appears to be hearsay or invention.[31]

Fort George was unable to feed so many during the winter. When McKenzie left in early October to go to Spokane, Alexander Ross described McKenzie's complement as a "medly of savages, Iroquois, Abenaki and Owhyhees…that marked the brigade as doomed."[32] But that was hindsight, written many years later, when Ross published his bias against Keith. As the Spokane brigade passed Okanogan, McKenzie informed Ross Cox that his request to retire had been approved by the Fort George council and then convinced him to stay on for another year.

29 William McGillivray and Henry MacKenzie, Agents for the North West Company to James Keith, Fort William, July 26, 1817, James Keith Papers (MSS Davidson & Garden) 2769/I/57/4, UA.

30 Disproving this shortcoming are letters McKenzie wrote to Ross Cox in February 1817, to George Simpson in 1823, to James Hargrave in 1831, to James Keith in 1833 and 1838, and in later years to Wilson Price Hunt concerning the estate of the trapper John Day. *See* Merk, ed., *Fur Trade and Empire*, 198-199. For McKenzie to Hargrave, 1831, *see* Glazebrook, ed., *The Hargrave Correspondence*, 86-87; Elliott, "Letter of Donald McKenzie to Wilson Price Hunt," 10-13, 194-197.

31 Cox, *Columbia River*, 247-48; Ross, *Fur Hunters*, 68-72.

32 Ross, *Fur Hunters*, 68-71, 78-81.

Cox recalled that when the boats to Okanogan and Spokane arrived in the summer 1817, Alexander Ross returned with them and "proceeded to Kamloops."[33] Given his attitude, Keith would not miss him.

At the beginning of the longest tenure of those in charge of Fort George, Keith made no comment in his memorandum book that McKenzie's appointment was unfair in a partnership of equals, and prohibited by the 1802 agreement. To his credit, Keith swallowed his differences about McKenzie's appointment and saw to it that the joint-management of the department was conducted as it should be. His responsibility was keeping the business in balance, calculations that came down to as mundane a consideration as "the Value of Potatoes at F^{t} Geo regulated by the cost of the articles in lieu of which they are issued."[34]

Despite differences within this split superintendence, the interior trade continued under the direction of experienced clerks like Finnan McDonald, James McMillan, and Nicholas Montour who were stationed in the sometimes threatened Salish country and keeping beaver hunters focused on trapping instead of being distracted by tribal war games, now made more deadly by the guns they sold.

The North West Company's expressed goal of increased fur production now depended on half-engaged trappers and experienced freemen. The Iroquois McKenzie brought with him were "professional" steel trappers who would soon clean out the tributaries of the Clark Fork or the spring creeks emanating from the wall of mountains along the east side of the Flathead Valley, any marshy places favorable to beaver.

---

33 Cox, *Columbia River*, 248.

34 It was a decade before Keith revealed his feelings about McKenzie in a letter to the Hudson's Bay Company concerning an inscription on a piece of silver plate. That would have to be changed from "...Partners of the late NW Company" to "Gentlemen connected with..." because of the addition of Donald McKenzie's name, he "never having been a NW Partner." Keith to Geddes McKenzie Simpson, November 3, 1828, Keith Papers, (MSS Davidson and Garden) 2769/I/57/4, UA. That was three years after Ross published his book.

Alexander Ross, Astorian and North West Company clerk.
From the 1855 edition of Ross's *Fur Hunters of the Far West: A Narrative of Adventures in the Oregon and Rocky Mountains* (London: Smith, Elder and Co., 1855).

Chapter Thirteen

Genesis of McKenzie's Snake Brigades

James Keith's notations in his memorandum book show a consistent, inquiring intellect and a man of scientific curiosity. Fort George had inherited an impressive library, left mostly by former Astorians, and Keith, like other clerks, drew upon that resource. His reading tended toward the abstractions of the physical world rather than the experimental and he surely consulted the half-dozen medical books to treat many of the depot complement for debilitating venereal complaints. But the cedar longhouses of lower Columbia Indians were no place for a gentleman and he preferred a bachelor's quiet life rather than another "cohabitation." His illusion of sole authority at Fort George was dispelled when he was harnessed to former Astorian Donald McKenzie, who had a reputation for insinuating himself in the business of others. Keith surely felt a tinge of resentment at the way McKenzie shouldered into the council and immediately began making reassignments.

McKenzie moved to Spokane House to spend the winter and consider how to implement his appointment. He could rely on the experienced inland traders: Finnan McDonald at Spokane, James McMillan at the Flatheads Post, and Nicholas Montour working among the Kutenai. But his immediate problem was feeding a large complement. In a February 12, 1817, letter to Ross Cox, McKenzie described the situation.

> On arriving here I found I had ninety souls to provide with the necessities of life, and therefore determined an excursion to Lewis River [the Snake].[1] Your friend Mr. McDonald accompanied me, and besides the Canadians, I took ten Sandwich Islanders whom I armed and accountred quite *en militaire*. The *Nez-Perces* did not half relish the swarthy

1 The large complement at Spokane included as many as forty men who Keith was unable to feed at Fort George. There is no indication how they were employed at Spokane and they went downstream with the spring brigade.

> aspect of these invincibles, and fancied I intended to resent former grudges. However, we did not see them all.[2]

Nez Perce and other tribes around the mouth of the Snake River previously experienced erratic behavior from fur traders. McKenzie's strong-armed demands for horses did little to dispel the lingering odor of the despised John Clarke, who had hung a Nez Perce for theft, or the later hostilities involving passing boat brigades that had alienated the Nimiipu.[3] Bullying Indians was a poor start to enlisting their cooperation in hunting and trapping.

By early February most of the Nez Perce horses McKenzie acquired had been consumed and there was not enough time for a second expedition before the downstream brigade began assembling. Getting an early start in March 1817, McKenzie arrived at Fort George on April 3, ready to implement his plan for a trapping adventure launched into Nez Perce territory.

McKenzie had no time to waste at Fort George, and Keith was better prepared to cooperate by making men and goods available for him. The flotilla that carried supplies to the upper river posts included "five Scotsmen, two English, one Irish, thirty-six Canadians, twenty Iroquois, two Nipissings, one Cree, three half-breeds, nine natives of the Sandwich Islands; with one boy, a servant, two women, and two children." They headed upriver in mid-April 1817 with eighty-six individuals crammed between ninety-pound bales of trade goods stowed in two barges and nine canoes (only two of bark).[4]

At the mouth of the Snake River McKenzie broke off with twenty-two men in three canoes to ascend to the Clearwater River and campaign for cooperation from the Nez Perce.[5] Accommodating Walla Wallas sold McKenzie nine horses for what was planned as a "tour to the Shoshone Indians," but he still had convince the Nimiipuu (Nez Perce), a self-suffi-

2 McKenzie to Cox, Spokane House, February 12, 1817, in Cox, *Columbia River*, 249.

3 Alexander Ross was not party to the events of that year because he was stationed at Kamloops. He may have read McKenzie's blithe letter in the book Cox published in 1831 and 1832, and improved on it in his somewhat marvelous 1855 description. Ross, *Fur Hunters*, 68-72.

4 Cox, *Columbia River*, 268.

5 Cox, *Columbia River*, 268-71. Cox counted twenty-two. Alexander Ross, who was on his way from Kamloops, says twenty-five, and that the party eventually grew to thirty-five, perhaps augmented by others coming from Spokane House with horses.

cient and therefore independently minded people, to forget the excesses he had previously inflicted on them.[6]

In their excursions east of the mountains Nez Perce risked confrontations with the Blackfeet. Raids toward the south clashed with Bannocks and Shoshones, fights that hardened their young warriors. They had a few worn-out guns passed to them by Crow middlemen before Lewis and Clark encouraged peaceful relations with neighbors, but as hostile encounters increased, more arms were in demand. In his history of the Nez Perce, Alvin Josephy wrote:

> [Donald McKenzie] established no permanent camp among the Nez Perce this time but for more than a month moved through their country, counseling with the headmen of different villages, pleading for good will and friendship, and examining the region and various routes to the south. At the same time, he realized that the hostility between the Sahaptan-speaking peoples and the Snake bands, renewed since the time of Lewis and Clark, would threaten his brigades with disruptions and attacks by both sides in the war areas to the south, and he realized that before he could launch his expeditions, he would have to try to bring about another peace treaty between the two peoples.[7]

The Astorians used an easy Indian trail that followed along the west side of the Snake River but McKenzie felt it could be vulnerable to Nez Perce interference. Before moving up the promising Snake River, he needed to placate those horsemen. Diplomacy might have benefitted from the services of an experienced clerk, but Angus Bethune and Duncan McDougall took three clerks with the Fort William express and other Salish country officers returned to their accustomed duty stations.

That included Alexander Ross, who was reassigned to Kamloops and would not return to Fort George until June 5, 1818.[8] What is known about Donald McKenzie's activities during 1817–18 depends on the description by Ross, who wasn't present and whose later recollections dangled on thirty-nine-year-old hearsay. Traveling with the upriver brigade gave him an opportunity to evaluate the party that turned up the Snake River, which he dismissed as thirty-five Iroquois "and other refuse," with only five trustworthy Canadians.[9]

6 Cox, *Columbia River*, 271.
7 Josephy, *The Nez Perce Indians*, 55.
8 Ross, *Fur Hunters*, 111, 116.
9 Ross, *Fur Hunters*, 109-10.

McKenzie wasn't all that fond of the Iroquois he brought west with him or found later around Spokane or Fort George. They soon made themselves a nuisance, when their leader, "Grand Pierre," got into a squabble over a horse. To settle the haggling, McKenzie paid the owner's price, drew his pistol, and shot the animal.[10] McKenzie had personally enlisted the Iroquois trappers in Lower Canada, but Ross maintained that they plotted to assassinate him. Warned by the interpreter Joachim, he dispersed three of the troublemakers, sending two to McMillan at Spokane and one on to Ross at Kamloops.[11] The rest were left under the supervision of an influential chief.

Alexander Ross provides the following uncorroborated account of McKenzie's activities:

> While with the remainder of his people [McKenzie] wheeled about in another direction, intending to carry on the project of hunting and of discovery for the season, although upon a more contracted scale. His primary object was to conclude an arrangement with the Nez Perces and in the Snake country to conciliate the Indians generally with reference to opening the way for extending the trade as soon as existing prejudices gave way; for he was surprised at the unfavorable change which the Indians had undergone during the short period the country had been under the domination of the North West Company and frequently observed to me that a change of system was as necessary to reduce the Indians to order as to reclaim the trade; both being on the brink of ruin.[12]

While McKenzie spent the winter of 1817-18 in the Nez Perce country experimenting with a moving brigade of trappers, his Iroquois were taking beaver that resident Nez Perce understood were valuable. After being bullied into selling their treasured spotted ponies to feed strangers, the horse breeders were reluctant to give over the animals that McKenzie needed to move into the Snake country. Nez Perce foresaw that trading outfits packed there by unwelcome strangers would include guns and ammunition to arm their enemies.

Although Ross was not present, he appears to distort facts to glorify McKenzie. He wrote that McKenzie traveled for three months in deep

10 "Grand Pierre" may have been Pierre Tevanitagon, later recognized as leader of a band that included two of his sons.

11 The warning may have come from Joachim Hubet who would show up later with Ogden's 1824–25 Snake Brigade.

12 Ross, *Fur Hunters*, 110.

snows "to traverse a rugged and mountainous country in order to keep up a good understanding with the strong and turbulent tribes inhabiting the south branch (lower Snake River)." It is a guess without confirmation that this snowshoe hike could have extended as far east as the Bitterroot, Frank Church and River of No Return Wilderness Areas bordering the Continental Divide, or south toward the headwaters of the Payette and Weiser Rivers. But the returns from McKenzie's trial run among the Nez Perce were not encouraging and he had used up the first year of his three-year contract with McTavish, McGillivray & Company without increasing production. If he was going to produce beaver, he had to move south into the dangerous Snake country.

At Fort William in summer 1818, the architect of the new system, William McGillivray, lacked a clear understanding of McKenzie's hunting plan. His July 20 response to Keith's objections about McKenzie's assignment betrayed uncertainty.

> I know not what M^r^ M^c^Kenzies intentions may be—the *three years*—in which it was intended the effect of our new System should be tried, will soon have elapsed—& I think by his agreement (for I have it not by me) that it is then optional on either Party to drop it—I should expect however from M^r^ M^c^Kenzie every cooperation and assistance in turning the Property to advantage, should the Business not go on.[13]

Now into the second year of the contract, departure of the brigade for the interior was delayed at Fort George for three months waiting for the arrival of a ship. It was mid-June 1818 before Captain Robson anchored the brig *Columbia.*[14] The delay must have been trying for McKenzie because he had decided to abandon Spokane and build a new depot closer to his projected operations. Needing a trustworthy clerk to support the brigade in the field, he settled on Alexander Ross.

Ross wrote later that the upriver boat brigade landed ninety-five men on a sandy plain about a half mile above the confluence of the Walla

---

13 William McGillivray to James Keith, Fort William July 20, 1818, James Keith Papers, Davidson & Garden mss. 2769/I/57/4, UA. Ironically, about the time that James Keith received McGillivray's letter, the Fort George master was returning the place to the Americans. *See* Merk, *The Oregon Question*.

14 Captain Robson brought the *Columbia* stocked with just enough goods to allow trading to continue. *See* LaRocque to McTavish, Thompson River, March 22, 1819, HBCA, F.3/2, fos.190-190d; McDonald to McTavish, Spokane House, April 9, 1819, HBCA, F.3/2, fos. 202-202d.

Walla and the Columbia Rivers, the place selected for the depot, on July 11, 1818. That was not far upstream from a narrow but impressive gap between high mountains. In the winter lodge stories of the river people, the two towering basalt pillars overlooking the Wallula Gap were the wives of the trickster Coyote. Geologically, they were water-carved reminders of ancient glacial floods from a time beyond recall now incorporated into oral tradition.

McKenzie intended that the new location would become a convenient outfitting depot for the Snake Country Hunting Brigade. To construct what Ross described as a wooden castle with a square compound about one hundred feet on a side, builders scattered as far as "a hundred miles" upstream in search of driftwood or timber. Ripping six-inch-thick by thirty-inch-wide sawn planks kept the Kanakas sweating in the sawpit. Long slabs of sawn planks were set in trenches to make a twelve- to fifteen-foot-high wall topped by a four-foot palisade and firing platform.[15] The emphasis was on defense because the brigade leader didn't trust the tribes and a second, lower inside wall was added in case the outer gates were breached. Post-on-sill houses were ranged against the walls.

Past hostile incidents necessitated a strong fort. The locals had watched the wealth of desirable trade goods passing without stopping, and had shown their disaffection. The NWC traders were concerned about future conflict. The large number of curious Indians that gathered to watch the construction anticipated a handy store. Actually, they were river-oriented people, salmon fishers more than warriors.

The new labor-intensive, time-consuming construction effort took two and a half months of precious time to build. Known as Fort Nez Perces, it was an expensive reflection of Donald McKenzie's determination to have a strong base of operations but delayed the departure of the second year's hunting brigade until the end of September.

After a year, Ross wrote to J. G. McTavish on April 20, 1819, explaining the difficulty of mounting the first Snake Brigade:

> This part of the Columbia so renowned for its number of Horses was partly a mistaken idea of people in general when we take into consideration the immence number of Natives which inhabit it and whose roving disposition obliges them to keep a considerable number; we find it

15 Archaeologists working in the 1950s were unable to define the original outline of the fort beneath a later rebuilding.

has been but a bare sufficiency for the natives themselves; for by the time we got a bare sufficiency to equip our worthy Trappers and fit M[r] M[c]K-enzie and party for the Snake quarter, we had to travel all the Country from the Upper Nez Perces to the [word missing] and then we were put to a thousand shifts and often at a nonplus to find a supper for our people and this with the expenditure of the Fort, including all furs. we required and have made use of the round number of 320 Horses which have been traded at this Fort, between the 1st Ap[l] 1818 and the 1st April 1819 so that at present we neither find them plenty nor cheap and when so much goods are [traded] away on horse flesh, is it to be wondered that the natives do not nor will not kill Beavers,[16]

Meeting with leaders from the Nez Perce, Cayuse, Walla Walla, and Umatilla bands, McKenzie gained their agreement for peace with the Snakes, providing he could get the Shoshones and Bannocks to agree.[17] The motivation behind his diplomacy was not altruistic: the route he planned to follow ran south along the west side of the Snake River. That trail was also used by war parties and there was a previous history of Astorians attacked and killed where the brigade would hunt. McKenzie needed to insure that his party could pass without fear of molestation.

Subtle political tactics were beyond the concern of expectant trappers tying packs on the skittish Cayuse ponies that would carry them to a promised beaver bonanza. Loads included rations to get them past the Blue Mountains rising in the south. After that they would depend on their abilities as hunters to feed themselves and their families.

When McKenzie rode off at the end of September, clerk Ross watched twenty-five Canadian freemen and thirty Iroquois trail toward the Blue Mountains.[18] They had a herd of 195 horses carrying 300 beaver traps and other gear. Alexander Ross's account of how the hunt unfolded indicates that he did not entertain a high opinion of the first Snake Brigade:

After the war business was set again or rather the making of peace, we set about filling out a ragamuffin Medley of Freemen, unparalleled for worthlessness and bad conduct for no sooner were they fitted out than they were destitute of almost everything by Trafficking with the natives.

---

16 Alexander Ross to J. G. McTavish, Fort Nez Perces, April 20, 1819, HBCA, F.3/2, fos. 208-9.

17 Ross, *Fur Hunters*, 124.

18 In his memorandum book James Keith noted that there were forty-nine Iroquois in the Columbia Department in 1818, so McKenzie took most of them on his first hunt.

Guns Horses and even their Traps went—as for the Iroquois Trappers of this quarter, they are out of the question Too great Cowards to Trap but in bands, and when numerous they neither do nor think of anything but mischief. The others being principally old superannuated creatures are also but of little account either to themselves or the Company. However they do as well as can be expected from persons of their age and character.[19]

Climbing out of the sandy bottom of the Columbia River and across the low hills along the Walla Walla River, the caravan headed toward the pine-forested Blue Mountains rising in the distance. Some believed McKenzie intended to hunt there but instead the brigade went on, threading an ancient trail worn deep by the horsemen going to the Grande Ronde River crossing.[20] Beyond, a long, broad valley promised easy traveling with grass and water for the horses and game innocent of the gun. They followed the Powder River until it turned east to carve through raw basalt toward the Snake River Canyon. Climbing a ladder of minor rivers, the brigade passed the mouths of the yet-to-be-named Weiser and Payette Rivers to the Skam-naugh (Boise River).

It had been five years since the Astorian clerk John Reed and eleven men were murdered by Bannocks.[21] Choosing not to trap up the Snake, or expose his followers to the bones of the slain Reed party, McKenzie followed the Boise River to the modest stream he called the "little River Skam-am-naugh" (Indian Creek). He remembered it from his starving experience with the overland Astorians.[22] His former PFC associate Robert Stuart wrote:

Opposite of our present station a large River [Boise] comes in from the East, is well fed, contains many beaver, and is the most renowned Fishing Place in this Country. It is consequently the resort of the majority of the Snakes, where immense numbers of Salmon are taken, forming after

19 Alexander Ross to J. G. McTavish, Fort Nez Perces, April 20, 1819, HBCA, F.3/2, fos. 208-9.

20 J. F. LaRocque to J. G. McTavish, Thompsons River, March 22, 1819, HBCA, F.3/2, fos. 190-190d.

21 Rollins, ed., *Discovery of the Oregon Trail*, 69n38, 99n138.

22 Rollins, ed., *Discovery of the Oregon Trail*, 75-100. Indian Creek comes into the Boise at the northwest edge of present-day Caldwell, Idaho.

the [esculent] Roots, the principal article of food which the natives of this Barren tract possess.[23]

Although usually depicted as a group process, brigade trapping was actually individualistic and dangerously lonely. A trapper, or better two or three men to watch each other's backs, scattered to make sets far enough apart to avoid interfering with those of others. The brigade leader selected campsites and protected the small assortment of supplies that traveled with him. Leading a brigade of hunters was a matter of patience carefully interspersed with a judicious exercise of command. For example, McKenzie dispensed only enough powder and ball for a few shots, insuring that hunters had to return to the base camp.

After crossing the Snake River, twenty-five of the thirty Iroquois convinced McKenzie to provide them with outfits so they could cut loose and trap on their own. Due to the trouble he previously had with their spendthrift habits and gambling with other tribes in the Nez Perce country, McKenzie was reluctant to release them. Their equipment had to be advanced on credit and repaid with peltry, but the independently-minded Iroquois expected a less formal relationship, resulting in McKenzie's exasperated declaration, after having to refit them, "Iroquois will never do in this country. In fact, their introduction was the signal of our disappointments."[24] But that was Ross's opinion and after questioning an Iroquois deserter named Oskonanton, James Keith noted that only eleven Iroquois deserted in the Snake country.[25]

Leaving the Iroquois to work beaver on Indian Creek, McKenzie took the rest of the brigade along the Boise River for twenty-five miles to what promised to be a rich field for taking beaver. Beyond the east side of present Boise, Idaho, McKenzie's winter camp was established along the river, where his "Woody Point" probably reflected the sharp bend of the *rivière des bois*, as his Canadians called it.[26] From there the Boise River broke up into the South, Middle, and North Forks. Anticipated beaver

23 Rollins, ed., *Discovery of the Oregon Trail*, 83. Ross mentions the large number of lodges assembled in that vicinity for a fishing camp. For a recent reconsideration of the 200th Anniversary of the Astorians *see* Hardee, *Proceedings of the 2012 Fur Trade Symposium*.

24 Ross, *Fur Hunters*, 136; "Abstract of People in the Columbia for the following outfits," Keith Memorandum Book, p. 48.

25 Alexander Ross to J. G. McTavish, Fort Nez Perces, April 20, 1819, HBCA, F.3/2, fos. 208-9.

26 Ross, *Fur Hunters*, 152. Ross wrote this reconstruction as a direct statement by McKenzie.

in Boise Mountain streams would keep freemen occupied for the next four months.[27]

Beaver began putting on thicker winter coats in October, and it was time to begin trapping. The remaining five Iroquois and twenty-five freemen would work out of the base camp while McKenzie scouted east.

> After disposing of my people to the best advantage, trading with the natives and securing the different chiefs to our interest, I left my people at the end of four months. Then taking a circuitous route along the foot of the Rocky Mountains, a country extremely dreary during the winter voyage, till I reached the headwaters of the great south branch [present Snake River], regretting every step I made that we had been so long deprived of the riches of such a country.[28]

Reconstructing the performance of the first Snake Expedition requires getting beyond Ross's admiring account of McKenzie's travels and checking details against clues in other contemporary records, or the map provided by William Kittson in 1824-25. Idaho historian Merle Wells shows that what Ross wrote years later cannot be taken as unchallenged fact. Ross incorporated later data and colored it with his need to reinvent McKenzie as a hero.[29]

After the first of the year 1819, McKenzie and a few engages explored in the mountains to the east. In his book, Ross wrote that McKenzie "undertook at a late season of the year a voyage of three months long in deep snows, to traverse a rugged and mountainous country in order to keep up a good understanding with the strong and turbulent tribes inhabiting the south branch, where some of the scenes of his former years had taken place."[30]

To do that McKenzie would have traveled six hundred miles mostly on snowshoes, averaging ten miles a day over rough terrain, much of it in unfamiliar country. That would have been a fair pace, especially for a large

---

27 "Route of Alexander Ross, 1824," Idaho State Historical Society Reference Series, no. 86, 1990, 8-9. This source places Ross about 20 miles west of Caldwell "but not quite as close to the site of Donald Mackenzie's 1819 winter camp post as his journal suggests." The journal referred to is Elliott, ed., "Journal of Alexander Ross," 369 and following.

28 Ross, *Fur Hunters*, 136.

29 Compare to the article, "An Interdisciplinary Approach to Alexander Ross: Astorian, Ethnographer, and Transitional Figure of the North American Fur Trade," *2012 Fur Trade Symposium*, 165-72.

30 Ross, *Fur Hunters*, 111. As noted previously, this may represent a trip McKenzie made in the Nez Perce country in the winter 1818–19.

man like McKenzie. A probable alternative is that McKenzie explored branches of the Boise River or the Payette River looking for future trapping grounds in the Sawtooth Mountain Range to which the next Snake Brigade might travel. It is unlikely McKenzie actually hiked east as far as Henry's Fork of the Snake—which he called the headwaters of the great south branch—because he already knew it from being there with the overland Astorians. Certainly he would not have travelled as far east as the Bear River.

Returning to Indian Creek, McKenzie found the Iroquois trappers scattered in small parties. Failing to connect with them, McKenzie and six engagés continued on snowshoes "only carrying their blankets on their backs" over the Blue Mountains and on to Fort Nez Perces. When McKenzie left the previous September, he had been unable to say where he would be to receive a new outfit. The long hike to the depot was necessary to arrange to resupply the brigade still hunting in the mountains. After resting for a week those travel-worn voyageurs stowed their gear in a bateau and paddled away to see if it was possible to boat supplies up the Snake River.

The river McKenzie followed in 1811 through Hell's Canyon had been a rock-strewn channel at low water. The early spring of 1819 reconfirmed its impassability by boat.[31]

Oddly, the letter Ross wrote to J. G. McTavish on April 20 gave no indication that McKenzie had visited Fort Nez Perces. After graphic descriptions of the danger from local Indians, Ross admitted "with regard to the Snake country in general I shall be silent as I know but very little about it, by accounts it is very promising.[32]

Trading from his plank castle with local tribes, Ross sent those returns to Fort George with the spring boats from Spokane and Okanogan. His accounts looked good because he rolled the Salish country contribution in with his own. When the boat brigade for the interior returned, Ross received goods to forward to McKenzie by June 5. Despite the potential for trouble with Indians, Ross gave that responsibility to a new hand, William Kittson. Unfortunately, the clerk's experience in the War of 1812 and his later competitive struggles with the Hudson's Bay Company had not included mountain packing.

31 Ross, *Fur Hunters*, 138.

32 Ross to McTavish, Fort Nez Perces, April 20, 1819, HBCA, F.3/2, fos. 208-9.

Departing from Fort Nez Perces, Kittson took twenty-six men from that complement, along with fifteen others recently sent up from Fort George to strengthen the second Snake Brigade. Although Ross gave Kittson a letter of instructions, the inexperienced clerk was inattentive about hobbling the horses. Raiders coming out of the darkness ran off twelve of the herd one night and returned a few days later for the rest. The supply brigade bogged down for two days and nights until ten men, sent by McKenzie, arrived. To Kittson's relief, they were driving some of the packhorses recovered from Indians they intercepted on the trail.[33]

The clerk's education was not complete. After delivering the new outfit and picking up the returns of the 1818–19 hunt, he started to return to the fort. On the way he lost two men killed by a Nez Perce war party.[34] The packs were delivered to Ross by July 7, but that was too late to catch the spring brigade on the way to Fort George and too late to ship the first Snake Brigade beaver to the Canton market.[35]

Ross wrote McTavish that his trade was 2,800 beavers and otters (actually 2,758 pelts), while 3,102 came from Spokane.[36] Having missed the sailing of the *Nautilus,* the next opportunity to ship beaver would have been on the *Levant*, another Perkins venture, which left the Columbia River on May 25, 1820. The consequence was that peltry intended to rescue the Columbia Adventure stayed in the Fort George warehouse for almost a whole year.[37] Nevertheless Alexander Ross wrote:

---

33 Ross, *Fur Hunters*, 139-41.

34 One of the slain was the former overland Astorian, Jean Baptiste Delorme, who went east in April 1814 and showed up at Fort Nez Perces in 1819. Nicole St. Onge, "Blue Beads, Vermillion and Scalpers: The Social Economy of the 1810-1812 Astorian Overland Expedition's French Canadian Voyageurs," a paper presented at the 2004 Rupert's Land Symposium, Rocky Mountain House, Alberta, Canada.

35 The spring brigade did not start from Spokane until after April 9, 1819. HBCA, F.3/2, fos. 202-202d. The Perkins' Boston ship *Nautilus* arrived on March 25, 1819, and sailed without the Snake Brigade returns.

36 Keith Memorandum Book, p. 30. McDonald wrote to J. G. McTavish from Spokane on April 9 that "Spokan Fort fal [fell] sort [short] of Packs on a count there is fort at the Wala Wala which those furs use to Come here and ad number to the Pack." HBCA, F.3/2, fos. 202-202d.

37 Haldane left Spokane on April 19, 1820, taking thirty-two packs, of which twenty-three came from the Flathead country. Some 9,940 pelts went on from Fort Nez Perces, and the Columbia department counted the largest returns in its history, 16,120 pelts. Keith, Memorandum Book, p. 30. The furs were shipped to China on the *Levant* from Fort George on May 25, but 13,537 beaver skins were unsalable at Canton. Perkins Company Papers, Vol. 19, 79-3734, pp. 161-87.

> The result of the Snake expedition put an end to the sharp conduct [criticism] which had for some years past divided the councils at Fort George. No sooner was McKenzie's success in the Snake Country known than his opponents were loud in his praise. It was pleasing to see this year [1820] the council at Fort George now enter so warmly and approve so strongly our measures in having established Fort Nez Perces, and in gaining so promising a footing in the Snake country.[38]

Although there were questions of what part of the country produced them, the returns of 1819 were the largest number of beaver skins yet produced by the Columbia Adventure. Ross's recitation of McKenzie's tribulations during this period was imaginative. To make an even more dramatic story, he added a postscript, "By a courier of last ev[g] we received the melancholy news that ten of our Iroquois were killed to a Man by the Black Feet near the Calarado [Colorado] quarter [—] how far this is true is yet to be ascertained." In fact, only one Iroquois had been killed in a scuffle with local Indians, seven remained with the Snakes, and two had deserted.

When McKenzie returned to Indian Creek in late February, he was disgusted to find the Iroquois scattered all over the country in twos and threes, "living with the savages, without horses, without traps, without furs and without clothing." Those sophisticated eastern Indians were not as good at playing the hand game as local gamblers who stripped them of their possessions.

After Kittson, now aided by ten men of the Snake Brigade, departed for Fort Nez Perces, McKenzie and three men remained at Indian Creek guarding the new outfit and waiting for missing Iroquois to reappear or Kittson to return.

---

38 Ross, *Fur Hunters*, 144.

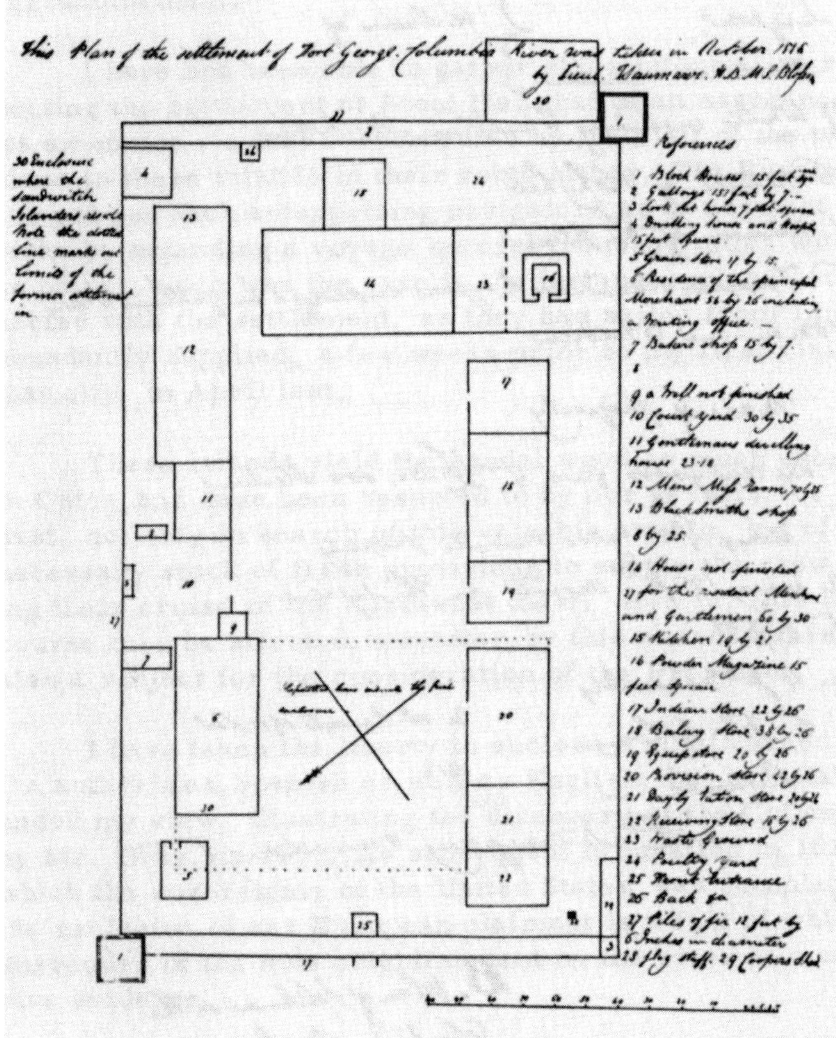

Plan of Fort George, 1818, by Lt. James Saumarez of the ship HMS *Blossom*. The enclosure labeled "30" outside the walls was for the Kanakas, or Sandwich Islanders. According to historian Barry Gough, "This wasn't racial exclusion so much as a financial reality for the company, for if you were within the walls you were on the payroll of the NWC and entitled to food, a place to sleep, medical care, etc." Rather than racial prejudice, the arrangement was a matter of employment status. (Private communication with publisher, 12/4/2015.) From B. C. Payette, *The Oregon Country Under the Union Jack* (Montreal: Payette Radio Limited, 1961).

Chapter Fourteen

The Restoration of Astoria

Although the War of 1812 gave the Nor'westers the opportunity to buy out the Pacific Fur Company, the peace of late 1814 seemed to nullify that purchase. The terms of the first article of the Treaty of Ghent stated, in part,

> All Territory, Places and Possessions whatsoever taken by either party from the other during the War, or which may be taken after the signing of this Treaty, excepting only the Islands hereinafter mentioned, shall be restored without delay, and without causing any destruction, or carrying away any of the Artillery or other public property originally captured in the said Forts or Places, and which shall remain therein upon the exchange of the Ratifications of this Treaty, or any Slaves or other private property.[1]

It didn't matter that a private partnership had purchased the assets of another private partnership before a naval representative of Great Britain took possession of Astoria/Fort George. Article I required that it be restored to the Americans.

As geographically remote as it seemed, the Columbia Adventure was not operating in a political vacuum. In the greater Canadian northwest, the North West Company was locked in a vicious struggle with the increasingly aggressive Hudson's Bay Company. Great Britain was economically drained by continental wars at a time when the NWC London agents felt that their government was inattentive and unsupportive. The London agents of the North West Company feared for the legal protection of the establishment on the Columbia River. They addressed

1 *Treaties and Agreements Affecting Canada in force between His Majesty and the United States of America with Subsidiary Documents 1814-1925* (Ottawa: F. A. Acland, 1927), 1.

the Secretary of State on August 9, 1815, and sent copies to McTavish, McGillivray & Company and to Sir Alexander Mackenzie & Company:

> As to the general question of Indian Trade in the territories of the United States, that is put to rest; no article in the commercial treaty stipulating our right to carry it on, is quite equivalent to one forbidding it, & where especially on such a subject & where the treaty is with such a state as America—It is also conclusive in our minds of the systematic deceit which has been practiced by our Government towards the Indians; their rights after the question of territory was decided, could only consist in the freedom of intercourse & trade, & then not being protected by the subsequent treaty, renders the article in that of Ghent equally absurd, & inefficient.[2]

Two decades after Jay's Treaty allowed British traders continued access to tribes in the northeastern United States, the London mercantile community hoped that the Treaty of Ghent would apply the same access to peoples of the Pacific Slope. But on July 23, 1815, the British *chargé de affaires* was informed of the American intention to reoccupy Astoria under the provisions of the treaty. He refused, citing three objections, the last being "the uncertainty whether any persons whatsoever remained on the site of Astoria."

That question was answered in a memorandum written by Simon McGillivray arguing that "Astoria did not fall within the formula of the Treaty of Ghent since it had been bought by British subjects, not captured."[3] The North West Company had known of the possibility of a potential controversy since the United States Congress approved the agreement in February 1815 and no doubt advised James Keith of it when he attended the annual meeting at Fort William in July.[4]

The downstream agents in Montreal tried to write their way out of yet another threat to their business by having their London representative, Simon McGillivray, resort to pamphleteering.[5] After the July 1815 meeting at Fort William, McGillivray returned to London where he wrote

2 Inglis, Ellice & Company (written by Edward Ellice) to McTavish, McGillivray & Company and Sir Alexander Mackenzie & Company, London, August 9, 1815, Baby Collection, u/5929, UM.

3 Merk, ed., *The Oregon Question*, 9.

4 The minutes of the 1815 summer meeting at Fort William are missing.

5 Without any immediate way of influencing public opinion, businesses printed handbills and pamphlets for distribution.

and published *A Narrative of Occurrences in the Indian Country of North America* in an attempt to muffle the violent trade war between the North West Company and the Hudson's Bay Company in Rupert's Land.

Then McGillivray concocted a second pamphlet, *Notice Respecting the Boundary between His Majesties Possessions in North America and the United States,* which raised the question of a boundary between Lake of the Woods and the Pacific Ocean.[6] McGillivray was goaded to take up his pen by the tardy distribution of an American map drawn by William Clark to accompany the 1814 publication of the journals of the Lewis and Clark Expedition, which was followed two years later by another, created by the cartographer John Melish. The later map delineated the northern boundary of Louisiana Territory as extending north to the drainage divide between the Saskatchewan and Missouri rivers, about 49°40′ north latitude. West of the Rocky Mountains, Melish imagined a U. S. territorial claim stretching from San Francisco Bay north to 52° north latitude.[7]

In trying to influence government policy on the location of a boundary, McGillivray relied on data gathered by the NWC clerk Alexander Ross during his exploration of the North Cascade Mountains in summer 1814. Before turning back, Ross descended a minor stream to its confluence with the Skagit River where his Indian guide told him it was a mere four days' travel to Puget Sound.[8] Ross passed his findings on to John George McTavish at Spokane and the information eventually reached Simon McGillivray, who had a fold-out map made as an insert for his 1817 pamphlet. Mostly a copy of the Melish map, the imaginative author added a large river which he named the Caledonia to show how a boundary along 49 degrees north latitude might sever a major stream.[9]

But there was no imaginary River Caledonia. Ross had failed to follow the Skagit to the sound, and all that McGillivray's deception accomplished was alerting the British ambassador in Washington,

6 Merk, ed., *The Oregon Question*, 60n21, 61n22.

7 Merk, ed., *The Oregon Question*, 62. This was essentially the same territory claimed by Captain Zackery Perch in 1807, which the NWC had managed to muffle.

8 Ross crossed Twisp Pass, descended Bridge Creek to the Stehekin River, and up that to Cascade Pass and down the Cascade River to its confluence with the Skagit, four days' travel to Puget Sound. Ross did not have had a clear understanding of his position or the extent of the streams he crossed. www.skagitriverjournal.com/Upriver/Cascades/Road/CascadeRoad02-Surveys1.html, accessed July 4, 2014.

9 Merk, ed., *The Oregon Question,* 59-61.

Charles Bagot, and the governor general of Canada of the consequences of losing a port on the Pacific Ocean if American authority returned to the Columbia. By October 1817 a United States warship was already underway to enforce the provisions of the Treaty of Ghent. The British were unaware of this until Simon McGillivray disclosed the departure to Bagot in mid-November. Given the distance and difficulties of communication, the NWC partner in charge at the mouth of the Columbia River was unaware and unprepared for a surprise.

On January 27, 1818, Lord Henry Bathurst, the British Colonial Secretary, sent this advice to the "Partners or Agents of the North West Company" residing on the Columbia River:

> Intelligence having been received that the United States Sloop of War *Ontario* has been sent by the American Government to reestablish a Settlement upon the Columbia River which was held by that State on the breaking out of the late war.[10] I am to acquaint you that it is the Prince Regent's Pleasure (without however admitting the right of that Government to the possession in question) that in pursuance of the 1st Article of the Treaty of Ghent, due facility should be given to the reoccupation of the said Settlement by the Officers of the United States and I am to desire that you would contribute as much as lies in your power to the execution of His Royal Highness's Commands.[11]

There remained disturbing questions as to how far American claims might extend northward and whether those pretensions might cut off other western harbors. The Foreign Office was ready to arbitrate a resolution to bothersome boundary questions, and negotiations began in London after July 1818. Writing from Fort William in mid-July, William McGillivray warned James Keith that the *Ontario* was coming to reestablish an American settlement on the Columbia River. But given the distance express canoes had to travel, Keith would not receive the warning for at least three months.

> All that I had to say on Business—generally, as well as what relates to the River Columbia in particular, has already been stated to you by the Agents—The visit from the Americans was not at all contemplated –

10 The *Ontario* debarked from New York on October 4, 1817. Judson, "British Side of the Restoration of Fort Astoria—II," 313.

11 Lord Bathurst to the Partners or Agents of the North West Company residing on the Columbia River, Downing Street, January 27, 1818, HBCA, F.3/2, fo. 149. Lord Bathurst served as the British Colonial Secretary.

> and the consequences we cannot now foresee—your own good sense & your experience must point out to you the line of conduct to be adopted in this difficult emergency—I fear that after all our sacrifices we shall be forced to relinquish our object, even after we are satisfied that the ultimate end of our exertions was within our reach.—Yet should we be driven from the Coast—the knowledge which has been acquired of the Country, will enable us to increase our Returns from the West side of the mountains by means of Hunters—and at the worst I shall expect your ideas on some plan of this kind next year.[12]

By October the ministers plenipotentiary were willing to agree that the international boundary would divide North America from Lake of the Woods east along the line of 49° north latitude to the continental crest. The far western region remained at an impasse. It was agreed to leave the Pacific Slope in a compromise of joint occupancy for ten years. But by the time this compromise was achieved, the *Ontario* had already arrived at the Columbia in August 1818.

It would be up to the Fort George factor to deal with the consequences of peace instead of a war. The British seizure of the mouth of the Columbia at the beginning of the War of 1812 displayed naval trappings of imperial dignity, but Keith could not have foreseen that the return of that territory to the United States under the conditions of the Treaty of Ghent would be blunt republicanism.

Captain James Biddle, commanding the *Ontario*, was a battle-tested veteran of the Barbary Wars as well as exchanges with the British during the recent conflict. His brother, Nicholas Biddle, had been the editor of journals of Lewis and Clark when those were published three years previously, along with William Clark's great map of the west. A family connection should have given Captain Biddle some degree of proprietary interest in the Pacific Northwest, but the seaman already had enough of dawdling diplomats and was unlikely to tarry for a ceremony flattering to the British whom he had recently engaged in battle.

Unwilling to trust the *Onatrio* to the infamous Columbia bar, the cautious captain kept his ship standing offshore, and climbed into one of three small boats to share the risk of that dangerous crossing with fifty of his tars. A surprised James Keith had to wait until mid-afternoon when

12 William McGillivray to James Keith, Fort William, July 20, 1818, James Keith Papers (MSS Davidson & Garden) 2769/I/57/4, UA.

Captain Biddle, his officers, and crew rowed to the fort. Raised in urban Philadelphia and educated at Princeton, Biddle must have been appropriately impressive in his high-collared, gold epauletted naval uniform, his tousled hair just a bit heroic, his long face unrevealing. Stiff, formal, but a good fellow, Keith always tried to be scrupulously correct. He managed to get on his black dress coat, but lacked enough time to use lime or powdered wood sorrel to get ink spots out of his white vest. That was the best he could do to uphold the appearance of a British gentleman.

Keith breathed easier when the little flotilla was sent over to Point George to cut timber for spars. Only the captain and the ship's surgeon remained for two hours of non-committal small talk that must have been trying for both men. As Keith wrote later, their conversation was "exceedingly social and polite," but the captain did not reveal "the most distant intimation of the object of his visit."[13] Keith recorded that

> towards 5 p. m. accompanied by another of my men in an Indian canoe rowed by the natives, Captain Biddle and surgeon set off to join their party, giving to understand they would go on board; however, learning that they had encamped where my people left them, I next morning dispatched the same two men with some fresh supplies, who soon after returning with accounts of their departure, reported having seen a board unusually painted and nailed upon a tree in a rather secluded and unfrequented place on Point George about one-half mile hence, whereon we found [the sign] inscribed in large characters.
>
> Taken possession of in the name and on
> the behalf of the United States
> by Captain James Biddle, commanding
> the United States Sloop of War, *Ontario*
> Columbia River, August 1818.[14]

The American sailors also nailed another sign on the other side of the river.[15] A trans-Allegheny long-hunter blazing trees to claim a corn-right in "Kaintucky" couldn't have done it any better.

Leaving the other two boats camped overnight to continue cutting spare spars, Captain Biddle had returned to his ship to sleep comfortably

13 James Keith to Frederick Hickey, Fort George, Columbia River, October 7, 1818, British Public Records Office, Foreign Office, 5, Vol. 147, published by Judson, "British Side of the Restoration of Fort Astoria II," 322-25.

14 Ibid.

15 That minor detail would be neglected when the British negotiators tried to draw the Oregon Boundary down the middle of the river in 1846.

in his cozy bunk. Without further exchanges, next day the *Ontario* set sail and departed.

As the United States disappeared over the horizon, the British traders gaped and reddened. The clerk Alexander McKenzie could not resist describing the curious behavior of "Brother Jonathan," as the British sometimes pejoratively referred to the Americans, and his abbreviated visit with just a hint of British superiority.

> Capt[n] [James] Biddle & the Doctor only landed upon which he ordered off his Boats & party about 40 in number to P[t] George there to await him after the cursory topics of salutation we escorted him to the Fort he remained only about half an hour at the Fort during which time he appeared studious to avoid any conversation that might lead to mention the object of his visit & M[r] Keith did not press him on that subject.
>
> he asked a few questions regarding the flour that was landed by the *Levant* belonging to him [which] he said he wished to dispose of it & would be glad if M[r] Keith took it off his hands. he asked this so often that M[r] Keith thinking it would be the means of bringing a subject of more consequence on the tapes agreed at length to purchase the flour and gave him Bills on Canada for the amount having gained his point, Jonathan wished to join his party at P[t] George. M[r] Keith naturally thinking he would be back shortly after did not think it prudent to make any enquiries regarding his visit until he came back. he encamped during the Night at P[t] George & early next morning himself & party went on board this was all we saw of Cap[t] Biddle.[16]

Finding the terse proceedings mystifying and unaccountable, Keith could not believe that a matter of such international consequence turned upon mere commodities. He kept the guns of Fort George shotted and small arms ready for all hands.

A formal but not particularly pompous man, the Fort George factor would remain deflated until a British bouquet was delivered in fall 1818. The pretty formalities of Article One were to be concluded by the United States' Special Agent to Peru and Chile, John B. Prevost, Esq., who was a friend of President Monroe and delegated representative of Secretary of State John Quincy Adams. He had been sent to Valparaiso on the United States warship *Ontario* in early 1818, but had taken a leisurely

16 Alexander McKenzie to J. G. McTavish, Fort George, March 31, 1819, HBCA, F.3/2, fos. 194-195d.

five months attending to State Department obligations. Prevost's duty included representing the United States of America in the restoration of Fort Astoria, but Captain Biddle was not a patient man. Having his ship swinging at anchor for that long was beyond endurance. He departed, as Frederick Merk wrote, "for the Columbia River in the *Ontairo* without his colleague." That explains the unceremonious brevity of his August visit to Fort George.[17]

Left essentially marooned on the Chilean shore, if Prevost was to complete his mission he would have to hitchhike. At Santiago he connected with Captain Frederick Hickey of *HMS Blossom*

> who had orders to proceed to the Columbia for the purpose of restoring Astoria to any representative of the United States who might be empowered to receive it. Prevost proposed to sail as a passenger with Captain Hickey to the Columbia, which hardly comported with his government's previous ideas of national dignity.[18]

The Special Agent and the naval officer might have saved a long trip by completing their obligations on the quarter-deck, but orders were orders. They had a nice companionable sail north to dignify the process.[19] The restitution of Fort George was, according to Keith, quite informal "saving the change of Flag, no Salutes, huzzas, regales or anything whatever ourselves only attending the ceremony."[20] The turnover was documented through an exchange of letters.

> In obedience to the commands of His Royal Highness the Prince Regent, signified in a dispatch from the Right Honorable Earl Bathurst addressed to the Partners or Agents of the North West Company bearing date 27th January 1818 and in obedience to subsequent orders dated the 24th July last from W. H. Sheriff Esqr Captain of His Majestys Ship *Andromache*. We the undersigned do in conformity to the first article of the Treaty of Ghent restore to the government of the United States thro its Agent J. B. Prevost Esqr the Settlement of Fort George on the River Columbia. Given under our hands in triplicate at Fort George (Columbia River) this Sixth day of October one thousand eight hun-

17 Merk, ed., *The Oregon Question*, 23.

18 Merk, ed., *The Oregon Question*, 23.

19 Merk, ed., *The Oregon Question*, 17-24.

20 Contrast Keith's description of the low-keyed affair with what often appears in the regional histories.

dred and eighteen. s/F. Hickey, Captain of His Majestys Ship *Blossom* and s/James Keith of the NW Company.[21]

Although the circumstances and staging might seem haphazard, this was a serious step in international relations. Prevost's acceptance was almost as terse as that previously expressed by Captain James Biddle.

> I do hereby acknowledge to have this day received on behalf of the Government of the United States the possession of the settlement designated on the other side in conformity to the first article of the Treaty of Ghent. Given under my hand in triplicate at Fort George (Columbia River) the sixth day of October one thousand eight hundred and eighteen.
>
> s/ J. B. Prevost, Agent for the U States[22]

However Prevost was a more outgoing and polished diplomat than his predecessor Biddle, and added a not-quite-reassuring note to Keith.

> In answer to your note of this morning I have the honor to state, that the principal object of the President in sending me thus far, was to obtain such information of the place, of its access and of its commercial importance, as might enable him to submit to the consideration of Congress measures for the protection and extension of the Establishment—From hence you will perceive that until the sense of the Government may be taken upon my report, any assurances I might offer to meet the wishes expressed by you, would be as unauthorized as unavailing—

Seeking a better assurance of where the North West Company was being left and what would become of its investment, Keith read on:

> I have sir however no hesitation in saying that should it hereafter comport with the views of the nation to foster the settlement, any claim of the Northwest Company justified by the usages of nations will be liquidated with great liberality; and that should its policy induce a system of exclusion it will never extend to your removal without sufficient notice to prevent loss and injury to the Company.
>
> I cannot conclude without expressing my approbation of the manner in which an establishment so precarious has been managed, nor without offering a hope that the same judicious course may be pursued under

21 HBCA, F.4/61, fo. 11.
22 HBCA, F.4/61, fo. 12d.

> the change of Flag for its success, until the pleasure of the President can be known.[23]

Keith was still uncertain how matters were going to play out for the North West Company, and still a bit miffed by what he considered Captain Biddle's rude behavior. However, his report to Captain Hickey concerning Mr. Prevost's conduct was laudatory.[24]

Captain Hickey also requested an account of the state and condition of Fort George. Always thorough, Keith fussed for another three days to complete the description and then reported,

> I shall first advert to the number of its inhabitants who (myself excepted) were and still are, under either written or verbal agreements, as servants of the North-West Company; consisting of two gentlemen clerks, and one surgeon of Scotch parent, one overseer, seventeen engagees, including mechanics, and mostly Canadians; twenty-six natives of Owhyhee, and one Indian boy (native of the soil) who added to two Owhyhees absent, and sixteen trappers, Canadians and Iroquois employed by the Company among the surrounding tribes to hunt skins, form a grand total of sixty-six persons, exclusive of women and children who may properly be said to belong to the settlement; and with regard to the minor establishments in the interior of this River, supplied from and dependent hereon, the number of people employed, the extent of our trade, annual produce, prospects, and mode of conducting it, it would too far exceed my intended limits to detail, and otherwise I presume is not altogether unknown to Government.[25]

Keith described the "progressive improvements and material changes the settlement had undergone subsequent to its purchase from the American Company in October, 1813" and the cost in labor and expenses to provide protection to persons and property from the weather or Indian attack. That added up to five years of quiet possession despite his view that the Astorians had essentially abandoned the place. The gross amount of property (buildings excluded) on Keith's rough estimate "cannot, I conceive be over rated at about £30,000."

23 J. B. Prevost to James Keith, Fort George Columbia River, October 6, 1818, HBCA, F.3/2, fos. 152-152d.

24 Ibid., James Keith to Frederick Hickey, Fort George, Columbia River, October 7, 1818.

25 The very existence of Fort George seems to have been unknown to the British Government in 1815 when they considered it probably abandoned. Keith was disingenuous in assuming the Government would know anything of its interior trading posts.

"Quiet possession" had required a curious armory of two long 18-pounders mounted in the square of the buildings, six 6-pounders and four 4-pounders, two 6-pound co-horn mortars capable of lobbing shells at an enemy, and seven swivels stationed in the blockhouses or on the platforms, besides blunderbusses, muskets, and fusils. There were eight-hundred round and canister shot for the cartridge guns, principally 18- and 6-pounders, together with a certain proportion of powder, ball, etc., part of which Keith considered indispensable for protecting the trade.

With a sense of improved expectations, Keith optimistically ordered the fort enlarged to 190 by 210 feet and the construction of a new 170-foot building about three hundred yards from the present structures. Those would now stand on ground to which the North West Company was a mere tenant at will of the United States.

Two days after the unceremonious return of the post, Keith undertook to inform the previously pessimistic Simon McGillivray of his actions. After crediting Prevost's suggestion that restraint was preferable to exciting ferment among the natives that might endanger the security of Fort George, Keith continued:

> The evening preceding the Restitution he showed me the sketch of a letter he intended addressing me the following day, which conveying no meaning intelligible to a British ear, much less to that of a British Nwester I told him plainly that his ideas & mine differed in very material points, on which I felt neither disposed nor authorised to enter into discussion; but that in order to simplify the business and curtail all extraneous matter I would merely submit to him a few queries to which he would make such reply as his powers or inclination suggested, hence my note following the Restitution to which I only received an answer towards Sunset—It is but justice to say that he observed throughout (during their stay of two days) a very modest, unassuming & accommodating deportment—no attempt at any exertion of Prerogative over me—[26]

Distant from headquarters and the decision makers, Keith could not say what changes had taken place elsewhere. During the last two years he had found his way through a shared command with a hireling of the

26 James Keith to Simon McGillivray, Fort George, October 8, 1818, HBCA, F.3/2, fos. 154-55.

downstream agents he didn't particularly like, and then a perplexing encounter with a rough-handed naval officer accustomed to delivering broadsides instead of courtesy. It appeared to him that the North West Company should give the place up as soon as possible. Two years earlier he expressed his reservations regarding the fort: "The more we persist the greater the expences & heavier the loss."[27] In that the bookkeeper was prescient, because after eleven years of the expansion of the trade, the bottom-line was not turning out as hoped.

Keith was just a business man trying to keep the Columbia Adventure accounts balanced. As the delegated nabobs of rival nations departed, it was time to get back to business. The plan to increase production appeared to be on a fast track, and with the completion of a substantial depot planned where the Walla Walla River entered the Columbia, Donald McKenzie should be able to exploit the beaver resources of the Snake River.

But Keith had not altered his opinion that "independent of other obstacles something appears wanting among ourselves in the internal management." He intended to express this long-held frustration to the Agents in Canada, "however I may be branded with after changing my Ideas."[28] Keith shared his feelings that the curious circumstances of the retrocession of the Columbia left bruises, if not to the imperial ego, then to the corporate sensibility.

The North West Company fared better than it expected in the changeover because "Brother Jonathan" was unprepared to occupy the ceded settlement. The NWC was allowed to remain in temporary possession "till the pleasure of the President be made known." Keith was disappointed that the British Government was not disposed to go to war (as a secretary of state formerly avowed) for the sake of the Columbia. "I can easily believe but that without having recourse to such desperate alternative they might have observed a little more faith and consistency [which] we had every reason to expect."

On a more optimistic note Keith continued that "our motions in this now famed corner though very slow are I believe progressive as regards

27 McGillivray to Keith, Fort William, July 28, 1816, Keith Papers, UA.

28 James Keith to Simon McGillivray, Fort George, October 8, 1818, HBCA, F.3/2, fos. 154-55.

Returns. The interior I am of opinion will more than compensate for any deficiency arising from our Trappers at this place."[29]

During the winter of 1818-19 Keith encountered an unfortunate situation that led to an embarrassing loss of life. A party sent toward Puget Sound returned with optimistic reports of finding more dens of beaver on the Cowlitz River. Nicholas Oskonanton, whose attitude in the Snake country alienated him from his fellow Iroquois, had been sent downriver to Fort George where James Keith sent him to hunt with other Iroquois on the Cowlitz. As they began trapping, the troublemaker could not resist meddling with a young Cowlitz woman and was murdered "by the Natives of that quarter & cut up in a manner too horrid to relate." Clerk Alexander McKenzie admitted, "Our little band was attacked & obliged to abandon the country,"[30] That required a punitive response and by then Keith had just the man to conduct it, Peter Skene Ogden.[31]

Reports of outrageous behavior against rival HBC traders at Ile a la Crosse by the bully Nor'westers Samuel Black and Peter Skene Ogden were so appalling that Ogden was sent across the mountains. When he arrived at Fort George with the 1819 spring brigade, Keith gave him the command of a punitive party of thirty or so Iroquois and freemen sent to confront the Cowlitz Indians about Oskonanton's murder. If justice was their concern, this posse was the worst possible combination Keith could have sent. The encounter ended in the slaughter of twelve innocent Cowlitz men, women, and children, a "lesson" that they have not forgiven to this day. Later, when the Cowlitz chief was induced to come to Fort George to receive condolence gifts, he was ambushed and nearly killed by jealous Chinooks.

29 James Keith to J. G. McTavish, Fort George, February 6, 1819, HBCA, F.3/2, fos. 186-87. Keith was right in anticipating an increase in returns from the interior as a result of Donald McKenzie's fur brigades.

30 Alexander McKenzie to J. G. McTavish, Fort George, March 31, 1819, HBCA, F.3/2, fos. 194-195d. Although Keith made several attempts to extend the trade of the lower Columbia, that did not prevent the harping Alexander Ross from writing that they "had not taken a single step to improve the trade...every one in turn made the best of not deviating from the steps of his predecessor but adhering as much as possible to the old habits and convenience while jaunting up and down the river in the old beaten path." Ross, *Fur Hunters*, 521-53.

31 Ogden was still at Ile a la Crosse on June 26, 1817, when the passing Ross Cox "bid adieu to the humerous, honest, eccentric, law-defying Peter Ogden, the terror of Indians, and the delight of all gay fellows." Cox, *Columbia River*, 309.

Keith seems unfortunate in his clerks at Fort George. Alexander Ross had been untrustworthy in his relationship with Donald McKenzie and the next clerk, Alexander McKenzie, could not wait to reveal this series of tragic events—so embarrassing to his superior that Keith tried to conceal it. The gossip-monger clerk reported that

> They paid dear for this affair. Immediately on hearing this news [of Oskonanton's murder] Mr Keith sent off a war party headed by Mr [Peter] Ogden you may believe under one of his general knowledge the expedition succeeded. I would willingly inform you what took place but Mr Keith made me pledge my word I would not mention a syllable of what transpired. I am afraid I have incured your displeasure for not doing so but I am sure you would not wish that I should hazard a falsehood & consequently lose Mr Keiths good Opinion. My Dear Sir—I know your great policy is truth.[32]

Keith never revealed a bias against Iroquois as Ross and McKenzie did. He knew that the unfortunate consequences of the punitive expedition reflected poorly upon his responsibility as a foreign trader operating in American territory, to keep the peace and protect the natives.[33]

The retrocession of Fort George to the Americans remained controversial. In June 1819 Thomas Thain, a partner in McTavish, McGillivray & Company, argued that Fort George was British property as a result of a legal sale, the same argument presented by Simon McGillivray to the British government, to no avail.[34] Thain alluded to another treaty; the recently concluded Convention of Commerce between Great Britain and the United States, signed on October 20, 1818. Article III of that Convention stated "any Country that may be claimed by either Party on the north-west coast of America, westward of the Stony Mountains, shall...be free and open for the term of 10 years from the date of the signature of the Present Convention, to the Vessels, Citizens and Subjects of the 2 powers."[35] Thain continued:

32 Alexander McKenzie to J. G. McTavish, Fort George, March 31, 1819, HBCA, F.3/2, fos. 194-195d.

33 Keith Papers, A-676, A-2, NAC.

34 Thomas Thain to James Keith, Montreal, June 7, 1819, Keith Papers, 769/I/57/3, UA.

35 Treaties and Agreements Affecting Canada (Ottawa: F. A. Acland, 1927), 16.

It now remains to be ascertained, whether anything can be made of the Trade under the Arrangement with Mess[rs] Perkins as it has been ascertained, that the Expense attending our Vessels cannot be supported—It would have saved the Concern several thousand Pounds—if the Old *Columbia* had been burnt, when she loaded her Cargo[36]—It is not intended to send anything to the Coast this Season, as it is supposed the Goods sent last year would suffice for two Years—I regret to inform you that the prospect for sales at Canton was very unfavorable last December—However our friends there would keep back the Furs in expectation of obtaining better prices.[37]—we are still without accounts of the Beaver Sale—But such is the present Commercial distress in England, that I expect only a small proportion of it would be sold, as we cannot afford to sell that article at very reduced prices—However I trust these difficulties will only be temporary & that Trade & Confidence will again revive—[38]

36 Thain's point was that the insurance on the ship and cargo would likely have returned more to the Company than could be expected from the Adventure itself.

37 Their "friends" in Canton consisted of Perkins and Company, agents for J. and T. H. Perkins and Company of Boston. The furs aboard the *Levant* sold for an average of $3.35 per pelt. *See* Perkins Company Papers, Vol. 19, 79-3734, p. 13.

38 Thain to Keith, Montreal, June 7, 1819. The Perkins Company sent the *Levant* again in 1819 carrying little except for flour, Indian corn, and a few articles of dry goods.

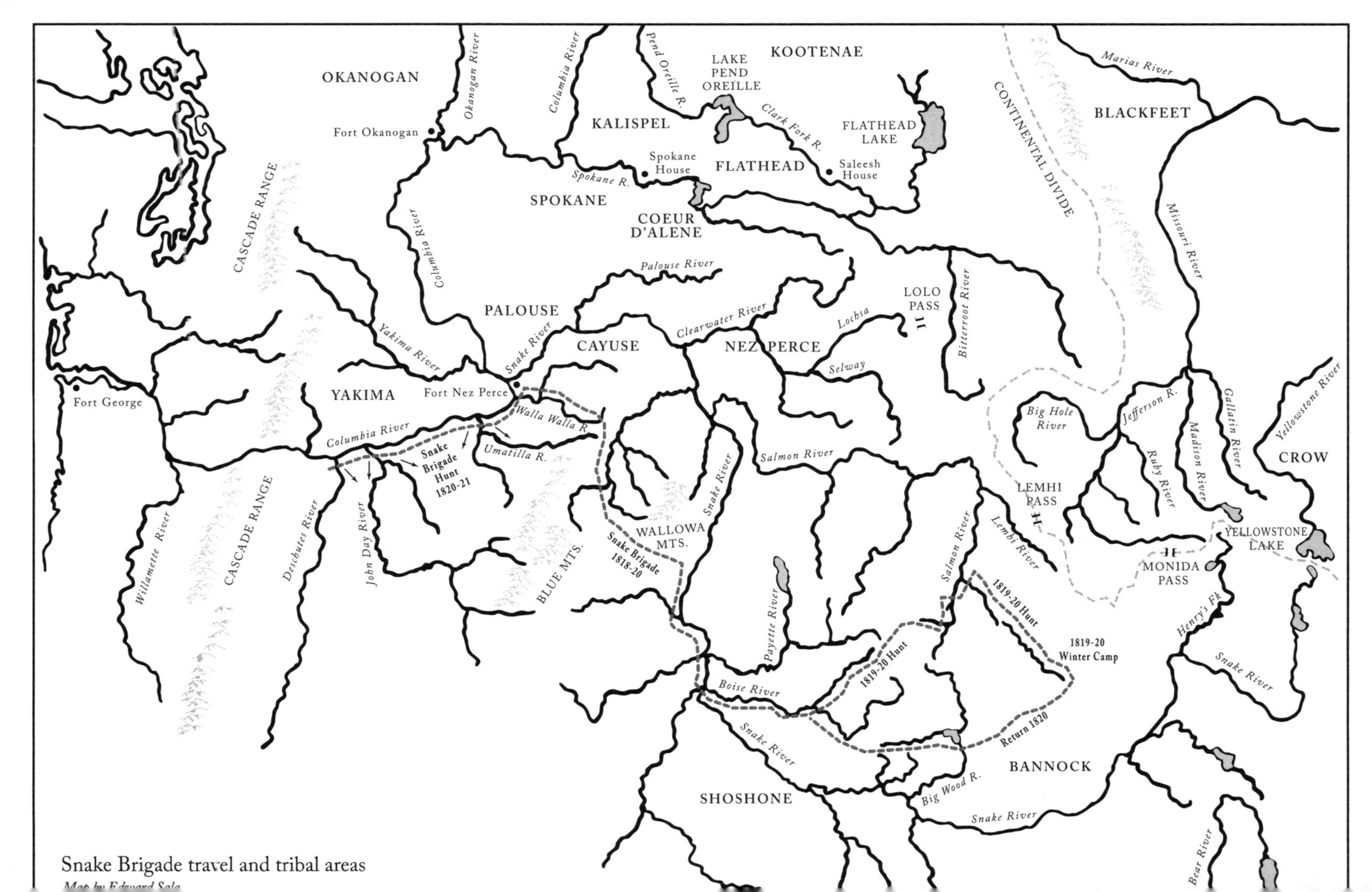

Snake Brigade travel and tribal areas

Map by Edward Sala

Chapter Fifteen

Fort Nez Perces and the Snake Country Hunting Brigades

ALTHOUGH THE DEVELOPMENT of the NWC Columbia Adventure seemed fixed on Fort George, the Salish country posts continued to send down substantial packs of beaver and other small furs, as did the caravans of limping packhorses trotting the trail from the Fraser River to Okanogan. Even the neglected Willamette River Valley contributed peltry that would give the Beaver State its modern-day catchphrase. But in 1819 the diminishing hopes of the concerned agency in distant Montreal were focused on the still uncertain increase in beaver production.

Recovering some degree of financial balance depended on the returns from the 1818–19 Snake Brigade hunt, but the packs that Donald McKenzie sent to Fort Nez Perces failed to go to Fort George with the spring brigade. James Keith was unable to give an accurate estimate of its value, but when those boats returned upstream, he forwarded the goods essential to resupply those hunters. Alexander Ross sent outfit 1819–20 on to McKenzie under charge of William Kittson.

In mid-April 1820 Donald McKenzie began trying to recall his scattered Iroquois trappers. After six weeks he accumulated almost 3,000 parchment (dry) beaver and otter at the place where the Boise entered the Snake. But he was unable to provide his hunters with new equipment until the new outfit arrived from Fort Nez Perces. Getting desperate, McKenzie sent ten men to meet Kittson's supply train, keeping just three freemen with him. His letter to Ross stated, "Although the natives are at present in a very unsettled state yet if the contemplated peace succeeds I hope that our success in this quarter next year will come up to the expectation of every reasonable man."[1] Until the packtrain arrived, the four

1 Ross, *Fur Hunters*, 143. The letter is missing but believed to be accurate.

men forted up behind the packs of beaver and nervously waited. They were not far from the place where John Reed and eight trappers had been killed by Bannocks five years previously.

Here was a good story that Ross repeated thirty-six years later when writing for publication. He thought that incident needed spicing up and described McKenzie's lonely vigil in dramatic detail. Hostiles were known to be in the area and, according to Ross, a party of Bannocks rode up to the edge of the river opposite their breastworks on an island. A desultory exchange of some trifles gave the Bannocks an opportunity to appraise the outfit and count the guns of the four men. Their demands turned aggressive and they threatened to step over the breastwork and help themselves to whatever property pleased them. In answer, McKenzie sprang forward, cradling a keg of gunpowder, brandishing a lighted match and threatening to blow everyone to hell. The desperate threat so terrified the belligerents that "the savages…took to flight."[2]

The anecdote made for exciting reading, but did it actually happen? A number of historians have thought so, including Hubert Howe Bancroft in his classic *History of the Northwest Coast*, David Lavender in *Land of Giants*, Alvin Josephy in *The Nez Perce Indians*, and William Goetzmann, who included it in his Pulitzer Prize-winning *Exploration and Empire*.[3] However, is there a lesson for unquestioning historians about being suspicious of this and similar stories when the protagonist is imbued with heroic qualities?

In the 1855 publication of *The Fur Traders of the Far West*, Alexander Ross claimed a role in the development of the Columbia Adventure by mixing questionable facts with a highly-charged repetition of this old chestnut. Travel narratives are notorious for blending fact with fiction. Percy G. Adams, author of *Travelers & Travel Liars, 1660-1800*, heads one of his chapters with this epigraph: "Seek the reasons that writers may have for deceiving themselves, for deceiving you. Be critical: Otherwise it will come to pass that people will give to the truth and to the lie the same degree of authority."[4]

---

2 Ross, *Fur Hunters*, 147-49.

3 The story is also repeated by Trenholm and Cary, *The Shoshonis*, 53-54; by Atkin, "Snake River Fur Trade," 301; and by Nielsen, "Donald McKenzie in the Snake Country Fur Trade," 173-74

4 (Berkeley: University of California Press, 1962), 223.

Anthropologist Bruce White has documented at least six different versions of this "gunpowder story," which he terms "occupational folklore." An early rendition was recorded in 1751. White concludes that the "presence of such elements are remnants of folktales that fur traders once told each other."[5] The Indian trader and interpreter John Long included a 1778 occurrence of the gunpowder threat in his *Voyages and Travels*. Ross liked the story so well that he used it three times, first on page 166 of his *First Settlers*, again on page 178, and finally in *Fur Hunters*. An oft-told tale spun around a campfire is innocuous in itself, but Ross employed it as a device to promote McKenzie's stature. What started out as occupational folklore became part of the "occupational fact" carried forward by new historians.[6] In this case, the lesson is to approach the data from Ross with caution.

McKenzie waited twenty-two days for Kittson to make the round trip between Fort Nez Perces and Indian Creek. When the additional men Keith sent from Fort George arrived, McKenzie was ready to move beyond his old winter camp with about seventy trappers and camp keepers.[7] Leaving Kittson to build two houses or hangars near the mouth of the Boise River, the brigade may have entered the mountains following the east fork of the Payette River or more likely the north fork of the Boise.[8]

A landmark was mentioned on September 10, 1819, when McKenzie wrote a letter to Ross and dated it "Black Bears' Lake." That alpine body is now known as Redfish Lake (referring to its Sockeye salmon run) and the nearby Bear River is now Valley Creek.[9] Although a scenic wonder surrounded by magnificent mountains, a body of water likely to freeze ice three feet thick was no place to winter either horses or trappers.[10]

5 White, "The Fear of Pillaging: Economic Folktales," 199-200.

6 In most of the versions, the threatening hostiles would not have understood the danger of an explosion.

7 The fifty-five trappers of the initial Snake Hunting Brigade had been reduced by ten Iroquois: one killed, two deserted, and seven runaways who went to live with the local Indians. The addition of fifteen new men plus two clerks totals seventy, although Ross put the 1819–20 brigade count at seventy-five.

8 Rich, ed., *Ogden's Snake Country Journals*, 91. Vandals soon burned the houses.

9 Benchmark Maps, *Idaho Road and Recreation Atlas* (Medford, Oregon: Benchmark Maps, 2010), map 53.

10 In 1824 Alexander Ross had men with him who had previously traveled with McKenzie and knew the present Valley Creek that joins the Salmon River at Stanley, Idaho, as Bear River. The Black Bears' Lake that McKenzie mentioned in September was the lake that drains into the Salmon River south of the Stanley Basin.

Because the previous year's hunt was made from a stationary camp near Woody Point, this was McKenzie's first experiment in employing a moving trapping brigade. A trapping party going about its business moved slowly, spreading out to make sets for a night or more and checking those traps in the morning. That meant the standard of a day's travel depended on an elastic mileage as McKenzie worked away from the Stanley Basin and down the Salmon River until the brigade turned up the Pahsimeroi branch. Crossing yet another rugged divide, the hunters eventually arrived on another of those streams that start out promising in the high places and end up being sucked down into ever-thirsty lava tubes of the Snake Plain.

Idaho historian Merle Wells concluded that Donald McKenzie's 1819-20 winter camp was located in the Little Lost River Valley.[11] The editor of Ogden's 1827-29 *Journals* put the location near Badger Creek. Trapper John Day's dedicated biographer, Nick Sheedy, has explored the area in detail and concluded that the camp would have been just below present Fallert Springs, perhaps along Uncle Ike Creek.[12]

Alluvial fans stretching down to the Little Lost River provided good grazing for buffalo or horse herds and trees along the stream or winter red brush growing thick around springs supported beaver havocs (workings). To the north trails from the Little Lost River connected to the Pahsimeroi; to the south Indian roads let to the Snake River plains, or west over another range of mountains to Big Lost River. A trail that started above Fallert Springs used Pass Creek through the Lemhi Range and dropped into the Birch Creek drainage. Those were traditional roads of the Shoshone and also used by raiders from the northern plains coming to steal horses or seek war-game glory.

The location of John Day's grave was a known landmark as late as 1827 when the HBC's Peter Skene Ogden arranged to meet the detachment of Thomas McKay there. Upon arriving, Ogden found that the site had been occupied by three hundred lodges sheltering as many as fifteen hundred Shoshone whose herd of three thousand horses had laid waste

11 Wells, "Donald Mackenzie's Little Lost River Campsite," 29-30, 224; Elliott, "Journal of Alexander Ross," 375-77.

12 *Idaho Road and Recreation Atlas*, map 66.

to the grazing lands. Lacking vegetation to support his failing horses, Ogden left a note for McKay and moved on.[13]

McKenzie located his Little Lost River winter camp of 1819–20 in a location favored by local tribes. References to the wintering place and the vicinity of John Day's burial site can be found in Ross's 1824 journal, Ogden's 1824–25 journal, and William Kittson's 1825 journal and map. Kittson, who had rejoined McKenzie by then, mentioned later that the winter camp included McKenzie, Kittson, James Birnie, and Jaco Finlay, as well as twelve engaged men and twenty-two trappers, for a total of thirty-eight men in all. But between thirty-two and thirty-seven other free trappers are unaccounted for and their location unknown.

The operative details of the beaver hunt were being worked out as they hunted, not by managerial geniuses in Montreal, not by struggling field supervisors, but by the trappers. An understanding was developing among mountaineers that about thirty men was a workable number for a trapping brigade, large enough to discourage hostiles and small enough to keep trappers from interfering with each other's sets. Sometime between 1818 and 1820 a party of thirty or so freemen following Michel Bourdon worked southeast to another river which they called the Bear. William Kittson, who was present in the 1819 winter camp, attributed the river discovery to Bourdon, which Peter Skene Ogden later confirmed and added a branch which was also known as Bourdon's Fork.[14]

Unnoticed in Alexander Ross's magnification of McKenzie's accomplishments was the presence on the trail of his country wife, Mary McKay. She must have accompanied the 1819–20 brigade because John Day is represented as having taken a shine to her infant daughter Rachel. When he was dying on February 15, 1820, it appears Day had a curious and legalistic will drawn up, naming Donald McKenzie as his executor and recipient of property Day owned west of St. Louis, Missouri. And further, the will read, "I give and bequeath to Miss Rachel McKenzie of Columbia River all and every my ready cash with the lawful interest rising therefrom, and lying in the hands of my former master, Mr. John

13 Glyndwr Williams, ed., *Peter Skene Ogden's Snake Country Journals 1827-28 and 1828-29*, Introduction and notes by David E. Miller and David H. Miller (London: The Hudson's Bay Record Society, 1971), 24, 171.

14 Rich, ed., *Ogden's Snake Country Journals*, 40, 229, 231-32.

Jacob Astor, Merchant of New York."[15] The will was witnessed by the clerks William Kittson and James Birnie and delivered to McKenzie for safe keeping. After they broke camp to undertake the 1820 spring hunt, the Little Lost River was also known as John Day's River.

McKenzie also set out from his winter base camp "on a trip of discovery towards the south," from which he returned after only ten days. To have traveled as far south as the Bear River and Bear Lake in the southeast corner of present Idaho or through the mountains to the Green River, McKenzie would have had to average fifty miles a day. In his Fort George memorandum book James Keith recorded "D[d] M[c]K supposed to have advanced to 43 ¼ N. Lat, 113 ½ W. Long."[16]

Those coordinates place McKenzie's furthest advance just south of today's Craters of the Moon National Monument and west of Big Southern Butte. Adjusting twenty miles or so eastward supports McKenzie's claim to have "crossed and recrossed many parts I had seen in 1811."[17] There was nothing at this particularly barren expanse to interest trappers unless Ogden was trying to connect with Shoshones. Or he could have sent an engagé or obliging tribesman, to make the approximately eighty-mile ride across the barren Snake Plain to the winter camps Shoshones favored near the mouth of the Portneuf River.[18] The explorer continued with comments on a circuitous winter trip to the headwaters of the great south branch (the Snake).

But it is also possible that Ross, not McKenzie, wrote those words based on what McKenzie told him later or what he learned in 1824 when he was accompanied by freemen who traveled with Bourdon to the Bear River and Bear Lake.

During the winter, four bands of Shoshones camped near the trappers, giving McKenzie the opportunity to meet with them and propose a peace. The reason for McKenzie's hasty return to camp after just ten days was "political," in modern parlance. The Snake country roiled with hostile

15 Naming McKenzie and his daughter Rachel as beneficiaries is suspect. The timing and careful legalese of Day's will suggest McKenzie may have been less than honorable years later in pressing the document's stipulations. Elliott, "Last Will and Testament of John Day."

16 James Keith, Memoranda Book, 27. James Keith Estate Papers, A-676, 27, NAC.

17 Ibid., 136.

18 Supposition based on later clues and the location of the present reservation.

"Portrait of Peter Skene Ogden," Henry J. Warre, ca. 1845. *Library and Archives Canada, C-27147.*

parties of Nez Perce, Bannocks, and Shoshones upon whom Blackfeet from the upper Missouri were now imposing. Shoshone leaders of the bands who wintered near the Little Lost River brigade camp told McKenzie they feared those northern plainsmen more than their traditional Nez Perce sparring partners.

McKenzie assumed responsibility for arranging a peace council that included influential chiefs of eastern, buffalo-hunting bands and fifty-four other considerable tribesmen. The Nez Perce had already agreed to a peace if Ogden could get the Shoshone to respond in kind. The bands who came welcomed the opportunity to lessen inter-tribal harassment, although they could not answer for others, such as the Bannocks, who did not attend. This "apostle of peace," as H. H. Bancroft styled McKenzie, used his unsurpassed knowledge of Indian character to establish peace among former enemies and conduct trade with Indians where none before him had yet succeeded.[19] Of course this conciliation didn't last: tribal elders, no matter how well meaning, were unable to control their young warriors.

The horse manure treaty (so called because dried turds were said to have been traditionally smoked to confirm an agreement), allowed Alexander Ross to claim that petty jealousy and lack of initiative on the part of the proprietors at Fort George needlessly impeded McKenzie's Snake

19 Bancroft, *History of the North West Coast*, 2:275-76.

Country brigades.[20] But as long as ships arrived on the Columbia River in time, and outfits were dispatched upriver from Fort George, McKenzie or Ross could not complain about a lack of trade goods or manpower.

The problem, since David Thompson's first crossing to the Pacific Slope, was getting tribesmen to forego war gamesmanship and convert to commercial beaver hunting. With herds of buffalo grazing on the Snake Plains and salmon seasonally ascending the river, proud horsemen saw no reason to step down to dig a beaver from its bank side den. Others stole traps from the freemen, learned to use them, or harassed the white strangers for stealing a valuable commodity from them.

Some tribal delegates may have remained with the winter camp, under the welcome protection of the trappers and their guns. What was later described as the "War Road of the Blackfeet" crossed the Lemhi Pass and hooked south down the Birch Creek Valley and around the end of the Lemhi Range. Those hardy northern plainsmen came in the dead of winter as well as during tortured summers to harry Snakes and capture horses. By making his winter camp on the Little Lost River, Donald McKenzie and his winter campers had been out of the way enough to avoid hostiles.

At the end of the second spring hunt, McKenzie had packs to deliver and a gnawing uncertainty about his three-year contract. It was a twenty-two-day trip to the Blue Mountain crossing and he hurried the brigade on a direct way between the Sawtooth Mountains on the right and the tortured Craters of the Moon on his left. Passing the ashes of Kittson's hangars at the mouth of the Boise River, McKenzie's last Snake Brigade arrived at Fort Nez Perces on June 22, 1820, two days later than the return date he had predicted the previous September. Seventy men and their families jogged on some of the 154 horses, accompanied by a band of friendly Cayuse Indians who fell in with them in the Blue Mountains. The two-mile long packtrain probably descended the Umatilla River to the Columbia and traveled east along the south shore through the Wallula Gap to the fort.

---

20 Ross did not criticize any of the North West Company partners by name and explicitly excluded James Keith from his critical remarks when he informed McKenzie, "Mr. Keith has been led astray by the zeal of his associates, left to himself he is a good man." Ross, *Fur Hunters*, 70.

The spring downriver flotilla conducted by the most recent Spokane postmaster, John Haldane, had already passed. That added 2,711 pelts from the Flathead trade to the returns from Outfit 1818-19 that had been held over, making a total of 9,940 beaver. When the trade at Fort George was added, the Boston ship *Levant* had sailed on May 25, 1820, carrying 16,120 pelts to China. Because Nicholas Montour was held up by deep snow coming from the Kutenai country, James McMillan would follow later with two canoes. As matters turned out, the returns of a good but not great 1819-20 hunt would be shipped to England.

McKenzie's introduction of a mobile hunting brigade to increase production was a moderately successful test, but he could not produce a miracle. Now the three-year contract with McTavish, McGillivray & Company was about to expire and the Snake Brigade leader would have to abandon a unique hunting experiment just as it was beginning to prove itself.

Alexander Ross optimistically wrote that "McKenzie was again at his post, and turning their faces once more toward the Snake country, they left Fort Nez Perces on July 4, 1820 after a short stay of only twelve days."[21] That might have seemed to be a heroic dedication to the experiment—until Finnan McDonald revealed that McKenzie did not return to the Snake country but dispersed the brigade along the south side of the Columbia River:

> I Receved a Letter the other day from M^r^ D M^c^Kenzey dated to December the 5th [1820] in the summer he wen down with the most Part of his men as far as the Falls on the south side of the Columbia near the Mountins and set them all at work with there traps after shoeing [showing] them the Cuntre and where Beaver was to be Kild and he Brought all the Horses Back with him and Left them with nothing but there Traps and Guns arrived at the Fort Walla Walla fue Days before the Bregade from Fort William got there—from there went down in the Bots to Fort George to have the Eye on the Bregade with Mr Barniey [James Birnie] he remane only 5 Days at fort George and start with 4 Boats Loded of Goods Let [Left] that Plase he had not a singil our [hour] of Drie wather til he Come be low the Big Dals [Dalles] and as he Came to the Falls the Cole wather Began to smoe [snow] and sharp

21 Ross, *Fur Hunters*, 182-83.

> wine [wind] which the river the next Day was ful of Ice and snoe and got grate deale of mesurey [misery] to Come to the Fort with the Crafts the Goods all wite [wet?] as if it was takin from the Bottom of the River.[22]

McKenzie scattered small groups of trappers on the south side of the Columbia at the present Umatilla River, Willow Creek, Rock Creek, John Day, and Deschutes Rivers as far downstream as The Dalles. After their horses were driven back to fatten on the rich grass of the Walla Walla Valley, those marooned pedestrians were expected to hunt without supervision. The tactic spread seventy experienced trappers along streams that drained into the Columbia instead of the Snake, and netted fewer than 2,150 pelts, a number significantly lower than the previous year.

Writing years later after knowing the results, Ross glossed over the truth about the third expedition because he knew that McKenzie was uncertain about his standing with the Montreal agents. Predictably, Ross inflated the results when he noted the brigade arrived at Fort Nez Perces in July, 1821 "with an increase of returns."[23] In his words,

> While these changes were passing on[,] who should arrive in health and high spirits at Nez Perces after another year's absence but McKenzie from the Snake country, on the 10th of July 1821, with an increase of returns and the good fortune not to lose a man. At this period his contract of five years had expired, and the object of his mission was fully accomplished; but being too late in the season to get out of the country he passed the winter with me at Fort Nez Perces and crossed the Rocky Mountains in the autumn of 1822.

The Fort Nez Perces clerk revised that claim when he penned his memoir thirty-five years later. When his *Fur Traders of the Far West* was published at London in 1855, it was obvious that the British Empire had lost the disputed Oregon Country to the United States. Ross's laudatory account of Donald McKenzie's success in the Snake country, obscured by gratuitous asides about natural history or geography, was an attempt to shift responsibility for a failure upon Keith. But memory betrayed Ross.

22 Finan McDonald to J. G. McTavish, Flat Head House, March 2, 1821, HBCA, F.3/2, fos. 234-35.

23 Ross, *Fur Hunters*, 185.

As the author, Ross may have been "bent on making a spoon or spoiling a horn" as he put it, by contriving to ladle out a stew of misinformation. In just one paragraph of the edification of his hero, there are six errors of fact.

As a last survivor of a great adventure Alexander Ross's book became the main source for the activities of the two Snake River hunting brigades. But, as those operations faded in memory, historians relying solely on an unchallenged source have been, and will continue to be, led astray by an old man's recollections.

Fort George (Astoria), c. 1848, H. J. Warre.
Library and Archives of Canada, C-001626.

Chapter Sixteen

"We cannot blame ourselves therefore"

A Financial Failure

The North West Company organized as a partnership of competing equals. As the simplicity of trading a skin and carrying packs into or out of the upper country became a complex, international business, the organization moved beyond the management abilities of isolated wintering partners. Business was conducted by downstream agencies in Montreal and London, which expanded the business to include shipping to foreign markets. After expensive development, the business plan to sell Pacific Northwest beaver was faltering because of the inability of the Canton market to keep absorbing inferior beaver. In desperation the Montreal agency, McTavish, McGillivray and Company, had disregarded regulations and alienated many wintering partners by hiring Donald McKenzie, an outsider and a former Astorian for a three-year experiment to increase production.

As the premise of the North West Company Columbia Adventure teetered on the edge of financial failure, no one understood the difficulties of the Canton market better than the sometime supercargo Angus Bethune. Dissidents were already approaching the rival Hudson's Bay Company about a merger when William McGillivray wrote to Fort George factor James Keith on July 13, 1820, admitting there was a strong idea among the wintering partners of withdrawing from the country:

> On the affairs of the Columbia I have little to say further than what has been stated to you in the communication from the agents—There you will perceive an idea strongly held out of withdrawing from the Country—no man can regret this necessity more than myself, & happy shall I be if things turn out more favorably than is now contemplated, but we

> are weary of experiments, and if the expenses cannot be brought to a scale considerably less than the returns—we must give it up—[1]

Access to seven years of Canton sales data should have provided the Montreal agents with enough data to see the pattern of low prices for beaver in that market. McGillivray was not blaming the exertions of James Keith or Donald McKenzie for increasing the returns of Columbia drainage beaver. The fault lay with the agency for not keeping informed of changes in world markets. In galling contrast, their chief American rival, John Jacob Astor, was doing just that and adjusting his trade accordingly.[2]

After inheriting the management of the partnership from their uncle Simon McTavish and directing operations for many years, William and Simon McGillivray were being left to play catch up in the negotiations for terms. At the Fort William meeting in 1820, Angus Bethune had been teamed with John McLoughlin as spokesmen for eighteen wintering partners who were dissatisfied how their interests were represented. Dispatched to London, upon arrival they inquired if the HBC would be interested in replacing McTavish, McGillivray & Company as agents for the North West Company. On March 26, 1821, the McGillivray brothers joined Edward Ellice of the London agency and, without consulting the wintering partners, agreed to "a deed of co-partnership" with the HBC.

When William McGillivray went to Fort William the following July, he regretfully wrote to a friend, "I have been an Agent and Director since 1794 and Chief Superintendent since 1799…I was the first English clerk engaged in the Service of the N. W. Co, on its first Establishment in 1784 and I have put my Hand and Seal to the Instrument which closes its career—and [its] name in 1821."[3] William McGillivray would not forget that his brother Duncan McGillivray, friend Donald McTavish, and associate Alexander Henry died trying to make the Columbia Adventure succeed.

When the merger of rival firms was agreed upon, thirty-two of the fifty-three commissioned officers in the reorganized Hudson's Bay Company, more than half, were former Nor'westers. Seven of the new chief

---

1 The current agreement between the Montreal agents and the wintering partners was due to elapse in 1822.

2 Haeger, *John Jacob Astor*, 82.

3 McGillivray to John Strachan, July 1821, Fort William, in MacKay, *The Honourable Company*, 148-53, 158-60, 163-64.

factors had served in the Columbia Department and understood why the business plan had failed. McTavish, McGillivray & Company did not grasp the inescapable problems of shipping less desirable peltry to a reluctant market. Managing the Columbia Adventure from a continent away and maritime intricacies from the shore, William McGillivray had been unable to answer the physical demands of a distant department or coordinate the efforts of disruptive partners. He and his brother Simon were still rationalizing the collapse on the first of September 1823 when Simon penned a memo:

> the restrictions imposed on the private trade by the E.I.Co [East India Company] and the disadvantageous manner of remittance caused expenses which the trade could not bear & subsequently in 1813 & 1814 the case was the same, when the NWCo sent the skins to Canton in British ships and subject to the regulations of the E.I.Co. In both cases the result was the same, the trade was thrown into the hands of the Americans & after paying their heavy charges & large commissions, it was still more profitable to the Proprietors than to continue it on their own acct.[4]

Simon's tardy excuse has the smell of the brothers inability to admit that they had missed (or ignored) a long list of negative indications. During their early careers, beaver had been the only fur to bear the expense of transport. Now the expense of shipping undesirable beaver to the only China market was too costly to maintain and increasing production only added expenses.

Simon's recognition was written two years after the best informed partner in the west, James Keith, arrived at the Fort William annual meeting in July and read a letter from Montreal stating "that an union had been effected with the Hudson's Bay Co. upon principles of equality as to division and in which provision was made for our wintering Partners...Not only every part of the Trade in the N.W. & H. Bay territory, but the Columbia, Temiscamingue, Kings Post, Grand River &c &c are included in the agreement"[5] Keith was already packed for a trip to London where he hoped to ingratiate himself with the new management. If

4 "Memo of Simon McGillivray, 1 September 1823." HBCA, A 7/1, fol. 39, in Gough, "The North West Company's 'Adventure to China'," 329.

5 John Richardson to James Keith, Montreal, June 9, 1821, James Keith Papers, MSS (Davidson & Garden) 2769/I/57/4, UA.

increased production was supposed to answer the problem of selling beaver in Canton, he knew that between 1816 and 1821, the annual Columbia returns had increased to an average of 13,045 skins, a 75% improvement during that period, but not all of that increase reflected the contribution of the Snake country brigades.

Keith knew that the other three-fourths came from other established and consistently productive posts. Donald McKenzie's efforts added significantly to each year's returns, but had not "revolutionized the fur trade in the Far Northwest" as some have since claimed.[6] Quite the contrary, the expenses incurred in the Snake country business coupled with depressed beaver prices in Canton and the costs of shipping to England instead, led the agents in Montreal to allow the trapping brigade arrangement with McKenzie to expire.[7]

If the intent was to increase profits rather than merely increase returns, Donald McKenzie's efforts had been a complete waste of resources and the North West Company would have been better off if the Snake country brigade experiment had never been attempted. The entire Columbia business was never profitable and the Snake country brigades only added to the expense.

Despite this obvious conclusion, historians, sifting what limited evidence they could find, have concluded instead that the North West Company's "Adventure to the Columbia" resulted in a devastating financial loss because of inept and unimaginative management.[8] For example, Frederick Merk accepted among the causes for the company's failure the absence of compelling leadership, jealousy and bickering between the wintering partners in the region, and the "lax and wasteful methods which had crept into the trade when the country was virgin and its opportunities rich."[9] William Goetzmann labeled the leadership as "ridiculously inept and shortsighted."[10] So did Canadian historian Arthur Morton, who also described the North West partners as shortsighted and "punctilious" in their myopia.[11] Hubert Howe Bancroft character-

6 Goetzmann, *Exploration and Empire*, 88.

7 McGillivray to Keith, July 13, 1820.

8 An exception is Gough, "The North West Company's 'Adventure of China'," 309-31.

9 Merk, ed., *Fur Trade and Empire*, xxiv-xxvi. Merk relied, in large measure, on George Simpson's views in 1824-25.

10 Goetzmann, *Exploration and Empire*, 80.

11 Morton, *A History of the Canadian West*, 618.

ized one proprietor as "possess[ing] a remarkable facility for bungling business."[12] John Galbraith argued that the Hudson's Bay Company later earned considerable profit from the returns of the Columbia, confirming that "the losses suffered by the North West Company had been caused primarily by bad management."[13]

Upon closer inspection, however, this widely held view is refuted by new evidence drawn from North West Company journals and letters written by or to the principals involved. Despite the commonly held historical interpretation to the contrary, the North West Company's "Adventure to the Columbia" did not fail because of mismanagement on the part of the concern's leadership at Fort George. It failed because of a factor over which the Company's agents had absolutely no control—the consistently low price offered for Columbia beaver in China.

In the beginning the Nor'Westers had good reason to be optimistic about their expansion plan. As late as 1808 their fine North American beaver had found its way to northern China through intermediaries and sold at a good price.[14] The company's agents in Montreal thought that London furs were selling in St. Petersburg, Russia, for transshipment to China. The Russians were willing to pay 25 percent more than that offered at the London auctions and despite tremendous transportation costs getting the furs some 5,000 miles to market, the Russians were still able to make a profit.[15] There seemed no reason profits could not be improved by selling directly to Canton.

McGillivray optimistically ignored the disadvantage created by the inability to sell Chinese goods on the London market. American merchants could sell porcelain, silk, teas, and other Chinese goods in home markets for additional profit, but that trade was denied the North West Company by the trading monopoly granted the East India Company by their royal charter. Their expensive license was nontransferable, and application had to be made anew with each adventure.[16] When the NWC

12 Bancroft, *History of the Northwest Coast*, 2:287.

13 Galbraith, *The Hudson's Bay Company as an Imperial Factor*, 81.

14 London Locked Private Letter Book, 1823-1846, HBCA, A.7/1, fos. 38d-90, pp. 26-27.

15 Ibid., fos. 26-29d, pp. 1-8. The distance from St. Petersburg to Peking was estimated by the Russians at 7,538 versts. One verst equaled a little more than one kilometer, or .6629 miles.

16 The North West Company did send two more ships to the North American coast in which it held at least a partial interest—the *Columbia* in 1815 and the *Colonel Allan* in 1816.

ship *Isaac Todd* left Canton, it was restricted from carrying any profitable Chinese goods for resale.

William McGillivray looked to the alternative of obtaining specie in Canton instead of bank notes, thereby enabling the cash-poor Nor'Westers to benefit by holding specie rather than paying a discount of 20 to 25 percent on notes.[17] Specie had disadvantages because gold and silver sold for a higher price in Canton than in London and the advantage of avoiding the discount was reduced proportionately. Moreover, the Nor'Westers could not carry it on their ships, but had to lodge it with the East India Company, taking bills of exchange on India or London banks. Bearing only an ordinary rate of interest and having no value as credit, holding these bills of exchange resulted in tying up considerable capital for months—with no opportunity for reinvestment.[18]

The North West Company invested some £40,000, or one-third of the total Outfit for 1813, in their maritime Adventure to the Columbia.[19] Added to this was the value of the company's ship, the cost of refitting her in Portsmouth, insurance, and various other costs, including the East India Company license.[20] With a venture this large, the anticipated returns had to be considerable. And indeed, William McGillivray estimated that beaver returns in Canton would bring as much as $5 to $6, or 25 to 30 shillings (sterling), per skin for beaver in Canton.[21] Instead, the results for Outfit 1813 were financially disastrous; the returns netted only £25,259 sterling and total losses amounted to £26,040.19.10.[22]

At that time no Columbia River furs had actually been traded. Prices realized never reached the anticipated level because the Canton market

17 British Columbia Archives (henceforth, BC Archives), Selkirk Papers, MSS 1468, pp. 9123-26.

18 M'Konochie, *A Summary View of the Statistics and Existing Commerce*, 69.

19 William McGillivray to J. G. McTavish, May 9, 1813. HBCA, F.3/2, fos. 115-1167.

20 The original cost of the *Isaac Todd* amounted to £6,920. Repairs and outfitting it for the voyage added another £6,140. With stores and provisions of £5,040, the total investment in the ship amounted to £18,074. The ship sold for £2,270, her guns brought another £360, and the remaining stores sold for £272, all of which resulted in a return of £7,942 on the investment in the ship. Apart from the investment in trade goods, the North West Company lost some £10,132 on the ship itself. Keith Memorandum Book, p. 48, Keith Papers, A-676, A.2, LAC.

21 McGillivray to Keith, July 28, 1816, James Keith Papers (MSS Davidson & Garden), 2769/I/57/4, UA.

22 Gough, "The North West Company's 'Adventure of China'," 325; BC Archives, Selkirk Papers, pp. 9209-10.

did want low quality felting furs typical of the Columbia. Until 1821 prices in Canton averaged $3.50 (or 17/6£ sterling) per skin when they could be sold at all.[23]

The next year was not much better. The company-owned schooner *Columbia* arrived on the river with an outfit invoiced at £15,810.8.2 and returned a loss of £19,276.18.2.[24] The Adventure to the Columbia went on to incur considerable losses each successive year the company attempted the business. When the Nor'Westers resorted to an arrangement with the Boston firm J. and T. H. Perkins and Company whereby the American concern would transport North West Company outfits to the Columbia and carry returns to Canton for one-fourth of the net proceeds, the partners felt relief at simply reducing their annual losses to around £6,000 to £7,000 per year.

The final ship to transport returns from the Columbia to Canton, the *Houqua*, obtained a price for peltry that surprised even the Canton agency of J. and J. N. Perkins and Company, and resulted in a net profit of £11,622.76.5.[25] Ironically, the beneficiary of this tardy improvement in the Canton market was the newly reorganized Hudson's Bay Company.

For nearly eight years, between 1813 and 1821, while beleaguered elsewhere, North West Company Montreal agency struggled to make a profit on the Columbia Adventure. In addition to the sizable outfits sent out every year, McTavish, McGillivray and Company committed the services of more men than were allocated to any other department of the business. With considerable money and manpower invested, with exceptional leadership committed to the enterprise, with competition eliminated, and with anticipation of an attractive market, management expectations for success ran high. Yet, for those eight years, it eluded them. Despite a steady infusion of capital, despite organizational innovation, and despite the labor of as many as 254 men, the Adventure to the Columbia disintegrated into a financial disaster.

What went wrong? The usual answer given is mismanagement. It appears to settle the issue with little controversy. Failure was attributed to timidity and petty jealousies on the part of the partners at Fort George.

23 London Inward Correspondence, 1816-1822, HBCA, A.10/2, fos. 337-38.

24 Baby Collection, G1/119, UM.

25 Merk, ed., *Fur Trade and Empire*, 191; London Correspondence Book Outward, Official, 1824-1828, HBCA, A.6/21, p. 8, H.B.C.

Occasional mention is made of other aspects: intractable natives, poor quality furs, the remoteness and isolation of the country, the "ruinous" competition then existing with the Hudson's Bay Company, and the interference of Lord Selkirk and his Red River Colony at present Winnipeg.[26] But those problems were incidental compared to the chronic management malaise which supposedly enfeebled those comfort-seeking managers on the Columbia.

The bickering that occurred among the personnel on the Columbia during this time, in fact, did not contribute significantly to the ultimate failure of the business. It had been bad luck that the death of Donald McTavish, the proprietor most closely associated with arrangements for their first ship, the *Isaac Todd,* coincided with the loss of the critical wintering trader Alexander Henry, who understood the failure of previous maritime adventures and might have intervened. Both drowned at a crucial moment.

But that tragic loss did not offset the reality that Columbian furs simply would not sell profitably in Canton. And increasing production only glutted the market. The expenses incurred in the hunt, coupled with depressed beaver prices in Canton, led the agents in Montreal to conclude, within a short period, that it was best to give up the Adventure to the Columbia.[27]

The returns of Outfit 1819–1820, Donald McKenzie's best year in the Snake country, had to be shipped to London by way of Boston, adding additional port charges and commissions to other already rising losses.[28] Considering that the ultimate intent was to increase profits rather than merely increase returns, Donald McKenzie's efforts in the Snake country were a waste of resources. During the same time James Keith extended the Fort George coastal trade, both north and south, bringing cargoes of goods or provisions to the Russians and the Spanish as well.[29] His local

26 The revitalized London management of the HBC included the recent investor Thomas Douglas, Lord Selkirk, whose concern for displaced Scottish highlanders led him to try establishing a colony on the lower Red River in Canada that would also interdict the NWC provision system. The consequences proved disastrous in June 1816 when NWC-instigated Métis killed the governor and twenty-one colonists.

27 William McGillivray to James Keith, 13 July 1820, James Keith Papers, (Mss Davidson and Garden), UA, 2769/I/57/4.

28 North West Company Account Book, 1820-1823, HBCA, F.4/57, fo. 31d.

29 Mackie, *Trading Beyond the Mountains,* has a brief summary of NWC operations and continued HBC operations on the coast.

and Willamette Valley returns added to the increase and the Fort George Indian trade held steadily at 2,500 to 3,000 pelts annually.

The clerks and trappers in the interior also did their part. Between 1816 and 1822, freemen swelled the returns of Fort George by an average of 2,037 skins per year. Despite having taken a total of 58,988 skins from the country, economic losses continued to mount because circumstances were controlled by market factors and not local management. It was not supply, but lack of demand that was the problem. As long as the North West Company insisted on trading Columbia furs at Canton, their losses were inevitable. The Canton market would never accommodate more than 12,000 to 15,000 beaver pelts and those at consistently lower prices. Only when that market was given up and the low-grade Columbia felting furs were shipped for sale in London, did the Columbia Adventure become profitable. But by then, the business belonged to the Hudson's Bay Company.

For the first two decades of the nineteenth century the history of the Pacific Northwest was the history of the North West Company. That dominance was already slipping by July 1820 when William McGillivray wrote "We are weary of experiments, and if the expenses cannot be brought to a scale considerably less than the returns—we must give it up."[30]

McGillivray could only hope a favorable decision would soon take place, but those matters were now in the hands of lawyers, not fur traders. Unlike the direct buyout that ended the Pacific Fur Company, the HBC/NWC merger of 1821 was contrived by absentee agents and a dismayed cabal of wintering partners who saw no reason to continue an economically destructive competition in Rupert's Land. HBC records show:

> The Deed Poll of 1821 had accepted and formalized two distinct features of North West Company practice—the taking into financial partnership of the more senior traders, and the regular participation of those officers in the management of the trade...forty per cent of the Company's profits, divided into eighty-five shares, were set aside for the traders in the field, who were selected from among the old 'field officers' of the Hudson's Bay Company and the former 'wintering partners' of the North West Company.[31]

30 William McGillivray to James Keith, Fort William, July 13, 1820, James Keith Papers, (MSS Davidson & Garden) 2769/I/57/4, UA.

31 Williams, *Hudson's Bay Miscellany*, 153.

The document of 1821 listed twenty-five chief factors of whom only John George McTavish, James Keith, Angus Bethune, and Donald McKenzie had participated in the actual operations of the Columbia Adventure. Twenty chief traders included Joseph McGillivray, Joseph Felix Larocque, and James McMillan. On July 17, 1821, the deputy governor of the Northern Department, George Simpson, produced the list of new assignments that sent Chief Factors John Haldane and J. D. Cameron and Chief Traders John Lee Lewes and James McMillan to the Columbia District with no specific instructions. A year later, at Norway House on June 24, 1822, Donald McKenzie was appointed to conduct the expedition to the South Branch of the Saskatchewan "to procure in addition to Furs, an indefinite quantity of Buffalo Tongues to be cured for the London market."

Chapter Seventeen

Revelations of Character

The adjustments being made in the Columbia Department related to the agencies' arrangement with the inland supervisor. After dispersing the Snake River trappers along the south side of the Columbia River, Donald McKenzie drove their horses to Fort Nez Perces, arriving just in time to intercept the fall express returning from Fort William. In the dispatch case was a letter from William McGillivray addressed to James Keith, and presumably another to McKenzie. Something in the correspondence caused the hunting brigade leader to accompany the express on to Fort George. When they met downriver, the sedentary downstream superintendent of depot operations and the peripatetic leader of the interior hunt absorbed the apparent failure of the Columbia Adventure.

What seems to have taken place between the two leaders at that crucial meeting challenges Ross's version of a feud between them. Keith may have initially bristled at McKenzie's appointment infringing on the NWC articles concerning a partnership among equals, or that McKenzie was guaranteed a larger salary for three years than other partners could expect. But after the management plan had been put into operation, support was forthcoming and helpful.[1] The interpretation of McKenzie's feelings toward Keith's "chilling and studied politeness" depended on the memory of Alexander Ross, a clerk who was not party to the meeting, and at best heard McKenzie's views second-hand and invented excuses

1 Memoranda Book, 48, 54-56, Keith Estate Papers, NAC; William McGillivray to James Keith, April 28, 1816, and July 26, 1817, Keith Papers, 2769/I/57/1-4, Special Collections, UA; Keith was not alone in his criticism of the agents' arrangement. Colin Robertson wrote that "the wintering partners felt sore on paying so large a salary to an enterprise that yielded nothing but fine letters, while they themselves were losing money," Rich, ed., *Colin Robertson's Correspondence Book*, 198.

years later. According to Ross, "The chief of the interior stood alone, I being the only person on the ground who seconded his views."[2]

Isolated at the edge of the continent, there wasn't much that management at Fort George could do about being unprepared to provide men, equipment, and supplies. Nor was a manpower shortage an entirely unforeseen problem. When the eastbound express of spring 1817 arrived at the Rainy Lake inland depot at the end of July, they found clerk Joseph LaRocque leaving for the Columbia "with a reinforcement of forty men, principally Iroquois Indians, from Canada."[3]

Although Ross counted seventy-two men and boys going inland, the brigade McKenzie took into the Nez Perce country in 1817-18 was only twenty-two trappers. Additional manpower was provided in the next year for the construction of Fort Nez Perces, and McKenzie took seventy to seventy-five trappers into the Snake country in fall 1818. Even more men were sent from Fort George to reinforce the 1819-20 brigade. Yet Ross carped that McKenzie was promised a hundred.[4] If there was a lack of support, it was not about manpower.

Between 1812 and 1822 Keith collected data in his memorandum book about the returns of the Columbia Department.[5] Comparing those with some of the assertions made by Ross reflect a tendency to exaggerate the contributions of Fort Nez Perces and the Snake Brigade. In his April 1819 letter to J. G. McTavish, before the Snake Brigade returns arrived, Ross claimed to have "made 2,800 Beaver & otter at Nez Perces."[6] But the total returns at Nez Perces only amounted to 2,758 and were inflated by furs from the Spokane district.[7] A closer look at Ross's total of 5,495 beaver for Outfit 1819–20 shows around 1,800 pelts were obtained in the environs of Fort Nez Perces and those received from the Snake country amounted to 3,695.[8] Donald McKenzie's second expedition into the Snake country

2 Ross, *Fur Hunters*, 68-72.

3 Cox, *Columbia River*, 221. On pages 135-36 of his Memorandum Book, Keith noted forty-five Iroquois in 1817.

4 The Keith memorandum book shows that sixty-seven additional men appeared on the Columbia for Outfit 1817–18 and an additional fourteen arrived with Outfit 1818–19, most destined for Mackenzie's brigades.

5 Memoranda Book, 30, 60, Keith Estate Papers, NAC.

6 HBCA, F.3/2, fos. 208-09.

7 Finnan McDonald noted as much in a letter to J. G. McTavish dated Spokan House April 9, 1819. *See* note 36, Chapter Thirteen.

8 Ross, *Fur Hunters*, 176.

was his most successful, although the actual returns reduce the count to merely a good season. Despite these modest gains, Ross crowed, "The Snake expedition turned out well, it made up for all the deficiencies elsewhere and gave a handsome surplus besides."[9]

According to the accounts Keith compiled at Fort George at the end of Outfit 1819-20, the total returns of the Columbia Department were 15,962 beaver and land otter including 6,022 from the Willamette and Umpqua Valleys. On November 13, 1820, James Keith wrote to Finnan McDonald at the Flathead Post complaining that the Snake River packs had missed the ship to China. Although the Snake River hunt was left neglected, business in the Salish country continued. John Haldane, Kittson, and Rivet were at Spokane and McMillan at the Kutenai.

When McDonald wrote again from the Flathead Post in March 1821, competition between the NWC pedlars from Montreal and the HBC chartered lords of Rupert's Land was grinding down in legal contests and compromises, and J. G. McTavish and other former Nor'westers were already scrambling for positions in a looming merger with the HBC. Keith's correspondent, John Richardson, reported that a union of the two rival operations was under way and representatives to oversee the coalition of goods had already arrived in the city. "The Trade under your superintendence appears to have assumed a character, from which much benefit might have been expected, if China Sales had kept up to their old level, but the whole commercial world seems at present involved in distress, and little hope or prospect of speedy amendment."

Keith read that missive when he arrived at Fort William and learned that he was being placed in the higher class of Chief Factors. He immediately arranged to take a furlough and consolidate his appointment with a trip to London, where he informed the Governor and Committee of the Hudson's Bay Company that he considered it his duty to give them such information about the Columbia Department as deserved notice.

> [P]ermit me first to direct your attention to the number of hands employed on my departure last Spring which including Clerks & Trappers & excluding Owhyhees amounted to 180, to which must be added those sent thither last fall say 25 or 30 forming a total of 220, whereof 150 are to be considered effective & paid & fed by the Company. The remaining 70 are supposed Trappers.

9 Ross, *Fur Hunters*, 142.

In addition to "7 or 8 trading Stations mostly occupied since 1813," he wrote, there was "a more distant branch lately abandoned called the Snake Country," which the N.W. Company had endeavored to explore and settle since 1816, but had only been hunted during the years of 1819 and 1820. Keith did not enlarge on the reasons for McKenzie's withdrawal from that expensive experiment when he continued:

> Therefore excluding this last branch for which an additional number of hands was temporarily reserved as too casual & contingent to be relied on, the whole business once the superfluous hands drained off would be comprised under the old establishments already mentioned, which would require an annual Outfit or supply including Provisions of £5,000 Stg or London cost & complement of 100 odd effective hands besides Trappers, to produce 10,000 skins."[10]

The information Keith provided to the Governor and Committee interested them in the potential of what appeared to be a neglected resource. After serving another twenty years in Athabaska, and the Montreal department, Keith would retire from HBC business in 1843 and return to Scotland where he married his second cousin. They were living in Aberdeen at the time of his death in early January 1851.[11] Biographer Philip Goldring described James Keith as belonging "to that class of men who are remembered not for striking or colorful achievements, but for long and competent service in a responsible, though unspectacular position."[12]

Keith's opposite on the Columbia, Donald McKenzie, was more spectacular, thanks in part to the career of his admiring amanuensis, Alexander Ross. Although his activities west of the mountains as an Astorian were questionable, after the winter 1816-17 he organized the Snake Brigade and successfully marshaled recalcitrant trappers to kill beaver under fatiguing and sometimes dangerous circumstances, opening an area rich in peltry for his employers. At the end of the Snake country

10 James Keith to The Governor and Committee of the Hudson's Bay Company, from his lodging at 4 Welbeck Street, Cavendish Square, February 12, 1822, HBCA, A.10/2, fos. 337-38.

11 Goldring, "James Keith," *Dictionary of Canadian Biography* 8:454-55.

12 Goldring, "James Keith," provided another proof of character—the bequest for Keith's two country daughters, who were identified in his will with the apology, "It having fallen to my lot, a much lamented though almost unavoidable consequence of the situation and the Country wherein I have passed such a length of time, and which I trust will be viewed with that Christian indulgence (due to human frailty and imperfection) to have two reputed children."

service, McKenzie wrote a letter to his former associate Wilson Price Hunt, confirming "by the tenour of my engagements with the present concern I was under the necessity of extending this branch of the company's business. I had also charge of the interior comprising eight establishments."[13] It was not the fault of a field leader that the product could not be marketed profitably.

Already looking to his future and expecting to be disengaged the following summer, Donald McKenzie sat out the winter 1821–22 at Fort Nez Perces or Spokane House and caught the spring express to York Factory where he was relieved to be presented with a commission as a Chief Factor in the newly combined Hudson's Bay Company. His reputation as a field leader led to his assignment as the conductor of a reinforced trapping expedition to the South Branch of the Saskatchewan River, also known as the Bow River. The new Lt. Governor of the Northern Department, George Simpson, intended to use discharged employees to expand beaver hunting as close as possible (or maybe closer) to United States territory.

Simpson imagined that a reinforced expedition to the Bow River branch of the South Saskatchewan should be able to attract Indians or freemen who trapped beaver in United States territory and carried it north to trade at British posts. Supervised by McKenzie and employing surplus workmen, the Bow River expedition established a post near the 49th parallel border, close enough to sneak traders or trappers across the boundary without being detected. But, faced with threatening northern plains tribes, the best McKenzie managed to accomplish was sending scouting parties toward the Marias River tributary of the upper Missouri.[14]

Simpson's plan turned into a financial disaster that became embarrassing when the Snake Brigade, now under the command of two mere clerks, swept down the upper Missouri as far as the Great Falls, taking the trade of the Indian hunters McKenzie failed to contact and adding those beaver to Flathead Post returns. The Governor shuffled the

---

13 McKenzie to Hunt, Fort Nez Perces, Columbia River, April 20, 1821, in Elliott, "Letter of Donald McKenzie to Wilson Price Hunt," 12.

14 John Edward Harriot, "Memoirs of Life and Adventures in Hudson's Bay Territories, 1819-1825," c. 1860. Transcribed from a microfilm copy of the original in Beinecke Rare Book and Manuscript Library, Yale University, New Haven, Ct. members.shaw.ca/ProustCards/Memoirs%20of%20J.E.%20%20Harriott.pdf. Accessed 7/10/14.

expedition leader to an inconsequential post in the Red River colony where McKenzie liked to sit on a mortar and amaze locals with his florid yarns about past times.[15] That status did not accommodate a country wife, and when McKenzie returned to Norway House on June 21, 1823, Mary McKay was put off on the young clerk William Sinclair, Jr.[16]

Ten years later the settlement was becoming socialized and McKenzie's criticism of J. G. McTavish for putting off his niece for an English bride was another embarrassment to Simpson. The Governor now described McKenzie as "the most useless mischievous Drone on the Face of the Earth, still enjoys his £200 p[er]. Ann[um]. From Lord Selkirk, while I am doing all the Work & he plotting intriguing, planning mischief and endeavoring to undo all I am doing."[17]

Finally humiliated by being put in charge of the largely abandoned Fort William, McKenzie presented a certificate of ill health and resettled his family in a more established community in western New York where he settled into the life of a country gentleman.[18] His family included the three children of his previous country marriage to Mary McKay. The age of his country daughter, Rachel, now eleven years old, confirmed that she had been born in 1822, well after John Day supposedly drew his will favoring her.[19] On October 28, 1836, McKenzie presented the will of John Day to the Surrogate Court of Mayville, Chautauqua Co., New York.

Suspect with errors and misrepresentations, the will drew upon details that John Day could not have known at the time of his demise.[20] McKenzie's correspondent Hunt must have forwarded the information necessary to reconstruct a convincing document that McKenzie then submitted to the New York probate court. It was the last small act of a big

15 "The Character Book of Governor George Simpson, 1832," Williams, ed., *Hudson's Bay Miscellany*, 179-80.

16 McKenzie, however, kept his three mixed-blood children with him, hiring a housekeeper (whom he later married) to care for them.

17 Simpson Character Book, 179-80 n. 4. Simpson was not a forgiving person.

18 E. H. Oliver, ed., *The Canadian North-West: Its Early Development and Legislative Records*, vol. II, (Ottawa: Government Printing Bureau, 1914), 690.

19 Stella M. Drumm, "More About the Astorians," *Oregon Historical Quarterly*, 24: 4, (December 1923), 354.

20 For example, the specific descriptions of property Day had in Missouri had not been confirmed when he left that part of the world with the overland Astorians. "Some information concerning the life of John Day," unpublished mss by Nick Sheedy of John Day, Oregon, updated February 2004.

man who died in early 1851, four years before Alexander Ross published his admiring book.[21]

During the ten years McKenzie and Alexander Ross lived in the Red River settlement, there must have been opportunities to meet and share the memories that would later appear in *The Fur Hunters of the Far West.* When McKenzie had appeared at Fort George in late 1816, Ross, then serving as a clerk, already nursed a dislike for James Keith that might have been envy. Years later, after the experiment for increasing production soured, Ross continued to extol the leader of the Snake Brigade.

> To travel a day's journey on snowshoes was his delight, but he detested spending five minutes scribbling in a journal. His traveling notes were often kept on a beaver skin written hieroglyphically with a pencil or piece of coal, and he would often complain of the drudgery of keeping accounts. When asked why he did not like to write his answer was, "We must have something for others to do." Few men could fathom his mind, yet his inquisitiveness to know the minds and opinions of others had no bounds. Every man he met was his companion: and when not asleep, he was always upon foot strolling backward and forward full of plans and projects, and so peculiar was this pedestrian habit that he went by the name of "Perpetual Motion."[22]

The question persists, why did Ross attempt to elevate McKenzie to a greater than deserved place in the history of those times? In his 1855 book Ross used his own experiences as well as common knowledge to fill out what he extracted from McKenzie's adventures, making it an untrustworthy conglomeration of fact and invention. Did the former clerk expect to ride the coattails of his hero to a higher place? Reduced to his old role as a school teacher, Ross became a figure in the Red River Settlement and an author of three books.

Connecting two parallel lines of inter-corporate gamesmanship requires stepping back in time to the return of the Snake Brigade to Fort Nez Perces in 1820. It could not be left in limbo and to prevent the trappers from wasting the winter hanging around and consuming provisions, Donald McKenzie distributed them along the south side of the Columbia as far downstream as The Dalles. They were left without horses

21 Sylvia Van Kirk, "Donald McKenzie," *Dictionary of Canadian Biography* 7:577-578. www.biographi.ca/en/bio/mckenzie_donald_8E.html, accessed July 11, 2014.

22 Ross, *Fur Hunters*, 187.

to hunt up tributary streams and when the disorganized hunters returned in spring 1821, they grounded on the loose sands around Fort Nez Perces.

Although Donald McKenzie's three year contract with McTavish, McGillivray & Company had expired, the brigade could not be allowed to fall apart. McKenzie recommended Michel Bourdon as the most capable man to lead the freemen and Iroquois, but Bourdon was sent east with the spring brigade of 1821. In an early July meeting at distant Norway House on Lake Winnipeg, the HBC council decided (pending a further reorganization of the Columbia River trade) "to engage in the capacity of a Conductor of Trappers, Michel Bourdon at the lowest rate for which he may agree."[23]

The initial influx of free trappers in the Salish country may have created several wandering Ishmaels, but Michel Bourdon was no orphan of the storms; he created them. A freeman from the Detroit area who came to the Salish country with the nominally-American trader Charles Courtin, Bourdon remembered Courtin's large cache of beaver secreted at the Three Forks of the Missouri River. His search for that cache with Finnan McDonald had led to a fight with Piikani and the resulting blockade of the Kootenai country. Despite the inconveniences he caused, David Thompson engaged Bourdon to go to the mouth of the Columbia with him, a downstream journey Bourdon repeated two years later as a Nor'wester supporting the purchase of Astoria. In the 1813–14 combined list of individuals, Bourdon was listed as a freeman engaged for seven hundred livres as an interpreter at the Flatheads. That contract would expire in late July 1816, so it is uncertain if Donald McKenzie reengaged him at Spokane House. During McKenzie's two Snake expeditions Bourdon led a party of trappers to the area of the Bear River and Lake. Bourdon was a logical choice to herd a disorderly tribe of freeman back to the Snake country where they had previously hunted.

Clues to where they hunted can be drawn from the 1824 account of Alexander Ross or from Peter Skene Ogden and William Kittson's Snake Brigade journals. Those suggest that Bourdon took the reassembled brigade across the Blue Mountains and down the Grande Ronde Valley to a crossing of the Snake. Following up the Boise River the trappers hunted

23 Merle Wells, "Michel Bourdon," in LeRoy R Hafen, *The Mountain Men and the Fur Trade of the Far West*, 10 volumes (Glendale, CA: Arthur H. Clark Co., 1965-1972), 3:54-59.

the Stanley Basin and moved on to the vicinity of present Challis, Idaho, where Bourdon briefly considered making boats to try floating packs down the Salmon and Snake Rivers. When it was time for the hunters to re-fit, they were closer to the Salish country than Fort Nez Perces and Bourdon led them down the Bitterroot Valley, bringing most of the freemen to Flatheads Post and Spokane House by September 1822.[24]

Michel Bourdon's only failing was in preventing some Iroquois and a few former Astorians from breaking away from the main party. Leaving about seven hundred beaver skins cached somewhere on the east end of the Snake Valley, they went shopping. Those dissidents had picked up rumors that a reactivated American trading post at the mouth of the Big Horn River might pay better prices than could be expected from the Hudson's Bay Company.[25]

Bourdon led the trappers to a second, short winter hunt on the headwaters of the Jefferson Branch of the Missouri, but on their return in 1823, responsibility for the trappers passed to Bourdon's former associate, Finnan McDonald. With Bourdon as his second, in 1823 McDonald was sent to recover that cache of beaver and scour the east end of the Snake Valley. Bourdon's small party was returning along the upper Lemhi River when lurking Blackfeet finally collected a blood debt from an old enemy. McDonald later described the killings of six trappers.[26]

> We had saviral Ballils with the nation on the other side of the mountain Poore Meshel Bordoe was kile with 5 more of the. Band there dath was revenge as well as we Could revenge it for no less than 68 of them remane in the Planes as Pray for the wolves and those fue that askape our shotes they had not Britch Clout to Cover them selves we shoe them whay war was they will not be so radey to attack People another time

The exciting fight on the west side of Lemhi Pass slaughtered ten Atsiina fleeing from burning cover. Re-crossing the continental divide

24 "Route of Alexander Ross, 1824," *Idaho State Historical Society Reference Series No. 86* (written by Idaho State Historian Merle Wells) and based on clues in Ross, "Snake Country Journal," HBCA, B202/a/1 and Flathead Post Journal, HBCA, B69/a/1.

25 Spokane House Journal 1822/23; HBCA, B208/a/1, fols. 12, 13; Spokane District Report 1822/23, HBCA, B208.e/1. Fo. 4; and O'Fallon to Pilcher, 1 August 1823, in Dale Morgan, *The West of William H. Ashley*, 51.

26 The attackers are usually identified as Piikani but Charles Mckay, a Piikani interpreter, later identified them as Gros Ventre (Atsiina).

McDonald took his large trapping brigade down the Jefferson Fork of the Missouri River and on to the Great Falls, not that far south of where the Bow River expedition under the direction of Donald McKenzie was supposed to penetrate.

The Bow River scheme failed in the face of Blackfoot and Atsiina belligerence, but McDonald and his followers had already scooped up peltry from those bands, as he explained in a letter to J. G. McTavish.

> we got last summer as far as the Croe Indian Cuntre on the rail Spanish river from where we return Back separate several time in two Bands on account of the Band being two Strong and we war only 45 free and six Engage men so you may se that the rivers is not altogather alive with Beaver but for all it is the richest Cuntrre that I noe on this side of the mountains and only the Cuntre that feee men is able to do sumthing for the Flat Head Cuntre is rouint [ruined] of Beaver for Free men to hunt I sa the Mussasoury last fall down as far as the falls in that Part of the Cuntre is rouint of Beaver By the Amaricans for they have fort there five years agoe about ½ mile beloe Cortais old Fort it is fine river all and about the size of the N. Parsey River vary strong Currant I surch for the Free men that remane in the Snake the year before I could never fine [find] them out nor the Snakes.[27]

The returning brigade followed Cokalarishkit, the Salish road to the buffalo in reverse back to Flatheads Post where the furs would be credited to Columbia Department accounts rather than McKenzie's Bow River enterprise.[28]

Ordered by the London management to go west and sort out the troubling Columbia Department, Governor George Simpson relied on J. G. McTavish and Donald McKenzie at York Factory for information. During the canoe trip he pumped Chief Trader James McMillan. In October 1824 Simpson appeared at Spokane and immediately began recording snap judgments about the people he found there. He recorded that the band of freemen was the very scum of country, unruly outcasts for misconduct, expecting to lay about for several months during the best hunting season.

27 McDonald refers to the Iroquois and freemen who broke away from Michel Bourdon when he brought the Snake Brigade east the previous year.

28 A. P. Nasatir, "The International Significance of the Jones and Immell Massacre" *Pacific Northwest Quarterly* 30 (January 1939), 77-108: Edmonton House Journal, 1822/23, HBCA, B60/a/21, fol. 17, 26d-28.

The clerk Alexander Ross, scheduled to lead the next Snake Brigade, had not the talent to make anything of them and Peter Skene Ogden would remain at Spokane to take over the hunters when Ross returned. Mr. Kittson assumed the Kutenai trade from the discharged Montour. That left Finnan McDonald to conduct business at the Flatheads Post, with the promise that he could retire the next fall.[29]

Finnan McDonald had the 1824-25 winter to adjust his thoughts before writing to J. G. McTavish that he was beginning to doubt the loyalty of the trappers.

> I got safe home from the Snacke Cuntre thank and when that Cuntre will se me agane the Beaver will have Gould skin as to keep free men in order and to there duty. I wood Prefare to have Band of Indians to Command than Band of Free men they thanks no man for an Advise nor will not Lasin to that [what] is told to them they naver thinks of their own Profit nor the Companey as long as they gate Buffaloe meat they ar a troublesum set round Fort spileing [spoiling] the natives Paying every Articles they Bye double the Prise that we give the natives which spiles [spoils] the Trade it is the thing that will not doe to keep the Freemen round Post there is Plenty Beaver in the Snake Cuntre and in the Fall of the year after they delivers up their furs and takes there advances they can Easley return to the Snake Cuntre before the snow wood [would] fall in the mountains, the Snake Cuntr is no so far off as People espect it to be.[30]

After sixteen years, Finnan McDonald realized that the only world he had known was changing into something he wasn't at all sure he could get along with:

> Your Laws and regalasion on the other side of the mountain give People a fright on this side I am in the hopes that People with there rooles [their roots] in the Cuntre the gentlemen of this Cuntre ought to writhe home and Adverisesment that all those after this year that was to come in the Indian Cuntre to be Cut and so they will be able to safe there [save their] money.[31]

29 Merk, ed., *Fur Trade and Empire*, 44-45.

30 Finnan McDonald to John G. McTavish, Spokane House, April 5, 1824, HBCA, B239/c/1, fol. 140-141d.

31 Ibid.

Since crossing the mountains with David Thompson, Finnan had watched the Columbia Adventure change from a bright promise to a disappointment born of unanticipated consequences. When businesses fail, management moves on. Leadership retirements and deaths, as well as company mergers, had not benefitted him. He remained a mere clerk.

During the preceding winter at Fort George, Simpson had taken until mid-March 1825 filling fifty-seven pages with analysis of how to proceed. Before leaving Spokane, Simpson had already ordered an excursion toward the Rio Colorado for Ogden and the Snake Brigade. They were to "pass the Winter and Spring [1826] there and hunt their way out by the Umpqua and Willamette Rivers to Fort George next summer sufficiently early to send the returns home on the Ship."[32] A second hunting brigade would proceed along the Willamette and Umpqua Rivers to a place where it could investigate reported beaver potential on a large lake somewhere toward the Spanish Rio Colorado. This would be led by Finnan McDonald and Thomas McKay.

When the new governor Simpson visited Spokane House in fall 1824, he took the opportunity to evaluate the clerk who had taken beaver away from the Bow River Expedition. Despite that success, Finnan McDonald was reluctant to return to the Snake country. But he was still too valuable to be allowed to retire and could be of service to a new trapping strategy.

After making a sixty-mile spring 1825 ride to meet Governor Simpson at the forks of the Spokane River, McDonald was pleased to hear that he was qualified to take charge of a second hunting brigade to the Umpqua country. But when the Governor went on, he was still a poorly paid clerk. McDonald would bring his family down to the newly built Fort Vancouver on the Columbia and be prepared for the creation of the second arm of the encirclement of the best beaver trapping.

> The outfit for the interior will therefore be taken by the people immediately belonging to those Establishments only, forming a Brigade of about Thirty Two officers & men, and the Supernumeraries or extra men in question will be equipped for a whole year and sent off from Fort George on a Trapping Expedition in the month of May accompanied by all the Freemen in this neighborhood so as to form a party of between Fifty & Sixty under the command of Mess[rs] Finnan McDonald & Thos

32 Merk, ed., *The Oregon Question*, 77-78.

> McKay their route will be up the Wilhamot River across a Mountainous Country which we know little about to the Umpqua River and from thence Hunt their way to the Banks of the Rio Colorado keeping either inland or towards the Coast as the state of the Country in regard to Fur bearing Animals and the means of living may direct; they will remain out all Winter and Spring and return to Fort George in the month of June following (1826) about the time the Ship will arrive from England.[33]

Finding he was elevated from a long serving clerk buried in the Flathead country to the command of a southern hunting brigade, McDonald might have smelled promotion. Governor Simpson wanted him to cooperate with Mr. Ogden's Snake Brigade in gathering the entire country to the south into an American-proof HBC hunting preserve. Simpson's intent was to trap out the beaver in the Snake River country, creating a fur desert unattractive to the American concerns. It was a strategy based on Governor Simpson's understanding of an unexplored and difficult geography and he expressed no concern that the two expeditions might infringe on Spanish possessions.

But as he returned east in spring 1825, Governor Simpson and his party passed the mouth of the Spokane River less than a month before his exploitation strategy started to fall apart. Ross had returned to Flatheads Post trailed by seven American trappers who would expose HBC intentions to competitors. Simpson had decided Ogden was a proven tough who would bring dissident freemen to heel and give them no rest. But on a May 23 encounter with the main body of pugnacious American mountaineers, the freemen packed up their furs and took them to better paying Americans. When Mr. Simpson's enforcer lost two-thirds of the trappers, the fur desert scheme was already mooted.[34] It was already apparent that the Bear River was not the head of the Rio Colorado although Ogden remained "sanguine" about still reaching the Columbia by way of the Umpqua.[35]

Because McDonald and McKay were delayed by manpower problems related to the construction of a new depot until August 1825, Chief Factor John McLoughlin was aware that Ogden's Snake Brigade had lost twenty-three freemen trappers to better American prices. In his ranting

33 Merk, ed., *Fur Trade and Empire*, 88.

34 Rich, ed., *Ogden's Snake Country Journals*, 49-55; Rich, ed., *Letters of McLoughlin*, 1:8-14.

35 Ogden to HBC, East Fork, Missouri, July 10, 1825, in Merk, *Oregon Question*, 87.

about the deserters to other Chief Factors and Chief Traders, those concerns were about property instead of people.

> I think the Engagees evinced the most disgracefull I might say criminal neglect of their Duty in not supporting Mr. Ogden to the utmost of their ability which had they done I am of the opinion we would not have suffered the Losses we have nor the Indignity of seeing people going off with our property and at the same time insulting us in the most opprobrious Language they could Express...they drew debt much against our will...at a time when we ran the risk of losing our property by their death.[36]

At that point, McLoughlin could only provide the Southern Brigade leaders with indefinite instructions on how they were to proceed. He expected Ogden would assemble a more trustworthy party, complete a connection with McDonald and McKay, and assume command of both parties.[37] After August 20 the "Southern Brigade" of twenty-two engaged men and six Indians, with only two freemen, moved up the Willamette Valley and over to the Umpqua River Valley. Crossing the Cascade Mountains via Santiam Pass to the Deschutes River, they turned toward the unexplored Klamath country to explore as far toward California as possible.

Finnan McDonald had never backed down from a fight, but his party was going into unknown territory and potentially hostile Indians. After finding the Klamath Lake area unproductive, McDonald and McKay turned back to the Deschutes and hunted their way down as far as the Warm Springs where Ogden found them on December 9, 1825.[38] The Umpqua Expedition returned with only 460 beaver.

The now combined party headed east again and arrived at the mouth of the Owyhee River on February 18, 1826. Planning to trap the south side of the Snake, the HBC officers met Indians on March 24 who had already traded with Americans and displayed that flag. Continuing to the Portneuf River, the Snake Brigade encountered a party of thirty American trappers and freemen. Convinced it would be counterproductive, even dangerous, to continue, Ogden turned back on April 10 but met

36 McLoughlin to Chief Factors and Chief Traders, Fort Vancouver, August 10, 1825, in Rich, ed., *Ogden's Snake Country Journals*, 303.

37 McLoughlin to McDonald, Fort Vancouver, August 17, 1825, HBCA, B223/b/1, fos. 22d-23d.

38 Rich, ed., *Ogden's Snake Country Journals*, 102; Merk, ed., *Fur Trade and Empire*, 89n146.

other Indians again near the Salmon Falls on May 21 who revealed that another large party had crossed behind the baymen about a month previously.[39]

Reduced to hunting again over southern tributaries to the Columbia, Ogden separated from McDonald, McKay, and Dears near present Huntington, Oregon. Those clerks reached Fort Nez Perces where Chief Factor William convinced McKay and Dears to carry the returns to Fort Vancouver by boat. But they only carried a letter from Finnan. McDonald had seen enough and apparently sent down his letter of resignation for Chief Factor John McLoughlin's reaction. He waited at Fort Nez Perces for his family to come there with the inland boat brigade.

McDonald waited to get McLoughlin's approval and wasted another month at Fort Colvile before getting a late start across Athabaska Pass. Writing to Simpson from Fort Edmonton on January 12, 1827,

> By Mr. McMillan I received your kind favor. I am sorry that I was not able to fulfil your wish. I have been long enough in the Country and explored the whole Country for the Company, still I am not further advanced than if I had not been from the Fireside in the Fort.[40]

Finnan repeated his reasons for not completing the plan for the Southern Expedition, and then went on down the Saskatchewan to Fort Carlton where his wrestling match with a wounded buffalo severely injured him and delayed the family's arrival in Glengarry County, Ontario. Finnan became an important member of that Scots community and probably forgot that he had turned his back on the opportunity to have become the first explorer of the Humboldt country, a geographical accomplishment later attributed to Ogden but named by an American military explorer. Or was he disgusted by the potential of trouble in Governor Simpson's fur desert theory?

Like his predecessors, the McGillivray brothers, Simpson was fixated on increasing production and leaving the shipping and sales of peltry to the London management. Initially the Hudson's Bay Company allowed the deal with Perkins & Company of Boston to continue, and when prices in Canton were better than expected, even shipped the more

39 Rich, ed., *Ogden's Snake Country Journals*, 148, 154, 168, 174.

40 McDonald to Simpson. Edmonton, January 12, 1827, HBCA, D4/120, fos. 32-33; Rich, ed., *Ogden's Snake Country Journals*, Appendix B, 265-66.

desirable beaver pelts from London to Boston and on to Fort George with the supply ship of the year.

Later those operations were sent in HBC ships, an arrangement continued for another two decades while the skin games evaporated and imperial pretensions for a favorable boundary resolution with the United States faced up to the inevitable impact of overland immigration from the United States. By 1846 corporate operations at Fort Vancouver on the north bank of the Columbia had shifted to a holding pattern of mercantile and agricultural emphasis. HBC headquarters moved north to Fort Victoria on Vancouver Island and imperial pretensions had to settle for New Caledonia, which was nostalgically renamed British Columbia.

Free Hunter, by Nicholas Point.
Manuscripts, Archives, and Special Collections, Washington State University Libraries, Pullman.

Wife of a trapper dressed in her finery ("My partner at a Grand Ball at Fort Victoria, October 6, 1845"), Henry J. Warre.
Library and Archives Canada, C-58104.

"Baptiste, Iroquois Bow Man, and our Canoe," 1845, Henry J. Warre.
Library and Archives Canada, C-55333.

Chapter Eighteen

Freemen

THE ECONOMIES NOW IMPOSED upon the fading Columbia Adventure were corporate-driven with little consideration for those individuals whose lives were abruptly changed. Formerly proud NWC engagés were re-cast as "servants" in an increasingly rank-conscious HBC hierarchy. Regulars around posts might be assigned quarters or allowed to cobble up something outside the palisades to shelter couples. On the rivers or trails boatmen, packers, and trappers spent their days and nights living in the open and sleeping under the stars. Because lodge poles were too cumbersome to take in a boat, voyageurs felt lucky to have an overturned canoe to shelter their heads. In bad weather or rain, they wore all their daily clothes under sailcloth tarps or buffalo hide robes.

Freemen continued with the hunting brigades because they had Indian wives and growing families to support. Their families also lived in the open. Trappers' wives were daughters of tribal mothers who raised them in coastal, riverine, or mountain environments. Child-women, sometimes as young as twelve or fourteen years, had already learned those cultural habits before being asked to serve husbands whose language was often almost incomprehensible to them. Taught by other women in their conglomerate traveling brigade, brides learned to manage pack-horses, erect heavy skin lodges, maintain a mobile household, and raise their babies on the trail. Girls as well as boys grew up traveling, and the oldest children of western marriages were still adolescents when field operations were taken over by the reorganized HBC. A month after Jaco Finlay's death at Spokane in 1828, three of his sons were offered places in Ogden's next brigade.[1]

1 Williams, ed., *Ogden's Snake Country Journals*, 96n2.

By the end of the NWC tenure, tribal hunters had been reconciled to the new mercantile economy and were producing more than two-thirds as many furs as freemen. They equipped themselves to compete with engaged or freemen by stealing set traps. However, most native-dressed furs came from the Fraser River trading posts where direct trapping by engagés was not encouraged.[2] Due to the lack of efficient traps and knowing how to use them, Kutenai and Salish beaver production had been initially disappointing although they continued to take beaver through the combination of nooses and deadfalls, or by trenching to expose animals in their dens.

After the turn of the nineteenth century, Montreal fur companies recruited three hundred Iroquois on three-year contracts as boatmen or independent trappers.[3] Equipped with steel traps and understanding the use of castoreum bait irresistible to beaver, those trappers could be highly productive. After generations of skin game experience, Iroquois excelled as steel trappers. Despite accusations concerning Iroquois misbehavior, evidence suggests they were good hunters and many intended to return to their homes at the end of their engagements. Although they were contractually guaranteed to be returned to their place of enlistment at the end of their service, many Iroquois married into local tribes and stayed on. As an example, the Iroquois Jacques Osterico developed a marital connection with the Kutenai and asked to be discharged among his wife's people at the end of his re-enlistment.

Iroquois were famous boatmen. Hired at Rainy Lake in 1813 to help drive express canoes westward, George Teewhattahownie jealously guarded his prerogative as an experienced Columbia River steersman. After refusing an order from a terrified clerk to shorten sail, he later tried to settle the insult to his authority in a drunken knife fight.[4] At the time of the 1821 merger, many of the sixty-six named Iroquois were boatmen. Four years later, after riding across the continent on the arms of a picked crew of Iroquois canoe drivers, the economy-minded HBC governor

2 45,912 pelts were contributed by the Indian trade between 1814 and 1821, to which trappers added 13,076 beaver making a total of 58,988 pelts.

3 Johnson, ed., *Saskatchewan Journals*, xci.

4 Cox, *Columbia River*, 364-66. In 1813-14 Geo Tewhattahewnie had been enlisted at Rainy Lake.

rewarded their kind by reducing bateau crews driving fifty pieces of cargo upstream from eight to seven paddlers.[5]

Iroquois trappers accompanied McKenzie's 1817-18 Snake Brigade and those that followed for the next two outfits. Others continued to trap independently.

As a distinct element in the peopling of the Pacific Northwest, Iroquois seem to survive in the abstract rather than individuals. Jan Grabowsky and Nicole St. Onge conclude in their study, *Montreal Iroquois Engagés in the Western Fur Trade 1800-1827*, that an option for individual Iroquois or small groups was integration into local tribes such as the Flatheads through marriage that resulted in the complete assimilation of their descendants. "The third adaptive strategy pursued by the Iroquois and seemingly the most popular was their integration into the fast growing freeman component of the North West's population and their participation in a process of ethnogenesis, the formation of the western Metis." The authors also cite Bruce Watson's study of 119 known Iroquois who arrived in the Columbia District between 1810 and 1858. Nearly two-thirds of them arrived after the 1821 union of the NWC and HBC.[6]

There are traces of what could be Iroquois cultural items or habits, but the voices, the songs, the stories are mostly lost.[7] Nevertheless their descendants are still with us.

Another body of workmen had been introduced by the Astorians. Although they were part of this "collision of cultures," the Hawaiians are mostly overlooked in this study because their history is treated fully in the recent publication by two dedicated northwest historians, Jean Barman and Bruce Watson.[8] Contracted Sandwich Islanders should have been excellent boatmen, but the colder climate was trying. Known in the northwest as Owyhees or Kanakas, they were contracted as hired laborers or boatmen in Hawaii and initially brought to the Columbia by the Pacific Fur Company, a practice the NWC and HBC continued.

5 Merk, ed., *Fur Trade and Empire*, 38.

6 Gerhard Ens, R. C. McLeod and Ted Binnema, eds., *From Rupert's Land to Canada* (Edmonton, Alberta: University of Alberta Press, 2001), 44-45, 49.

7 Jennifer E. Jameson, "Iroquois of the Pacific Northwest Fur Trade: Their Archaeology and History." Master of Arts in Interdisciplinary Studies in Anthropology, Design and Human Environment, and Anthropology, December 5, 2007, Oregon State University.

8 Barman and Watson, *Leaving Paradise*.

Most often noted, John Cox arrived at the Columbia on the *Tonquin* in 1811, helped paddle a canoe across the continent and returned from London on the *Isaac Todd* and *Racoon* to serve as a pilot across the Columbia bar.[9] The Fort George sawyer Charles Cawanaia came from Hawaii probably in 1817 on a North West Company ship as his name does not appear on the 1813-14 list of persons living on the Columbia. He wasted no time in forming a relationship with an Indian woman there, which soon produced a son and a daughter. Taking no chances with strange gods, the children were baptized Methodist, Anglican, and Catholic. Charles Cawanaia Jr. settled on the north Tualatin Plains of Oregon and married a young mixed-blood woman, Amelia Johnson, in 1862, whose father was an employee of the HBC.[10] Amelia was still living on their neighboring farm in 1931 when family lore holds that she rocked this author when he was a baby.

To native peoples, who had long ago worked out living comfortably in the Northwest environment, the first traders had seemed benign and were welcomed for the useful articles they exchanged for furs. The strangers also introduced new weaponry, and upset the balance of power between tribes on both sides of the continental divide. What that meant for solitary trappers working a side stream could be deadly.

Bannock Indians were troublesome to the Astorians and massacred the Reed party near the mouth of the Boise River in the winter of 1813-14. In addition to threatening McKenzie, raiders killed three men of the packtrain bringing new outfits. Generally the first Snake Brigades trapped without serious hostilities, but the opportunities for ambush had increased by 1824 when intimations of a looming American presence initiated a competitive strategy concocted at York Factory by Governor Simpson, relying on the experience of the former Nor'westers J. G. McTavish, Donald McKenzie, and James McMillan.

Without having seen the country and goaded by an even less geographically informed London management, Simpson arrived in the West prepared to send trapping brigades capable of dominating the hunt and depleting beaver to keep American competitors away. But when Ross returned to the HBC Flathead Post trailed by seven Americans, another distant management scheme was already mooted. American mountain

9 Kittleson, "John Coxe: Hawaii's First Soldier of Fortune," 213-18.

10 Barman and Watson, *Leaving Paradise*, 234-35.

men associated with the Ashley/Henry partnership were soon swarming into the Bear River country and immediately drew away two-thirds of Ogden's Snake Brigade freeman trappers to exciting promises and better prices.

Perhaps it may be historically presumptuous to attribute so much to so few, but there may be a turning point here revealing something about the character and continued heritage in the peopling of the Pacific Northwest. Appendix A that follows is an imperfect listing of those freemen who had trapped for years with the Pacific Fur Company or North West Company. After the merger they had no option except dealing with a suddenly imperious Hudson's Bay Company. When the opportunity was presented, they went over to the Ashley/Henry partnership and continued hunting with Smith, Jackson & Sublette, or on their own personal initiative. Freemen continued to trade with the Salish and Kutenai or occasionally with placative-minded Blackfeet. They roistered with American mountaineers at summer rendezvous where French accents and voyageur's songs were heard. Although they were key producers of beaver, those indispensable trappers continued to be disparaged as deserters in HBC records.

After gaining access to the archives of the Hudson's Bay Company, London, the Harvard scholar Frederick Merk became interested in tracing the transition from North West Company operations to a new corporate vision through his editing of Governor Simpson's immediate evaluation of the western freemen. After their conquest of New France, the British had the audacity to describe *Canadiens* as "new subjects." The founders of the northwest fur trade demonstrated a new degree of initiative in confronting the sternly institutionalized Hudson's Bay Company. That initiative crossed the Rocky Mountains with the North West Company and infected the thinking of men who went free on the Columbia River drainage and were now resisting a corporation that found ideas of personal determination inconvenient. This attitude was clearly expressed in a note in Merk's much quoted *Fur Trade and Empire:*

> Freemen in the language of the fur trade were ex-servants of the fur companies free in the sense of being no longer under indenture. They were usually worn-out voyageurs, differing from ordinary discharged engages in that they did not retire to Red River Colony or to Canada, but chose to remain in the Indian country living among the natives.

> Shiftless and irresponsible, they found in the Indian country refuge both from necessity of regular labor and the restraints of civilized life. They were usually tied to the wilderness also by Indian wives and half-breed children.[11]

When Merk began his research in the mid-1920s, in addition to the HBC corporate documents made available to him, the editor could also read the reactions of former Astorian clerks Gabriel Franchère, Ross Cox, and Alexander Ross whose writings set a negative tone about the freemen who soon became an essential factor in the development of Hudson's Bay Company competitive plans.

At least four of the men who initially crossed the mountains with David Thompson passed into the service of the Hudson's Bay Company. Clerks like Nicholas Montour and Finnan McDonald had been in the country so long that they had almost forgotten how to get out of it. Free trappers like Jaco Finlay or Francois Rivet had no other homes to return to.

Jacques Raphael "Jaco" Finlay, the country son of a founder of the Saskatchewan River trade, actually began his western career as an articled clerk of the North West Company. He and another mixed-blood clerk, Nicholas Montour, were sent across the mountains during the winter of 1806–07 to prepare a packroad for the NWC expansion. But David Thompson, as noted earlier, was critical of Jaco's performance as a trail cutter and canoe builder and recommended that he lose at least half of his wages of £150 per annum plus a clerk's equipment.

During the intervening years, Finlay sometimes trapped on his own or was rehired by the NWC as a clerk or interpreter. In 1824 at Jasper's House on the Athabaska Pass route, HBC Governor Simpson suspected that Jaco and his band of freemen were trafficking furs in order to intercept the Suswaps trade for their own advantage. In an early forecast of how matters in the Columbia Department would go, Simpson wrote:

> These freemen are a pest in this country, having much influence over the Natives...but if such measures as I have recommended...they will soon be quite at our disposal as their very extistence depends on us...as their present independence and high toned importance is very injurious and in my opinion frought with danger to the concern.[12]

11 Merk, ed., *Fur Trade and Empire*, 2, 44.
12 Merk, ed., *Fur Trade and Empire*, 31.

Before the governor left the country he decided to close Spokane House and build a new receiving depot at Kettle Falls. Reluctant to abandon a location he knew so well, Finlay took over the old post as his home and lived there until 1828, when three of his sons, Augustin, Mitikom, and Pinetse were trapping with Ogden's Snake Brigade. Used up by the skin game, their sixty-year-old mixed-blood father was buried under a bastion of the fort. He left his wife and more than a dozen children, whose descendants are now reputed to number in the thousands.[13]

Not all the free trappers in the Pacific Northwest came there through North West Company service. Other free hunters had been introduced to the Salish heartland by two earlier American parties.[14] Francois Rivet, who remained living along the Clark Fork River with the hospitable Salish, had been associated with Captain Zackery Perch's large party, and later traveled as a freeman with the Snake Brigades. In late June 1831, Rivet's family came down the Columbia from Fort Colvile with a party that demonstrated a melancholy aspect of close fur-trade relationships. Several in this extended family were making that long boat trip to honor the grave of a first-born son named Francois Rivet Jr. who had drowned in a boating accident.

Rivet's aging wife, Therese Tete Platte (Flathead) was accompanied by her two sons, Antoine and Joseph, and her daughter, Julia Ogden, with two small sons. They were escorted by the son of Nicholas Montour, as well as the Indian mother-in-law of HBC trader John Work.[15] Eight years later, old Rivet and two grown sons followed other retiring traders and trappers to the Willamette Valley. The big son roped, bulldogged, and branded half-wild cattle not that far from the ranch of Rivet's aging companion, Nicholas Montour.

As the merger negotiations between the HBC and NWC became finalized, the terms were unlikely to provide for the Columbia freemen who had no contractual connection to the North West Company beyond

13 Jameson, "Iroquois of the Pacific Northwest Fur Trade," has a description of the archeological excavation of Jaco's grave.

14 Louis Joseph Houle dit Capois, Michel Bourdon, Francois Gregoire, and Francois SansFacon.

15 Stern, ed., *Chiefs and Chief Traders*, 130-31. Others lost at the Dalles of the Columbia must have been buried there, but because young Rivet was a relation, Ogden had the body carried back to Fort Nez Perces.

repaying the debts they owed. They were "free" to try to earn a living by trapping on their own, as they had been doing for some time, but not so free to find a competitive market for their packs.

Despite elevated positions in the new HBC, Governor George Simpson and Chief Factor John McLoughlin were still fur traders with no authority to dictate to free men who had survived as trappers for fifteen years and whose children by native wives were beginning to enter that hunt. The 137 individuals (later amended to 150 or a total of 220) listed as the 1821 legacy were mostly boatmen and provision hunters. James Keith left out an uncertain number of other hunters, supposed to be about seventy trappers whose only relationship with the new order were the furs they took and the ammunition and tools they needed to support that way of life and their families. The arrangement was not that much different from what Indians could expect at the trade shop window.

After the imperious Governor Simpson returned east in spring 1825, Chief Factor McLoughlin faced the implementation of economies. He understood the limitations of his authority over freemen was tenacious and a larger business strategy reduced non-contracted trappers to a system of debt servitude. That would have to change as American trappers and traders appeared in the central Rocky Mountains and began holding summer trade fairs where more generous allowances on furs or supplies were available.

Freemen's wealth was in their packs. They spent those "plus" (a prime beaver pelt) to buy what they needed to continue trapping, and then whatever remained on foofaraws for their wives, sugar for the children, and drinks all around. Unless they were paid in coin at a rendezvous, freemen or Iroquois never saw a Spanish dollar. Instead, they wore their savings as silver crosses, broaches, or heavy pendants in their ears. The only bank was the company book that the brigade clerk carried and who saw no reason to waste paper writing out promissory notes to illiterates.

Another example of false economies grew out of the convoluted career of Finlay's former associate, Nicholas Montour. It was no longer significant that he was the country son of a founder of the North West Company and had served it faithfully as a clerk with the Kutenai for nineteen years. Governor Simpson considered Montour a disposable supernumerary leaving him with no option except to accompany the

1824 Snake Brigade as a common trapper with his wife and two growing sons.[16]

Equipped with fifteen traps, three guns, and ten horses, Montour shared the informal leadership of the freemen with Charles Gros Louis and the Iroquois leaders Martine Mieguin and Old Pierre Tevanitagon. The older Montour children, ten-year-old George, eight-year-old Robert, and six-year-old Isabelle, also jogged on not-entirely-gentle ponies over rough mountain trails and dangerous crossings of flooding mountain streams. Brigade leader Ross listed Montour and his son George as free trappers.

They returned to Flatheads Post on December 20, 1824, just in time for the Montour family to accompany Ogden's 1825 Snake Brigade, which included thirty women and thirty-five children. As the party descended the Lemhi River on February 17, 1825, Mme. Susanne Montour gave birth to a boy who was later christened Toussaint. The brigade stayed in camp for two days, not from any consideration of the mother or the child, but because snow was falling and a bitter east wind whipped their skin lodges. When the shivering hunters broke camp, Susanne Montour mounted her horse with the newborn wrapped inside her blanket capot. Later she would "put him to the moss," in a cradleboard tied to her tall saddle horn.

In camp, while their parents set the poles to support the heavy buffalo skin lodge cover, children helped unpack camp gear and searched for firewood. Cooking over a small fire, the women boiled or roasted meats, boiled stiff black tea, and sometimes added ascorbic wild greens or roots to the stewpot. In her spare moments Madam Montour sewed, mended, and did other chores. The North West Company brigades appreciated women as essential in camp and on the brigade trail, taking over duties that freed their husbands to trap away from camp. But when the HBC took over and the new governor had to send an officer with a deranged wife back across the mountain, Simpson saw them as an unnecessary expense, as he wrote in the spring of 1825 at Okanogan:

> almost every man in the District has a Family, which is productive of serious injury and inconvenience on account of the great consumption of Provisions: but by changing the men this evil will be remedied and

16 Ross, "Snake Country Journal," HBCA, B202/a/1 and Flathead Post Journal, HBCA, B69/a/1.

> the Women and Children sent to their Indian relatives. We must put a stop to the practice of Gentlemen bringing their Women and Children from the East to the West side of the Mountain, it is attended with much expense and inconvenient on the Voyage, [when] business must give way to domestick consideration.[17]

Life on the brigade trail must have been trying for women, and nights in skin lodges were not always harmonious. Ogden's clerk William Kittson described the death of one of Martin Miaquin's band of four Iroquois. Louis Kanatagan had been considered unfit for the 1824 Brigade. During the night in his lodge, Kanatagan was killed by the "accidental" discharge of his gun in the hands of his Pend d'Oreille wife. Next day she moved into the lodge of the only witness to the "accident."[18]

A stingy HBC management provided Ogden with only twelve engaged men to help conduct the 1824–25 hunt. The other forty-six were free hunters who had been advanced pricy supplies on credit and were obligated to turn in their beaver at the end of the hunt. Some hunters had to deliver as many as 150 skins just to clear a debt. A reminder that this was serious business came on April 8 when five trappers checking traps from a raft were attacked by a war party of Bloods. Antoine Benoit was trying to lead a horse away when he was killed, mutilated, and scalped. Two days later the body was recovered and buried on the east bank of the Snake River, casting gloom over the brigade camp. Ogden calculated the loss as one man, three horses, and twelve beaver, plus gunpowder and ball. About the same time the seven Americans decided to break away and go to find their friends who wintered on the Bear River.[19]

On May 23 the Brigade was in camp along the South Fork of what is now known as Odgen's River when a mob of belligerent American trappers appeared and invited the freemen and Iroquois to bring their packs and join them. Nicholas Montour evened the score for his demotion when he joined twenty-three freemen who left Ogden's brigade for the better paying Americans.[20] Montour went to the American rendezvous and traded forty-five beaver pelts to buy his wife, Susanne, beads, rings,

17 Merk, ed., *Fur Trade and Empire*, 131.
18 Rich, ed., *Ogden's Snake Country Journals*, 20n1.
19 Rich, ed., *Ogden's Snake Country Journals*, 34-35; Williams, ed., *Ogden's Snake Country Journals*, xlvii, 76 and note.
20 Rich, ed., *Ogden's Snake Country Journals*, 49-55, 233-36.

ribbons, four yards of scarlet cloth, and lest this sound too sentimental, a two-gallon copper pot.

Left with too few men to risk going on to the "real Spanish River" as Governor Simpson expected, Ogden turned north and eventually came out at Fort Nez Perces. A year later, after Ogden's Snake Brigade and Finnan McDonald's Southern Brigade regrouped to trap up the Snake River, they met a party of Americans and Iroquois at the Portneuf River, again blunting British ambitions. Ogden met most of the deserters "who expressed themselves sorry (at least in conversation with our men) that they had left us." Other freemen were unconvinced by the measures taken to draw them back to the HBC with slightly better prices for their beaver and lower costs for outfits. As early as September 1, 1826, Chief Factor McLoughlin reported "servants" (hired trappers) attached to Ogden brought in 2,188 beaver at a total cost of 13 shillings 4 pence each.

> Had we not employed these men in this way the Whole of the Snake Expedition would have been broken up, as for the deserters of Mr. Odgen's men and the Saskatchewan Freemen abandoning the party, the Remainder were too few to Venture to the Snake Country."[21]

Calculating future possibilities, the Chief Factor thought a hundred additional trappers could be employed for three years—eighty at Henry's Fork of the Snake, twenty in the Flathead country to as far north as old Kootenae House—killing twelve thousand beaver annually until that country was exhausted. To get freeman to return, McLoughlin offered to pay ten shillings for every full grown beaver, half for a cub, and to allow them to purchase necessaries at reduced prices. However, during the 1827-28 winter, the HBC trader at Flatheads Post observed fourteen deserters who were still conducted by the Smith, Jackson, and Sublette clerk Robert Campbell. When some of them came down to Fort Vancouver, McLoughlin was embarrassed to find that he lacked goods to resupply them.[22]

Montour had completed his separation from the HBC by paying off his, and an associates debts, with the funds still riding in the Columbia

21 "McLoughlin to Governor, Deputy Governor and Committee, Fort Vancouver, 1 September 1826," in Rich, ed., *Letters of McLoughlin*, 27-28, 34, 36.

22 Rich, ed., *Letters of McLoughlin*, 41.

Department's account books.[23] But his separation was short-lived when McLoughlin, at Fort Vancouver, was obliged to rehire him to regain influence over freemen and to travel with the Flatheads and keep them from going to the Americans. Later Montour and an American trapper named Ferris were surreptitiously slipped into the American rendezvous to test the possibility of sending trade goods there to compete with those "sly Yankees." To lessen the risk, the investment was secured by Montour's life savings in the Fort Vancouver account books. Nevertheless, he continued to serve the HBC as a clerk until about 1838 when he took his family to the French Prairies of the Willamette Valley to try living as a rancher.

Historians relying on HBC versions of what followed are still arguing the consequences, but American records provide evidence that a lot of peltry trapped by HBC brigades and meant to create a fur desert barrier actually trotted on packhorses to St. Louis. Smith, Jackson, and Sublette continued until it appeared that the bonanza beaver hunt was over. In 1830 the American wagons rolled to a rendezvous where the Popo Agie joined the Wind River and hauled away furs taken in the Flathead and Snake country from as far west as approaches to Fort Nez Perces.

Despite the unhappy fate of some freemen, thirteen are known to have been hunting for ten to eighteen years when Ogden took them with his 1827–28 and 1828–29 Snake Brigades. By then the brigade leader believed that "every part of the country is now more or less in a ruined state [trapped out]" and the only way to continue getting any beaver at all was by separating into small groups, a risky undertaking in a country increasingly hostile to trappers.[24] When Joseph Paul sickened on the trail, the brigade had to keep moving. Faced with leaving Paul behind, Joseph Portneuf, his wife, and children agreed to stay until he died.[25] Ogden noted in his journal that Paul was "only 29 years of age, a steady man and a good trapper," to which he added "there remains only one man living of all the Snake men of 1819 and rather extraordinary all have been killed, with the exception of two who died a natural death and [their graves] are scattered all over the Snake Country."[26]

23 Rich, ed., *Letters of McLoughlin*, 350.

24 Williams, ed., *Ogden's Snake Country Journals* 1, 96.

25 Williams, ed., *Ogden's Snake Country Journals* 98 n.6.

26 Williams, ed., *Ogden's Snake Country Journals*, Introduction, lvii. Pierre Bercier may have been the survivor who led Ogden to that false conclusion. Aged fifty-nine, he had served twenty-nine years in the country after crossing the mountains in 1806.

The Snake Brigade hunters took a heavy hit when Ogden returned to Fort Walla Walla (Nez Perces) from his final 1829-30 hunting expedition and decided to send the furs downstream in a boat paddled by trappers. In passing the lower part of The Dalles, their boat was sucked down and among the nine who drowned were the compassionate Joseph Portneuf, his wife, and their two children. Another victim was the namesake son of the elderly Francois Rivet, Ogden's father-in-law. Because of the family connection, the upriver brigade carried his body back to Fort Walla Walla for burial.[27] That was enough for Ogden, who turned north to New Caledonia and established Fort Simpson on the Nass River.

The 1831 brigades to the Snake produced fewer beaver skins and too much conflict with Blackfeet and others. Beaver was no longer the fur that paid its way; the price of human lives was adding to the cost.[28]

During eight years most of the former Columbia Adventure engagés and freeman had been incorporated into the Hudson's Bay Company. There was even a failed scheme to organize another brigade recruited from Red River mixed-bloods and send them west. Trapping continued under the provisions of the boundary compromise extension of 1827 that allowed joint occupation until one of the nations gave twelve months' notice of termination. But that "tenancy at will" was now threatened by American mountaineers, competing trading companies, and finally permanent posts like Fort Laramie and Fort Hall.[29] Within a few years missionaries, retiring mountaineers, and overland pioneers were seen as interfering with fur trade operations.

Although Governor Simpson's intention of creating a "fur desert" to hold rivals at bay was not quite as successful as accepted understanding would have us believe, it was ironic in 1838 that the British government finally got around to awarding the Hudson's Bay Company exclusive trading rights to the western trade. HBC Outfit 1844 amassed 40,437 beaver because more than two-thirds of the total returns came from distant New Caledonia—only 12,893 from the disputed Oregon Country. Whether Governor Simpson's much-published, often misunderstood

27 Ibid., 181.

28 Ibid., 62-63.

29 John C. Jackson and Carl D. W. Hays, "Research Material on David Edward Jackson, 1786-1989," Collection no. 09997, American Heritage Center, University of Wyoming, Laramie, Wyoming.

strategy for holding off American competitors actually succeeded is open to question, it continues to be asserted by historians.[30]

30 Mackie, *Trading Beyond the Mountains*, 114, 118; for an alternative argument see Jennifer Ott, "Ruining the River of the Snake Country: The HBC's Fur Desert Policy," *Oregon Historical Quarterly*, 104:2 (2003).

Chapter Nineteen

The Human Legacy

HIDDEN BEHIND THE SCRIM of business accounting and geopolitics, the dramatic contributions of western freemen to the British and American fur trade and to the growth of a unique Pacific Northwest cultural heritage are still buried in company ledgers and field books. Those pages record the names or incidents, but rarely the full story of men who were brought across the mountains to serve commerce, who married native women, and who stayed on to become the first settlers. Some were Iroquoian and Algonkian speakers, some transplanted Sandwich Islanders, but most were *Canadiens* whose passage is still marked by the Francophone names they laid on many of the native tribes, and on landmarks of the geography. Trapping beaver could be dangerous work and sometimes their scalps fluttered on a *Pied Noir* coupe stick. Sometimes their legacy was a simple note in an HBC account book. Most of their graves are long since forgotten. The authors felt the importance of compiling an admittedly incomplete list of those neglected individuals who became the first citizens of a new world.

Theirs was an adventure in the truest sense, the epic creation of a small French-speaking community. As long as a man had a horse, a gun and ammunition for hunting or defense, and traps, he was independent, an early mountain man. He was "free" to care for his family, free to run buffalo with his wife's tribesmen, free to make what he could of himself in what was rightfully considered a "river of fortune." The extended drainage of the Columbia River was a factory of furbearing animals.[1]

For over twenty years the North West Company tried to extract a profit by shipping packs of beaver skins to the Chinese market at Canton. Prices were never enough to pay the expenses and in 1821 the trade

1 Paraphrasing Gough, *Fortune's A River.*

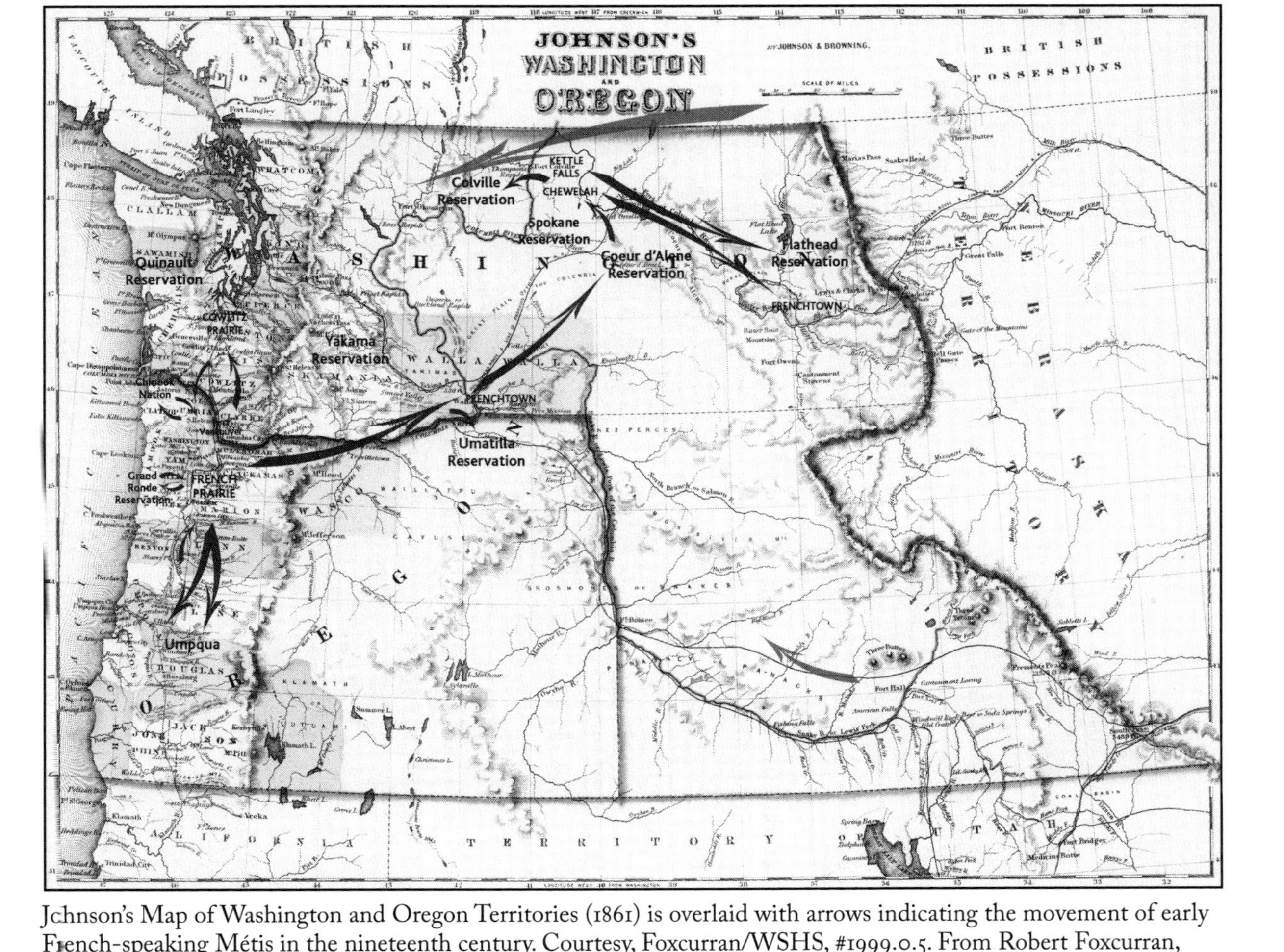

Johnson's Map of Washington and Oregon Territories (1861) is overlaid with arrows indicating the movement of early French-speaking Métis in the nineteenth century. Courtesy, Foxcurran/WSHS, #1999.0.5. From Robert Foxcurran, "Les Canadíens: Resettlement of the Métis into the Backcountry of the Pacific Northwest," *Columbia: The Magazine of Northwest History* 26, no. 3 (Fall 2012): 24.

was taken over by a reorganized Hudson's Bay Company. Returns at Spokane House show that freemen traded 4,450 large and small beaver plus other small skins although there were never enough credits riding on the account books to clear the debits on goods advanced to those hard-working men. At the end of the North West Company's disappointing Columbia Adventure a cadre of experienced beaver trappers passed to the Hudson's Bay Company. Arriving in late 1824 to inspect western operations, the new governor confidently expected that, if properly managed, those hunters would answer his requirements for increased production and the protection of the resource from American competitors. Instead, in trying to squeeze additional profits out of the indispensable trappers, he alienated them. In May 1825, the Snake Brigade trappers found the initiative to leave HBC service, and the term freeman took on a larger meaning.

Freeman trappers became pawns in a poorly conceived competitive game to check American mountain men until a distant HBC London management ordered the abandonment of the increasingly dangerous and unprofitable Snake Brigades in the summer 1834; Governor Simpson closed down California and Southern Brigade operations in 1842.[2] In the declining last years, British goods had been smuggled to the Yankee rendezvous until Nathaniel Wyeth, a self-defeated New England iceman, left a permanent trading post, Fort Hall, on the Snake River plain that was soon matched by the HBC's Fort Boise. Wagon tires of the overlanders soon engraved a trail from jumping off places on the coasts of Missouri, across the plains and down the Snake River all the way to Fort Vancouver and the French Prairies of the Willamette Valley.

In those enigmatic years, it may be incorrect to assume that the Pacific Northwest was initially opened by British subjects: independently minded French speaking freemen did it as engagés and freemen. After dropping out of the traveling skin games, they found places to settle and build permanent homes for their mixed-blood families. Freemen broke the sod of places like the French Prairies of the Willamette Valley or at several interior locations in the present states of Washington and western Montana that strangers called Frenchtowns. Once located, *Canadiens*

2 Rich, ed., *Letters of McLoughlin*, xcv; *second series, 1838-44* (Toronto: Champlain Society, 1943), 267.

became a unique subculture, smoking their clay pipes and watching their offspring grow up in the country they had helped open.

Meanwhile, the business of the HBC fur trade in New Caledonia continued coming down the Columbia to Fort Vancouver.[3] Other former workers and freemen were making permanent homes and turning to ranching and farming on the French Prairies of the Willamette Valley. Thirteen of them were listed on December 1, 1837, showing the dates of their settlement and that they were now in possession of land claims and were farming a combined total of 796 acres.

They had been rarely mentioned in the fading brown ink of travel-stained trip journals or carefully copied reports to London. It would take a delightful Scottish lady, Harriet Duncan Munnick, to recapture the lives of the French communities in the seven volumes of the Catholic Church Records of the Pacific Northwest that she carefully transcribed. Her work preserves untold stories of personal dedication, births, baptisms, marriages, deaths, and burials.[4]

Their parish priests recorded how those mixed-blood families intermarried, multiplied, and persevered through the last half of the nineteenth century. Families coming from the brigade trail or remote posts were pleased to locate homes and productive fields close to neighbors who also spoke French, who walked on trails across the fields to hear mass, and sometimes gathered to hear the fiddlers and time-worn voyageur's songs, even dance a jig while the blanket-wrapped babies slept in the hay of someone's log barn. Young men raced their best ponies and dark-eyed neighbor girls dutifully admired them.

In those pioneer communities, most *Canadiens* were illiterate and had to make their marks on the Provisional and Territorial government declarations claiming a fair share of the once disputed Oregon Country. French remained the operative language and, like their Catholicism, the retired trappers held to it. On March 23, 1838, eighteen heads of households who had fifty-nine children among them signed a petition that was delivered to the Bishop of Juliopolis at the Red River settlement, asking that they be provided with religious guidance. Their plea was answered

3 Landerholm, trans., *Notices & Voyages*, 25.

4 For a sampling of the complexities of these country arrangements and their progeny, *see* Mikell de Lores Wormell Warner and Harriet Duncan Munnick, eds., *Catholic Church Records of the Pacific Northwest: Vancouver and Stellamaris Mission* (St. Paul, Oregon: French Prairie Press, 1972). Hereafter *CCRPN*.

by two Catholic priests, Fathers Francois Norbert Blanchet and Modeste Demers, who arrived at Fort Vancouver later that year, after laying a string of baptisms and marriages at trading posts and other stops along the upper Columbia River.

Descending the upper Columbia from Athabaska Pass, the priests faced the problem of coming up with Christian names when baptizing so many women with tribal names. Many wives or mothers were recorded as Josephte Cree or Susanne Okanogan, or just "a woman of the country."

At the Fort of the Lakes, the tardy marriage of postmaster John McKay and Josephte Boucher, a Métisse, was sanctified. At Fort Colvile the engagé Joseph Hubert married Josephte Kanhopitsa of the Kettle Falls. Seventeen children of several couples were also baptized and seven more at Okanogan and Fort Walla Walla, although no more marriages were performed until the boats arrived at Fort Vancouver. On November 24, 1838, Catharine Humpreville, about age thirty-three and the wife of the Fort Nez Perces master Pierre Chrisologue Pambrun, was baptized along with their three children, ranging in age from twelve years to sixteen months. The marriage of Pierre and Catharine on December 8 was witnessed by the officers of the fort. Chief Factor John McLoughlin had been baptized Jean Baptiste by his French speaking mother and continued to speak it at home with his Métisse wife and her son Thomas McKay.

Twenty-three days later, the Protestant Thomas McKay married Isabelle, the daughter of Nicholas Montour and Susanne Humpherville.[5] The bride Isabelle's brother George Montour would in the future return to the interior and marry a Flathead Valley Métisse named Angelle Ashley. His death seemed to end the name Montour, but there was a daughter, Rosette, whose marriages to two Finlay grandsons generated a combined total of 567 deceased and living family connections, many who would continue to live on the Flathead and Colville Indian Reservations.[6] Unlike the country arrangements of gentleman officers who "put off" their companions, the marriages of most engagés or freemen persisted.

5 Notes in Warner and Munnick, *CCRPN: Vancouver and Stellamaris Mission.*

6 Author's interviews with Gene Felsman of Pablo, Montana, and C (Chauk) Courchane of Wenatchee, Washington.

The census the priests made at Fort Vancouver included seventy-six Catholic Canadian and Iroquois men, women, and children. Father Blanchet traveled north to the HBC Cowlitz farm, near present Toledo, Washington, where he baptized children of Latour, Coutenoir, and Plamondon, free men, and a natural child of Pierre Bercier and Emélie Finlay, a granddaughter of old Jaco. Moving across the Columbia River to the families settled on the French Prairies of the Willamette Valley, Blanchet confirmed the informal country relationships with Indian or Métisse wives that had over the years produced around thirty-seven children. A belief system that had lain dormant for so many years required parish churches and schools. From the beginning, the Catholic Mission of the "Walamette" was a French speaking institution and remained so for several decades.

Past marital arrangements were overlooked because when husbands died and their children needed a new protector, the widows remarried. Now older, those who learned the arts of camp and trail were asked to adapt again, to a sedentary life among strangers. Church records preserve only bare facts of those relationships without revealing how those women felt when their progeny were absorbed into the increasingly dominant white pioneer community or retreated to reservations to live with tribal kinsmen.

In 1836 and 1838 Protestants, supported by the American Board of Commissioners for Foreign Missions, established not entirely successful missions along what would become the Oregon Trail, in the Nez Perce country, or near old Spokane.[7] The 1841 arrival of the first small party of overland immigrants from the United States was matched by the appearance of an HBC-sponsored group of colonists from the Red River Settlement (now Winnipeg, Manitoba). They were French and British mixed-bloods whom Governor Simpson considered an "undesirable element," but might be politically useful to strengthen the Hudson's Bay Company's argument for making the Columbia River the boundary between British and United States territorial pretensions.[8] When the Columbia Department was unable to meet the contractual obligations,

7 Jill R. Otman, "1836 and 1838: When White Girls Crashed the Party," *The Rocky Mountain Fur Trade Journal*, vol. 8 (2014), 62-81, provides a view of how white women were received at rendezvous.

8 Jackson, *Children of the Fur Trade*, 99-128.

the disillusioned colonists abandoned their assigned pastures on the Cowlitz River or the unbroken, stony farm lands near Fort Nisqually and moved south to the French Prairies or North Tualatin Plains. When the disputed Oregon Question was settled diplomatically at the 49th parallel of north latitude, those French speakers had the option of becoming Americans. Most would.

Although initial settlement focused on the Willamette Valley, the Flathead country was not neglected. In 1842 a Jesuit party traveled from St. Louis to the east end of the Snake River plain, guided by the son of the Iroquois trapper John Grey who had settled in a community of other Iroquois at the mouth of the Kansas River. Another former trapper, Gabriel Prudhomme, whose debt Nicolas Montour paid to the HBC, met the priests and took them on to the Bitterroot Valley. During the construction of St. Mary's Mission of the Bitterroot Valley, the "Black Robes" conducted an estimated 654 baptisms of Indians.

The retired freemen who hoped to find contentment on a piece of land of their own soon experienced new problems as overland immigration from the United States poured across the mountains and into the disputed Oregon Country where earlier *Canadien* trappers were already developing choice land claims. Arriving in large numbers in 1842 and 1843, overland immigrants from the United States soon threatened to overwhelm the French-speaking community. Covered wagon pioneers had completed a trying journey across half of the continent with the expectation of taking free land claims in Oregon. Instead, they found choice locations were already taken by retired "Frenchmen" with queer habits and an unfamiliar language. Jealously disparaged as squawmen, half-Indians, or halfbreeds, to many new arrivals those British subjects seemed an accident of preemption that needed to be corrected.

The log churches at St. Paul, St. Louis, Gervais, and Oregon City were difficult for pious Protestant neighbors to bear. Ranchers couldn't continue to let their cattle range on "commons" where crooked rail fences failed to contain the half-wild cows that the HBC or a Yankee mountaineer named Ewing Young drove north from California. Legal problems around Young's estate led to the need for a political organization. Catholic priests cautioned that transplanted *Canadiens* were still British subjects, but astute French settlers recognized the language barrier could prevent them from participating in the decision process. In the vote to form a provisional government, it turned out that there were as many reluctant French as aggressive Methodists from the nearby Willamette Mission. The forty-six French Prairie residents in opposition lost their first experience in democracy by two votes. Etienne Lucier, a former Astorian, and Francois X. Matthieu, a fugitive from Canadian politics, were the only two Frenchmen favoring a government.[9]

Taxation in the territory had been voluntary in 1843, but in the next year a tax was levied on "all male citizens over the age of 21 years, being the descendent of a white man." The tax collector was Sheriff Joseph Meek, a former mountain man who had known many of the French during his days in the mountains. Meek took the broader view when some refused to pay, perhaps because they were technically British subjects but more likely because they were poor. Payment remained essentially voluntary until 1845 when it was stated that "any person refusing to pay a tax as in this act required shall have no benefit of the laws of Oregon and shall be disqualified from voting in any election in the country."[10]

The Territorial Judge of Elections was reminded that Article 4, Section 2 of the Organic Laws held that "anyone descended from a white man who has resided in Oregon for six months could vote in any election as long as he has paid his taxes."[11] Uncollected small debts did not prevent Canadian volunteers from serving in the punitive force raised in the settlements to chastise the Cayuse Indians for murdering the Whitman missionaries. The veterans rode home just as news of the discovery of gold in California reached the Willamette Valley.

The bonanza became a disaster for many Oregonians who rushed into the mining regions during the fall and winter of 1848. But those that survived the imported diseases and foul working conditions returned with cash and new options to buy or sell land claims. The enfranchisement of French-speaking Canadians was still a question when the Federal Donation Land Act of 1850 allowed single men to claim 320 acres of land and another 320 in the name of his wife as long as they were citizens or produced a documented statement of their intention to become such.

9 S. A. Clarke, *Pioneer Days of Oregon History* (Portland, OR: J. K. Gill Company, 1905).

10 Leslie M. Scott, "First Taxes in Oregon, 1844," *The Oregon Historical Quarterly* 31 (1), (March 1930): 1-24.

11 Charles H. Carey, *General History of Oregon, 1971*, as cited in Eliza Canty-Jones, "Voting Rules 1843," Oregon History Web Project; www.ohs.org/education/oregonhistory/index.cfm, accessed June 22, 2014.

The cutoff date of 1853, extended to 1855, triggered a last minute rush of overland immigrants who offered irresistible prices to buy the choice land holdings of *Canadiens*. Because a 640-acre claim was larger than a pioneer family could expect to clear, break, and plant, many French speakers were tempted to cash in their preemptions and move to new locations.

Voting rights remained an issue in the newly organized Washington Territory. However after a vigorous and often intolerant debate, by a vote of nine ayes to four nays Washington Territory legislators finally accepted the same solution previously hammered out in the Oregon Legislature allowing *Canadiens* to vote.

Determined pockets of *Canadiens* continued to gather for worship in their tiny churches, or came together to sing the old boatmen's songs and dance Red River jigs. But as the pioneer community sorted out social and religious differences, the French language slipped into the background. Schools used English instead of French, and it would be several generations before the disquieting question of racial origins was gradually submerged. Going to an Oregon City store instead of the Fort Vancouver trade window confirmed that French was no longer the operative language in the Oregon Country.

Feeling social pressure from Protestant missionaries and land-greedy settlers, the French were being submerged in the overwhelming population of unsympathetic overlanders. Many Métis moved to less socially discriminatory locations in the Umpqua, Walla Walla, or lower Bitterroot valleys and started over. Others returned to the Flathead Valley or the vicinity of Fort Colvile where social pressures were slower to develop. Today the thread of those disrupted lives makes a fabric that genealogists are still untangling.[12]

After the Rogue River Indian War and treaty removals cleared out most of the native inhabitants, other Métis located in the vicinity of what would be called the "French Settlement" on the South Umpqua River, or on claims scattered west toward the Coast Range.[13] Although the

12 Bruce McIntyre Watson, *Lives Lived West of the Divide: A Biographical Dictionary of Fur Traders Working West of the Rockies, 1793-1858*, 3 vols. (Kelowna, B.C.: Centre for Social, Spatial, and Economic Justice, University of British Columbia, 2010).

13 Ella Mae Young, "French Settlement," *Umpqua Trapper* (Roseburg, OR: Quarterly of the Douglas County Historical Society, 1980), 16:4, p. 75. The French Settlement was seven miles northwest of present Roseburg and is now known as Melrose.

Roseburg Land Office eventually counted 2,141 Donation Land Claims, only a few were attributable to mixed-bloods who located at the end of the decade. In 1858 when Archbishop François Norbert Blanchet set out from Oregon City to ride circuit to the Umpqua, he found about thirty settlers with familiar French names whose cabins and cleared fields could be called farms. Basil Courville's wife was baptized Marian Tlikakate (Klickatat); Alexander Dumond was wed to Métisse Josepthe Finlay. Some families flourished—the names of Antoine Dumont and Margaret Quintal's family required thirty-eight entries in an index of church records.[14] The last of the Montour and McKay lineages also moved to the Umpqua drainage and submerged into backwoods obscurity.

North of the Columbia River, James Keith's error of placing Peter Skene Ogden in command of a band of pugnacious Iroquois trappers had resulted in the deaths of several Cowlitz tribesmen. Tribal resentment simmered for many years, but the portage corridor linking the Columbia River to Puget Sound could not be denied. After helping build Fort Langley on the lower Fraser River, the carpenter Simon Plamondon was sent to the most southern part of Puget Sound to establish Fort Nisqually as an HBC way station.[15] There he acquired a Cowlitz wife and stayed. When Father Blanchet visited that area in 1838, there were enough French speaking Catholics at the HBC's Cowlitz Farms to justify baptisms and marriages.[16]

The HBC also appropriated land for farming and ranching to support another enterprise beyond the fur trade, the Puget Sound Agriculture Company. The mix of servants and freemen at the Cowlitz farm included English speaking overseers who issued orders in French, Hawaiian, and the Chinook trade jargon to local native laborers. Later, when the United States Exploring Expedition anchored off Fort Nisqually, Lt. Charles Wilkes observed that a half dozen Canadians had married Indians or Métisse and settled there. The farms of about twenty-three French-speaking heads of household were eventually patented under the Donation Lands Act where a generation of Métisse

14 Munick, *CCRPN*; Roseburg Register and Missions, 1853-1911, Annotations.

15 Bruce A. McKelvie, *Fort Langley: Birth Place of British Columbia* (Victoria, B.C.: Porcepic Books Ltd, 1991).

16 John C. Jackson, "Mixed Bloods on the Cowlitz," *Columbia* (Spring 1998), 12-16.

grandmothers or great-grandmothers continued speaking French until the end of the 20th century.[17]

After failing to negotiate an international boundary at the Columbia River, the HBC withdrew farther north, to a new headquarters on Vancouver Island. Even there, in a proper English-speaking place like Fort Victoria, the governor's lady, the half-Cree Amelia Douglas, conducted her afternoon teas conversing in the French she learned as a child. However, her husband, James Douglas, sent their daughter to England for a proper early Victorian education.

Moving was less of an exodus than a gradual withdrawal to familiar places where there were like speakers and like believers, where the old traditional ways were still intact.

Two of the places where former trappers and traders decided to congregate became known as Frenchtowns: one near present Walla Walla, Washington, and another west of present Missoula, Montana, in the lower Bitterroot Valley. Settlement began in the Walla Walla Valley when Fort Nez Perces postmaster Alexander Ross sent herders to pasture horses on the lush meadows in the loops of the Walla Walla River. During 1820-21, after Donald McKenzie allowed the Snake Hunting Brigade to falter, stranding many trappers, it is believed that Joseph Sebastian Larocque and his wife Lisette Walla Walla may have located up the valley. However in 1830, Larocque was still working in the Snake country when he petitioned to be sent back to Fort Walla Walla.

Six years later, when Marcus and Narcissa Whitman founded their small Protestant mission at Waiilatpu (west of present Walla Walla), they were reluctant to acknowledge that about a dozen *Canadien* settlers were living nearby. Three years later, Larocque and his associate Narcisse Raymond were still listed in the 1839 Snake District with the notation, "No married man to be permitted to leave the Establishment unless for good & all."[18] After a failed attempt to settle in the Willamette Valley, the

17 Robert Foxcurran interview with Michael Hubbs, Cowlitz Tribal member, Métis and genealogist, July 2013.

18 James Douglas, "Establishment of the Columbia District, 1839," James Douglas Correspondence, AG 206 26, Archives of British Columbia. Raymond led some of the last excursions of the old Snake Brigade.

Larocque family moved back to the Walla Walla Valley where the community, soon to be called Frenchtown, had already developed.

The French-speaking Catholic families had grown to about fifty persons by October 1847 when an overland party of *Canadien* priests and several Oblates of Mary Immaculate from France stopped at Fort Walla Walla. A hospitable Cayuse leader, Tauitau, provided Father J. B. A. Brouillet with an 18 x 30 foot cabin along the Umatilla River so he could open Mission St. Anne for Tauitau's people, who were dying. The medicine of Dr. Marcus Whitman failed to save them and the mission couple was attacked and killed by other Cayuse. The horrified priest rode to the massacre site to bury the bodies as best he could, but his Christian kindness was poorly rewarded.[19] Although the community was tolerated by their Walla Walla tribal neighbors, the coincidental arrival of the priests and the massacre of respected Protestant missionaries cast a shadow over Frenchtown.

In the 1850s conflicts resulted in violence and forced pacification of the plateau tribes. Some French settlers, mistrustful of the increasing American population, moved farther inland.[20]

Others, confident of their right to remain where they had settled, and trusting in the protection of their church, stayed. The Frenchtown community grew to around three hundred individuals who were promised a mission school where their children would be taught in French. But a mining boom in Idaho in the early 1860s brought more believers, non-believers, and dollars to the growing town of Walla Walla. It was some time before a county school came to Frenchtown, and when it did, it too was taught in English rather than in French.

For many years all that remained of Frenchtown was a tall monument on a hillside listing names of those who were buried in the St. Rose cemetery, and a few French sounding names on roadside mail boxes. That is now changing as a dedicated group of Walla Walla Valley historians, the Frenchtown Historical Foundation, works to restore a visitor's center and historic structures that are attracting the return of descendants.[21]

19 Ruby and Brown, *The Cayuse Indians*, 106-08, 114.

20 Jackson, *A Little War of Destiny*; Robert Ignatius Burns, S.J., *The Jesuits and the Indian Wars of the Pacific Northwest* (New Haven, CT: Yale University Press, 1966), 258-67, 298-311.

21 For a more complete description visit frenchtownpartners.org.

After the end of the Indian wars, settlement around Walla Walla crowded the Frenchtown settlement. But former trappers remembered the open country in the lower end of the long Bitterroot Valley where the Salish and Snake Brigades rallied before risking the Blackfeet. At the Hellgate Treaty, held west of present Missoula, Montana, in 1855, the Bitterroot Salish ceded their lands in the long valley in exchange for a reservation just over the mountains in the Flathead Valley. The Black Robes from St. Mary's Mission of the Bitterroot would follow them.

Because the *Canadien* Louis Brown and his wife Emily Pend d'Oreille were in the process of moving their mixed-blood family from a farm in the Colville Valley to the lower end of the Bitterroot Valley, they missed being included in the 1860 census of oversize Spokane County, Washington Territory, but gained the reputation of being founders of this second Frenchtown.[22] As miners streamed up the Clark Fork and little Blackfoot River in search of gold instead of beaver pelts, the settlement, along that route, became part of a vibrant new place of passing cowboys, miners, soldiers, road builders, and individuals seeking the main chance.

French-speaking Catholics emigrated from eastern Canada to join the small community, and a church served by lay brothers from St. Ignatius in the Flathead Valley allowed the community to maintain its Catholic faith and French language for some time. In the 1880s the rival city of Missoula, Montana, only twenty-two miles to the east, gained importance. Forty years later in 1920, a teacher commented that "the county superintendent of schools came to visit and forbade me to speak any French in the classroom. Most of my pupils were bi-lingual, but a few could speak French only." As late as 1924, children in other schools continued speaking French.[23]

Since the first appearance of traders and trappers, the Salish country had always been the crucible where Salish and French speakers merged. As the years passed the Flathead Valley remained a multicultural reservoir of a human heritage in retreat, a mountain-sheltered heartland offering refuge to Frenchmen who couldn't live comfortably when closely

---

22 Father Demers thought Brown a virtuous man for teaching Christian prayers to the natives.

23 *Frenchtown Valley Footprints*, [3] (Missoula, MT: Mountain Press Printing, 1976), 86, 92.

crowded by strangers with little interest in understanding their history or accommodating their uniqueness.[24]

In Oregon, reservations had been created at Grand Ronde, Siletz, Warm Springs, and Umatilla Rivers. North of the Columbia River free-roaming plateau tribes of Washington were impounded on the Yakama, Spokane, Coeur d'Alene, and Colville Reservations. Along the shores of the Salish Sea (Puget Sound), every salmon stream supported extended families, making assignment to centralized reserves almost impossible. Some authorities suspected that *Canadiens* were responsible for encouraging tribal resistance to treaty terms. Only later, when interior reservation lands were opened to outside settlement, did the government reverse itself by deciding that the example set by French-speaking, mixed-bloods made them the right kind of intermediaries for encouraging reservation Indians to settle down as good Christian farmers and ranchers.

Three interior reservations took in significant French populations: the Flathead in western Montana, the Colville in Washington, and the Umatilla in northeast Oregon. Adoption by any one of the three Umatilla Reservation tribes would entitle individual members of a Métis family to a free allotment of up to 160 acres of land on the north part of the Umatilla Reservation. Another change occurred in 1881, when the Umatilla Agent was informed that a person with any portion of Indian blood was to be considered an Indian and entitled to reservation benefits.[25] The Coeur d'Alene, Nez Perce, and Yakama reservations adopted smaller numbers of families.

Five years later, on the Umatilla Reservation there were 723 full-blood Indians and 196 mixed-bloods. Métis were attracted by land allotments and the agency expected their "inherent capacities" would encourage farming.[26] Most of those French-speaking families traced mothers or grandmothers to tribes that were now isolated on other reserves. Later, a one-fourth blood quantum rule gradually excluded many mixed-blood

24 Robert Bigart and Clarence Woodcock, *In the Name of the Salish & the Kootenai Nation: The 1855 Hell Gate Treaty and the Origin of the Flathead Indian Reservation* (Pablo, MT: Salish Kootenai College Press, 1996).

25 Ibid. Whites also married Indian women to gain allotments, but the language in those households was not always English.

26 James B. Kennedy, "The Umatilla Indian Reservation, 1855-1975: Factors Contributing to a Diminished Land Resource," Ph.D. Thesis, Oregon State University, 1977, p. 48.

descendants from moving to resettle near kinsmen on other reservations. A 1906 Bureau of Indian Affairs report stated, "There were about 1,200 Indians residing on this [Umatilla] reservation, of which number about one-fourth were of mixed blood, principally of Canadian-French descent." On the Flathead Reservation, the implementation of the Dawes Act came in a final round of adoptions preceding distribution of allotments that brought the total number of mixed-bloods in 1905 to 1,183 or 55 percent of the enrollees.

One hundred and sixty years after the 1850 census identified mixed-bloods, and the 1860 census began to track their relocation, the 2010 national count revealed greater social understanding of the outmoded concept of race as a distinguishing factor in populations. In their quiet way, the human heritage of the fur trade was the forerunner of a refreshing new Pacific Northwest multiculturalism.

That is a remarkable contribution by the initial small population of a great region. A chapter of anecdotes about individuals and an imperfect list of names does little more than begin to identify the freemen. In the years that followed the decline of the fur trade and the rise of a modern Pacific Northwest, those mostly anonymous people were more than a corporate inheritance; they became its lasting heritage. Part-tribal, part-European bloodlines made them the original inhabitants of the region: a French-speaking, Catholic base upon which a vital new population has grown and quietly flourished. On a much larger international scale, that is the same question the region and its new inhabitants are meeting now.

The long-neglected record of the fur trade in the Pacific Northwest generated a fragmented history: part Astorian in the beginning, part HBC at the end, but with a missing historical link which this narrative connects. Perhaps the previously unexamined documentary evidence may stimulate new scholarly interest. If there is a lesson in the completion of the last corner of a great continental nation, might it be that getting beyond the smoke of failed business plans and the oppression of incorporation demands a deeper appreciation of a basic humanity.

Pour de bon

On August 13, 1866, the Astoria farmer James Taylor was called as a witness before the joint U.S./British commissioners evaluating Hudson's

Bay Company property claims. Negotiations were setting the value of the fur trade improvements that the Hudson's Bay Company left behind when it moved the shipping port to Fort Victoria on Vancouver Island and the remaining trade of New Caledonia to the newly conceived British Columbia. The boundary agreement stipulated that the British company should be reimbursed for the improvements it had abandoned. Asked to give his idea of the value of Fort George, Taylor described a sagging warehouse partly used as a dwelling, and several small, old buildings "somewhat advanced in wear." Made of square hewn timber, he estimated those might be worth $600 to $700. The two acres they were on, fronting the Columbia, weren't much good for agriculture, but might be worth another $2,000.[27] The price of the buildings he estimated when sold to the North West Company on March 10, 1814, had been £200.

27 *Evidence for the United States in the matter of the claim of the Hudson's Bay Company pending before the British and American Joint commissioners...* (Washington, D.C.: McGill and Withrow, Printers, 1867), 197-98.

Appendix A

Columbia People

Listing names sifted from old letters and journals is an unsatisfying attempt at identifying the 220 workmen and unknown number of obscure freemen who the North West Company turned over to the tender mercies of an economy-minded distant British corporation. Naming all the individuals whose lives played out in the Pacific Northwest edges toward sometimes risky misinterpretation. Perhaps historians willing to consult a missing link, or descendants following a forbearer, may find it of value.

List of engagés who crossed the mountains with David Thompson from 1807 to 1812. These are extracted from Thompson's journals and cannot be accurately verified as some were tripmen who returned to the Fort des Prairies Department.

The 1800-01 pointmen:
La Gassé (Charles?)
Le Blanc (Jean Baptise?)

The 1806-07 trail builders:
Jacques Raphael Finlay dit Jaco
Nicolas Montour
Jules Maurice Quesnel
Michel Boulard
Bercier
Joseph Daniel
Drummond
Forcier
Finlay's Saulteur brother-in-law

Americans who crossed in 1807 with Captain Perch or in 1809 with Charles Courtin.

Francois Rivet
Louis Joseph Houle dit Capois
Michel Bourdon
Francois Gregoire
Francois SansFacon

Thompson's 1807 to 1814 parties:

Beaulieu
Bellanger
Berger
Beriere
Boisverd
Bostonae
Boulard
Brier
Buche
Cadien
Canada
Carrow
Charles Loyer
Clement
Crepeau
Dejarlais
Delcour
Drummond
Dupre
F. Gabriel
Forcier
Françcois Rivet
Franchmontagné
Gagnon

Grondeau
Hamelin
Hoole
Ignace Shoriawane
Iroquois Ignace
Iroquois Jacques
Iroquois Joseph
Iroquois Martin
Iroquois Paul
Iroquois Pierre
J. Durand
J. Gaudeaux
Joseph Coté
Joseph Daniel
La Fortune
LeCamble
Lolo
Lussier
Major
Mercier
Methode
Michel Allaire
Michel Bourdeaux dit Bourdon
Michel Kinville
Mousseau
Namilla (drowned 1811)
P. Daniels
Pierre Parielle
Raymond
Regis Bellaire, (may have come with Courtin)
Regis Bruguiere.
Richette
Roberge
Sans Façon
Saulteurs (2)
Valard dit Prince
Vandette
Villard

James Keith record of the twenty-two Iroquois engaged along the St. Laurence River. His tally shows he had difficulty sorting out factions in his "Abstract of People in the Columbia during the foll^{g} Outfits."[1]

	1814	15	16	17	18	19	20
Total including Owh^{s} & Iroquois	157	168	156	223	237	254	239
Deduct Owhyhees	14	17	17	64	61	56	38
Total Whites & Iroquois	143	151	139	159	176	198	201
Deduct those classed as Iroq^{s} & Abenaks	11	33	38	45	49	65	66
Total Whites includ^{g} Prop^{s} &c &c	132	118	101	114	127	133	135

11 Iroq^{s} deserted in Snakes—5 Sent to
N. Caled w^{t} 2 Whites & 2 Owhy^{s}
2 d^{o} sent across w^{t} 5 Whites are not
included in total of 1820

Abstract of People in the Columbia, Outfits from 1814 through 1820. James Keith, comp.

1 Keith, Memorandum Book, 135-36.

James Keith's list of twenty-five Iroquois enlisted by Donald McKenzie to serve in the west. Columbia 1816 to NWComp^{y} 1816[2]

Amount bro^{t} forward			2681	3
Jos. Mokaman	Cash paid his wife		60	
Ignace Madotehisam	d^{o}		24	–
Nicolas Oskononton	d^{o}		24	–
Thomas Oraquanandagan	d^{o}		45	–
Fran^{s} Payette	Cash p^{d} Gardeper		150	–
Augustine Roussil	" " B. Gibb		114	–
Michel Rashahitita	" his Sister		30	–
Louis Shonagarata	" his wife		99	–
Louis Shoegaskatsa	" his mother		30	–
J^{n} B^{te} Shoreohenton	" his wife		30	–
Thomas Sacahand-8-ta	" his mother		30	–
Henri Tasehaheri	" his wife		45	–
Charles Toherongeagheton	" his wife		45	–
Thomas Tawatoan	" his wife		30	–
Charles Tecawsateron	" his mother		30	–
Frs X. Tarihanye	" his mother		24	–
Michel Tecanarane	" his wife		45	–
Michel Tcharongwatie	" his mother		30	–
Thomas Tie-8[ou]-ne	" his wife		30	–
Joseph Monique Sund: Pr Eng: Bk		163.-		
	Cash paid his mother	57.-	220	
Dom: Monique Sund: Pr Eng: Bk		277.10		
	Cash paid his mother	57.-	334	
Martin Kanomswasse Sund:Pr Eng Bk		347.17		10
	Cash paid his wife	30.--	377	
Etienne Hotesse adv. at Fort W^{m}			585	17
Charles Landreville	d^{o} at Montreal		355	15
Olivier Roquebrune	d^{o} at Montreal and Fort William		455	
				7
	Livres NWCurr^{y}		5725	
				2
	Equal to H^{x}			
			£493	
				11

2 HBCA, F.4/7, p. 31.

List of Persons engaged in the Service of the North West Company in the department of the Columbia River and whose engagements for Service have been transferred to the Governor and Company of Adventurers of England trading into Hudson's Bay, Shewing the rate of Salary or Wages payable to the said Persons, the Balances due to or from them respectively and the Amount to be carried to the Credit of the North West Company as part of Capital for account of the Same.[3] Viz[t]

N°	Names	Capacity	Wages
1	Aubichon Alexis	Middleman	400.-
2	Bernier Julien	Steersman	600.-
3	Bercier Pierre	Middleman	300.-
4	Bourdignon Antoine	d°	300.-
5	Buland J. B[te]	d°	350.-
6	Cardinal Jacques	d°	350.-
7	Connor Patrick	d°	
8	Cartier Joseph	Interpreter	1000.-
9	Cotenoir Michel	Middleman	400.-
10	Cardinal Gillaume	Steersman	600.-
11	Chalifoux André	d°	600.-
12	Cox John	Middleman	288.-
13	Cook James	d°	288.-
14	Dubreville J. B[te]	Milieu	460.-
15	DeGrais Pierre Philip	d°	500.-
16	Finlay Bonhomme	Interpreter	565.
17	Grenier Joseph	Milieu	-
18	Groslin Charles	d°	
19	Hodgsons Frans. W[m]	Blacksmith	48.-
20	Jimo	Milieu	288.-
21	Kancratsoak Joshua	d°	288.-
22	Kanak Frank	d°	288.-
23	Kanonsavassé Martin	d°	400.-
24	Kitson William	Clerk	
25	Kassawessa Pierre	Boute	600.-
26	La Forte Michel	d°	600.-
27	La Gassé Charles	d°	574.10
28	La Vallé Louis	d°	600.-
29	La Boute Louis	Milieu	400.-
30	LaFramboise Michel	Milieu	500.-
31	Laurent Francois	Bout	600.-
32	La Chapelle André	Milieu	400.-
33	M[c]Donald Finan	Clerk	1800.-
34	M[c]Kenzie Alexander	d°	1200.-
35	Martial François	Milieu	300.-
36	Madotehisane Ignace	d°	100.-
37	Milwood	d°	288.-
38	Moreau Joseph	d°	400.-
39	Namokakay	d°	288.-

3 HBCA, F.4/46, p. 26-29. These men appear to be boatmen and do not include freeman trappers.

40	Noah Harry Bell	d°	288.-
41	Onore J. B^te	d°	500.-
42	Oketown Harry	d°	288.-
43	Proreau J. B^te	d°	400.-
44	Plante Charles	d°	127.
45	Poirier Bazil	d°	500.-
46	Paul Louis	d°	400.-
47	Poah Paul	d°	288.-
48	Powrowrie Joseph	d°	288.-
49	Pahwack Racoon	d°	288.-
50	Paget Antoine	d°	138.-
51	Pix Joseph	d°	400.-
52	Plouff Joseph	d°	400.-
53	Piette Francois dit Famant	d°	400.-
54	Quesnell Amable	d°	150.-
55	Rivet Francois	Bout	600.-
56	Roussil Augustin	Blacksmith	1000.-
57	Ross Alexander	Clerk	1200.-
58	St Martin Joseph	Milieu	400.-
59	Satakarass Pierre	Bout	750.-
60	Servant Jacques	Milieu	400.-
61	Tewhattahorance George	d°	100.-
62	Tawanadion Michel	Bout	600.-
63	Toussin Jean (Loupin?)	Milieu	400.-
64	Umfreville Carroté	Bout	600.-
65	Vellandare Pierre	Milieu	400.-
66	Wilson William	Bout	600.-
67	Anywarion Louis	d°	750.-
68	Dauphine Louis	Milieu	500.-
69	Kanationha Louis	d°	400.-
70	Molle Jean Marie	Taylor	750.-
71	Kakaragueron Pierre	Milieu	150.-
72	Le Fang Pierre	d°	332.
73	Le Vine Francois	Bout	600.-
74	Bruyeres Narcisse	Blacksmith	450.-
75	Charpentier Francois	Milieu	400.-
76	Monjon F. C.	d°	400.-
77	Birnie James	Clerk	240.-
78	McDermid Archibald	Carpenter	780.-
79	McKay Thomas	Clerk	1200.-
80	Apissasis	Bout	600.-
81	Annance F. Noel	Interpreter	600.-
82	André Louis	Milieu	400.-
83	Joseph Jean B^te	d°	150.-
84	Charles Pierre	d°	100.-

85	Perrault J. Bte	Bout	600.-
86	Amiot Alexis	d°	600.-
87	Aubichon Pierre	Milieu	400.-
88	Johnson William	d°	214.10-
89	Poirier Toussaint	Bout	600.-
90	Rondeau Louis	Milieu	400.-
91	Farriant St Valier	Bout	750.-
92	Le Brun Benjamin	Milieu	400.-
93	Portneuf Joseph	d°	332.10-
94	Portneuf Louis	d°	150.-
95	Paget Charles	d°	300.-
96	Le Pirier Pierre	d°	400.-
97	Danis Louis	d°	500.-
98	Tyaquaseche J. Bte	d°	400.-
99	Boulard Michel	d°	350.-
100	Cire Joseph	d°	400.-
101	Deslard Joseph	Bout	600.-
102	Grenier Charles	Milieu	300.-
103	Karonhetehego Lauarent	Bout	600.-
104	Kennedy John	Milieu	400.-
105	La Course Pierre	Bout	650.-
106	La Prade Alexis	Milieu	400.-
107	La Fontasie Jacques	d°	400.-
108	Montour Nicholas	Clerk	3781. 1(savings)
109	Moineau Antoine	Milieu	300.-
110	Montigny Ovid	Interpreter	900.-(3273. 2 savings)
111	Pion Louis	d°	1000.-
112	Piccard André	Milieu	400.-
113	Paul Joseph	d°	200.-
114	Portelamé Joseph Roy	d°	300.-
115	La Belle Pierre	Bout	600.-
116	Vellandris Alexis	Milieu	400.-
117	Pensonault Jos. B.	d°	400.-
118	Benoit Antoine	d°	400.-
119	Brunelle Louis	d°	400.-
120	Potoin Jacques	d°	400.-
121	Arpent Noel	d°	350.-
122	Bellveau François	d°	350.-
123	Bellevenalle J. Bte	d°	350.-
124	Cardin J Bte	d°	350.-
125	Champagne François	d°	350.-
126	Depot Pierre	d°	350.-
127	Drehamet Pierre	d°	350.-
128	Gingras Jean	d°	350.-
129	Lonctin Eustache	Bout	600.-

130	Lonctin André	Milieu	500.-
131	La Batte Michel	Guide	850.-
132	Prudhomme Bazil	Milieu	350.-
133	Rondeau Pierre	d°	350.-
134	Rondeau Joseph	d°	350.-
135	Vivet Louis	d°	450.-
136	Wagner Peter	d°	350.-
137	Ross Clarke	Clerk	946.14
	Total		62534.5

Dr 64278.8 Cr 33170.3 Credit to NWC 26852.17

James Keith compiled the above list before he left Fort George as the count had changed when he wrote advising the London Governor and Committee. "Clerks & Trappers & excluding Owhyhees amounted to 180, to which must be added those sent thither last fall say 25 or 30 forming a total of 220, whereof 150 are to be considered effective & paid & fed by the Company. The remaining 70 are supposed Trappers.

Names not given in the Fort George legacy list reconstructed to some degree through lists of individuals accompanying the trapping brigades led by Michel Bourdon in 1822, Finnan McDonald in 1823, and Alexander Ross in 1824.

Hunters presumed to be with Bourdon 1822 and who returned to Flatheads Post were:
Laurent Karowtowshow

Jacques Osistericha (remains with the Kutenais).
Antoine Paget
Jos. Perrault
Francois Sansfacon
Sauteau St. Germain
Fran. Sasanirie
Baptise Sowenge
Pierre Tavenitogen (Old Pierre) & two sons
Pierre Tennotiessin
Jacque Thataracton
11 named men and boys

Fourteen trappers who did not return to Flatheads that fall but went off seeking better prices:

Joseph St. Armand
Pierre Cassawasa [reached Fort Atkinson]
Fran. H. Frenetorosue
J. Gardipee
Franc. Wm. Hodgens
J. McLeod [survived to return 1825].
Francois Method [survived to return 1825].
Thos. Nakarsheta
Patrick O'Conner [killed returning in 1825]
Ignace Sokhonie [Big Ignace La Mousse?]
Ignace Sokhonie's stepson
Louis St. Michel
Ignace Tahekeurate
Lazard Teycaleyecourigi [survived to return 1825][4]

4 -23, Spokane House Report, HBCA, B208/e/1.

The men who accompanied Finnan and Michel Bourdon in spring 1823 (presumably older Columbia Freemen):

J. Bte Bouchard
Alex Carson
Ignace Dehodionwasse
Charles Groslui
Jean Bpt. Grandriau
Antoine Godin
Ignace Katcheiorongueshe
Louis Kanota
Louis Konitagen [Kanitagan, killed 6 Feb 1825]
Ignace Konitagen
Lazard Hayaiguarelita
Charles Loyer
Charles LaGasse
Martin Miaquin
Jacques Osistericha (remains with the Kutenais).
Antoine Paget, [hunter, Flatheads, 1813-14 at Spokane House, an old hunter in 1822].
Jos. Perrault
Francois Sansfacon
Sauteau St. Germain
Fran. Sasanirie
Baptise Sowenge
Pierre Tavenitogen (Old Pierre) & two sons
Pierre Tennotiessin
Jacque Thataracton
Laurent Karowtowshow

Add to that number those who came across fall 1823 from the Saskatchewan and who accompany Mr. McDonald [and Bourdon] this spring to the Snake Country. Of the above as Finnan McDonald wrote …poore Meshel Bordoe was kile with 5 more of the Band[5]

Thomas Anderson [killed]
J. B. Beauchamp
Antoine Clement
Antoine Crevois
Charles Crevois
Keyakik Finlay
J.B. Grandeau
J. Bte. Prudhomme
Michel Uneau
Antoine Valle
Louis Valle

5 1822-23, Spokane House Report, HBCA, B208/e/1.

List of engagés and freemen who accompanied Alexander Ross in 1824 as the best list of those remaining from the initial Snake Brigade.[6]

HBC officers, interpreter and servants.
Alexander Ross…1 gun, 6 traps, 16 horses
Francois Rivet…2 guns, 6 traps, 15 horses, 1 lodge.
Joseph Annance…1 gun, 3 traps, 2 horses
Pierre Depot…1 gun, 3 traps, 2 horses
Francois Faniiaint…1 gun, 3 traps, 2 horses
Jean Baptiste Gadaira…1 gun, 3 traps, 2 horses [died Oct. 12, 1824, age 65]
Thyery Godin…1 gun, 3 traps, 2 horses, [since 1820]
Louis Paul…1 gun, 3 traps, 2 horses
Laurent Quintal…1 gun, 3 traps, 2 horses [Iroquois]
Antoine Sylvaille…1 gun, 3 traps, 2 horses
Joseph Vail…1 gun, 3 traps, 2 horses

The freemen leaders were:
Charles Gros Louis…3 men, 16 traps, 4 guns, 10 horses
Martine Mieguin…4 men, 14 traps, 5 guns, 20 horses
Nicholas Montour…3 men, 15 traps, 3 guns, 10 horses
Vieux Pierre…3 men, 15 traps, 4 guns, 11 horses

The freemen, mostly Fort des Prairies transfers were:
Cadiac dit Grandreau…4 men, 11 traps, 4 guns, 7 horses
Robas Cass…4 men, 16 traps, 4 guns, 13 horses
[Antoine] Clements…2 men, 8 traps, 2 guns, 22 horses
Creverss…3 men, 8 traps, 3 guns, 8 horses
Francois…2 men, 9 traps, 2 guns, 11 horses
John Grey…2 men, 7 traps, 2 guns, 7 horses
George Gros Louis…3 men, 12 traps, 3 guns, 9 horses
Indian…2 men, 9 traps, 2 guns, 10 horses
Jacques, 1 man, 5 traps, 3 guns, 7 horses
Charles Loyer…2 men, 6 traps, 2 guns, 5 horses
Antoine Paget…2 men, 12 traps, 2 guns, 13 horses
[J. Bpte.] Prudhomme…2 men, 12 traps, 4 guns, 10 horses
Antoine Valle…1 man, 7 traps, 1 gun, 7 horses

6 Elliott, *Journal of Alexander Ross.*

Freemen who left Ogden in May 1825. Kittson names the following individuals as deserting between May 24–30, 1825. Kittson's journal stopped on June 1 but there may have been more desertions later in the season. The names with an asterisk were probably Iroquois.

Alexander Carson
Charles Duford
Martin Miaquin*
Pierre Tevaiiitagon*
Jacques Osteaceroko*
Ignace Deohdiouwassere*
Ignace Hatchiorauquasha (John Grey)*
Laurent Karahouton*
Baptise Sawenrego*
Lazard Kayenquaretcha*
Joseph Perreault
Louis Kanota*
Nicholas Montour
Antoine Clement
Annance
Prudhomme
Sansfacon*
Thiery Goddin
J. Bte. Gervais
Fras. Sasanare*

Those still hunting with the 1828-29 Snake Brigade and with the 1829-30 party:

Pierre Bercier
Alexander Carson
Francois Champagne
Antoine Cantara drowned 1830
Jerome Cloutier
Pierre Depot
Joseph Despard
Augustin Finlay
Mitikom Finlay
Pinetse Finlay
Bache Goodriche drowned 1830
Joseph Grenier drowned 1830
Louis Kanota
Jean Baptiste Lefevre
Michel Laforte
Jacques Launge
Antoine Letendre
Andre Lonctain
Joseph Paul died on trail
Francois Payette
Charles Plante
Joseph Portneuf drowned 1830
Jacques Porvin drowned 1830
Laurent Quintal
Francois Rivet Jr. drowned 1830
Charles Rondeau
John Saunders
Antoine Sylvaille drowned 1830
Jean Baptiste Tyeguariche

Those remaining in the Snake District Establishment in October 1839:

Clerks
Francis Ermatinger
Francis Payette
C[ourtney] Mede Walker

Servants
George Adams
Charles Carpentiuhis
Corbeau
James Craigie
Deschamp
John Favel
Nicholas Finlay
Thomas Geoige
Hoolapa
William Johnson
Joseph Larocque
Joe Manoa
Maxeme Mathe
Narcisse Montique
Louis Miscuman
Jim Paparee
Joseph Pineau
Narcisse Raymond
Joseph Sagoyinhas
J. B. Sylvstre
Talar
Tatoota
Tasutos
Louis Tetreau
Joseph Tehongagarati
Nicolas Alki
Jean Abrais
Joseph Dejarley
Lavisdure
McDophine
Louis Pincette, hunter on the books

[No married man to be permitted to leave the District unless for good and all]

Those who hunted with the 1839 Southern Party (Willamette Valley and south) conducted by Michel Laframboise and Joseph McLoughlin:

Thomas Agoniasta
Antoine Azure
Alexis Aubichon
Joseph Beaulieu
Ignace Canasawarette
Francois Champagne
J. B. Corbeil
Joseph Cornoyer
Jacques Dahonti
Antoine Dechampe
J. B. Dubreuille
J. B. Gardipee
Jospeh Gendron
Louis Kanota
Thomas Pisk Kipling
Francis X Liard
Jim Manucka
Fabien Malois
Ohpoonuay
Louis Onskanha
Louis Ossin
J. B. Petite dir Gobin
Laurent Quintal
Louia Rondeau
Louis Shaigoskatsa
Thomas Tewatcon
John Tolyak
J.B. Tyeguariche
Louis Vivet
[Indians]
Andre's step son
Palkanoot
Qutteh
Wassayac

From the 1839 lists it can be seen that most of the old hands have disappeared and they have been replaced by contracted Hawaiians.

Appendix B

Business Records

Table 1. Returns of the Columbia Outfits 1812-1822

Outfit	District	Returns		
1812	Interior	3,667		
1813	Fort George			
	Indian Trade	650		
	Willamette	976	1,626	
	Interior	2,000	3,626	
1814	Fort George	2,319		
	Interior	4,192	6,511	
1815	Fort George	4,217		
	Interior	5,285	9,502	
1816	Fort George	4,240		
	Interior	5,665	9,905	
1817	Fort George	4,864		
	Interior	6,672	11,536	
1818	Fort George	4,002		
	Interior			
	Nez Perces	2,758		
	Spokane	3,102		
	Thompson's River	2,808	8,668	
1819	Fort George	12,570		
	Interior	6,500		
	Nez Perces	16,598		
	Spokane	5,495	9,940	
	Thompson's River	158		
1820	Fort George		6,500	
	Interior			
	Nez Perces	2,150		
	Spokane	3,800		
	Thompson's River	1,858	7,808	
			(14,308)	
	[669 pelts cached in Snake Country		669	14,377
1821	Fort George	5,592		
	Interior			
	Nez Perces	1,247		
	Spokane	8,109		
	Thompson's River	2,416	11,772	17,364
1822	[less 669 pelts cached in 1819/1820 but taken out this Outfit]	-669		16,695
	Fort George	7,343		
	Interior	1,369		
	Nez Perces	7,041		
	Spokane	2,933	11,343	
	Thompson's River	1,379		18,686
	[plus land otters]	20,065		

Data for Outfits 1812 to 1821 are taken from NAC, Keith Papers, Memoranda Book, 30, 60. Data for Outfit 1822 are taken from HBCA, B.76/z/1, fos.5-6d.

Table 2: Fort George Returns, Outfits 1814-1821

Outfit	Indian Trade	Trappers' Hunts
1814	1,741	578
1815	2,599	1,800
1816	3,096	897
1817	2,595	2,295
1818	2,527	1,507
1819	3,163	2,556
1820	3,337	2,933
1821	4,100	600

Table 3. Columbia Department Profit and Loss 1813-1821

Outfit	Gain	Loss
1813		£26,040.19.10
1814		£19,276.18.2
1815	£9,000	
1816		£6,247.3.9
1817		£6,904.10.1
1818	$285.12.1	
1819		£6,821,13.4
1820	not salable in Canton	not salable in Canton
1821	£11,622.7.5	

The data in this table are extracted from NAC, James Keith Papers, A-676, Memorandum Book, p. 53.

Table 4. Ships Movements at Fort George 1813 - 1822[a]

Ship	Arrival	Departure	Destination	Company	Captain
HMS *Racoon*	30 Nov 1813c	31 Dec 1813	Sandwich Islands	Royal Navy	Black
Isaac Todd	22 Apr 1814	26 Sep 1814	Canton	NWC	Smith
Schooner *Columbia*	7 Jul 1814	14 Aug 1814	Norfolk Sound	NWC	Robson
Schooner *Columbia*	? Oct 1814	? Nov 1814	Monterey, S. I., & Canton	NWC	Robson
Schooner *Columbia*	1 Jul 1815	? Aug 1815	Monterey	NWC	Jennings
Schooner *Columbia*	? Sep 1815	16 Sep 1815	Norfolk Sound	NWC	Jennings
Schooner *Columbia*	25 Oct 1815	13 Nov 1815	S.I., Canton, & Rus. Am.	NWC	Jennings
Colonel Allan	? Jun 1816	? Aug 1816	Monterey	I. E. & NWC	McLennan
Schooner *Columbia*	? Aug 1816	10 Jan 1817	S. I. & Nor. Sound	NWC	Jennings
Colonel Allan	? Oct 1816	? Nov 1816d	London	I.E. & NWC	McLennan
Alexander	12 Jun 1817	12 Jul 1817	Canton	Perkins	Bancroft
Schooner *Columbia*	17 Jun 1817	12 Jul 1817	Coastal Trade	NWC	Jennings
Schooner *Columbia*	10 Oct 1817	14 Nov 1817	Sandwich Islands	NWC	Jennings
Brig *Columbia*	19 Jun 1818		Russ. Am. & Monterey	Robson	Robson
Levant	8 Jul 1818		Canton	Perkins	Carey
USS *Ontario*	19 Aug 1818	20 Aug 1818		USN	Biddle
HMS *Blossom*	2 Oct 1818	12 Oct 1818		Royal Navy	Hickey
Nautilus	25 Mar 1819		Canton	Perkins	Pearson
Levant	? ? 1820	25 May 1820	Canton	Perkins	Carey
Alexander	? Apr 1821	Hawaii 5 July	Canton	Perkins	Comerford
Houqua	? Apr 1822	Hawaii Aug	Canton	Perkins	Nash

[a]Data contained in this table were derived from N.A.C., Keith Papers, Memorandum Book; Corney, 1965; Ross, 1986; O'Neil, 1930; Payette, ????; Lamb, 1969; H.B.C.A., F.3/2 series.

Table 5. Comparative Prices for Beaver Skins, London, Canton, and St. Petersburg

Outfit	London[a] seasoned beaver	Canton seasoned beaver	St. Petersburg fine beaver
1815	32/11	19/ to 19/6	
1816	29/11 to 33/	17/6	
1817	29/6	17/6	43/
1818	27/6	17/6	44/11
1819	28/2 to 32/1	not salable in Canton	38/7
1820	35/8	17/6	43/4
1821	31/9	23/9	41/4
1822	brought in at 27/1 to 29/	20/	33/2

[a] These prices are taken as the average for seasoned and damaged beaver skins on the London market (see Table 4). They reflect the spring auction prices which were always higher than those in the fall. London prices are figured by the pound rather than by the skin. Canton prices are given by the pelt. HBCA, A.7/1,fo.27, p.3; A.10/2, fo. 338, B.239/c/1, fo. 71.

Table 6. Currency Conversion Table

To change –multiply by:

	Dollars	Sterling	Army Sterling	Halifax Currency	Quebec Currency	York Currency	NWC Livres
Dollar	1.0000	0.2250	0.2333	0.2500	0.3000	0.4000	6.0000
Sterling	4.4444	1.0000	1.0371	1.1 11 1	1.3333	1.7778	26.6664
Army Sterling	4.2857	0.9643	1.0000	1.0714	1.2857	1.7143	25.7147
Halifax Currency	4.0000	0.9000	0.9333	1.0000	1.2000	1.6000	24.0000
Quebec Currency	3.3333	0.7500	0.7778	0.8333	1.0000	1.3333	19.9998
York Currency	2.5000	0.5625	0.5833	0.6250	0.7500	1.0000	15.0000
Livres	0.1667	0.0375	0.0389	0.0417	0.0500	0.0667	1 .0000

Example: To convert $11.00 to Quebec currency, multiply $11.00 by .3 to get 3.30 or 31 610 Quebec currency. From 1825, the conversion rate for army sterling varies

Because of western Canada's relative isolation, its currency system developed independently of eastern Canadian systems. In general, within the territories granted or leased to the Hudson's Bay Company, sterling was the accepted money of account. About the middle of the eighteenth century the fur traders based in Montreal developed a special money of account called Grand Portage or Northwest currency in which 12 livres was equal to Halifax currency. How widespread the use of the currency was is not known, but it disappeared when the North-West Company united with the Hudson's Bay Company in 1821. The Hudson's Bay Company developed a special commodity money of account, the "made beaver," based on the relative value of the furs it traded which was used principally in keeping accounts with Indian trappers. Because the relative value of a "made beaver" varied with time and place it is impossible to establish any general conversion factor between it and sterling. A.B. McCullogh, "Currency Conversion in British North America, 1760-1900" Archivia 16 (Summer 1983), 91-92.

Bibliography

Abbreviations

AU	Aberdeen University
DCB	Dictionary of Canadian Biography
DNB	Dictionary of National Biography
HBCA	Hudson's Bay Company Archives
HU	Harvard University
LAC	Library and Archives of Canada
NAC	National Archives of Canada
UM	Université de Montréal

Manuscript Collections

Archives nationales du Québec, Montréal
CN1-29: Calendar of Notorial Documents from Etude Beek

Baker Library, Harvard University Graduate School of Business Administration, Boston, Massachusetts
Russell Company Papers, Perkins Letter Book, Vol. 19, 79-3734, Pos. C9 box 49 #4 and Vols. 20-21, 66-3871, Pos. C9 box 49 #5

Hudson's Bay Company Archives (Provincial Archives of Manitoba), Winnipeg
Section A: Headquarters Records
A.6/20: [complete]
A.7/1: [complete]
A.10/2: [complete]
Section B: Post Records
B.60/a/9: Edmonton House Journal, 1810-11.
B.76/d/1: Fort George Account Book, 1821
B.76/z/1: Fort George Miscellaneous Items 1821-1848
B.119/a/1: Fort McLeod Post Journal, 1823-24.
Section D: Governor's Papers
D.4/1: [complete]
D.4/116: [complete]
D.4/117: [complete]
Section E: Miscellaneous Records
E.24/2: John Stuart Copy Book of Letters Inward to Council of Northern Department of Rupert's Land, 1825-1826
E.3/2: Peter Fidler's Journal, 1792.
Section F: Records of Allied and Subsidiary Companies
F.3/2: North West Company Correspondence, etc., 1800-1827
F.4/4: [complete]
F.4/46: North West Company Account Book, 1821
F.4/54: North West Company Account Book, 1821
F.4/61: North West Company - Miscellaneous Accounts, 1808-1827

Archives of Ontario, Toronto

American Heritage Center, University of Wyoming, Laramie, Private Papers, John C. Jackson and Carl D. W. Hays, Collection no. 09997. Research Material on David Edward Jackson, 1786-1989

Library and Archives Canada, Ottawa

- Edward Ellice Papers, microfilm A-19
- James Keith Papers, microfilm A-676
- MG 19. Fur Trade and Indians
- C. Fur Trade, Collections
  - 1. Masson Collection
    - Vol. 14. Journal of the Rocky Mountain Fort, Fall 1799
    - Vol. 40. Miscellaneous Papers: Arrangements of the Proprietors, Clerks, Interpreters &c of the North West Company in the Indian Department, 1799
- E. Red River Settlement 99
  - 1. Selkirk, Thomas Douglas, 5th Earl of (Selkirk Papers)
    - Vol. 30. Various letters from Simon and William McGillivray, 1811-1812. Vol. 31. Archibald McGillivray's 1806-1807 Rocky Mountain Portage Journal, 9309-27.
- F: Private papers
  - 1. F 443. David Thompson Notebooks and Journals. Journal No. 18-19. Microfilm MS 4426
  - 2. F 443. David Thompson Notebooks and Journals. Journal No. 35 Microfilm MS 4428

Beinecke Rare Book and Manuscript Library, Yale University, New Haven, Connecticut

- Coe Collection of Western Americana
- John Jacob Astor Papers

National Archives of Canada, Ottawa

- MG 19: Fur trade and Indians
  - A: Fur trade, general
    - 19: Edward Ellice Papers, 54, No. 19
    - 41: Keith, James, microfilm A-676
  - C: Fur trade, collections
    - 1: Masson collection
      - Vol. 34: Correspondence between Joseph McGillivray and John McKenzie, 1813
  - E: Red River settlement
    - 1: Selkirk, Thomas Douglas, 5th Earl of (Selkirk Papers)
      - Vol. 31: Canton Sales 1815, 9209-9210
      - Letter dated London 25 May 1811 from Simon McGillivray to William McGillivray, 9119-9120
      - Letter dated London 9 April 1812 from William McGillivray to Wintering Partners of the North West Company, 9121-9126
      - Letter dated London 9 April 1812 from Simon McGillivray to Wintering Partners of the North West Company, 9108-9111

National Archives, London

- Public Records Office, Colonial Office Papers, 42/149/95; 42/ 82; 42/149/141; 5/208/156-58.
- British Library, *Isaac Todd – 1815 Journal*, L/MAR/B/186A; British Library, Surrey, 1815, Journal of Chief Mate Samuel Rodman Chace, L/MAR/B/191.

Royal Commonwealth Society Library, Cambridge, England

- Narrative of the Establishment on the Sources of the Columbia, addressed to Mr. Duncan McGillivray, Director to the N.W. Co^{y}, and the Gentlemen of the upper Fort des Prairies.

University of Aberdeen, Special Collections Library, Aberdeen, Scotland
James Keith Papers (MSS Davidson and Garden) 2769/I/57-1-4
Université de Montréal, Division des archives historiques, Montréal
François-Louis-Georges Baby Collection
G1: Grandes compagnies – fourrures

U.S. Congress
1823. *Message from the President communicating the Letter of Mr. Prevost and other Documents Relating to an Establishment made at the Mouth of the Columbia River.* 17th Cong. 2 sess. H. doc 45., Washington, D.C.: Gales and Seaton.

Books, Articles, Theses, and Dissertations

Aarstad, Rich. "This Unfortunate Affair: An 1810 Letter From the Three Fork." *Montana: The Magazine of Western History* 58:4 (Winter 2008): 62-67.

Allaire, Gratien. "Thomas Thain." *DCB* 6: 764-766.

Anon. 1823. *Message from the President of the United States, communicating the Letter of Mr. Prevost, and other Documents, relating to an establishment at the mouth of Columbia River.* Washington: Gales and Seaton, 1823.

Anon. 1927. Treaties and Agreements Affecting Canada in Force between His Majesty and the United States of America with Subsidiary Documents 1814-1925. Ottawa: F. A. Acland.

Atcheson, Nathaniel. *On the Origin and Progress of the North-West Company of Canada, with a History of the Fur Trade, as Connected with That Concern, and Observations on the Political Importance of the Company's Intercourse With, and Influence Over the Indians or Savage Nations of the Interior, and on the Necessity of Maintaining and Supporting the System from Which That Influence Arises, and by Which Only It Can be Preserved.* London: Cox, Son, and Baylis, 1811.

Atkin, W. T. "Snake River Fur Trade, 1816-24." *The Oregon Historical Quarterly* 35: 295-312.

Avery, Mary W. "An Additional Chapter on Jane Barnes." *Pacific Northwest Quarterly* 42 (1951): 330-332.

Bancroft, Hubert Howe. *History of the Northwest Coast.* 2 vols. New York: The Bancroft Company, 1884.

———. *The Works of Hubert Howe Bancroft, History of California.* Vol. 2 of 7. 1885. Reprint, Santa Barbara: Wallace Hebberd, 1966.

Barman, Jean, and Bruce Watson. *Leaving Paradise: Indigenous Hawaiians in the Pacific Northwest, 1787-1898.* Honolulu: University of Hawaii Press, 2006.

———. "An Extraordinary Canoe Race from Astoria in 1811." *The Washington Historical Quarterly* 21 (1930): 294-296.

———. "Early Oregon Country Forts: A Chronological List." *Oregon Historical Quarterly* 46 (1945): 101-111.

Barry, J. Neilson. "Ko-come-ne Pe-en, the Letter Carrier." *The Washington Historical Quarterly* 20 (1929): 201-203.

Beaglehole, J. C., ed. *The Journals of Captain James Cook on His Voyages of Discovery: The Voyage of the 'Resolution' and 'Discovery' 1776-1780.* Vol. 2 of 4. London: Cambridge University Press, 1967.

Belyea, Barbara. "The 'Columbian Enterprise' and A. S. Morton: A Historical Exemplum." *BC Studies* 86 (1990): 3-27.

Belyea, Barbara. *Columbia Journals: David Thompson.* Montreal: McGill-Queen's University Press, 1994.

Binns, Archie. *Peter Skene Ogden: Fur Trader.* Portland: Binfords and Mort, 1967.

Bowsfield, Hartwell. "Owen Keveny." *DCB* 5: 465-466.

Boyd, Robert. 1994. "Smallpox in the Pacific Northwest: The First Epidemics." *BC Studies* 101 (Spring 1994): 8-13.

Boyd, Robert. *The Coming of the Spirit of Pestilence: Introduced Infectious Diseases and Population Decline among Northwest Coast Indians, 1774-1874*. Seattle: University of Washington Press, 1999.

Bridgwater, Dorothy W. "John Jacob Astor Relative to his Settlement on the Columbia River." *Yale University Library Gazette* 24 (1949): 47-69.

Brown, Jennifer S. H. "Duncan McDougall." *DCB* (1983) 5: 525-527.

Brown, William C. "Old Fort Okanogan and the Okanogan Trail." *The Quarterly of the Oregon Historical Society* 15:1 (March 1914): 1-38.

Brunton, Bill B. "Kooternai." In vol. 12, *Handbook of North American Indians*, ed. Deward E. Walker Jr. Washington: Smithsonian Institution, 1998.

Bryce, George, ed. "Letters of a Pioneer, Alexander Ross," *Transaction of the Historical and Scientific Society of Manitoba*, 63. Winnipeg: Free Press, 1903.

Bulley, Anne. *The Bombay Country Ships 1790-1833*. Richmond, Surrey: Curzon, 2000.

Bumsted, J. M. *Canadian History before Confederation: Essays and Interpretations*. 2nd ed. Georgetown, Ontario: Irwin-Dorsey Limited, 1979.

Bumsted, J. M., ed. *The Collected Writings of Lord Selkirk 1810-1820*. Vol. II. Winnipeg: The Manitoba Record Society Publication no. 9, 1987.

Burley, David and Scott Hamilton. "Rocky Mountain Fort: Archaeological Research and the Late Eighteenth-century North West Company Expansion into British Columbia." *BC Studies* 88 (1990-91): 3-20.

Burley, David V., et.al. *Prophecy of the Swan: The Upper Peace River Fur Trade of 1794-1823*. Vancouver: University of British Columbia Press, 1996.

Burroughs, Peter. "Sir George Prevost." *DCB* 5: 693-698.

Busch, Briton C. and Barry M. Gough, eds. *Fur Traders from New England: The Boston Men in the North Pacific, 1787-1800*. Spokane: Arthur H. Clark Co., 1997.

Campbell, Marjorie Wilkins. *McGillivray, Lord of the Northwest*. Toronto: Clarke, Irwin and Company, 1962.

———. *The North West Company*. Vancouver: Douglas and McIntyre, 1957.

Cebula, Larry. *Plateau Indians and the Quest for Spiritual Power, 1700-1850*. Lincoln: University of Nebraska Press, 2003.

Chittenden, Hiram Martin. *The American Fur Trade of the Far West: A History of the Pioneer Trading Posts and Early Fur Companies of the Missouri Valley and the Rocky Mountains and of the Overland Commerce with Santa Fe*, 2 vols., 1902. Reprint, Lincoln: University of Nebraska Press, 1986.

Cline, Gloria Griffin. *Peter Skene Ogden and the Hudson's Bay Company*. Norman: University of Oklahoma Press, 1974.

Clyde, Paul H. and Burton F. Beers. *The Far East: A History of Western Impacts and Eastern Responses, 1830–1975*. 6th ed. Englewood Cliffs, New Jersey: Prentice-Hall, 1975.

Colthart, James M. "Edward Ellice." *DCB* 9:233-239.

Cook, Ramsay, et al. *Dictionary of Canadian Biography*. 16 volumes. Toronto: University of Toronto Press, 1965-1998. Throughout listed as DCB, and available online at www.biographi.ca/en/index.php. Accessed 10/5/2015.

Cook, Warren L. *Flood Tide of Empire: Spain and the Pacific Northwest, 1543–1819*. New Haven: Yale University Press, 1973.

Corney, Peter. *Early Voyages in the North Pacific 1813-1818*. 1821; Fairfield, WA: Ye Galleon Press, 1965.

———. *Voyages in the Northern Pacific, Narrative of Several Trading Voyages from 1813 to 1818, between the Northwest Coast of America, the Hawaiian Islands and China, with a description of the Russian establishments on the Northwest Coast, Interesting early account of Kamehameha's realm; manners and customs of the people, etc., and Sketch of a Cruise of the Independents of South America in 1819, by Peter Corney*. Honolulu: Thomas G. Thrum, publisher, 1896.

Coues, Elliott, ed. *New Light on the Early History of the Greater Northwest: The Manuscript Journals of Alexander Henry and of David Thompson*. 2 vols. 1897; reprinted, Minneapolis: Ross and Haines, 1965.

———. *The Explorations of Zebulon Montgomery Pike, To Headwaters of the Mississippi River, Through Louisiana Territory, and in New Spain, During the Years 1805 – 6 –7*. 2 vols. 1810 and 1895. Minneapolis: Ross and Haines, 1965.

Cox, Ross. *The Columbia River*. Edited by Edgar I. and Jane R. Stewart. 1831. Norman: University of Oklahoma Press, 1957.

Cross, Michael S. "The Lumber Community of Upper Canada, 1815-1867." *Canadian History Before Confederation: Essays and Interpretations*, ed. J. M. Bumsted. 2nd ed. Georgetown, Ontario: Irwin-Dorsey, 1979.

Davidson, Gordon Charles. *The North West Company*. 1918. Reprint, New York: Russell and Russell, 1967.

Davis, William Heath. *Seventy-five years in California*. 1889, repr. San Francisco: John Howell, 1967.

Dermigny, Louis. *La Chine et l'occident: Le commerce à Canton au xviiie siècle 1719–1833*. Paris: S. E. V. P. E. N., 1964.

Dernberger, Robert F. et al., eds. *The Chinese: Adapting the Past, Building the Future*. Ann Arbor: University of Michigan Center for Chinese Studies, 1986.

Douglas, Jesse S., ed. "Matthews' Adventures on the Columbia: A Pacific Fur Company Document." *The Oregon Historical Quarterly* 40 (1939): 105-148.

Drury, Clifford M., ed. *The Diaries and Letters of Henry H. Spalding and Asa Bowen Smith relating to the Nez Perce Mission 1838–42*. Glendale, CA: Arthur H. Clark Co., 1958.

Duckworth, Harry, ed. *The English River Book: A North West Company Journal and Account Book of 1786*. Montreal: McGill-Queens University Press, 1990.

Duckworth, Harry. "British Capital in the Fur Trade: John Strettell and John Fraser." *The Fur Trade Revisited: Selected Papers of the Sixth North American Fur Trade Conference, Mackinac Island, Michigan, 1991*. Jennifer S. H. Brown et al., eds. East Lansing: Michigan State University Press, 1994.

Duff, Wilson. *The Indian History of British Columbia: The Impact of the White Man*. Vol. 1, 2nd ed. Victoria: British Columbia Provincial Museum, 1969.

Dunham, Aileen. *Political Unrest in Upper Canada, 1815-1836*. Westport, CT: Greenwood Press, 1975.

Eldredge, Zoeth Skinner. *The Beginnings of San Francisco*. 2 vols. San Francisco: Zoeth S. Skinner, 1912.

Elliott, T. C. "David Thompson and Beginnings in Idaho." *The Quarterly of the Oregon Historical Quarterly* 21 (1929): 49-61.

———. "David Thompson Pathfinder and the Columbia River." *The Quarterly of the Oregon Historical Society* 26 (1925): 191-202.

———. "David Thompson, Pathfinder, and the Columbia River." *The Quarterly of the Oregon Historical Society* 12 (1911): 195-205.

———. "Introduction to David Thompson's Narrative: The Discovery of the Source of the Columbia." *The Quarterly of the Oregon Historical Society* 26 (1925): 23-49.

———. "Last Will and Testament of John Day, Editorial Notes," *Oregon Historical Quarterly* 17 (1916): 373-79.

———. "Letter of Roseman and Perch, July 10th, 1807." *Oregon Historical Quarterly* 38 (1937): 391.

———. "David Thompson's Journeys in Idaho." *The Washington Historical Quarterly* 11:2-3 (1920): 97-103, 163-73.

———. "David Thompson's Journeys in the Pend Oreille Country." *The Washington Historical Quarterly* 33 (1932): 173-176.

———. "David Thompson's Journeys in the Spokane Country." *The Washington Historical Quarterly* 8:3-4 (1917): 183-87, 261-64; 9:1-4 (1918): 11-16, 103-06, 169-73, 284-87; 10:1 (1919): 17-20.

———. "Journal of Alexander Ross: Snake Country Expedition, 1824." *The Quarterly of the Oregon Historical Society* 14 (1913): 366-85.

———. "Journal of David Thompson." *The Quarterly of the Oregon Historical Society* 15:1-2 (1914): 39-63; 104-25.

———. "Letter of Donald McKenzie to Wilson Price Hunt," *The Oregon Historical Quarterly* 53 (1942): 10-13.

———. "Peter Skene Ogden, Fur Trader." *The Quarterly of the Oregon Historical Society* 11 (1910): 229-278.

———. "Sale of Astoria, 1813," *The Oregon Historical Quarterly*, 33 (1932): 44-46.

———. "The Fur Trade in the Columbia River Basin prior to 1811." *The Quarterly of the Oregon Historical Society* 15 (1914): 241-251.

———. "The Fur Trade in the Columbia River Basin Prior to 1811." *The Washington Historical Quarterly* 6 (1915): 3-10.

———. "The Gun Powder Story by Archibald McKinlay." *The Quarterly of the Oregon Historical Society* 12:4 (1911): 369-74.

———. "The Strange Case of David Thompson and Jeremy Pinch." *The Oregon Historical Quarterly* 40 (1939): 188-199.

———. "The Surrender at Astoria in 1818." *The Quarterly of the Oregon Historical Society* 19 (1918): 271- 282.

Farr, William E. "Going to Buffalo: Indian Hunting Migrations Across the Rocky Mountains." *Montana* 53:4 (2003): 2-21.

Fisher, Robin. *Contact and Conflict: Indian-European Relations in British Columbia, 1774–1890*. Vancouver: University of British Columbia Press, 1977.

Fladmark, K. R. "Early Fur-trade Forts of the Peace River Area of British Columbia." *BC Studies* 65 (1985): 48-65.

Fleming, R. Harvey, ed. *Minutes of Council Northern Department of Rupert's Land, 1821-31*. Vol. 3 of 33. London: The Champlain Society for the Hudson's Bay Record Society, 1940.

Fleming, R. Harvey. "The Origin of 'Sir Alexander Mackenzie and Company'." *Canadian Historical Review* 9 (1928): 137-155.

Foster, J. E. "William Auld." *DCB* 6: 17-18.

Franchère, Gabriel. *Journal of a Voyage on the West Coast of North America during the Years 1811, 1812, 1813 and 1814*. Transcribed and translated by Wessie Tipping Lamb, and edited by W. Kaye Lamb. Toronto: The Champlain Society, 1957.

French, David H., and Kathrine S. French. "McTavish Frobisher and Company of Montreal." *Canadian Historical Review* 10: 136-152.

———. "Wasco, Wishram, and Cascades." In vol. 12, *Handbook of North American Indians*, ed. Deward E. Walker Jr. Washington: Smithsonian Institution, 1998.

Galbraith, John S. *The Hudson's Bay Company as an Imperial Factor, 1821-1869*. Berkeley: University of California Press, 1957.

Gates, Charles M., ed. *Five Fur Traders of the Northwest*. 1933. Reprinted St. Paul: Minnesota Historical Society, 1965.

Gibson, James R. *Farming the Frontier: The Agricultural Opening of the Oregon Country, 1786-1846*. Seattle: University of Washington Press, 1985.

———. *Otter Skins, Boston Ships, and China Goods: The Maritime Fur Trade of the Northwest Coast, 1785-1841*. Seattle: University of Washington Press, 1992.

———. *The Lifeline of the Oregon Country: The Fraser-Columbia Brigade System, 1811-47*. Vancouver: University of British Columbia Press, 1997.

Glazebrook, D. P. De T. *The Hargrave Correspondence 1821-1843*. Toronto: The Champlain Society, 1938.

Glover, Richard, ed. *David Thompson's Narrative 1784-1812*. 2 vols. Toronto: The Champlain Society Publication no. 40, 1963.

Goetzmann, William H. *Exploration and Empire: The Explorer and the Scientist in the Winning of the American West*. New York: Vintage Books, 1966.

Goldring, Philip. "James Keith." *DCB* 8:454-455.

Gough, Barry M. "Alexander Henry." *DCB* 5: 418-419.

———. *Distant Dominion: Britain and the Northwest Coast of North America, 1579-1809*. Vancouver and London: University of British Columbia Press, 1980.

———. *First Across the Continent: Sir Alexander Mackenzie*. Norman and London: University of Oklahoma Press, 1997.

———. *Fortune's a River: The Collision of Empires in Northwest America*. Madeira Park, B.C.: Harbour Publishing Company, 2007.

———. "Peter Pond." *DCB* 5:681-686.

———. *The Journal of Alexander Henry the Younger 1799-1814*. 2 vols. Toronto: The Champlain Society Publication no. 56 (1988) and 57 (1992).

———. "The North West Company's 'Adventure to China'." *Oregon Historical Quarterly* 76 (1975): 309-331.

Grabowski, Jan and Nicole St. Onge. *Montreal Iroquois engagés in the Western Fur Trade, 1800-1821*. In *From Rupert's Land to Canada*, eds. Theodore Binnema, Gerhard Ens, and R. C. Macleod. Edmonton: University of Alberta Press, 2001.

Green, Larry G. "An Analysis of the *Autobiographical Notes of John McDonald of Garth*." Master's thesis, University of Saskatchewan, Saskatoon, 1999.

Greenwood, F. Murray. "John Richardson." *DCB* 6:639-647.

Haeger, John Denis. "Business Strategy and Practice in the Early Republic: John Jacob Astor and the American Fur Trade." *Western Historical Quarterly* 19 (1988): 183-202.

———. *John Jacob Astor: Business and Finance in the Early Republic*. Detroit: Wayne State University Press, 1991.

Haig, Bruce, ed. *Journal of a Journey over Land from Buckingham House to the Rocky Mountains in 1792 & 3*. Lethbridge, Alberta: Historical Research Centre, 1990.

Hanson, James A., *When Skins Were Money: A History of the Fur Trade* (Chadron, NE: Museum of the Fur Trade, 2005).

Hardee, James, ed., *Proceedings of the 2012 Fur Trade Symposium, September 5-8, Pinedale, Wyoming*. Pinedale: Museum of the Mountain Man, 2013.

Haywood, Carl W. *Sometimes Only Horses to Eat: David Thompson, The Saleesh House Period, 1807-1812*. Thompson Falls: Rockman's Trading Post, 2008.

Henry, Alexander. *Travels and Adventures in Canada and the Indian Territories Between the Years 1760 and 1776*. Edited by James Bain. 1809. Reprint, Rutland, VT: Charles E. Tuttle Co., 1969.

Holman, Frederick V. "Discovery and Exploration of Fraser River." *The Quarterly of the Oregon Historical Society* 10 (1909): 1-15.

Howay, F. W. *A List of Trading Vessels in the Maritime Fur Trade, 1785-1825*. Edited by Richard A. Pierce. Kingston, Ontario: The Limestone Press, 1973.

———. "A Yankee Trader on the Northwest Coast, 1791-1795." *Washington Historical Quarterly* 21: (1930): 89-91.

———. "David Thompson's Account of his First Attempt to Cross the Rockies." *Queen's Quarterly* 40:337.

———. "Origin of the Chinook Jargon on the Northwest Coast." *Oregon Historical Quarterly* 44:1 (1943): 27-55.

———, ed. *Voyages of the 'Columbia' to the Northwest Coast 1787-1790 and 1790-1795*. 1941. Reprint, Portland: Oregon Historical Society Press, 1990.

Howay, F. W., and T. C. Elliott. "Voyages of the *Jenny* to Oregon, 1792-94." *Oregon Historical Quarterly* 30:3 (1929): 197-206.

Hunn, Eugene S. *Nch'i-Wana, "The Big River": Mid-Columbian Indians and Their Land*. Seattle: University of Washington Press, 1990.

Hussey, John A. ed. *The Voyage of the Racoon: A Secret Journal of a Visit to Oregon, California, and Hawaii, 1813–1814*. San Francisco: The Book Club of California, 1958.

———. *The History of Fort Vancouver and its Physical Structure*. Tacoma: Washington State Historical Society, 1957.

Hyatt. A. M. J. "Henry Procter." *DCB* 6:616-618.

Innis, Harold A. *Peter Pond: Fur Trader and Adventurer*. Toronto: Irwin and Gordon, Ltd., 1930.

———. *The Fur Trade in Canada*. 1930, Reprint, New Haven: Yale University Press, 1964.

Irving, Washington. *Astoria; or, Anecdotes of an Enterprise beyond the Rocky Mountains*, 1836. Rev. ed. London: Henry G. Bohn, 1850.

Jackson, Donald, ed. *Letters of the Lewis and Clark Expedition, with Related Documents: 1783-1854*, 2 vols. Urbana: University of Illinois Press, 1978.

Jackson, John C. *A Little War of Destiny: The Yakima Walla Walla Indian War of 1855-56*. Fairfield, WA: Ye Galleon Press, 1996.

———. *By Honor and Right: How One Man Boldly Defined the Destiny of a Nation*. Amherst, N. Y.: Prometheus Books, 2010.

———. *Children of the Fur Trade: Forgotten Métis of the Pacific Northwest*. Missoula: Mountain Press, 1995.

———. *The Piikani Blackfeet: A Culture Under Siege*. Missoula: Mountain Press, 2000.

Jameson, Jennifer E., "Iroquois of the Pacific Northwest Fur Trade: Their Archaeology and History." Master of Arts in Interdisciplinary Studies in Anthropology, Design and Human Environment, and Anthropology, Oregon State University, 2005.

Johnson, Alice M., ed. *Saskatchewan Journals and Correspondence: Edmonton House, 1795-1800, Chesterfield House, 1800-1802*. London: The Hudson's Bay Record Society, 1967.

Jones, Robert F., ed. *Annals of Astoria: The Headquarters Log of the Pacific Fur Company on the Columbia River, 1811-1813*. New York: Fordham University Press, 1999.

———. *Astorian Adventure: The Journal of Alfred Seton, 1811-1815*. New York: Fordham University Press, 1993.

Josephy, Alvin M., Jr. *The Nez Perce Indians and the Opening of the Northwest*. New Haven: Yale University Press, 1965.

Judson, Katharine B. "The British Side of the Restoration of Fort Astoria." *The Quarterly of the Oregon Historical Society* 20 (1929): 243-260.

———. "British Side of the Restoration of Fort Astoria - II." *The Quarterly of the Oregon Historical Society* 20: 321-325.

Karamanski, Theodore J. "The Iroquois and the Fur Trade of the Far West." *The Beaver* 312: 4: 4-13.

Keay, John. *The Honourable Company: A History of the English East India Company*. London: HarperCollins, 1991.

Keith, Alexander. *A Thousand Years of Aberdeen*. Aberdeen, Scotland: Aberdeen University Press, 1972.

Keith, H. Lloyd. "'Shameful Mismanagement, Wasteful Extravagance, and the Most Unfortunate Dissention': George Simpson's Misconceptions of the North West Company," *Oregon Historical Quarterly* 102 (2001): 434-453.

———. "The Adventure Narrative as History: Alexander Ross and *The Fur Hunters of the Far West*." *Columbia* 18 (2006):2:24-29.

———, ed. *North of Athabaska: Slave Lake and Mackenzie River Documents of the North West Company, 1800-1821*. Montreal: McGill-Queens University Press, 1999.

Kinkade, M. Dale et al. *Languages*. In vol. 12 of *Handbook of North American Indians*, ed. Deward E. Walker Jr. Washington: Smithsonian Institution, 1998.

Kittleson, David. "John Coxe: Hawaii's First Soldier of Fortune," *Hawaii Historical Review* 1 (1965): 10.

Kyba, Daniel A. "David Thompson's 1801 Attempt to Cross the Rocky Mountains." *Alberta History* 46: 15-25.

———. "Duncan McGillivray's 1800 Reconnaissance of the Upper Brazeau River." *Alberta History* 49: 17-24.

Lamb, W. Kaye, ed. *Sixteen Years in the Indian Country: The Journal of Daniel Williams Harmon, 1800-1816*. Toronto: Macmillan of Canada, 1957.

———. *The Letters and Journals of Simon Fraser, 1806-1808*. Toronto: Macmillan of Canada, 1960.

———. *Journal of a Voyage on the North West Coast of North America during the Years 1811, 1812, 1813 and 1814 by Gabriel Franchère*. Toronto: The Champlain Society Publication no. 45, 1969.

———. *The Journals and Letters of Sir Alexander Mackenzie*. London: Cambridge University Press, 1970.

Landerholm, Carl, trans., *Notices & Voyages of the Famed Quebec Mission to the Pacific Northwest, Being the Correspondence, Notices, etc. of Fathers Blanchet and Demers, together with those of Fathers Bolduc and Langlois... 1838 to 1847*. Portland: Oregon Historical Society, 1956.

Lavender, David. *Land of Giants: The Drive to the Pacific Northwest 1750-1950*, 1956. Reprint, Edison, NJ: Castle Books, 2001.

Lee, Henry. "The Magee Family and the Origins of the China Trade." In *Proceedings of the Massachusetts Historical Society*, Boston: Massachusetts Historical Society 81 (1970): 104-119.

Livermore, C. M., and N. Anick. "John McDonald." *DCB* 9:481-483.

Losey, Elizabeth Browne. 1999. *Let Them Be Remembered: The Story of the Fur Trade Forts*. New York: Vantage Press, 1999.

M'Konochie, Captain. *A Summary View of the Statistics and Existing Commerce of the Principal Shores of the Pacific Ocean*. London: J. M. Richardson and W. Blackwood, 1818.

MacKay, Donald. *The Honourable Company*. Toronto: McClelland and Stewart Limited, 1966.

Mackenzie, Alexander. *Voyages from Montreal on the River St. Lawrence through the Continent of North America to the frozen and Pacific Oceans in the Years 1789 and 1793*. 1801. Facsimile Reprint, n.p.: Readex Microprint Corporation, 1966.

Mackie, Richard Somerset. *Trading Beyond the Mountains: The British Fur Trade on the Pacific, 1793-1843*. Vancouver: University of British Columbia, 1997.

MacMillan, David S. "Joseph Forsyth." *DCB* 5: 325-327.

Malloy, Mary. *Boston Men on the Northwest Coast: The American Maritime Fur Trade, 1788-1844*. Fairbanks, AK: The Limestone Press, 1998.

Masson, L. R., ed. *Les Bourgeois de la Compagnie du Nord-Ouest*. 1889-1890. Reprint, New York: Antiquarian Press, 1960.

McDonald, Lois Halliday. *Fur Trade Letters of Francis Ermatinger Written to his Brother Edward during his service with the Hudson's Bay Company 1818-1853*. Glendale, CA: Arthur H. Clark Co., 1980.

Merk, Frederick, ed. *Fur Trade and Empire: George Simpson's Journal*. Rev. ed. Cambridge, MA: Harvard University Press, Belknap Press, 1968.

———. *The Oregon Question: Essays in Anglo-American Diplomacy and Politics*. Cambridge: Harvard University Press, 1968.

Meyers, Jacob. A. "Finan McDonald—Explorer, Fur Trader and Legislator." *The Washington Historical Quarterly* 13 (1922): 196-208.

———. "Jacques Raphael Finlay." *The Washington Historical Quarterly* 10 (1919): 163-167.

Miller, Jay. *Middle Columbia River Salishans*. In vol. 12, *Handbook of North American Indians*, ed. Deward E. Walker Jr. Washington: Smithsonian Institution, 1998.

Miller, Robert J. *Native America, Discovered and Conquered: Thomas Jefferson, Lewis and Clark, and Manifest Destiny*. Paperback edition, Lincoln and London: University of Nebraska Press, 2008.

Moreau, William E. ed., *The Writings of David Thompson*. Vol. 1. Toronto: The Champlain Society, 2009.

Morgan, Murray. *Puget's Sound: A Narrative of Early Tacoma and the Southern Sound*. Seattle: University of Washington Press, 1979.

Morison, Samuel Eliot, et al. *The Growth of the American Republic*. 7th ed. 2 vols. New York: Oxford University Press, 1980.

Morison, Samuel Eliot. *The Maritime History of Massachusetts 1783-1860*. 1921. Reprint, Boston: Northeastern University Press, 1979.

Morris, Grace Parker. "Some Letters from 1792-1800 on the China Trade." *Oregon Historical Quarterly* 42: 48-87.

Morrison, Jean. "Kenneth MacKenzie." *DCB* 5:543-544.

———. "Donald McTavish." *DCB* 5:559-560.

———, ed. *The North West Company in Rebellion: Simon McGillivray's Fort William Notebook, 1815*. Thunder Bay, Ontario: Thunder Bay Historical Museum Society, 1988.

Morse, Eric W. *Fur Trade Canoe Routes of Canada/Then and Now.* Toronto: University of Toronto Press, 1969.

Morse, Hosea Ballou. *The Chronicles of the East India Company Trading to China, 1638–1834.* Cambridge: Harvard University Press, 1929.

Morton, Arthur S. "The North West Company's Columbian Enterprise and David Thompson." *Canadian Historical Review* 17 (1936): 266-288.

———. *A History of the Canadian West to 1870-71.* Toronto: Thomas Nelson and Sons Ltd., 1939.

———. *The Journal of Duncan M'Gillivray of the North West Company at Fort George on the Saskatchewan, 1794-5.* Toronto: The Macmillan Company of Canada, Ltd, 1929.

Moulton, Gary E., ed. *The Journals of the Lewis and Clark Expedition.* 13 vols. Lincoln: University of Nebraska Press, 1983-2001.

Munnick, Harriett Duncan. *Catholic Church Records of the Pacific Northwest: St. Paul, Oregon, 1839-1898,* 3 vols. Portland, Oregon: Binford and Mort, 1979.

Nicks, Trudy. "The Iroquois and the Fur Trade in Western Canada." In *Old Trails and New Directions: Papers of the Third North American Fur Trade Conference,* eds. Carol M. Judd and Arthur J. Ray. Toronto: University of Toronto Press, 1980.

Nielsen, Jean C. "Donald McKenzie in the Snake Country Fur Trade, 1816-1821." *Pacific Northwest Quarterly* 31 (1940): 161-179.

Nisbet, Jack. *Mapmaker's Eye; David Thompson on the Columbia Plateau.* Pullman: Washington State University Press, 2005.

———. *Sources of the River: Tracking David Thompson Across North America.* Seattle: Sasquatch Books, 1995, rev. ed., 2007.

O'Neil, Marion. "The Maritime Activities of the North West Company, 1813–1821." *The Washington Historical Quarterly* 21 (1930): 243-267.

———. "The Peace River Journal, 1799-1800." *The Washington Historical Quarterly* 19 (1928): 250-270.

Oglesby, Richard Edward. "Pierre Menard, Reluctant Mountain Man." *The Bulletin of the Missouri Historical Society,* vol. 24.

———. *Manuel Lisa and the Opening of the Missouri Fur Trade.* Norman: University of Oklahoma Press, 1984.

Ouellet, Fernand. "Simon McGillivray." *DCB* 7:561-562.

———. "William McGillivray." *DCB* vol. 6.

Payette, B. C., ed. *The Northwest.* Montreal: Payette Radio Limited, 1964.

———. *The Oregon Country Under the Union Jack.* Postscript ed. Montreal: Payette Radio Limited, 1962.

Pendergast, Russell Anthony. "The XY Company 1798-1804." Unpublished doctoral dissertation, University of Ottawa, Rochester, New York, 1957.

Perrine, Fred S. "Early Days on the Willamette." *The Quarterly of the Oregon Historical Society* 25 (1924): 295-312.

Phelps, William Dane. "Solid Men of Boston in the Northwest." In *Fur Traders from New England, The Boston Men in the North Pacific, 1787-1800, The Narratives of William Dane Phelps, William Sturgis and James Gilchrist Swan.* Spokane, WA: Arthur H. Clark Co., 1997.

Phillips, Paul C. *The Fur Trade.* 2 vols. Norman: University of Oklahoma Press, 1961.

Porter, Kenneth W. "Jane Barnes, First White Woman in Oregon." *Oregon Historical Quarterly* 31 (1939): 125-135.

———. *John Jacob Astor: Business Man.* 2 vols. Cambridge, Harvard University Press, 1931.

Priestley, J. B. *The Prince of Pleasure and His Regency.* New York: Harper and Row, 1969.

Quaife, Milo M., ed. *The John Askin Papers.* Vol. 1. 1747-1795. Detroit: Detroit Library Commission, 1928.

Quimby, George I. "The Wife of Portsmouth's Tale, 1813-1818: An Apology to Miss Jane Barnes." *Pacific Northwest Quarterly* 71 (1980): 127-130.

Reid, John Phillip. "Restraints of Vengeance: Retaliation-in-Kind and the Use of Indian Law in the Old Oregon Country." *Oregon Historical Quarterly* 95:1 (1994): 48-92.

Reid, John Phillip. *Patterns of Vengeance: Crosscultural Homicide in the North American Fur Trade.* Pasadena: Ninth Judicial Circuit Historical Society, 1999.

Rich, E. E., ed. *Cumberland House Journals and Inland Journal 1775-82*. First Series, 1775-79. Publication no. 14. London: The Hudson's Bay Record Society, 1951.

———. *Peter Skene Ogden's Snake Country Journals 1824-25 and 1825-26.* London: The Hudson's Bay Record Society, 1950.

———. *The Fur Trade and the Northwest to 1857.* Toronto: McClelland and Stewart, 1967.

———. *The History of the Hudson's Bay Company 1670-1870*. Vol. 2: 1763-1870. London: The Hudson's Bay Record Society, 1959.

———, ed. *Colin Robertson's Correspondence Book, September 1817 to September 1822.* London: Hudson's Bay Record Society Publication no. 2, 1939.

———, ed. *Part of Dispatch from George Simpson Esqr Governor of Ruperts Land to the Governor & Committee of the Hudson's Bay Company London; March 1, 1829. Continued and Completed March 24 and June 5, 1829.* Publication no. 10. London: The Champlain Society for The Hudson's Bay Record Society, 1947.

———, ed. *The Letters of John McLoughlin from Fort Vancouver to the Governor and Committee: First Series 1825-38.* London: Hudson's Bay Record Society Publication no. 4, 1941.

Roe, Michael, ed. *The Journal and Letters of Captain Charles Bishop on the North-West Coast of America, in the Pacific and in New South Wales 1794-1799.* London: Cambridge University Press, 1967.

Rollins, Philip Ashton, ed. *Discovery of the Oregon Trail: Robert Stuart's Narratives of his Overland Trip Eastward from Astoria in 1812-13.* 1935. Reprint, Lincoln and London: University of Nebraska Press, 1995.

Ronda, James P. *Astoria and Empire*. Lincoln: University of Nebraska Press, 1990.

Roquefeuil, Camille de. *Voyage Around the World, 1816-1819, and Trading for Sea Otter Fur on the Northwest Coast of America.* 1823. Reprint, Fairfield, WA: Ye Galleon Press, 1981.

Ross, Alexander. 1986. *Adventures of the First Settlers on the Oregon or Columbia River, 1810-1813.* 1849. Lincoln: University of Nebraska Press, 1986.

———. *The Fur Hunters of the Far West.* Kenneth A. Spaulding, ed. 1855; repr. Norman: University of Oklahoma Press, 1956.

Ruby, Robert H., and John A. Brown. *Indians of the Pacific Northwest.* Norman: University of Oklahoma Press, 1981.

———. *The Cayuse Indians: Imperial Tribesmen of Old Oregon.* Norman: University of Oklahoma Press, 1972.

———. *The Chinook Indians: Traders of the Lower Columbia River.* Norman: University of Oklahoma Press, 1976.

———. *The Spokane Indians: Children of the Sun.* Norman: University of Oklahoma Press, 1970.

———. *The Cayuse Indians: Imperial Tribesmen of Old Oregon.* Norman: University of Oklahoma Press, 1972.

Russell, Hilary. "Angus Bethune." *DCB* 8:85-86.

———. "The Chinese Voyages of Angus Bethune." *Beaver* 307 (Spring 1977): 22-31.

Schaeffer, Claude. "The Kutenai Female Berdache: Courier, Guide, Prophetess, and Warrior." *Ethnohistory* 12:3 (1964): 193-236.

Silverstein, Michael. *Chinookans of the Lower Columbia.* In vol. 7, *Handbook of North American Indians*, ed. Wayne Suttles. Washington: Smithsonian Institution, 1990.

Sladkovskii, M.L. *History of Economic Relations between Russia and China.* M. Roublev, trans. Jerusalem: Israel Program for Scientific Translations, 1966.

Sloan, William A. "The Role of Native People in Extension of the Fur Trade on the Upper Saskatchewan and through the Rocky Mountains 1784-1807." Unpublished Paper, n.d.

Smiley, H. D. "The Dalliance of David Thompson." *The Beaver* (1972), 303:40-47.

Smith, Allan H. "An Ethnohistorical Analysis of David Thompson's 1809–1811 Journeys in the Lower Pend Oreille Valley, Northeastern Washington." *Ethnohistory* 8: 309-381.

Sperlin, O. B. "Exploration of the Upper Columbia." *The Washington Historical Quarterly* 4 (1913): 3-11.

———. "Two Kootenay Women Masquerading as Men? Or Were They One?" *The Washington Historical Quarterly* 21 (1930):120-130.

Sprague, Roderick. *Palouse*. In vol. 12, *Handbook of North American Indians*, ed. Deward E. Walker Jr. Washington: Smithsonian Institution, 1998.

Stark, Peter. *Astoria: John Jacob Astor and Thomas Jefferson's Lost Pacific Empire: A Story of Wealth, Ambition, and Survival*. New York: Harper Collins Publishers, 2014.

Stern, Theodore. *Cayuse, Umatilla, and Walla Walla*. In vol. 12, *Handbook of North American Indians*, ed. Deward E. Walker Jr. Washington: Smithsonian Institution, 1998.

———. *Chiefs and Chief Traders: Indian Relations at Fort Nez Perces, 1818-1855*. Corvallis: Oregon State University Press, 1993.

———. *Columbia River Trade Network*. In vol. 12, *Handbook of North American Indians*, ed. Deward E. Walker Jr. Washington: Smithsonian Institution, 1998.

Sturtevant, William C., gen. ed. *Handbook of North American Indians*, vols. 7, 12. Washington: Smithsonian Institution, 1990, 1998.

Suttles, Wayne, ed. *Northwest Coast*. Vol. 7, *Handbook of North American Indians*. Washington: Smithsonian Institution, 1990.

Swan, James G. *The Northwest Coast or, Three Years' Residence in Washington Territory*. 1857. Reprint, Seattle: University of Washington Press, 1969.

Thompson, Lawrence, and M. Dale Kinkade. *Languages*. In vol. 7, *Handbook of North American Indians*, ed. Wayne Suttles. Washington: Smithsonian Institution, 1990.

Tikhmenev, P. A. *A History of the Russian-American Company*. Trans. and ed. by Richard A. Pierce and Alton S. Donnelly. Seattle: University of Washington Press, 1978.

Tracy, Nicholas, ed., *The Naval Chronicle: The Contemporary Record of the Royal Navy at War*. Vol. 5, 1811–1815. London: Stackpole Books, Chatham Publishing, 1999.

Trenholm, Virginia Cole, and Maurine Cary. *The Shoshonis: Sentinels of the Rockies*. Norman: University of Oklahoma Press, 1964.

Tulchinsky, Gerald J. J. "John Forsyth." *DCB* 7: 309-311.

———. "Alexander Auldjo." *DCB* 6:18-20.

Tyrrell, J. B. "David Thompson and the Columbia River." *Canadian Historical Review* 18 (1937): 12-27.

———. *David Thompson: Narrative of his Explorations in Western America*. Toronto: The Champlain Society, 1916.

———, ed. *Journals of Samuel Hearne and Philip Turnor*. Publication no. 21. Toronto: The Champlain Society, 1934.

Van Kirk, Slyvia, *"Many Tender Ties," Women in Fur-Trade Society, 1670-1870*. Winnipeg, Manitoba: Watson & Dwyer Publishing Ltd., 1980.

———. "John George McTavish." *DCB* 7:577-578.

Vancouver, George. *A Voyage of Discovery to the North Pacific Ocean and Round the World 1791-1795*. Edited by W. Kaye Lamb. 4 vols. 1798. London: The Hakluyt Society, 1984.

Vibert, Elizabeth. *Traders' Tales: Narratives of Cultural Encounters in the Columbia Plateau, 1807–1846*. Norman: University of Oklahoma Press, 1997.

Walker, Deward E., Jr. and Roderick Sprague. *History Until 1846*. In vol. 12, *Handbook of North American Indians*, ed. Deward E. Walker Jr. Washington: Smithsonian Institution, 1998.

Wallace, J. N. *The Wintering Partners on Peace River*. Ottawa: Thorburn and Abbott, 1929.

Wallace, W. Stewart, ed. *Documents Relating to the North West Company*. Toronto: The Champlain Society, 1934.

———. *The Pedlars from Quebec and Other Papers on the Nor'Westers*. Toronto: The Ryerson Press, 1954.

Watson, Bruce McIntyre Watson. *Lives Lived West of the Divide: A Biographical Dictionary of Fur Traders Working West of the Rockies, 1793-1858*, vols. 1-3. Kelowna, BC: Centre for Social, Spatial, and Economic Justice, University of British Columbia, 2010.

Wells, Merle. "Donald Mackenzie's Little Lost River Campsite, 1819-20." Boise: Idaho Historical Society Reference Series, Number 902, 1988.

White, Bruce. "The Fear of Pillaging: Economic Folktales of the Great Lakes Fur Trade," in *The Fur Trade Revisited: Selected Papers of the Sixth North American Fur Trade Conference, Mackinac Island, Michigan, 1991.* eds. Jennifer S. H. Brown et al. East Lansing: Michigan State University Press, 1994. 199-200.

White, M. Catharine, ed. *David Thompson Journals Relating to Montana and Adjacent Regions 1808-12.* Missoula: Montana State University Press, 1950.

———. "Saleesh House: The First Trading Post Among the Flathead." *The Pacific Northwest Quarterly* 33 (1942): 251-264.

White, Richard and William Cronon. *Ecological Change and Indian-White Relations.* In vol. 4, *Handbook of North American Indians*, ed. Wilcomb E. Washburn. Washington: Smithsonian Institution, 1988.

Williams, Glyndwr, ed. *Hudson's Bay Miscellany, 1670-1870.* Winnipeg: Hudson's Bay Record Society, 1975.

———. *Peter Skene Ogden's Snake Country Journals, 1827-28 and 1828-29.* London: Hudson's Bay Record Society, 1971.

Woodward, Llewellyn. *The Age of Reform: 1815-1870.* 2nd. ed. Oxford: Clarendon Press, 1962.

Index

Illustration pages noted in *italics*

About the Authors

John C. Jackson (1931-2015) authored nine books and numerous articles focusing on early American exploration, the fur trade, and the Pacific Northwest. His first career was as an independent advertising designer and art director. He then turned to his passion in American history. He was a recipient of a Rockefeller Foundation grant to write his first book, *Shadow on the Tetons: David E. Jackson and the Claiming of the American West*.

H. Lloyd Keith (1938-2008) was professor of history and sociology at Shoreline (Washington) Community College. His published books include *North of Athabasca: Slave Lake and Mackenzie River Documents of North West Company, 1800-1821* and *Bibliography for History of the Pacific Northwest and of Canada*. He authored numerous articles and was recognized as a preeminent expert on the history of the nineteenth century.